STUDY GUIDE

Richard O. Straub

University of Michigan, Dearborn

to accompany

Kathleen Stassen Berger

The Developing Person Through Childhood and Adolescence

Seventh Edition

WORTH PUBLISHERS

Study Guide
by Richard O. Straub
to accompany
Berger: **The Developing Person Through Childhood and Adolescence,** Seventh Edition

© 2006, 2003, 2000, 1995, 1991, 1986, 1980 by Worth Publishers

ISBN-13: 978-0-7167-6806-7
ISBN-10: 0-7167-6806-2

Second Printing

Worth Publishers
41 Madison Avenue
New York, NY 10010
www.worthpublishers.com

Contents

Preface

This Study Guide is designed to be used with *The Developing Person Through Childhood and Adolescence*, Seventh Edition, by Kathleen Stassen Berger. It is intended to help you to evaluate your understanding of that material, and then to review any problem areas. "How to Manage Your Time Efficiently, Study More Effectively, and Think Critically" provides detailed instructions on how to use the textbook and this Study Guide for maximum benefit. It also offers additional study suggestions based on principles of time management, effective note-taking, evaluation of exam performance, and an effective program for improving your comprehension while studying from textbooks.

Each chapter of the Study Guide includes a Chapter Overview, a set of Guided Study questions to pace your reading of the text chapter, a Chapter Review section to be completed after you have read the text chapter, and three review tests. One chapter in each section of the text includes a crossword puzzle that provides an alternative way of testing your understanding of the terms and concepts. The review tests are of two types: Progress Tests that consist of questions focusing on facts and definitions and a Thinking Critically Test that evaluates your understanding of the text chapter's broader conceptual material and its application to real-world situations. For all three review tests, the correct answers are given, followed by textbook page references (so you can easily go back and reread the material), and complete explanations not only of why the answer is correct but also of why the other choices are incorrect.

I would like to thank Betty and Don Probert of The Special Projects Group for their exceptional work in all phases of this project. My thanks also to Danielle Pucci and Stacey Alexander for their skillful assistance in the preparation of this Study Guide. We hope that our work will help you to achieve your highest level of academic performance in this course and to acquire a keen appreciation of human development.

Richard O. Straub
September 2005

How to Manage Your Time Efficiently, Study More Effectively, and Think Critically

How effectively do you study? Good study habits make the job of being a college student much easier. Many students, who *could* succeed in college, fail or drop out because they have never learned to manage their time efficiently. Even the best students can usually benefit from an in-depth evaluation of their current study habits.

There are many ways to achieve academic success, of course, but your approach may not be the most effective or efficient. Are you sacrificing your social life or your physical or mental health in order to get A's on your exams? Good study habits result in better grades *and* more time for other activities.

Evaluate Your Current Study Habits

To improve your study habits, you must first have an accurate picture of how you currently spend your time. Begin by putting together a profile of your present living and studying habits. Answer the following questions by writing *yes* or *no* on each line.

_____ 1. Do you usually set up a schedule to budget your time for studying, recreation, and other activities?

_____ 2. Do you often put off studying until time pressures force you to cram?

_____ 3. Do other students seem to study less than you do, but get better grades?

_____ 4. Do you usually spend hours at a time studying one subject, rather than dividing that time between several subjects?

_____ 5. Do you often have trouble remembering what you have just read in a textbook?

_____ 6. Before reading a chapter in a textbook, do you skim through it and read the section headings?

_____ 7. Do you try to predict exam questions from your lecture notes and reading?

_____ 8. Do you usually attempt to paraphrase or summarize what you have just finished reading?

_____ 9. Do you find it difficult to concentrate very long when you study?

_____ 10. Do you often feel that you studied the wrong material for an exam?

Thousands of college students have participated in similar surveys. Students who are fully realizing their academic potential usually respond as follows: (1) yes, (2) no, (3) no, (4) no, (5) no, (6) yes, (7) yes, (8) yes, (9) no, (10) no.

Compare your responses to those of successful students. The greater the discrepancy, the more you could benefit from a program to improve your study habits. The questions are designed to identify areas of weakness. Once you have identified your weaknesses, you will be able to set specific goals for improvement and implement a program for reaching them.

Manage Your Time

Do you often feel frustrated because there isn't enough time to do all the things you must and want to do? Take heart. Even the most productive and successful people feel this way at times. But they establish priorities for their activities and they learn to budget time for each of them. There's much in the saying "If you want something done, ask a busy person to do it." A busy person knows how to get things done.

If you don't now have a system for budgeting your time, develop one. Not only will your academic accomplishments increase, but you will actually find more time in your schedule for other activities. And you won't have to feel guilty about "taking time off," because all your obligations will be covered.

Establish a Baseline

As a first step in preparing to budget your time, keep a diary for a few days to establish a summary, or baseline, of the time you spend in studying, socializing, working, and so on. If you are like many students, much of your "study" time is nonproductive; you may sit at your desk and leaf through a book, but the time is actually wasted. Or you may procrastinate. You are always getting ready to study, but you rarely do.

Besides revealing where you waste time, your time-management diary will give you a realistic picture of how much time you need to allot for meals, commuting, and other fixed activities. In addition, careful records should indicate the times of the day when you are consistently most productive. Table 1 shows a sample time-management diary.

Plan the Term

Having established and evaluated your baseline, you are ready to devise a more efficient schedule. Buy a calendar that covers the entire school term and has ample space for each day. Using the course outlines provided by your instructors, enter the dates of all exams, term paper deadlines, and other important academic obligations. If you have any long-range personal plans (concerts, weekend trips, etc.), enter the dates on the calendar as well. Keep your calendar up to date and refer to it often. I recommend carrying it with you at all times.

Develop a Weekly Calendar

Now that you have a general picture of the school term, develop a weekly schedule that includes all of your activities. Aim for a schedule that you can live with for the entire school term. A sample weekly schedule, incorporating the following guidelines, is shown in Table 2.

1. Enter your class times, work hours, and any other fixed obligations first. *Be thorough.* Using information from your time-management diary, allow plenty of time for such things as commuting, meals, laundry, and the like.

Table 1   Sample Time-Management Diary

Activity	Monday	
	Time Completed	Duration Hours: Minutes
Sleep	7:00	7:30
Dressing	7:25	:25
Breakfast	7:45	:20
Commute	8:20	:35
Coffee	9:00	:40
French	10:00	1:00
Socialize	10:15	:15
Videogame	10:35	:20
Coffee	11:00	:25
Psychology	12:00	1:00
Lunch	12:25	:25
Study Lab	1:00	:35
Psych. Lab	4:00	3:00
Work	5:30	1:30
Commute	6:10	:40
Dinner	6:45	:35
TV	7:30	:45
Study Psych.	10:00	2:30
Socialize	11:30	1:30
Sleep		

Prepare a similar chart for each day of the week. When you finish an activity, note it on the chart and write down the time it was completed. Then determine its duration by subtracting the time the previous activity was finished from the newly entered time.

2. Set up a study schedule for each of your courses. The study habits survey and your time-management diary will direct you. The following guidelines should also be useful.

(a) Establish regular study times for each course. The 4 hours needed to study one subject, for example, are most profitable when divided into shorter periods spaced over several days. If you cram your studying into one 4-hour block, what you attempt to learn in the third or fourth hour will interfere with what you studied in the first 2 hours. Newly acquired knowledge is like wet cement. It needs some time to "harden" to become memory.

(b) Alternate subjects. The type of interference just mentioned is greatest between similar topics. Set up a schedule in which you spend time on several *different* courses during each study session. Besides reducing the potential for interference, alternating subjects will help to prevent mental fatigue with one topic.

(c) Set weekly goals to determine the amount of study time you need to do well in each course. This will

Table 2   Sample Weekly Schedule

Time	Mon.	Tues.	Wed.	Thurs.	Fri.	Sat.
7–8	Dress Eat	Dress Eat	Dress Eat	Dress Eat	Dress Eat	
8–9	Psych.	Study Psych.	Psych.	Study Psych.	Psych.	Dress Eat
9–10	Eng.	Study Eng.	Eng.	Study Eng.	Eng.	Study Eng.
10–11	Study French	Free	Study French	Open Study	Study French	Study Stats.
11–12	French	Study Psych. Lab	French	Open Study	French	Study Stats.
12–1	Lunch	Lunch	Lunch	Lunch	Lunch	Lunch
1–2	Stats.	Psych. Lab	Stats.	Study or Free	Stats.	Free
2–3	Bio.	Psych. Lab	Bio.	Free	Bio.	Free
3–4	Free	Psych.	Free	Free	Free	Free
4–5	Job	Job	Job	Job	Job	Free
5–6	Job	Job	Job	Job	Job	Free
6–7	Dinner	Dinner	Dinner	Dinner	Dinner	Dinner
7–8	Study Bio.	Study Bio.	Study Bio.	Study Bio.	Free	Free
8–9	Study Eng.	Study Stats.	Study Psych.	Open Study	Open Study	Free
9–10	Open Study	Open Study	Open Study	Open Study	Free	Free

This is a sample schedule for a student with a 16-credit load and a 10-hour-per-week part-time job. Using this chart as an illustration, make up a weekly schedule, following the guidelines outlined here.

depend on, among other things, the difficulty of your courses and the effectiveness of your methods. Many professors recommend studying at least 1 to 2 hours for each hour in class. If your time-management diary indicates that you presently study less time than that, do not plan to jump immediately to a much higher level. Increase study time from your baseline by setting weekly goals [see (4)] that will gradually bring you up to the desired level. As an initial schedule, for example, you might set aside an amount of study time for each course that matches class time.

(d) Schedule for maximum effectiveness. Tailor your schedule to meet the demands of each course. For the course that emphasizes lecture notes, schedule time for a daily review soon after the class. This will give you a chance to revise your notes and clean up any hard-to-decipher shorthand while the material is still fresh in your mind. If you are evaluated for class participation (for example, in a language course), allow time for a review just before the class meets. Schedule study time for your most difficult (or least motivat-

ing) courses during hours when you are the most alert and distractions are fewest.

(e) Schedule open study time. Emergencies, additional obligations, and the like could throw off your schedule. And you may simply need some extra time periodically for a project or for review in one of your courses. Schedule several hours each week for such purposes.

3. After you have budgeted time for studying, fill in slots for recreation, hobbies, relaxation, household errands, and the like.

4. Set specific goals. Before each study session, make a list of specific goals. The simple note "7–8 PM: study psychology" is too broad to ensure the most effective use of the time. Formulate your daily goals according to what you know you must accomplish during the term. If you have course outlines with advance assignments, set systematic daily goals that will allow you, for example, to cover fifteen chapters before the exam. And be realistic: Can you actually

expect to cover a 78-page chapter in one session? Divide large tasks into smaller units; stop at the most logical resting points. When you complete a specific goal, take a 5- or 10-minute break before tackling the next goal.

5. Evaluate how successful or unsuccessful your studying has been on a daily or weekly basis. Did you reach most of your goals? If so, reward yourself immediately. You might even make a list of five to ten rewards to choose from. If you have trouble studying regularly, you may be able to motivate yourself by making such rewards contingent on completing specific goals.

6. Finally, until you have lived with your schedule for several weeks, don't hesitate to revise it. You may need to allow more time for chemistry, for example, and less for some other course. If you are trying to study regularly for the first time and are feeling burned out, you probably have set your initial goals too high. Don't let failure cause you to despair and abandon the program. Accept your limitations and revise your schedule so that you are studying only 15 to 20 minutes more each evening than you are used to. The point is to identify a regular schedule with which you can achieve some success. Time management, like any skill, must be practiced to become effective.

Techniques for Effective Study

Knowing how to put study time to best use is, of course, as important as finding a place for it in your schedule. Here are some suggestions that should enable you to increase your reading comprehension and improve your note-taking. A few study tips are included as well.

Using SQ3R to Increase Reading Comprehension

How do you study from a textbook? If you are like many students, you simply read and reread in a *passive* manner. Studies have shown, however, that most students who simply read a textbook cannot remember more than half the material ten minutes after they have finished. Often, what is retained is the unessential material rather than the important points upon which exam questions will be based.

This *Study Guide* employs a program known as SQ3R (Survey, Question, Read, Recite, and Review) to facilitate, and allow you to assess, your comprehension of the important facts and concepts in *The Developing Person Through Childhood and Adolescence*, Seventh Edition, by Kathleen Stassen Berger.

Research has shown that students using SQ3R achieve significantly greater comprehension of textbooks than students reading in the more traditional passive manner. Once you have learned this program, you can improve your comprehension of any textbook.

Survey   Before reading a chapter, determine whether the text or the study guide has an outline or list of objectives. Read this material and the summary at the end of the chapter. Next, read the textbook chapter fairly quickly, paying special attention to the major headings and subheadings. This survey will give you an idea of the chapter's contents and organization. You will then be able to divide the chapter into logical sections in order to formulate specific goals for a more careful reading of the chapter.

In this Study Guide, the *Chapter Overview* summarizes the major topics of the textbook chapter. This section also provides a few suggestions for approaching topics you may find difficult.

Question   You will retain material longer when you have a use for it. If you look up a word's definition in order to solve a crossword puzzle, for example, you will remember it longer than if you merely fill in the letters as a result of putting other words in. Surveying the chapter will allow you to generate important questions that the chapter will proceed to answer. These question correspond to "mental files" into which knowledge will be sorted for easy access.

As you survey, jot down several questions for each chapter section. One simple technique is to generate questions by rephrasing a section heading. For example, the "Preoperational Thought" head could be turned into "What is preoperational thought?" Good questions will allow you to focus on the important points in the text. Examples of good questions are those that begin as follows: "List two examples of . . . ." "What is the function of . . . ?" "What is the significance of . . . ?" Such questions give a purpose to your reading. Similarly, you can formulate questions based on the chapter outline.

The *Guided Study* section of this Study Guide provides the types of questions you might formulate while surveying each chapter. This section is a detailed set of objectives covering the points made in the text.

Read   When you have established "files" for each section of the chapter, review your first question, begin reading, and continue until you have discovered its answer. If you come to material that seems to answer an important question you don't have a file for, stop and write down the question.

Using this Study Guide, read the chapter one section at a time. First, preview the section by skimming it, noting headings and boldface items. Next, study the appropriate section objectives in the *Guided Study*. Then, as you read the chapter section, search for the answer to each objective.

Be sure to read everything. Don't skip photo or art captions, graphs, marginal notes. In some cases, what may seem vague in reading will be made clear by a simple graph. Keep in mind that test questions are sometimes drawn from illustrations and charts.

Recite When you have found the answer to a question, close your eyes and mentally recite the question and its answer. Then *write* the answer next to the question. It is important that you recite an answer in your own words rather than the author's. Don't rely on your short-term memory to repeat the author's words verbatim.

In responding to the objectives, pay close attention to what is called for. If you are asked to identify or list, do just that. If asked to compare, contrast, or do both, you should focus on the similarities (compare) and differences (contrast) between the concepts or theories. Answering the objectives carefully will not only help you to focus your attention on the important concepts of the text, but it will also provide excellent practice for essay exams.

Recitation is an extremely effective study technique, recommended by many learning experts. In addition to increasing reading comprehension, it is useful for review. Trying to explain something in your own words clarifies your knowledge, often by revealing aspects of your answer that are vague or incomplete. If you repeatedly rely upon "I know" in recitation, you really may not know.

Recitation has the additional advantage of simulating an exam, especially an essay exam; the same skills are required in both cases. Too often students study without ever putting the book and notes aside, which makes it easy for them to develop false confidence in their knowledge. When the material is in front of you, you may be able to recognize an answer, but will you be able to recall it later, when you take an exam that does not provide these retrieval cues?

After you have recited and written your answer, continue with your next question. Read, recite, and so on.

Review When you have answered the last question on the material you have designated as a study goal, go back and review. Read over each question and your written answer to it. Your review might also include a brief written summary that integrates all of your questions and answers. This review need not

take longer than a few minutes, but it is important. It will help you retain the material longer and will greatly facilitate a final review of each chapter before the exam.

In this Study Guide, the *Chapter Review* section contains fill-in and one- or two-sentence essay questions for you to complete after you have finished reading the text and have written answers to the objectives. The correct answers are given at the end of the chapter. Generally, your answer to a fill-in question should match exactly (as in the case of important terms, theories, or people). In some cases, the answer is not a term or name, so a word close in meaning will suffice. You should go through the Chapter Review several times before taking an exam, so it is a good idea to mentally fill in the answers until you are ready for a final pretest review. Textbook page references are provided with each section title, in case you need to reread any of the material.

Also provided to facilitate your review are two *Progress Tests* that include multiple-choice questions and, where appropriate, matching or true–false questions. These tests are not to be taken until you have read the chapter, written answers to the objectives, and completed the *Chapter Review.* Correct answers, along with explanations of why each alternative is correct or incorrect, are provided at the end of the chapter. The relevant text page numbers for each question are also given. If you miss a question, read these explanations and, if necessary, review the text pages to further understand why. The *Progress Tests* do not test every aspect of a concept, so you should treat an incorrect answer as an indication that you need to review the concept.

Following the two Progress Tests is a *Thinking Critically Test*, which should be taken just prior to an exam. It includes questions that test your ability to analyze, integrate, and apply the concepts in the chapter. As with the *Progress Tests*, answers for the *Thinking Critically Test* are provided at the end of each chapter, along with relevant page numbers.

The chapter concludes with *Key Terms*, either in list form only or also in a crossword puzzle. In either form, as with the *Guided Study* objectives, it is important that the answers be written from memory, and in list form, in your own words. The *Answers* section at the end of the chapter gives a definition of each term, sometimes along with an example of its usage and/or a tip to help you remember its meaning.

One final suggestion: Incorporate SQ3R into your time-management calendar. Set specific goals for completing SQ3R with each assigned chapter. Keep a record of chapters completed, and reward yourself for being conscientious. Initially, it takes more time and effort to "read" using SQ3R, but with practice, the steps will become automatic. More importantly, you will comprehend significantly more material and retain what you have learned longer than passive readers do.

Taking Lecture Notes

Are your class notes as useful as they might be? One way to determine their worth is to compare them with those taken by other good students. Are yours as thorough? Do they provide you with a comprehensible outline of each lecture? If not, then the following suggestions might increase the effectiveness of your note-taking.

1. Keep a separate notebook for each course. Use standard notebook pages. Consider using a ring binder, which would allow you to revise and insert notes while still preserving lecture order.

2. Take notes in the format of a lecture outline. Use roman numerals for major points, letters for supporting arguments, and so on. Some instructors will make this easy by delivering organized lectures and, in some cases, by outlining their lectures on the board. If a lecture is disorganized, you will probably want to reorganize your notes soon after the class.

3. As you take notes in class, leave a wide margin on one side of each page. After the lecture, expand or clarify any shorthand notes while the material is fresh in your mind. Use this time to write important questions in the margin next to notes that answer them. This will facilitate later review and will allow you to anticipate similar exam questions.

Evaluate Your Exam Performance

How often have you received a grade on an exam that did not do justice to the effort you spent preparing for the exam? This is a common experience that can leave one feeling bewildered and abused. "What do I have to do to get an A?" "The test was unfair!" "I studied the wrong material!"

The chances of this happening are greatly reduced if you have an effective time-management schedule and use the study techniques described here. But it can happen to the best-prepared student and is most likely to occur on your first exam with a new professor.

Remember that there are two main reasons for studying. One is to learn for your own general academic development. Many people believe that such knowledge is all that really matters. Of course, it is possible,

though unlikely, to be an expert on a topic without achieving commensurate grades, just as one can, occasionally, earn an excellent grade without truly mastering the course material. During a job interview or in the workplace, however, your A in Cobol won't mean much if you can't actually program a computer.

In order to keep career options open after you graduate, you must know the material and maintain competitive grades. In the short run, this means performing well on exams, which is the second main objective in studying.

Probably the single best piece of advice to keep in mind when studying for exams is to *try to predict exam questions.* This means ignoring the trivia and focusing on the important questions and their answers (with your instructor's emphasis in mind).

A second point is obvious. How well you do on exams is determined by your mastery of both lecture and textbook material. Many students (partly because of poor time management) concentrate too much on one at the expense of the other.

To evaluate how well you are learning lecture and textbook material, analyze the questions you missed on the first exam. If your instructor does not review exams during class, you can easily do it yourself. Divide the questions into two categories: those drawn primarily from lectures and those drawn primarily from the textbook. Determine the percentage of questions you missed in each category. If your errors are evenly distributed and you are satisfied with your grade, you have no problem. If you are weaker in one area, you will need to set future goals for increasing and/or improving your study of that area.

Similarly, note the percentage of test questions drawn from each category. Although exams in most courses cover both lecture notes and the textbook, the relative emphasis of each may vary from instructor to instructor. While your instructors may not be entirely consistent in making up future exams, you may be able to tailor your studying for each course by placing additional emphasis on the appropriate area.

Exam evaluation will also point out the types of questions your instructor prefers. Does the exam consist primarily of multiple-choice, true–false, or essay questions? You may also discover that an instructor is fond of wording questions in certain ways. For example, an instructor may rely heavily on questions that require you to draw an analogy between a theory or concept and a real-world example. Evaluate both your instructor's style and how well you do with each format. Use this information to guide your future exam preparation.

Important aids, not only in studying for exams but also in determining how well prepared you are, are the Progress and Thinking Critically Tests provided in this Study Guide. If these tests don't include all of the types of questions your instructor typically writes, make up your own practice exam questions. Spend extra time testing yourself with question formats that are most difficult for you. There is no better way to evaluate your preparation for an upcoming exam than by testing yourself under the conditions most likely to be in effect during the actual test.

A Few Practical Tips

Even the best intentions for studying sometimes fail. Some of these failures occur because students attempt to work under conditions that are simply not conducive to concentrated study. To help ensure the success of your time-management program, here are a few suggestions that should assist you in reducing the possibility of procrastination or distraction.

1. If you have set up a schedule for studying, make your roommate, family, and friends aware of this commitment, and ask them to honor your quiet study time. Close your door and post a "Do Not Disturb" sign.

2. Set up a place to study that minimizes potential distractions. Use a desk or table, not your bed or an extremely comfortable chair. Keep your desk and the walls around it free from clutter. If you need a place other than your room, find one that meets as many of the above requirements as possible—for example, in the library stacks.

3. Do nothing but study in this place. It should become associated with studying so that it "triggers" this activity, just as a mouth-watering aroma elicits an appetite.

4. Never study with the television on or with other distracting noises present. If you must have music in the background in order to mask outside noise, for example, play soft instrumental music. Don't pick vocal selections; your mind will be drawn to the lyrics.

5. Study by yourself. Other students can be distracting or can break the pace at which your learning is most efficient. In addition, there is always the possibility that group studying will become a social gathering. Reserve that for its own place in your schedule.

If you continue to have difficulty concentrating for very long, try the following suggestions.

6. Study your most difficult or most challenging subjects first, when you are most alert.

7. Start with relatively short periods of concentrated study, with breaks in between. If your attention starts to wander, get up immediately and take a break. It is better to study effectively for 15 minutes and then take a break than to fritter away 45 minutes out of an hour. Gradually increase the length of study periods, using your attention span as an indicator of successful pacing.

Critical Thinking

Having discussed a number of specific techniques for managing your time efficiently and studying effectively, let us now turn to a much broader topic: What exactly should you expect to learn as a student of developmental psychology?

Most developmental psychology courses have two major goals: (1) to help you acquire a basic understanding of the discipline's knowledge base, and (2) to help you learn to think like a psychologist. Many students devote all of their efforts to the first of these goals, concentrating on memorizing as much of the course's material as possible.

The second goal—learning to think like a psychologist—has to do with critical thinking. Critical thinking has many meanings. On one level, it refers to an attitude of healthy skepticism that should guide your study of psychology. As a critical thinker, you learn not to accept any explanation or conclusion about behavior as true until you have evaluated the evidence. On another level, critical thinking refers to a systematic process for examining the conclusions and arguments presented by others. In this regard, many of the features of the SQ3R technique for improving reading comprehension can be incorporated into an effective critical thinking system.

To learn to think critically, you must first recognize that psychological information is transmitted through the construction of persuasive arguments. An argument consists of three parts: an assertion, evidence, and an explanation (Mayer and Goodchild, 1990).

An assertion is a statement of relationship between some aspect of behavior, such as intelligence, and another factor, such as age. Learn to identify and evaluate the assertions about behavior and mental processes that you encounter as you read your textbook, listen to lectures, and engage in discussions with classmates. A good test of your understanding of an assertion is to try to restate it in your own words. As you do so, pay close attention to how important terms and concepts are defined. When a researcher asserts that "intelligence declines with age," for example, what does he or she mean by "intelligence"? Assertions such as this one may be true when a critical term ("intelligence") is defined one way (for example, "speed of thinking"), but not when defined in another way (for example, "general knowledge"). One of the strengths of psychology is the use of *operational* definitions that specify how key terms and concepts are measured, thus eliminating any ambiguity about their meaning. "Intelligence," for example, is often operationally defined as performance on a test measuring various cognitive skills. Whenever you encounter an assertion that is ambiguous, be skeptical of its accuracy.

When you have a clear understanding of an argument's assertion, evaluate its supporting evidence, the second component of an argument. Is it *empirical*? Does it, in fact, support the assertion? Psychologists accept only *empirical (observable) evidence* that is based on direct measurement of behavior. Hearsay, intuition, and personal experiences are not acceptable evidence. Chapter 1 discusses the various research methods used by developmental psychologists to gather empirical evidence. Some examples include surveys, observations of behavior in natural settings, and experiments.

As you study developmental psychology, you will become aware of another important issue in evaluating evidence—determining whether or not the research on which it is based is faulty. Research can be faulty for many reasons, including the use of an unrepresentative sample of subjects, experimenter bias, and inadequate control of unanticipated factors that might influence results. Evidence based on faulty research should be discounted.

The third component of an argument is the explanation provided for an assertion, which is based on the evidence that has been presented. While the argument's assertion merely *describes* how two things (such as intelligence and age) are related, the explanation tells *why*, often by proposing some theoretical mechanism that causes the relationship. Empirical evidence that thinking speed slows with age (the assertion), for example, may be explained as being caused by age-related changes in the activity of brain cells (a physiological explanation).

Be cautious in accepting explanations. In order to think critically about an argument's explanation, ask yourself three questions: (1) Can I restate the explanation in my own words?; (2) Does the explanation make sense based on the stated evidence?; and (3) Are there alternative explanations that adequately explain the assertion? Consider this last point in relation to our sample assertion: It is possible that the slower thinking speed of older adults is due to their having less recent experience than younger people with tasks that require quick thinking (a disuse explanation).

Because psychology is a relatively young science, its theoretical explanations are still emerging, and often change. For this reason, not all psychological arguments will offer explanations. Many arguments will only raise additional questions for further research to address.

Some Suggestions for Becoming a Critical Thinker

1. Adopt an attitude of healthy skepticism in evaluating psychological arguments.

2. Insist on unambiguous operational definitions of an argument's important concepts and terms.

3. Be cautious in accepting supporting evidence for an argument's assertion.

4. Refuse to accept evidence for an argument if it is based on faulty research.

5. Ask yourself if the theoretical explanation provided for an argument "makes sense" based on the empirical evidence.

6. Determine whether there are alternative explanations that adequately explain an assertion.

7. Use critical thinking to construct your own effective arguments when writing term papers, answering essay questions, and speaking.

8. Polish your critical-thinking skills by applying them to each of your college courses, and to other areas of life as well. Learn to think critically about advertising, political speeches, and the material presented in popular periodicals.

Some Closing Thoughts

I hope that these suggestions help make you more successful academically, and that they enhance the quality of your college life in general. Having the necessary skills makes any job a lot easier and more pleasant. Let me repeat my warning not to attempt to make too drastic a change in your life-style immediately. Good habits require time and self-discipline to develop. Once established they can last a lifetime.

Chapter One

Introduction

Chapter Overview

The first chapter introduces the study of human development. The first two sections define development, identify five characteristics of the scientific study of human development, and explain different aspects of the overlapping contexts in which people develop. The story of David illustrates the effects of these contexts.

The next section discusses the strategies developmentalists use in their research, beginning with the scientific method and including scientific observation, experiments, surveys, and case studies. To study people over time, developmentalists have created several research designs: cross-sectional, longitudinal, and cross-sequential. The ecological-systems approach—Bronfenbrenner's description of how the individual is affected by, and affects, many other individuals, groups of individuals, and larger systems in the environment—can be used with any research strategy or any combination of strategies.

The final section discusses several common mistakes that can be made in interpreting research, including the mistake of confusing correlation with causation, and the ethics of research with humans. In addition to ensuring confidentiality and safety, developmentalists who study children are especially concerned that the benefits of research outweigh the risks.

NOTE: Answer guidelines for all Chapter 1 questions begin on page 11.

Guided Study

The text chapter should be studied one section at a time. Before you read, preview each section by skimming it, noting headings and boldface items. Then read the appropriate section objectives from the following outline. Keep these objectives in mind and, as you read the chapter section, search for the information that will enable you to meet each objective. Once you have finished a section, write out answers for its objectives.

Defining Development (pp. 5–6)

1. Define development, focusing on three elements of its scientific study.

Five Characteristics of Development (pp. 6–17)

2. Identify five characteristics of development.

3. Discuss two aspects of the social context that affect development.

4. Discuss the multidisciplinary approach to the study of development, focusing on understanding childhood psychopathology and noting the three domains into which development is divided.

5. Using the multicontextual approach, discuss the origins of childhood resilience.

Developmental Study as a Science (pp. 18–27)

6. List and describe the basic steps of the scientific method.

7. Describe scientific observation as a research strategy, noting at least one advantage (or strength) and one disadvantage (or weakness).

8. Describe the components of an experiment, and discuss the main advantage of this research method.

9. Describe surveys and case studies, noting at least one advantage (or strength) and one disadvantage (or weakness) of each.

10. (Thinking Like a Scientist) Define and differentiate ethnicity, race, and culture.

11. Describe three basic research designs used by developmental psychologists.

12. Describe the ecological-systems approach to the study of human development, and explain how this approach leads to an understanding of the overlapping contexts in which people develop.

Cautions from Science (pp. 28–32)

13. Describe two common mistakes made in the interpretation of research.

14. Briefly summarize some of the ethical issues involved in conducting research with humans.

Chapter Review

When you have finished reading the chapter, work through the material that follows to review it. Complete the sentences and answer the questions. As you proceed, evaluate your performance for each section by consulting the answers beginning on page 11. Do not continue with the next section until you understand each answer. If you need to, review or reread the appropriate section in the textbook before continuing.

Defining Development (pp. 5–6)

1. The scientific study of human development can be defined as the science that seeks to understand

   _____

   _____.

2. Development is characterized by _____, characteristics that are unchanging, and by _____, or characteristics that change over time.

Five Characteristics of Development (pp. 6–17)

The five developmental characteristics embodied within the science of development are that development is

   a. _____

   b. _____

   c. _____

   d. _____

   e. _____

3. Four important insights emerging from the fact that development is multidirectional are that

   a. human development is _____ .

   b. each aspect of life is _____ .

   c. the _____ _____ , in which even a tiny change in one system can have a profound effect on the other systems of development.

   d. the power of _____ , in which even large changes seemingly have no effect.

4. A group of people born within a few years of each other is called a _____ . These people tend to be affected by history in _____ (the same way/different ways).

5. A contextual influence that is determined by a person's income, education, place of residence, and occupation is called _____ _____ , which is often abbreviated _____ .

6. The values, technologies, customs, and patterns of behavior as well as the physical objects that a group of people have adopted as a design for living constitute a _____ .

7. People can belong to _____ (only one/more than one) culture, with the particular choice dependent on their immediate _____ .

8. The study of human development can be divided into three domains: _____ , _____ , and _____ .

9. Multiple disciplines are needed to understand development because people develop in several _____ , multifaceted _____ , and diverse _____ .

10. Although the fear response is localized in the brain area known as the _____ , fearfulness is also more likely in people who inherit the _____ (shorter/longer) version of the serotonin transporter gene. Research from the new field of _____ _____ _____ has revealed that each person's past _____ and the immediate _____ affect activity in the amygdala.

11. One of the most encouraging aspects of the science of development is that development is characterized by _____ , or the ability to change. One remarkable example is _____ , or the ability of some children to overcome severe threats to their development.

12. Although poverty is a useful signal for severe problems throughout life, other variables, such as the nature of the family life and the child's _____ , play a crucial role in determining individual development. Another variable is _____ _____ , which refers to the degree to which neighbors create a functioning, informal network of people who show concern for each other.

13. (A Case) Because his mother contracted the disease _____ during her pregnancy, David was born with a heart defect and cataracts over both eyes. Thus, his immediate problems centered on _____ problems. However, because he was born at a particular time, he was already influenced by the larger _____ context. Particularly in the church community, the _____-_____ context benefited him. David's continuing development of his skills is a testimony for _____ .

Developmental Study as a Science (pp. 18–27)

14. In order, the basic steps of the scientific method are

    a. _____

    b. _____

    c. _____

    d. _____

    e. _____

15. A specific, testable prediction that forms the basis of a research project is called a _____ .

16. To repeat an experimental test procedure and obtain the same results is to _____ the test of the hypothesis.

17. In designing research studies, scientists are concerned with four issues: _____ , or whether a study measures what it purports to measure; _____ , or whether its measurements are accurate; _____ , or whether the study applies to other populations

and situations; and _____ , or whether it solves real-life problems.

18. When researchers observe and record, in a systematic and objective manner, what research participants do, they are using _____ _____ .

19. In the science of human development, people may be observed in a _____ setting or in a _____ .

20. A chief limitation of observation is that it does not indicate the _____ of the behavior being observed.

21. The method that allows a scientist to determine cause and effect is the _____ . In this method, researchers manipulate a(n) _____ variable to determine its effect on a(n) _____ variable. Sometimes, results are reported by _____ size, and sometimes tests of _____ are used to indicate whether the results might have occurred by chance.

22. In an experiment, the participants who receive a particular treatment constitute the _____ _____ ; the participants who do not receive the treatment constitute the

    _____ _____ .

23. In a(n) _____ , scientists collect information from a large group of people by personal interview, written questionnaire, or some other means.

24. Potential problems with this research method are that those being questioned are not _____ of the group of interest, the _____ and _____ of the questions may influence people's answers, and respondents may give answers that make them seem wise or good.

25. (Thinking Like a Scientist) A collection of people who share certain attributes, such as ancestry, national origin, religion, and language and, as a result, tend to have similar beliefs, values, and cultural experiences is called a(n) _____ _____ . Biological

traits used to differentiate people whose ancestors come from different regions is the definition of _____ .

26. An intensive study of one individual is called a(n) _____ _____ . An advantage of this method is that it makes it possible to understand a particular individual very well. Other important uses are that it provides a good _____ _____ for other research and that it can illustrate _____ .

27. Research that involves the comparison of people of different ages is called a _____-_____ research design.

28. With cross-sectional research it is very difficult to ensure that the various groups differ only in their _____ . In addition, every cross-sectional study will, to some degree, reflect _____ _____ .

29. Research that follows the same people over a relatively long period of time is called a _____ research design.

State three drawbacks of this type of research design.

30. The research method that combines the longitudinal and cross-sectional methods is the _____-_____ research method.

31. The approach that emphasizes the influence of the systems that support the developing person is called the _____-_____ approach. This approach was emphasized by _____ .

32. According to this model, the family, the peer group, and other aspects of the immediate social setting constitute the _____ .

33. Systems that link one microsystem to another constitute the _____ .

34. Community institutions such as school and church make up the _____ .

35. Cultural values, political philosophies, economic patterns, and social systems make up the _____ .

36. The final system in this model is the _____ , which emphasizes the importance of historical time on development.

Cautions from Science (pp. 28–32)

37. A number that indicates the degree of relationship between two variables is a _____ . To say that two variables are related in this way _____ (does/does not) necessarily imply that one caused the other. A correlation is _____ if both variables tend to _____ together; a correlation is _____ if one variable tends to _____ when the other _____ ; a correlation is _____ if there is no evident connection between the two variables.

38. Because numbers can be easily summarized and compared, scientists often rely on data produced by _____ research. This method may be particularly limiting when researchers describe _____ , and so many developmental researchers use _____ research that asks _____-_____ questions.

39. Developmental researchers work from a set of moral principles that constitute their _____ _____ _____ . Researchers who study humans must obtain _____ _____ , which refers to written permission, and ensure that their participants are not _____ and that they are allowed to stop at any time.

40. To ensure that research is not unintentionally slanting, scientific _____ , _____ , and replication are crucial.

Progress Test 1

Multiple-Choice Questions

Circle your answers to the following questions and check them against the answers on page 12. If your answer is incorrect, read the explanation for why it is incorrect and then consult the appropriate pages of the text (in parentheses following the correct answer).

1. The scientific study of human development is defined as the study of:
   a. how and why people change or remain the same over time.
   b. psychosocial influences on aging.
   c. individual differences in learning over the life span.
   d. all of the above.

2. The research method that involves the use of open-ended questions and obtains answers that are not easily translated into categories is:
   a. the case study.
   b. qualitative research.
   c. cross-sectional study.
   d. quantitative research.

3. Which of the following is *not* an important aspect of the social context mentioned in the text?
   a. historical
   b. socioeconomic
   c. cultural
   d. racial

4. Which of the following describes a neighborhood in which people pitch in to keep children safe, keep trash off the streets, and generally show concern for one another?
   a. cohort effect
   b. collective efficacy
   c. resilience
   d. butterfly effect

5. The ecological-systems approach to developmental psychology focuses on the:
   a. biochemistry of the body systems.
   b. macrosystems only.
   c. internal thinking processes.
   d. overall environment of development.

6. The science of development focuses on:
   a. the sources of continuity from the beginning of life to the end.
   b. the sources of discontinuity throughout life.

   c. the "nonlinear" character of human development.
   d. all of the above.

7. Neuroscientists have discovered that the brain's amygdala is a major source of which emotion?
   a. joy
   b. sadness
   c. fear
   d. anger

8. A hypothesis is a:
   a. conclusion.
   b. prediction to be tested.
   c. statistical test.
   d. correlation.

9. A developmentalist who is interested in studying the influences of a person's immediate environment on his or her behavior is focusing on which system?
   a. mesosystem   c. microsystem
   b. macrosystem   d. exosystem

10. Socioeconomic status is determined by a combination of variables, including:
    a. age, education, and income.
    b. income, ethnicity, and occupation.
    c. income, education, and occupation.
    d. age, ethnicity, and occupation.

11. Developmentalists refer to the ability of some children to become happy, healthy, and productive adults despite growing up in terrible circumstances as:
    a. the butterfly effect.
    b. resilience.
    c. continuity.
    d. discontinuity.

12. In an experiment testing the effects of group size on individual effort in a tug-of-war task, the number of people in each group is the:
    a. hypothesis.
    b. independent variable.
    c. dependent variable.
    d. level of significance.

13. Which research method would be most appropriate for investigating the relationship between parents' religious beliefs and their attitudes toward middle-school sex education?
    a. experimentation
    b. longitudinal research
    c. naturalistic observation
    d. the survey

14. To establish cause, which type of research study would an investigator conduct?
    a. an experiment
    b. a survey
    c. scientific observation
    d. a case study

15. Developmentalists who carefully observe the behavior of schoolchildren during recess are using a research method known as:
    a. the case study.
    b. cross-sectional research.
    c. scientific observation.
    d. cross-sequential research.

True or False Items

Write T (*true*) or F (*false*) on the line in front of each statement.

_____ 1. Scientists rarely repeat an experiment.
_____ 2. (A Case) The case study of David clearly demonstrates that for some children only nature (or heredity) is important.
_____ 3. Observation usually indicates a clear relationship between cause and effect.
_____ 4. Each social context influences development independently.
_____ 5. Cohort differences are an example of the impact of the social context on development.
_____ 6. Every trait of an individual can be molded into different forms and shapes.
_____ 7. Because of its limitations, qualitative research is rarely used in developmental research.
_____ 8. The influences between and within Bronfenbrenner's systems are unidirectional and independent.
_____ 9. People of different ethnic groups can all share one culture.
_____ 10. Longitudinal research is particularly useful in studying development over a long age span.

Progress Test 2

Progress Test 2 should be completed during a final chapter review. Answer the following questions after you thoroughly understand the correct answers for the Chapter Review and Progress Test 1.

Multiple-Choice Questions

1. An individual's personal sphere of development refers to his or her:
   a. microsystem and mesosystem.
   b. exosystem.
   c. macrosystem.
   d. microsystem, mesosystem, exosystem, macrosystem, and chronosystem.

2. Developmental psychologists explore three domains of development:
   a. physical, cognitive, psychosocial.
   b. physical, biosocial, cognitive.
   c. biosocial, cognitive, psychosocial.
   d. biosocial, cognitive, emotional.

3. The most important principle of the developmental research code of ethics is:
   a. never physically or psychologically harm those who are involved in research.
   b. maintain confidentiality at all costs.
   c. obtain informed consent from all participants.
   d. ensure that participants do not understand the true purpose of their research study.

4. When developmentalists speak of the "butterfly effect," they are most directly referring to the idea that:
   a. a small event may have a powerful impact on development.
   b. development is fundamentally a nonlinear event.
   c. each context of development is a dynamic system.
   d. each context of development interacts with the others.

5. According to the ecological-systems approach, the macrosystem would include:
   a. the peer group.   c. cultural values.
   b. the community.   d. the family.

6. When developmentalists speak of the "power of continuity," they are referring to the insight that:
   a. a change in one developmental system often affects many other things.
   b. a small change can become huge.
   c. a large change may have no perceptible effect.
   d. all of the above occur.

7. Professor Cohen predicts that because "baby boomers" grew up in an era that promoted independence and assertiveness, people in their 40s and 50s will respond differently to a political survey than will people in their 20s and 30s. The professor's prediction regarding political attitudes is an example of a(n):
   a. replication.
   b. hypothesis.
   c. independent variable.
   d. dependent variable.

8. A cohort is defined as a group of people:
   a. of similar national origin.
   b. who share a common language.
   c. born within a few years of each other.
   d. who share the same religion.

9. In a test of the effects of noise, groups of students performed a proofreading task in a noisy or a quiet room. To what group were students in the noisy room assigned?
   a. experimental   c. randomly assigned
   b. comparison   d. dependent

10. (Thinking Like a Scientist) In differentiating ethnicity and culture, we note that:
    a. ethnicity is an exclusively biological phenomenon.
    b. an ethnic group is a group of people who were born within a few years of each other.
    c. people of many ethnic groups can share one culture, yet maintain their ethnic identities.
    d. racial identity is always an element of culture.

11. If developmentalists discovered that poor people are happier than wealthy people are, this would indicate that wealth and happiness are:
    a. unrelated.
    b. correlated.
    c. examples of nature and nurture, respectively.
    d. causally related.

12. The plasticity of development refers to the fact that:
    a. development is not always linear.
    b. each human life must be understood as embedded in many contexts.
    c. there are many reciprocal connections between childhood and adulthood.
    d. human characteristics can be molded into different forms and shapes.

13. In an experiment testing the effects of noise level on mood, mood is the:
    a. hypothesis.
    b. independent variable.
    c. dependent variable.
    d. scientific observation.

14. People who inherit the shorter of two alleles of the serotonin transporter gene:
    a. are more likely to score higher in clinical tests for fearfulness.
    b. have less active amygdalas.
    c. are more likely to engage in thrill-seeking and other acts of fearlessness.
    d. are characterized by all of the above.

15. (Thinking Like a Scientist) Which of the following statements concerning ethnicity and culture is *not* true?
    a. Ethnicity is determined genetically.
    b. Race is a social construction.
    c. Racial identity is an element of ethnicity.
    d. Ethnic identity provides people with shared values and beliefs.

Matching Items

Match each definition or description with its corresponding term.

Terms

_____ 1. independent variable
_____ 2. dependent variable
_____ 3. culture
_____ 4. replicate
_____ 5. chronosystem
_____ 6. exosystem
_____ 7. mesosystem
_____ 8. socioeconomic status
_____ 9. cohort
_____ 10. ethnic group
_____ 11. cross-sectional research
_____ 12. longitudinal research

Definitions or Descriptions

a. group of people born within a few years of each other
b. determined by a person's income, education, occupation, and so on
c. research study comparing people of different ages at the same time
d. the historical conditions that affect development
e. collection of people who share certain attributes, such as national origin
f. shared values, patterns of behavior, and customs maintained by people in a specific setting
g. local institutions such as schools
h. the variable manipulated in an experiment
i. connections between microsystems
j. to repeat a study and obtain the same findings
k. the variable measured in an experiment
l. research study retesting one group of people at several different times

Thinking Critically About Chapter 1

Answer these questions the day before an exam as a final check on your understanding of the chapter's terms and concepts.

1. Dr. Ahmed is conducting research that takes into consideration the relationship between the individual and the environment. Evidently, Dr. Ahmed is using the:
   a. ecological-systems approach.
   b. longitudinal method.
   c. cross-sectional method.
   d. case study method.

2. In order to study the effects of temperature on mood, Dr. Sanchez had students fill out questionnaires in very warm or very cool rooms. In this study, the independent variable consisted of:
   a. the number of students assigned to each group.
   b. the students' responses to the questionnaire.
   c. the room temperature.
   d. the subject matter of the questions.

3. Jahmal is writing a paper on the role of the social context in development. He would do well to consult the writings of:
   a. Piaget.   c. Bronfenbrenner.
   b. Freud.   d. Skinner.

4. Summarizing her presentation on race and biology, Trisha notes that:
   a. a racial group is a collection of people who share ancestral heritage.
   b. race is a biological construction defined by the genetic traits of a group of people.
   c. social scientists recognize that all racial categories are imprecise.
   d. all of the above are true.

5. Esteban believes that high doses of caffeine slow a person's reaction time. In order to test his belief, he has five friends each drink three 8-ounce cups of coffee and then measures their reaction time on a learning task. What is wrong with Esteban's research strategy?
   a. No independent variable is specified.
   b. No dependent variable is specified.
   c. There is no comparison condition.
   d. There is no provision for replication of the findings.

6. Your roommate is skeptical when you tell her that development is characterized by continuity. To illustrate, you give the example of:
   a. mastering a new language.
   b. overcoming an addiction.
   c. learning to play the piano as an adult.
   d. temperament.

7. Research on the roots of fear has revealed that:
   a. fear depends on past learning.
   b. fear is caused by genes.
   c. fear depends on an individual's current context.
   d. biology, psychology, and sociology all help explain why some people feel threatened in situations that others perceive as harmless.

8. Professor Jorgenson believes development is plastic. By this she means that:
   a. change in development occurs in every direction, not always in a straight line.
   b. human lives are embedded in many different contexts.
   c. there are many cultures that influence development.
   d. every individual, and every trait within each individual, can be altered at any point in the life span.

9. Karen's mother is puzzled by the numerous discrepancies between the developmental psychology textbook she used in 1976 and her daughter's contemporary text. Karen explains that the differences are the result of:
   a. the lack of regard by earlier researchers for the scientific method.
   b. changing social conditions and cohort effects.
   c. the widespread use of cross-sectional research today.
   d. the widespread use of longitudinal research today.

10. If height and body weight are correlated, which of the following is true?
    a. There is a cause-and-effect relationship between height and weight.
    b. Knowing a person's height, one can predict his or her weight.
    c. Both a. and b. are true.
    d. Neither is true.

11. An example of longitudinal research would be when an investigator compares the performance of:
    a. several different age groups on a memory test.
    b. the same group of people, at different ages, on a test of memory.
    c. an experimental group and a comparison group on a test of memory.
    d. several different age groups on a test of memory as each group is tested repeatedly over a period of years.

12. For her developmental psychology research project, Lakia decides she wants to focus primarily on qualitative data. You advise her to conduct:
    a. a survey.
    b. an experiment.
    c. a cross-sectional study.
    d. a case study.

13. Professor Johnson warns her students to be skeptical of the results of a controversial study because it has not been replicated. By this she means that:
    a. there was no experimental group.
    b. there was no comparison group.
    c. the study has not yet been repeated by other researchers in order to verify the original findings.
    d. the results are statistically insignificant.

14. Dr. Weston is comparing research findings for a group of 30-year-olds with findings for the same individuals at age 20, as well as with findings for groups who were 30 in 1990. Which research method is she using?
    a. longitudinal research
    b. cross-sectional research
    c. case study
    d. cross-sequential research

15. To find out whether people's attitudes regarding an issue vary with their ages, Karen distributes the same survey to groups of people in their 20s, 30s, 40s, 50s, and 60s. Karen is evidently conducting:
    a. longitudinal research.
    b. cross-sectional research.
    c. cross-sequential research.
    d. a case study.

Key Terms

Using your own words, write a brief definition or explanation of each of the following terms on a separate piece of paper.

1. science of human development
2. continuity
3. discontinuity
4. butterfly effect
5. cohort
6. socioeconomic status (SES)
7. resilience
8. scientific method
9. hypothesis
10. replicate
11. scientific observation
12. experiment
13. independent variable
14. dependent variable
15. experimental group
16. comparison group
17. survey
18. ethnic group
19. race
20. case study
21. cross-sectional research
22. longitudinal research
23. cross-sequential research
24. ecological-systems approach
25. correlation
26. quantitative research
27. qualitative research
28. code of ethics

ANSWERS

CHAPTER REVIEW

1. how and why people—all people, everywhere—change or remain the same over time
2. continuity; discontinuity
   a. multidirectional
   b. multicontextual
   c. multicultural
   d. multidisciplinary
   e. plastic
3. a. dynamic; static
   b. multidirectional
   c. butterfly effect
   d. continuity
4. cohort; the same way
5. socioeconomic status; SES
6. culture
7. more than one; context
8. biosocial; cognitive; psychosocial
9. domains; contexts; cultures
10. amygdala; shorter; social cognitive neuroscience; experience; context
11. plasticity; resilience
12. personality; collective efficacy
13. rubella; physical; historical; cultural-ethnic; plasticity
14. a. formulate a research question;
    b. develop a hypothesis;
    c. test the hypothesis;
    d. draw conclusions;
    e. make the findings available.
15. hypothesis
16. replicate
17. validity; reliability; generalizability; usefulness
18. scientific observation
19. naturalistic; laboratory
20. cause
21. experiment; independent; dependent; effect; significance
22. experimental group; comparison group (control group)
23. survey
24. representative; phrasing; order
25. ethnic group; race
26. case study; starting point; more general truths
27. cross-sectional
28. ages; cohort differences
29. longitudinal

Over time, some participants may leave the study. Some people may "improve" simply because they are familiar with the goals of the study. The biggest problem is the changing historical context.

30. cross-sequential
31. ecological-systems; Urie Bronfenbrenner
32. microsystem
33. mesosystem

34. exosystem

35. macrosystem

36. chronosystem

37. correlation; does not; positive; increase; negative; increase; decreases; zero

38. quantitative; children; qualitative; open-ended

39. code of ethics; informed consent; harmed

40. training; collaboration

PROGRESS TEST 1

Multiple-Choice Questions

1. **a.** is the answer. (p. 5)

   b. & c. The study of development is concerned with a broader range of phenomena, including physical aspects of development, than these answers specify.

2. **b.** is the answer. (p. 29)

   a. In this research method, one individual is studied intensively.

   c. In this research method, groups of people who differ in age are compared.

   d. This type of research provides data that can be expressed with numbers.

3. **d.** is the answer. (pp. 8, 10)

4. **b.** is the answer. (p. 15)

5. **d.** is the answer. This approach sees development as occurring within five interacting levels, or environments. (p. 27)

6. **d.** is the answer. (pp. 6–7)

7. **c.** is the answer. The amygdala is also a source of anxiety. (p. 12)

8. **b.** is the answer. (p. 18)

9. **c.** is the answer. (p. 27)

   a. This refers to systems that link one microsystem to another.

   b. This refers to cultural values, political philosophies, economic patterns, and social conditions.

   d. This includes the community structures that affect the functioning of smaller systems.

10. **c.** is the answer. (p. 9)

11. **b.** is the answer. (p. 15)

12. **b.** is the answer. (p. 20)

    a. A possible hypothesis for this experiment would be that the larger the group, the less hard a given individual will pull.

    c. The dependent variable is the measure of individual effort.

    d. Significance level refers to the numerical value specifying the possibility that the results of an experiment could have occurred by chance.

13. **d.** is the answer. (p. 21)

    a. Experimentation is appropriate when one is seeking to uncover cause-and-effect relationships; in this example the researcher is only interested in determining whether the parents' beliefs *predict* their attitudes.

    b. Longitudinal research would be appropriate if the researcher sought to examine the development of these attitudes over a long period of time.

    c. Mere observation would not allow the researcher to determine the attitudes of the participants.

14. **a.** is the answer. (p. 20)

    b., c., & d. These research methods do not indicate what causes people to do what they do.

15. **c.** is the answer. (pp. 18–19)

    a. In this method, *one* person is studied over a period of time.

    b. & d. In these research methods, two or more *groups* of participants are studied and compared.

True or False Items

1. F   Just the opposite. Scientists always try to replicate their or other people's work. (p. 18)

2. F   The case study of David shows that both nature and nurture are important in affecting outcome. (p. 14)

3. F   A disadvantage of observation is that the variables are numerous and uncontrolled, and therefore cause-and-effect relationships are difficult to pinpoint. (p. 19)

4. F   Each social context affects the way a person develops, and each is affected by the other contexts. (p. 15)

5. T (p. 8)

6. T (p. 13)

7. F   Qualitative research often reveals information that would be lost if an observation were expressed in numbers. (p. 29)

8. F   Quite the reverse is true. (p. 27)

9. T (pp. 11, 22)

10. T (p. 25)

PROGRESS TEST 2

Multiple-Choice Questions

1. **d.** is the answer. (p. 27)
2. **c.** is the answer. (p. 11)
3. **a.** is the answer. (p. 30)

    b. & c. Although these are important aspects of the code of ethics, protecting participants from harm is the most important.

4. **a.** is the answer. (p. 7)

    b., c., & d. Although these are true, they are not the butterfly effect.

5. **c.** is the answer. (p. 27)

    a. & d. These are part of the microsystem.

    b. This is part of the exosystem.

6. **c.** is the answer. (p. 7)

    a. This is the insight of interacting systems.

    b. This insight is the butterfly effect.

7. **b.** is the answer. (p. 18)

    a. Replication refers to the repetition of a scientific study.

    c. & d. Variables are treatments (independent) or behaviors (dependent) in *experiments*, which this situation clearly is not.

8. **c.** is the answer. (p. 8)

    a., b., & d. These are attributes of an ethnic group.

9. **a.** is the answer. The experimental group is the one in which the variable or treatment—in this case, noise—is present. (p. 20)

    b. Students in the quiet room would be in the comparison condition.

    c. Presumably, all students in both groups were randomly assigned to their groups.

    d. The word *dependent* refers to a kind of variable in experiments; groups are either experimental or control.

10. **c.** is the answer. (pp. 11, 22)

    a. & d. Ethnicity refers to shared attributes, such as ancestry, national origin, religion, and language.

    b. This describes a cohort.

11. **b.** is the answer. (p. 28)

    a. Wealth and happiness clearly *are* related.

    c. For one thing, poverty is clearly an example of nurture, not nature.

    d. Correlation does not imply causation.

12. **d.** is the answer. (p. 13)

13. **c.** is the answer. (p. 20)

    a. Hypotheses make *specific*, testable predictions.

    b. Noise level is the independent variable.

    d. Scientific observation is a research method in which participants are watched, while their behavior is recorded unobtrusively.

14. **a.** is the answer. (pp. 12–13)

    b. In fact, they tend to have more active amygdalas.

    c. Just the opposite is true.

15. **a.** is the answer. Ethnic identity is a product of the social environment and the individual's consciousness. (p. 22)

Matching Items

1. h (p. 20)
2. k (p. 20)
3. f (p. 10)
4. j (p. 18)
5. d (p. 27)
6. g (p. 27)
7. i (p. 27)
8. b (p. 9)
9. a (p. 8)
10. e (p. 22)
11. c (p. 24)
12. l (p. 25)

THINKING CRITICALLY ABOUT CHAPTER 1

1. **a.** is the answer. (p. 27)
2. **c.** is the answer. Room temperature is the variable being manipulated. (p. 20)

    a. & d. These answers are incorrect because they involve aspects of the experiment other than the variables.

    b. This answer is the dependent, not the independent, variable.

3. **c.** is the answer. (p. 27)

    a. Piaget is notable in the area of cognitive development.

    b. Freud was a pioneer of psychoanalysis.

    d. Skinner is notable in the history of learning theory.

4. **c.** is the answer. (p. 22)

    a. This is an ethnic group.

    b. Race is a social construction.

5. **c.** is the answer. In order to determine the effects of caffeine on reaction time, Esteban needs to measure reaction time in a comparison group that does not receive caffeine. (p. 20)

    a. Caffeine is the independent variable.

    b. Reaction time is the dependent variable.

    d. Whether or not Esteban's experiment can be replicated is determined by the precision with which he reports his procedures, which is not an aspect of research strategy.

6. **d.** is the answer. (p. 21)

   a., b., & c. Each of these is an example of discontinuity in development.

7. **d.** is the answer. (p. 13)

8. **d.** is the answer. (p. 13)

   a. This describes the multidirectional nature of development.

   b. This describes the multicontextual nature of development.

   c. This describes the multicultural nature of development.

9. **b.** is the answer. (pp. 8–9)

   a. Earlier developmentalists had no less regard for the scientific method.

   c. & d. Both cross-sectional and longitudinal research were widely used in the 1970s.

10. **b.** is the answer. (p. 28)

    a. Correlation does not imply causation.

11. **b.** is the answer. (p. 25)

    a. This is an example of cross-sectional research.

    c. This is an example of an experiment.

    d. This type of study is not described in the text.

12. **d.** is the answer. (pp. 23, 29)

    a., b., & c. These research methods generally yield *quantitative,* rather than qualitative, data.

13. **c.** is the answer. (p. 18)

    a., b., & c. Although any of these may be true, none has anything to do with replication.

14. **d.** is the answer. (p. 26)

    a. & c. In these research methods, only one group of people is studied.

    b. Dr. Weston's design includes comparison of groups of people of different ages *over time.*

15. **b.** is the answer. (p. 24)

    a. In longitudinal research, the same individuals are studied over a long period of time.

    c. In cross-sequential research, groups of people of different ages are followed over a long period of time.

    d. In a case study, one person is studied intensively.

KEY TERMS

1. The **science of human development** seeks to understand how and why all people, everywhere, change or remain the same over time. (p. 6)

2. **Continuity** is the tendency of certain developmental characteristics to persist from one age to the next. (p. 6)

3. **Discontinuity** is the tendency of certain developmental characteristics to change from one age to the next (p. 6)

4. The **butterfly effect** is the insight that even a small event or thing (such as the breeze created by the flap of a butterfly's wings) may set off a series of changes that create a major event. (p. 7)

5. A **cohort** is a group of people who, because they were born within a few years of each other, experience many of the same historical changes. (p. 8)

6. An individual's **socioeconomic status (SES)** is determined by his or her income, education, place of residence, occupation, and other factors. (p. 9)

7. **Resilience** is the ability of some people to adapt, and even thrive, in the face of severe threats to their development. (p. 13)

8. The **scientific method** is a way to answer questions that requires empirical research and data-based conclusions. The five basic steps of the scientific method are (1) formulate a research question; (2) develop a hypothesis; (3) test the hypothesis; (4) draw conclusions; and (5) make the findings available. (p. 18)

9. In the scientific method, a **hypothesis** is a specific, testable prediction. (p. 18)

10. To **replicate** a study is to repeat a test of a research hypothesis and try to obtain the same results using a different but related group of participants or procedures in order to test the study's validity. (p. 18)

11. **Scientific observation** is the unobtrusive watching and recording of participants' behavior in a systematic and objective manner, either in the laboratory or in a natural setting. (p. 18)

12. The **experiment** is the research method designed to untangle cause from effect by manipulating one variable to see the effect on another variable. (p. 20)

13. The **independent variable** is the variable that is manipulated in an experiment to see what effect it has on the dependent variable. (p. 20)

14. The **dependent variable** is the variable that may change as a result of whatever new condition or situation is added in an experiment. (p. 20)

    Example: In the study of the effects of a new drug on memory, the participants' memory is the dependent variable.

15. The **experimental group** of an experiment is one in which participants are exposed to the independent variable being studied. (p. 20)

16. The **comparison group/control group** of an experiment is one in which the treatment of interest, or independent variable, is withheld so that comparison to the experimental group can be made. (p. 20)

17. The **survey** is the research method in which information is collected from a large number of people, either through written questionnaires, personal interviews, or some other means. (p. 21)

18. An **ethnic group** is a collection of people whose ancestors were born in the same region, usually sharing a language and religion. (p. 22)

19. **Race** is a misleading social construction for a group of people who are regarded (by themselves or others) as genetically distinct on the basis of physical appearance. (p. 22)

21. The **case study** is the research method involving the intensive study of one person. (p. 23)

22. In **cross-sectional research,** groups of people who differ in age but share other important characteristics are compared with regard to the variable under investigation. (p. 24)

23. In **longitudinal research,** the same group of individuals is studied over a period of time to measure both change and stability as they age. (p. 25)

24. **Cross-sequential research** follows a group of people of different ages over time, thus combining the strengths of the cross-sectional and longitudinal methods. (p. 26)

25. The **ecological-systems approach** to developmental research takes into consideration the relationship between the individual and the environment. (p. 27)

26. **Correlation** is a number indicating the degree of relationship between two variables such that one is likely (or unlikely) to occur when the other occurs or one is likely to increase (or decrease) when the other increases (or decreases). (p. 28)

27. **Quantitative research** collects data that are expressed with numbers. (p. 29)

28. **Qualitative research** collects non-numerical descriptions of participants' characteristic behaviors and ideas. (p. 29)

29. Developmental psychologists and other scientists work from a **code of ethics,** which is a set of moral principles that guide their research. (p. 30)

Chapter Two

Theories of Development

Chapter Overview

Developmental theories are systematic statements of principles and generalizations that provide a coherent framework for studying and explaining development. Many such theories have influenced our understanding of human development. This chapter describes and evaluates five broad theories—psychoanalytic theory, behaviorism, cognitive theory, sociocultural theory, and epigenetic theory—that will be used throughout the book to present information and to provide a framework for interpreting events and issues in human development. Each of the theories has developed a unique vocabulary with which to describe and explain events as well as to organize ideas into a cohesive system of thought.

Three of the theories presented—psychoanalytic theory, behaviorism, and cognitive theory—are "grand theories" that are comprehensive in scope but inadequate in the face of recent research findings. Two of the theories—sociocultural and epigenetic—are considered "emergent theories" because they may become the comprehensive theories of the future. Rather than adopt any one theory exclusively, most developmentalists take an eclectic perspective and use many or all of the theories.

As you study this part of the chapter, consider what each of the theories has to say about your own development, as well as that of friends and relatives in other age groups. It is also a good idea to keep the following questions in mind as you study each theory: Which of the theory's principles are generally accepted by contemporary developmentalists? How has the theory been criticized? In what ways does this theory agree with the other theories? In what ways does it disagree?

NOTE: Answer guidelines for all Chapter 2 questions begin on page 29.

Guided Study

The text chapter should be studied one section at a time. Before you read, preview each section by skimming it, noting headings and boldface items. Then read the appropriate section objectives from the following outline. Keep these objectives in mind and, as you read the chapter section, search for the information that will enable you to meet each objective. Once you have finished a section, write out answers for its objectives.

What Theories Do (pp. 35–36)

1. Define developmental theory, and describe how developmental theories help explain human behavior and development. In your answer, be sure to differentiate grand theories, minitheories, and emergent theories.

Grand Theories (pp. 36–48)

2. Discuss the major focus of psychoanalytic theories, and describe the conflicts that could occur during Freud's stages of psychosexual development.

3. Describe the crises of Erikson's theory of psychosocial development, and contrast them with Freud's stages.

4. Discuss the major focus of behaviorism, and explain the basic principles of classical and operant conditioning.

5. (Thinking Like a Scientist) Discuss Harlow's research with infant monkeys, and explain how it contributed to revisions of psychoanalytic theories and behaviorism.

6. Discuss social learning theory as an extension of behaviorism.

7. Identify the primary focus of cognitive theory, and briefly describe Piaget's stages of cognitive development.

8. Discuss the process that, according to Piaget, guides cognitive development.

Emergent Theories (pp. 49–57)

9. Discuss the basic ideas of Vygotsky and the sociocultural theory of development.

10. Discuss the basic ideas of epigenetic theory.

11. (In Person) Discuss the ethology of infant social instincts and adult caregiving impulses.

What Theories Contribute (pp. 58–62)

12. Summarize the contributions and criticisms of the major developmental theories, and describe the eclectic perspective of contemporary developmentalists.

13. Explain the nature–nurture controversy as it pertains to hyperactivity and sexual orientation.

Chapter Review

When you have finished reading the chapter, work through the material that follows to review it. Complete the sentences and answer the questions. As you proceed, evaluate your performance for each section by consulting the answers beginning on page 29. Do not continue with the next section until you understand each answer. If you need to, review or reread the appropriate section in the textbook before continuing.

What Theories Do (pp. 35–36)

1. A systematic statement of principles and generalizations that provides a coherent framework for understanding how and why people change as they grow older is called a(n)

_____ _____ .

2. Developmental theories form the basis for educated guesses, or _____ , about behavior; they generate _____ , and they offer _____ guidance.

3. Developmental theories fall into three categories: _____ theories, which traditionally offer a comprehensive view of development; _____ theories, which explain a specific area of development; and _____ theories, which may be the comprehensive theories of the future.

Grand Theories (pp. 36–48)

4. Psychoanalytic theories interpret human development in terms of inner _____ and _____ , many of which are _____ (conscious/ unconscious) and _____ .

5. According to Freud's _____ theory, children experience sexual pleasures and desires during the first six years as they pass through three stages. From infancy to early childhood to the preschool years, these stages are the _____ stage, the _____ stage, and the _____ stage. One of Freud's most influential ideas was that each stage includes its own potential _____ between child and parent.

Specify the focus of sexual pleasure and the major developmental need associated with each of Freud's stages.

oral _____

_____

anal _____

_____

phallic _____

_____

genital _____

_____

6. Erik Erikson's theory of development, which focuses on social and cultural influences, describes _____ (number) developmental stages, each characterized by a particular developmental _____ related to the person's relationship to the social environment. Unlike Freud, Erikson proposed stages of development that _____ (span/do not span) a person's lifetime.

Complete the following chart regarding Erikson's stages of psychosocial development.

Age Period	Stage
Birth to 1 yr.	trust vs. _____
1–3 yrs.	autonomy vs. _____
3–6 yrs.	initiative vs. _____
7–11 yrs.	_____ vs. inferiority
Adolescence	identity vs. _____
Young adulthood	_____ vs. isolation
Middle adulthood	_____ vs. stagnation
Older adulthood	_____ vs. despair

7. A major theory in American psychology, which directly opposed psychoanalytic theory, was _____ . This theory, which emerged early in the twentieth century under the influence of _____ , is also called _____ theory because of its emphasis on how we learn specific behaviors.

8. Behaviorists have formulated laws of behavior that are believed to apply _____ (only at certain ages/at all ages). The learning process, which is called _____ , takes two forms: _____ _____ and _____ _____ .

9. In classical conditioning, which was discovered by the Russian scientist _____ and is also called _____ conditioning, a person or an animal learns to associate a(n) _____ stimulus with a meaningful one.

10. According to _____ , the learning of more complex responses is the result of _____ conditioning, in which a person learns that a particular behavior produces a particular _____ , such as a reward. This type of learning is also called _____ conditioning.

11. The process of repeating a consequence to make it more likely that the behavior in question will recur is called _____ . The consequence that increases the likelihood that a behavior will be repeated is called the _____ . Consequences that make a behavior less likely are called aversive consequences, or _____ .

12. (Thinking Like a Scientist) The behavior of infant monkeys separated from their mothers led researcher _____ to investigate the origins of _____ in infant monkeys. These studies, which demonstrated that infant monkeys clung more often to "surrogate" mothers that provided _____ (food/contact comfort), disproved _____ theory's idea that infants seek to satisfy oral needs and _____ view that reinforcement directs behavior.

13. The extension of behaviorism that emphasizes the ways that people learn new behaviors by observing others is called _____ _____ . The process whereby a child patterns his or her behavior after a parent or teacher, for example, is called _____ .

14. This process is most likely to occur when an observer is _____ or _____ and when the model is _____ . This type of learning is also affected by the individual's _____ . Human social learning is related to _____ , _____ , _____ , and feelings of _____ .

15. The structure and development of the individual's thought processes and the way those thought processes affect the person's understanding of the world are the focus of _____ theory. A major pioneer of this theory is _____ .

16. In Piaget's first stage of development, the _____ stage, children experience the world through their senses and motor abilities. This stage occurs between birth and age _____ .

17. According to Piaget, during the preschool years (up to age _____), children are in the _____ stage. A hallmark of this stage is that children begin to think _____ . Another hallmark is that sometimes the child's thinking is _____ , or focused on seeing the world solely from his or her own perspective.

18. Piaget believed that children begin to think logically in a consistent way at about _____ years of age. At this time, they enter the _____ _____ stage.

19. In Piaget's final stage, the _____ _____ stage, reasoning expands from the purely concrete to encompass _____ thinking. Piaget believed most children enter this stage by age _____ .

20. According to Piaget, cognitive development is guided by the need to maintain a state of mental balance, called _____ _____ .

21. When new experiences challenge existing understanding, creating a kind of imbalance, the individual experiences _____ _____ , which eventually leads to mental growth.

22. According to Piaget, people adapt to new experi-ences either by reinterpreting them to fit into, or _____ with, old ideas. Some new experiences force people to revamp old ideas so that they can _____ new experiences.

Emergent Theories (pp. 49–57)

23. In contrast to the grand theories, the two emergent theories draw from the findings of _____ (one/many) discipline(s).

24. Sociocultural theory sees human development as the result of _____ _____ between developing persons and their surrounding society and _____ .

25. A major pioneer of this perspective was _____ , who was primarily interested in the development of _____ competencies.

26. Vygotsky believed that these competencies result from the interaction between _____ and more mature members of the society, acting as _____ , in a process that has been called an _____ _____ _____ .

27. In Vygotsky's view, the best way to accomplish the goals of apprenticeship is through _____ _____ , in which the tutor engages the learner in joint activities.

28. According to Vygotsky, a mentor draws a child into the _____ _____ _____ _____ , which is defined as the range of skills that a person can acquire with _____ but cannot master independently.

Cite a contribution and a criticism of sociocultural theory.

29. The newest of the emergent theories, _____ theory, emphasizes the interaction between

_____ and the _____ .

This idea contrasts sharply with the idea of _____ , according to which everything is set in advance by genes.

30. In using the word _genetic_, this theory emphasizes that we have powerful _____

and abilities that arise from our _____ heritage.

31. The prefix "epi" refers to the various _____ factors that affect the expression of _____

_____ . These include _____ factors such as injury, temperature, and crowding. Others are _____ factors such as nourishing food and freedom to play.

32. Some epigenetic factors are the result of the evolutionary process called _____

_____ , in which, over generations, genes for useful traits that promote survival of the species become more prevalent.

33. "Everything that seems to be genetic is actually epigenetic." This statement highlights the fact that _____ (some/most/all) genetic expressions are affected by the environment.

34. (In Person) The study of animal patterns of behavior as they are related to the survival of a species is called _____ . Newborn animals and human infants are genetically programmed for _____

_____ and forming

_____ _____

_____ as a means of survival. Similarly, adult animals and humans are genetically programmed to _____

_____ .

What Theories Contribute (pp. 58–62)

35. Which major theory of development emphasizes:

    a. the importance of culture in fostering development? _____

    b. the ways in which thought processes affect actions? _____

    c. environmental influences? _____

    d. the impact of unconscious impulses on development? _____

    _____

    e. the interaction of genes and environment? _____

    _____

36. Which major theory of development has been criticized for:

    a. being too mechanistic?

    _____

    b. undervaluing genetic differences?

    _____

    c. being too subjective?

    _____

    d. neglecting society?

    _____

    e. neglecting individuals?

    _____

37. Because no one theory can encompass all of human behavior, most developmentalists have a(n) _____ perspective, which capitalizes on the strengths of all the theories.

38. The debate over the relative influence of heredity and environment in shaping personal traits and characteristics is called the

_____–_____ controversy. Traits inherited at the moment of conception give evidence of the influence of _____ ; those that emerge in response to learning and environmental influences give evidence of the effect of _____ .

39. Developmentalists agree that, at every point, the _____ between nature and nurture is the crucial influence on any particular aspect of development.

40. Children who are especially impulsive, restless, and unable to attend to anything for more than a moment may be suffering from

_____-_____/

_____   _____ . This
disorder is more common in _____
(girls/boys).

State several pieces of evidence that genetic inheritance is responsible for ADHD.

41. Most social scientists once considered homosexuality to be the product of _____ (nature/nurture). However, new research suggests that it is at least partly due to _____ (nature/nurture). This has also led researchers to draw a distinction between _____ _____ , which encompasses erotic _____ and _____ , and _____ _____ , which encompasses sexual _____ .

Progress Test 1

Multiple-Choice Questions

Circle your answers to the following questions and check them with the answers on page 30. If your answer is incorrect, read the explanation for why it is incorrect and then consult the appropriate pages of the text (in parentheses following the correct answer).

1. The purpose of a developmental theory is to:
   a. provide a broad and coherent view of the complex influences on human development.
   b. offer guidance for practical issues encountered by parents, teachers, and therapists.
   c. generate testable hypotheses about development.
   d. do all of the above.

2. Which developmental theory emphasizes the influence of unconscious drives and motives on behavior?
   a. psychoanalytic   **c.** cognitive
   b. behaviorism   **d.** sociocultural

3. Which of the following is the correct order of the psychosexual stages proposed by Freud?
   a. oral stage; anal stage; phallic stage; latency; genital stage
   b. anal stage; oral stage; phallic stage; latency; genital stage
   c. oral stage; anal stage; genital stage; latency; phallic stage
   d. anal stage; oral stage; genital stage; latency; phallic stage

4. Erikson's psychosocial theory of human development describes:
   a. eight crises all people are thought to face.
   b. four psychosocial stages and a latency period.
   c. the same number of stages as Freud's, but with different names.
   d. a stage theory that is not psychoanalytic.

5. Which of the following theories does *not* belong with the others?
   a. psychoanalytic   **c.** sociocultural
   b. behaviorism   **d.** cognitive

6. An American psychologist who explained complex human behaviors in terms of operant conditioning was:
   a. Lev Vygotsky.   **c.** B. F. Skinner.
   b. Ivan Pavlov.   **d.** Jean Piaget.

7. Pavlov's dogs learned to salivate at the sound of a bell because they associated the bell with food. Pavlov's experiment with dogs was an early demonstration of:
   a. classical conditioning.
   b. operant conditioning.
   c. positive reinforcement.
   d. social learning.

8. The nature–nurture controversy considers the degree to which traits, characteristics, and behaviors are the result of:
   a. early or lifelong learning.
   b. genes or heredity.
   c. heredity or experience.
   d. different historical concepts of childhood.

9. Modeling, an integral part of social learning theory, is so called because it:
   a. follows the scientific model of learning.
   b. molds character.
   c. follows the immediate reinforcement model developed by Bandura.
   d. involves people's patterning their behavior after that of others.

10. Which developmental theory suggests that each person is born with genetic possibilities that must be nurtured in order to grow?
   a. sociocultural
   c. behaviorism
   b. cognitive
   d. epigenetic

11. Vygotsky's theory has been criticized for neglecting:
   a. the role of genes in guiding development.
   b. developmental processes that are not primarily biological.
   c. the importance of language in development.
   d. social factors in development.

12. Which is the correct sequence of stages in Piaget's theory of cognitive development?
   a. sensorimotor, preoperational, concrete operational, formal operational
   b. sensorimotor, preoperational, formal operational, concrete operational
   c. preoperational, sensorimotor, concrete operational, formal operational
   d. preoperational, sensorimotor, formal operational, concrete operational

13. When an individual's existing understanding no longer fits his or her present experiences, the result is called:
   a. a psychosocial crisis.
   b. equilibrium.
   c. disequilibrium.
   d. negative reinforcement.

14. In explaining the origins of homosexuality, most social scientists have traditionally emphasized:
   a. nature over nurture.
   b. nurture over nature.
   c. a weak father and overbearing mother.
   d. the individual's voluntary choice.

15. The zone of proximal development refers to:
   a. a stage during which the child exhibits preoperational thinking.
   b. the influence of a pleasurable stimulus on behavior.
   c. the range of skills a child can exercise with assistance but cannot perform independently.
   d. the tendency of a child to model an admired adult's behavior.

True or False Items

Write T (*true*) or F (*false*) on the line in front of each statement.

_____ 1. Behaviorists study what people actually do, not what they might be thinking.

_____ 2. Erikson's eight developmental stages are centered not on a body part but on each person's relationship to the social environment.

_____ 3. Most developmentalists agree that the nature–nurture controversy has been laid to rest.

_____ 4. Few developmental theorists today believe that humans have instincts or abilities that arise from our species' biological heritage.

_____ 5. Of the major developmental theories, cognitive theory gives the most emphasis to the interaction of genes and experience in shaping development.

_____ 6. New research suggests that homosexuality is at least partly genetic.

_____ 7. According to Piaget, a state of cognitive equilibrium must be attained before cognitive growth can occur.

_____ 8. In part, cognitive theory examines how an individual's understandings and expectations affect his or her behavior.

_____ 9. According to Piaget, children begin to think only when they reach preschool age.

_____ 10. Most contemporary researchers have adopted an eclectic perspective on development.

Progress Test 2

Progress Test 2 should be completed during a final chapter review. Answer the following questions after you thoroughly understand the correct answers for the Chapter Review and Progress Test 1.

Multiple-Choice Questions

1. Which developmental theorist has been criticized for suggesting that every child, in every culture, in every nation, passes through certain fixed stages?
   a. Freud
   c. Piaget
   b. Erikson
   d. all of the above.

2. Of the following terms, the one that does *not* describe a stage of Freud's theory of childhood sexuality is:
   a. phallic.
   b. oral.
   c. anal.
   d. sensorimotor.

3. We are more likely to imitate the behavior of others if we particularly admire and identify with them. This belief finds expression in:
   a. stage theory.
   b. sociocultural theory.
   c. social learning theory.
   d. Pavlov's experiments.

4. How do minitheories differ from grand theories of development?
   a. Unlike the more comprehensive grand theories, minitheories explain only a part of development.
   b. Unlike grand theories, which usually reflect the thinking of many researchers, minitheories tend to stem from one person.
   c. Only the recency of the research on which they are based keeps minitheories from having the sweeping influence of grand theories.
   d. They differ in all the above ways.

5. According to Erikson, an adult who has difficulty establishing a secure, mutual relationship with a life partner might never have resolved the crisis of:
   a. initiative versus guilt.
   b. autonomy versus shame and doubt.
   c. intimacy versus isolation.
   d. identity versus role confusion.

6. Who would be most likely to agree with the statement, "anything can be learned"?
   a. Jean Piaget   c. John Watson
   b. Lev Vygotsky   d. Erik Erikson

7. Classical conditioning is to _____ as operant conditioning is to _____ .
   a. Skinner; Pavlov   c. Pavlov; Skinner
   b. Watson; Vygotsky   d. Vygotsky; Watson

8. Behaviorists have found that they can often solve a person's seemingly complex psychological problem by:
   a. analyzing the patient.
   b. admitting the existence of the unconscious.
   c. altering the environment.
   d. administering well-designed punishments.

9. According to Piaget, an infant first comes to know the world through:
   a. sucking and grasping.
   b. naming and counting.
   c. preoperational thought.
   d. instruction from parents.

10. According to Piaget, the stage of cognitive development that generally characterizes preschool children (2 to 6 years old) is the:
    a. preoperational stage.   c. oral stage.
    b. sensorimotor stage.   d. psychosocial stage.

11. In Piaget's theory, cognitive equilibrium refers to:
    a. a state of mental balance.
    b. a kind of imbalance that leads to cognitive growth.
    c. the ultimate stage of cognitive development.
    d. the first stage in the processing of information.

12. You teach your dog to "speak" by giving her a treat each time she does so. This is an example of:
    a. classical conditioning.   c. reinforcement.
    b. respondent conditioning.   d. modeling.

13. A child who must modify an old idea in order to incorporate a new experience is using the process of:
    a. assimilation.
    b. accommodation.
    c. cognitive equilibrium.
    d. guided participation.

14. Which of the following is a common criticism of sociocultural theory?
    a. It places too great an emphasis on unconscious motives and childhood sexuality.
    b. Its mechanistic approach fails to explain many complex human behaviors.
    c. Development is more gradual than its stages imply.
    d. It neglects developmental processes that are not primarily social.

15. A major pioneer of the sociocultural perspective was:
    a. Jean Piaget.   c. Lev Vygotsky.
    b. Albert Bandura.   d. Ivan Pavlov.

Matching Items

Match each theory or term with its corresponding description or definition.

Theories or Terms

_____ 1. psychoanalytic theory
_____ 2. nature
_____ 3. behaviorism
_____ 4. social learning theory
_____ 5. cognitive theory
_____ 6. nurture
_____ 7. sociocultural theory
_____ 8. conditioning
_____ 9. emergent theories
_____ 10. modeling
_____ 11. epigenetic theory

Descriptions or Definitions

a. emphasizes the impact of the immediate environment on behavior
b. relatively new, comprehensive theories
c. emphasizes that people learn by observing others
d. environmental influences that affect development
e. a process of learning, as described by Pavlov or Skinner
f. emphasizes the "hidden dramas" that influence behavior
g. emphasizes the cultural context in development
h. emphasizes how our thoughts shape our actions
i. the process whereby a person learns by imitating someone else's behavior
j. emphasizes the interaction of genes and environmental forces
k. traits that are inherited

Thinking Critically About Chapter 2

Answer these questions the day before an exam as a final check on your understanding of the chapter's terms and concepts.

1. Many songbirds inherit a genetically programmed species song that enhances their ability to mate and establish a territory. The evolution of such a trait is an example of:
   a. selective adaptation.
   b. epigenetic development.
   c. accommodation.
   d. assimilation.

2. When a pigeon is rewarded for producing a particular response, and so learns to produce that response to obtain rewards, psychologists describe this chain of events as:
   a. operant conditioning.   c. modeling.
   b. classical conditioning.   d. reflexive actions.

3. Professor Swenson, who believes that a considerable amount of development involves the developing person coming to associate neutral stimuli with meaningful stimuli, would most likely agree with the writings of:
   a. Freud.
   b. Erikson.
   c. Vygotsky.
   d. Pavlov.

4. Dr. Ivey's research focuses on the biological forces that shape each child's characteristic way of reacting to environmental experiences. Evidently, Dr. Ivey is working from a(n) _____ perspective.
   a. psychoanalytic   c. sociocultural
   b. cognitive   d. epigenetic

5. Which of the following is the best example of guided participation?
   a. After watching her mother change her baby sister's diaper, 4-year-old Brandy changes her doll's diaper.
   b. To help her son learn to pour liquids, Sandra engages him in a bathtub game involving pouring water from cups of different sizes.
   c. Seeing his father shaving, 3-year-old Kyle pretends to shave by rubbing whipped cream on his face.
   d. After reading a recipe in a magazine, Jack gathers ingredients from the cupboard.

6. A child who calls all furry animals "doggie" will experience cognitive _____ when she encounters a hairless breed for the first time. This may cause her to revamp her concept of "dog" in order to _____ the new experience.
   a. disequilibrium; accommodate
   b. disequilibrium; assimilate
   c. equilibrium; accommodate
   d. equilibrium; assimilate

7. A confirmed neo-Freudian, Dr. Thomas strongly endorses the views of Erik Erikson. She would be most likely to disagree with Freud regarding the importance of:
   a. unconscious forces in development.
   b. irrational forces in personality formation.
   c. early childhood experiences.
   d. sexual urges in development.

8. After watching several older children climbing around a new junglegym, 5-year-old Jennie decides to try it herself. Which of the following best accounts for her behavior?
   a. classical conditioning
   b. modeling
   c. guided participation
   d. reinforcement

9. I am 8 years old, and although I understand some logical principles, I have trouble thinking about hypothetical concepts. According to Piaget, I am in the _____ stage of development.
   a. sensorimotor
   b. preoperational
   c. concrete operational
   d. formal operational

10. Two-year-old Jamail has a simple understanding for "dad," and so each time he encounters a man with a child, he calls him "dad." When he learns that these other men are not "dad," Jamail experiences:
    a. conservation.
    b. cognition.
    c. equilibrium.
    d. disequilibrium.

11. (In Person) Most adults become physiologically aroused by the sound of an infant's laughter. These interactive reactions, in which caregivers and babies elicit responses in each other:
    a. help ensure the survival of the next generation.
    b. do not occur in all human cultures.
    c. are the result of conditioning very early in life.
    d. are more often found in females than in males.

12. The school psychologist believes that each child's developmental needs can be understood only by taking into consideration the child's broader social and cultural background. Evidently, the school psychologist is working within the _____ perspective.
    a. psychoanalytic
    b. epigenetic
    c. social learning
    d. sociocultural

13. Four-year-old Bjorn takes great pride in successfully undertaking new activities. Erikson would probably say that Bjorn is capably meeting the psychosocial challenge of:
    a. trust vs. mistrust.
    b. initiative vs. guilt.
    c. industry vs. inferiority.
    d. identity vs. role confusion.

14. Dr. Cleaver's developmental research draws upon insights from several theoretical perspectives. Evidently, Dr. Cleaver is working from a(n) _____ perspective.
    a. cognitive
    b. behaviorist
    c. eclectic
    d. sociocultural

15. Dr. Bazzi believes that development is a lifelong process of gradual and continuous growth. Based on this information, with which of the following theories would Dr. Bazzi most likely agree?
    a. Piaget's cognitive theory
    b. Erikson's psychosocial theory
    c. Freud's psychoanalytic theory
    d. behaviorism

Key Terms

Writing Definitions

Using your own words, write a brief definition or explanation of each of the following terms on a separate piece of paper.

1. developmental theory
2. grand theories
3. minitheories
4. emergent theories
5. psychoanalytic theory
6. behaviorism
7. conditioning
8. classical conditioning
9. operant conditioning
10. reinforcement
11. social learning theory
12. modeling
13. self-efficacy
14. cognitive theory
15. cognitive equilibrium

16. sociocultural theory
17. apprenticeship in thinking
18. guided participation
19. zone of proximal development
20. epigenetic theory
21. preformism

22. selective adaptation
23. eclectic perspective
24. nature
25. nurture
26. sexual orientation

Cross-Check

After you have written the definitions of the key terms in this chapter, you should complete the crossword puzzle to ensure that you can reverse the process—recognize the term, given the definition.

ACROSS

2. Behaviorism focuses on the sequences and processes involved in the _____ of behavior.
8. An instinctive or learned behavior that is elicited by a specific stimulus.
11. All the genetic influences on development.
12. Developmental perspective that accepts elements from several theories.
14. Influential theorist who developed a stage theory of cognitive development.
17. All the environmental (nongenetic) influences on development.
19. Type of theory that brings together information from many disciplines into a comprehensive model of development.

DOWN

1. Theory that focuses on some specific area of development.
3. Theory that emphasizes the interaction of genetic and environmental factors in development.
4. The process by which the consequences of a behavior make the behavior more likely to occur.
5. Comprehensive theory of development that has proven to be inadequate in explaining the full range of human development.
6. Theory of personality and development that emphasizes unconscious forces.
7. Learning process that occurs through the association of two stimuli or through the use of reinforcement.
9. Influential theorist who outlined the principles of operant conditioning.
10. The study of behavior as it relates to the evolution and survival of a species.
13. An early and especially strong proponent of learning theory in America.

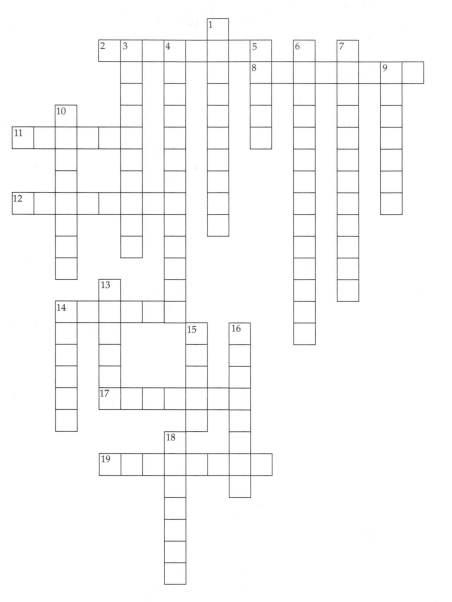

14. Russian scientist who outlined the principles of classical conditioning.
15. The developer of psychoanalytic theory.
16. The process of learning by imitating another person's behavior.
18. Psychoanalytic theorist who viewed development as a series of psychosocial crises.

ANSWERS
CHAPTER REVIEW

1. developmental theory
2. hypotheses; discoveries; practical
3. grand; mini; emergent
4. motives; drives; unconscious; irrational
5. psychoanalytic; oral; anal; phallic; conflicts

Oral stage: The mouth is the focus of pleasurable sensations as the baby becomes emotionally attached to the person who provides the oral gratifications derived from sucking.

Anal stage: Pleasures related to control and self-control, initially in connection with defecation and toilet training, are paramount.

Phallic stage: Pleasure is derived from genital stimulation.

Genital stage: Mature sexual interests that last throughout adulthood emerge.

6. eight; crisis (challenge); span

Age Period	Stage
Birth to 1 yr.	trust vs. **mistrust**
1–3 yrs.	autonomy vs. **shame and doubt**
3–6 yrs.	initiative vs. **guilt**
7–11 yrs.	**industry** vs. inferiority
Adolescence	identity vs. **role confusion**
Young adulthood	**intimacy** vs. isolation
Middle adulthood	**generativity** vs. stagnation
Older adulthood	**integrity** vs. despair

7. behaviorism; John B. Watson; learning
8. at all ages; conditioning; classical conditioning; operant conditioning
9. Ivan Pavlov; respondent; neutral
10. B. F. Skinner; operant; consequence; instrumental
11. reinforcement; reinforcer; punishments
12. Harry Harlow; attachment; contact comfort; psychoanalytic; behaviorism's
13. social learning; modeling
14. uncertain; inexperienced; admirable and powerful, nurturing, or similar to the observer; self-understanding; self-confidence; social reflection; self-efficacy
15. cognitive; Jean Piaget
16. sensorimotor; 2
17. 6; preoperational; symbolically; egocentric
18. 6; concrete operational
19. formal operational; abstract (hypothetical); 12
20. cognitive equilibrium
21. cognitive disequilibrium
22. assimilate; accommodate
23. many
24. dynamic interaction; culture
25. Lev Vygotsky; cognitive
26. novices; mentors (or tutors); apprenticeship in thinking
27. guided participation
28. zone of proximal development; assistance

Sociocultural theory has emphasized the need to study development in the specific cultural context in which it occurs. The theory has been criticized for neglecting the importance of developmental processes that are not primarily social, such as the role of biological maturation in development.

29. epigenetic; genes; environment; preformism
30. instincts; biological
31. environmental; genetic expression; stress; facilitating
32. selective adaptation
33. all
34. ethology; accepting help; attachments to caregivers; nurture babies
35. a. sociocultural
    b. cognitive
    c. behaviorism
    d. psychoanalytic
    e. epigenetic
36. a. behaviorism
    b. cognitive
    c. psychoanalytic
    d. epigenetic
    e. sociocultural
37. eclectic
38. nature–nurture; genes (nature); nurture
39. interaction
40. attention-deficit/hyperactivity disorder (ADHD); boys

    ADHD children:
    - often have close male relatives with the same problem
    - are overactive in every context
    - calm down when they take stimulants

41. nurture; nature; sexual orientation; inclinations; thoughts; sexual expression; activities

PROGRESS TEST 1

Multiple-Choice Questions

1. **d.** is the answer (pp. 35–36)

2. **a.** is the answer. (p. 37)

    b. Behaviorism emphasizes the influence of the immediate environment on behavior.

    c. Cognitive theory emphasizes the impact of *conscious* thought processes on behavior.

    d. Sociocultural theory emphasizes the influence on development of social interaction in a specific cultural context.

3. **a.** is the answer. (pp. 37, 38)

4. **a.** is the answer. (pp. 3, 39)

    b. & c. Whereas Freud identified four stages of psychosexual development, Erikson proposed eight psychosocial stages.

    d. Although his theory places greater emphasis on social and cultural forces than Freud's did, Erikson's theory is nevertheless classified as a psychoanalytic theory.

5. **c.** is the answer. Sociocultural theory is an emergent theory. (p. 49)

    a., b., & d. Each of these is an example of a grand theory.

6. **c.** is the answer. (p. 41)

7. **a.** is the answer. In classical conditioning, a neutral stimulus—in this case, the bell—is associated with a meaningful stimulus—in this case, food. (pp. 40–41)

    b. In operant conditioning, the consequences of a voluntary response determine the likelihood of its being repeated. Salivation is an involuntary response.

    c. & d. Positive reinforcement and social learning pertain to voluntary, or operant, responses.

8. **c.** is the answer. (p. 59)

    a. These are both examples of nurture.

    b. Both of these refer to nature.

    d. The impact of changing historical concepts of childhood on development is an example of how environmental forces (nurture) shape development.

9. **d.** is the answer. (p. 45)

    a. & c. These can be true in all types of learning.

    b. This was not discussed as an aspect of developmental theory.

10. **d.** is the answer. (pp. 52–53)

    a. & c. Sociocultural theory and behaviorism focus almost entirely on environmental factors (nurture) in development.

    b. Cognitive theory emphasizes the developing person's own mental activity but ignores genetic differences in individuals.

11. **a.** is the answer. (p. 52)

    b. Vygotsky's theory does not emphasize biological processes.

    c. & d. Vygotsky's theory places considerable emphasis on language and social factors.

12. **a.** is the answer. (pp. 46, 47)

13. **c.** is the answer. (p. 46)

    a. This refers to the core of Erikson's psychosocial stages, which deals with people's interactions with the environment.

    b. Equilibrium occurs when existing schemes *do* fit a person's current experiences.

    d. Negative reinforcement is the removal of a stimulus as a consequence of a desired behavior.

14. **b.** is the answer. (p. 60)

    c. This is only true of psychoanalytic theory.

    d. Although the grand theories have emphasized nurture over nature in this matter, no theory suggests that sexual orientation is voluntarily chosen.

15. **c.** is the answer. (p. 51)

    a. This is a stage of Piaget's cognitive theory.

    b. This describes positive reinforcement.

    d. This is an aspect of social learning theory.

True or False Items

1. T (p. 40)

2. T (p. 39)

3. F Although most developmentalists believe that nature and nurture interact in shaping development, the practical implications of whether nature or nurture plays a greater role in certain abilities keep the controversy alive. (pp. 58–59)

4. F This assumption lies at the heart of epigenetic theory. (p. 52)

5. F Epigenetic theory emphasizes the interaction of genes and experience. (p. 52)

6. T (p. 61)

7. F   On the contrary, *dis*equilibrium often fosters greater growth. (p. 46)

8. T (p. 46)

9. F   The hallmark of Piaget's theory is that, at every age, individuals think about the world in unique ways. (p. 46)

10. T (p. 58)

PROGRESS TEST 2

Multiple-Choice Questions

1. **d.** is the answer. (pp. 37, 39, 46)

2. **d.** is the answer. This is one of Piaget's stages of cognitive development. (pp. 37, 46)

3. **c.** is the answer. (p. 45)

4. **a.** is the answer. (p. 36)

   b. *Grand* theories, rather than minitheories, usually stem from one person.

   c. This describes emergent theories.

5. **d.** is the answer. (p. 38)

6. **c.** is the answer. (p. 40)

   a. Piaget formulated a cognitive theory of development.

   b. Vygotsky formulated a sociocultural theory of development.

   d. Erikson formulated a psychoanalytic theory of development.

7. **c.** is the answer. (pp. 40, 41)

8. **c.** is the answer. (p. 41)

   a. & b. These are psychoanalytic approaches to treating psychological problems.

   d. Behaviorists generally do not recommend the use of punishment.

9. **a.** is the answer. These behaviors are typical of infants in the sensorimotor stage. (p. 46)

   b., c., & d. These are typical of older children.

10. **a.** is the answer. (pp. 46, 47)

   b. The sensorimotor stage describes development from birth until 2 years of age.

   c. This is a psychoanalytic stage described by Freud.

   d. This is not the name of a stage; "psychosocial" refers to Erikson's stage theory.

11. **a.** is the answer. (p. 46)

   b. This describes *dis*equilibrium.

c. This is formal operational thinking.

d. Piaget's theory does not propose stages of information processing.

12. **c.** is the answer. (p. 42)

   a. & b. Teaching your dog in this way is an example of operant, rather than classical (respondent), conditioning.

   d. Modeling involves learning by imitating others.

13. **b.** is the answer. (p. 47)

   a. Assimilation occurs when new experiences do *not* clash with existing ideas.

   c. Cognitive equilibrium is mental balance, which occurs when ideas and experiences do *not* clash.

   d. This is Vygotsky's term for the process by which a mentor engages a child in shared learning activities.

14. **d.** is the answer. (p. 52)

   a. This is a common criticism of psychoanalytic theory.

   b. This is a common criticism of behaviorism.

   c. This is a common criticism of psychoanalytic and cognitive theories that describe development as occurring in a sequence of stages.

15. **c.** is the answer. (p. 49)

Matching Items

1. f (p. 37)	**5.** h (p. 46)	**9.** b (p. 36)
2. k (p. 58)	**6.** d (p. 59)	**10.** i (p. 45)
3. a (p. 40)	**7.** g (p. 49)	**11.** j (p. 52)
4. c (p. 45)	**8.** e (p. 40)	

THINKING CRITICALLY ABOUT CHAPTER 2

1. **a.** is the answer. (p. 54)

   b. This term was not used to describe development.

   c. & d. These terms describe the processes by which cognitive concepts incorporate (assimilate) new experiences or are revamped (accommodated) by them.

2. **a.** is the answer. This is an example of operant conditioning because a response recurs due to its consequences. (p. 41)

   b. & d. In classical conditioning, the individual learns to associate a neutral stimulus with a meaningful stimulus.

c. In modeling, learning occurs through the observation of others, rather than through direct exposure to reinforcing consequences, as in this example.

3. **d.** is the answer. In classical conditioning, an organism comes to associate a neutral stimulus with a meaningful one and then responds to the former stimulus as if it were the latter. (pp. 40–41)

4. **d.** is the answer. (p. 52)

   a. Psychoanalytic theorists focus on the role of unconscious forces in development.

   b. Cognitive theorists emphasize how the developing person actively seeks to understand experiences.

   c. Sociocultural theorists focus on the social context, as expressed through people, language, and customs.

5. **b.** is the answer. (p. 50)

   a. & c. These are both examples of modeling.

   d. Guided participation involves the coaching of a mentor. In this example, Jack is simply following written directions.

6. **a.** is the answer. (pp. 46, 47)

   b. Because the dog is not furry, the child's concept of dog cannot incorporate (assimilate) the discrepant experience without being revamped.

   c. & d. Equilibrium exists when ideas (such as what a dog is) and experiences (such as seeing a hairless dog) do *not* clash.

7. **d.** is the answer. (p. 39)

8. **b.** is the answer. Evidently, Jennie has learned by observing the other children at play. (p. 45)

   a. Classical conditioning is concerned with the association of stimuli, not with complex responses, as in this example.

   c. Guided participation involves the interaction of a mentor and a child.

   d. Reinforcement is a process for getting a response to recur.

9. **c.** is the answer. (p. 47)

10. **d.** is the answer. When Jamail experiences something that conflicts with his existing understanding, he experiences disequilibrium. (p. 46)

    a. Conservation is the ability to recognize that objects do not change when their appearances change.

    b. Cognition refers to all mental activities associated with thinking.

    c. If Jamail's thinking were in equilibrium, all men would be "dad"!

11. **a.** is the answer. (p. 56)

    b. & c. Infant social reflexes and adult caregiving impulses occur in all cultures (b), which indicates that they are the product of nature rather than nurture (c).

    d. The text does not address the issue of gender differences in infant reflexes or caregiving impulses.

12. **d.** is the answer. (p. 49)

13. **b.** is the answer. (p. 38)

    a. According to Erikson, this crisis concerns younger children.

    c. & d. In Erikson's theory, these crises concern older children.

14. **c.** is the answer. (p. 58)

    a., b., & d. These are three of the many theoretical perspectives upon which someone working from an eclectic perspective might draw.

15. **d.** is the answer. (p. 40)

    a., b., & c. Each of these theories emphasizes that development is a discontinuous process that occurs in stages.

KEY TERMS

Writing Definitions

1. A **developmental theory** is a systematic statement of principles and generalizations that provides a coherent framework for understanding how and why people change as they grow older. (p. 35)

2. **Grand theories** are comprehensive theories of psychology, which have traditionally inspired and directed psychologists' thinking about child development. Examples of grand theories are psychoanalytic and cognitive theories and behaviorism. (p. 36)

3. **Minitheories** are less general and comprehensive than grand theories, focusing instead on some specific area of development. (p. 36)

4. **Emergent theories,** such as sociocultural theory and epigenetic theory, are newer comprehensive theories that bring together information from many disciplines but are not yet a systematic and comprehensive whole. (p. 36)

5. **Psychoanalytic theory,** a grand theory, interprets human development in terms of inner drives and motives, many of which are irrational and unconscious. (p. 37)

6. **Behaviorism,** a grand theory, emphasizes the laws and processes by which behavior is learned; also called *learning theory*. (p. 40)

7. **Conditioning** is the learning process that occurs either through the association of two stimuli (classical conditioning) or through the use of positive or negative reinforcement or punishment (operant conditioning). (p. 40)

8. **Classical conditioning** is the process by which a neutral stimulus becomes associated with a meaningful one so that both are responded to in the same way. (p. 41)

9. **Operant conditioning** is the process by which a response is gradually learned through reinforcement or punishment. (p. 41)

10. **Reinforcement** is the process by which the consequences of a particular behavior make it more likely that the behavior will be repeated. (p. 42)

11. An extension of behaviorism, **social learning theory** emphasizes that people often learn new behaviors through observation and imitation of other people. (p. 45)

12. **Modeling** refers to the process by which we observe other people's behavior and then pattern our own after it. (p. 45)

13. In social learning theory, **self-efficacy** is the belief that one is effective. (p. 45)

14. **Cognitive theory,** a grand theory, emphasizes that the way people think and understand the world shapes their attitudes, beliefs, and behaviors. (p. 46)

15. In Piaget's theory, **cognitive equilibrium** is a state of mental balance, in which a person's thoughts about the world seem not to clash with each other or with his or her experiences. (p. 46)

16. **Sociocultural theory,** an emergent theory, seeks to explain development as the result of a dynamic interaction between developing persons and the surrounding social and cultural forces. (p. 49)

17. In sociocultural theory, an **apprenticeship in thinking** is the process by which novices develop cognitive competencies by interacting with more skilled parents, teachers, or other mentors. (p. 49)

18. In sociocultural theory, **guided participation** is a learning process in which the learner is tutored, or mentored, through social interaction with a skilled teacher. (p. 50)

19. According to Vygotsky, developmental growth occurs when mentors draw children into the **zone of proximal development,** which is the range of skills, knowledge, and concepts the child can acquire with assistance but cannot master independently. (p. 51)

20. **Epigenetic theory,** an emergent theory, emphasizes the genetic origins of behavior but also stresses that genes, over time, are directly and systematically affected by environmental forces. (p. 52)

21. **Preformism** is the idea that every aspect of development is set in advance by genes and then gradually emerges in the course of maturation, but it is through time, not experience, that they emerge. (p. 52)

22. **Selective adaptation** is the evolutionary process through which useful genes that enhance survival become more common within individuals. (p. 54)

23. Developmentalists who work from an **eclectic perspective** accept elements from several theories, instead of adhering to only a single perspective. (p. 58)

24. **Nature** refers to all the traits, capacities, and limitations that a person inherits from his or her parents at the moment of conception. (p. 59)

25. **Nurture** refers to all the environmental influences that affect a person's development following the moment of conception. (p. 59)

26. **Sexual orientation** refers to a person's impulses and personal direction regarding sexual interest toward persons of the same sex, of the other sex, or of both sexes. (p. 60)

Cross-Check

ACROSS	DOWN
2. learning	1. minitheory
8. response	3. epigenetic
11. nature	4. reinforcement
12. eclectic	5. grand
14. Piaget	6. psychoanalytic
17. nurture	7. conditioning
19. emergent	9. Skinner
	10. ethology
	13. Watson
	14. Pavlov
	15. Freud
	16. modeling
	18. Erikson

Chapter Three

Heredity and Environment

Chapter Overview

Conception occurs when the male and female reproductive cells—the sperm and ovum, respectively—come together to create a new, one-celled zygote with its own unique combination of genetic material. The genetic material furnishes the instructions for development—not only for obvious physical characteristics, such as sex, coloring, and body shape but also for certain psychological characteristics, such as bashfulness, moodiness, and vocational aptitude.

Every year scientists make new discoveries and reach new understandings about genes and their effects on the development of individuals. This chapter presents some of their findings, including that most human characteristics are polygenic and multifactorial, the result of the interaction of many genetic and environmental influences. Perhaps the most important findings have come from research into the causes of genetic and chromosomal abnormalities. The chapter discusses the most common of these abnormalities and concludes with a section on genetic counseling. Genetic testing before and after conception can help predict whether a couple will have a child with a genetic problem.

Many students find the technical material in this chapter difficult to master, but it *can* be done with a great deal of rehearsal. Working through the Chapter Review several times and mentally reciting terms are both useful techniques for rehearsing this type of material.

NOTE: Answer guidelines for all Chapter 3 questions begin on page 46.

Guided Study

The text chapter should be studied one section at a time. Before you read, preview each section by skimming it, noting headings and boldface items. Then read the appropriate section objectives from the following outline. Keep these objectives in mind and, as you read the chapter section, search for the information that will enable you to meet each objective. Once you have finished a section, write out answers for its objectives.

The Genetic Code (pp. 65–70)

1. Identify the mechanisms of heredity.

2. Describe the process of conception and the first hours of development of the zygote.

3. Explain how sex is determined.

From One Cell to Many (pp. 70–78)

4. Differentiate genotype from phenotype, and describe the Human Genome Project.

5. Describe the processes of duplication, division, and differentiation.

6. Explain the polygenic and multifactorial nature of human traits.

7. Explain the additive and nonadditive patterns of genetic interaction, giving examples of the traits that result from each type of interaction.

8. Discuss X-linked genes in terms of genotype and phenotype.

9. (Thinking Like a Scientist) Discuss the benefits of genetic diversity.

10. Distinguish between monozygotic and dizygotic twins and between monozygotic twins and clones.

11. (In Person) Discuss issues related to the use of assisted reproductive technology for infertile couples.

From Genotype to Phenotype (pp. 79–85)

12. Discuss the interaction of genes and environment, focusing on the development of schizophrenia, addiction, and nearsightedness.

13. Discuss the practical implications of research on nature–nurture interactions.

Chromosomal and Genetic Abnormalities (pp. 85–94)

14. Describe the most common chromosomal abnormalities, including abnormalities involving the sex chromosomes.

15. Identify two common genetic disorders, and discuss reasons for their relatively low incidence of occurrence.

16. Describe four situations in which couples should seek genetic testing and counseling.

Chapter Review

When you have finished reading the chapter, work through the material that follows to review it. Complete the sentences and answer the questions. As you proceed, evaluate your performance for each section by consulting the answers beginning on page 46. Do not continue with the next section until you understand each answer. If you need to, review or reread the appropriate section in the textbook before continuing.

The Genetic Code (pp. 65–70)

1. The work of body cells is done by _____ , under the direction of instructions stored in molecules of _____ , each of which is called a _____ .

2. Each normal person inherits _____ chromosomes, _____ from each parent. The genetic instructions in chromosomes are organized into units called _____ , each of which contains instructions for a specific _____ , which in turn is composed of chemical building blocks called _____ _____ . The sum total of these genetic instructions for a given species is called its _____ .

3. The human reproductive cells, which are called _____ , include the male's _____ and the female's _____ .

4. When the gametes' nuclei fuse, a living cell called a _____ is formed.

5. This new cells receives _____ chromosomes from the father and _____ from the mother.

6. An organism's entire genetic inheritance is called its _____ .

7. The chromosomes in a pair are generally identical or similar. Some genes come in several slight, normal variations called _____ .

8. The developing person's sex is determined by the _____ pair of chromosomes. In the female, this pair is composed of two _____-shaped chromosomes and is designated _____ . In the male, this pair includes one _____ and one _____ chromosome and is therefore designated _____ .

9. The critical factor in the determination of a zygote's sex is which _____ (sperm/ovum) reaches the other gamete first. In a stressful pregnancy, _____ (XX/XY) embryos are more likely to be expelled in a miscarriage, or _____ .

10. (text and Issues and Applications) At birth, the overall sex ratio has always _____ (favored males/favored females/been roughly equal). In countries such as China, prenatal tests that show the sex of the child have been used to _____ .

From One Cell to Many (pp. 70–78)

11. The actual appearance and manifest behavior of the person is called the _____ .

12. Within hours after conception, the zygote begins to _____ and _____ . At about the eight-cell stage, the cells start to _____ , with various cells beginning to specialize and reproduce at different rates. Genes affect this process through _____-_____ _____ mechanisms that code for specific proteins.

13. Most human characteristics are affected by many genes, and so they are _____ ; and by many factors, and so they are _____ .

14. (text and Thinking Like a Scientist) The international effort to map the complete human genetic code is referred to as the _____ _____ _____ . This effort found most importantly that all living creatures _____ (have different/share) genes.

15. A phenotype that reflects the sum of the contributions of all the genes involved in its determination illustrates the _____ pattern of genetic interaction. Examples include genes that affect _____ and _____ .

16. Less often, genes interact in a _____ fashion. In one example of this pattern, some genes are more influential than others; this is called the _____–_____ pattern. In this pattern, the more influential gene is called _____ , and the weaker gene is called _____ .

17. Some recessive genes are located only on the X chromosome and so are called _____-_____ . Examples of such genes are the ones that determine _____ . Because they have only one X chromosome, _____ (females/males) are more likely to have these characteristics in their phenotype.

18. Complicating inheritance further is the fact that dominant genes sometimes do not completely _____ the phenotype. This may be caused by _____ , _____ , or other factors.

19. Twins who begin life as two separate zygotes created by the fertilization of two ova are called _____ twins. Such twins have approximately _____ percent of their genes in common.

20. Dizygotic births may occur about once in every _____ births, but generally one embryo dies and just one baby is born. The incidence of dizygotic twins varies by _____ .

21. Identical twins, who develop from one
_____ , _____ (are/are
not) genetically identical.

22. An artificially created organism that is exactly the
same genotype as another organism that is
already alive is called a _____ .

23. Multiple births have higher rates of
_____ , _____ , and
_____ than single births.

24. (In Person) Couples that have been unable to produce a baby after at least one year of trying are
troubled by _____ . For such cou-
ples, _____ _____
_____ can help in conceiving and
then sustaining a pregnancy.

25. (In Person) One simple treatment for infertility is
to use _____ to cause ovulation. If
the male partner is infertile, donor sperm may be
inserted into the female's uterus in a process
called _____ _____ . A
more complicated method, involving fertilization
in a laboratory dish, is called _____
_____ _____ .

From Genotype to Phenotype (pp. 79–85)

State three general principles of genetic influences on
development that virtually all developmentalists
accept.

26. A person who has a gene in his or her genotype
that is not expressed in the phenotype but that
can be passed on to the person's offspring is said
to be a _____ of that gene.

27. Mental illnesses, or _____ such as
schizophrenia, are the results of _____–
_____ and _____–
_____ interaction. One predisposing factor is birth during _____
_____ , probably because a certain
_____ is more prevalent at this time
of year. It is suspected that a crucial factor in the
development of schizophrenia is an experience at
or before birth such as _____
_____ .

Schizophrenia may also develop in part as a
response to experiences after birth, such as
_____ _____ .

28. Some people's inherited biochemistry makes
them highly susceptible to each kind of
_____ . Certain _____
traits are also correlated with addiction, including
_____ .
Thus, alcoholism is _____ . Another
important factor, which makes alcoholism
_____ , is _____ .

29. The most common vision problem in children is
_____ , also called
_____ . This problem may be
caused by genes, by physical _____
or _____ , and by poor
_____ . The alarming increase in the
rate of this vision problem among children in
some parts of the world has been attributed to the
increasing amount of time spent by children in
the _____ .

30. On a practical level, knowing that a particular
genetic disorder runs in the family can help parents take _____ measures to reduce
their children's vulnerability. For instance, type 2
diabetes does not begin unless a person is
_____ vulnerable and has more
_____ _____ than is
ideal for his or her age and height.

Chromosomal and Genetic Abnormalities (pp. 85–94)

Researchers study genetic and chromosomal abnormalities for three major reasons. State them.

31. Chromosomal abnormalities occur during the formation of the _____ , producing a sperm or ovum that does not have the normal complement of chromosomes.

32. The variable that most often correlates with chromosomal abnormalities is _____ _____ . When cells in a zygote end up with more or fewer than 46 chromosomes, the result is a person who is _____ .

33. Most fetuses with chromosomal abnormalities are _____ _____ . Nevertheless, about 1 in every _____ newborns has one chromosome too few or one too many, leading to a cluster of characteristics called a _____ .

34. The most common extra-chromosome syndrome is _____ _____ , which is also called _____-_____ . People with this syndrome age _____ (faster/more slowly) than other adults. By middle age, people with Down syndrome almost invariably develop _____ , which severely impairs their already limited _____ skills.

List several of the physical and psychological characteristics associated with Down syndrome.

35. About 1 in every 500 infants is either missing a _____ chromosome or has two or more such chromosomes. One resulting syndrome is _____ , in which a girl inherits only one _____ chromosome; another is _____ _____ , in which a boy inherits the _____ chromosome pattern.

36. Most of the known genetic disorders are _____ (dominant/recessive). Genetic disorders usually _____ (are/are not) seriously disabling. These disorders are _____ (common/rare) because people with these disorders usually _____ (do/do not) have children.

37. Two exceptions are the central nervous system disease called _____ and the disorder that causes its victims to exhibit uncontrollable tics and explosive outbursts, called _____ .

38. In some individuals, part of the X chromosome is attached by such a thin string of molecules that it seems about to break off; this abnormality is called _____ _____ syndrome.

39. Three common recessive disorders that are not sex-linked are _____ , _____ , and _____-_____ _____ .

40. Through _____ _____ , couples today can learn more about their genes and about their chances of conceiving a child with chromosomal or other genetic abnormalities.

41. List four situations in which genetic counseling is strongly recommended.

   a. _____

   b. _____

   c. _____

   d. _____

Progress Test 1

Circle your answers to the following questions and check them against the answers beginning on page 47. If your answer is incorrect, read the explanation for why it is incorrect and then consult the appropriate pages of the text (in parentheses following the correct answer).

Multiple-Choice Questions

1. When a sperm and an ovum merge, a one-celled _____ is formed.
   a. zygote   c. gamete
   b. reproductive cell   d. monozygote

2. Genes are separate units that provide the chemical instructions that each cell needs to become:
   a. a zygote.
   b. a chromosome.
   c. a specific part of a functioning human body.
   d. deoxyribonucleic acid.

3. In the male, the 23rd pair of chromosomes is designated _____ ; in the female, this pair is designated _____.
   a. XX; XY   c. XO; XXX
   b. XY; XX   d. XXY; XO

4. Since the 23rd pair of chromosomes in females is XX, each ovum carries an:
   a. XX zygote.   c. XY zygote.
   b. X zygote.   d. X chromosome.

5. When a zygote splits, the two identical, independent clusters that develop become:
   a. dizygotic twins.   c. fraternal twins.
   b. monozygotic twins.   d. trizygotic twins.

6. Which of the following is a predisposing factor for schizophrenia?
   a. birth during late winter
   b. having a close relative with the illness
   c. inadequate oxygen at birth
   d. Each of the above is a predisposing factor.

7. Most of the known genetic disorders are:
   a. dominant.   c. seriously disabling.
   b. recessive.   d. sex-linked.

8. When we say that a characteristic is multifactorial, we mean that:
   a. many genes are involved.
   b. many environmental factors are involved.
   c. many genetic and environmental factors are involved.
   d. the characteristic is polygenic.

9. Genes are segments of molecules of:
   a. genotype.
   b. deoxyribonucleic acid (DNA).
   c. karyotype.
   d. phenotype.

10. The potential for genetic diversity in humans is so great because:
    a. there are approximately 8 million possible combinations of chromosomes.
    b. when the sperm and ovum unite, genetic combinations not present in either parent can be formed.
    c. just before a chromosome pair divides during the formation of gametes, genes are exchanged, producing recombinations.
    d. of all the above reasons.

11. A chromosomal abnormality that affects males only involves a(n):
    a. XO chromosomal pattern.
    b. XXX chromosomal pattern.
    c. YY chromosomal pattern.
    d. XXY chromosomal pattern.

12. Some developmentalists believe that the epidemic increase in myopia among children in Hong Kong, Taiwan, and Japan is partly the result of:
    a. the recent epidemic of rubella.
    b. vitamin A deficiency.
    c. the increasing amount of time spent by children in close study of books and papers.
    d. mutations in the Pax6 gene.

13. Babies born with trisomy-21 (Down syndrome) are often:
    a. born to older parents.
    b. unusually aggressive.
    c. abnormally tall by adolescence.
    d. blind.

14. To say that a trait is polygenic means that:
    a. many genes make it more likely that the individual will inherit the trait.
    b. several genes must be present in order for the individual to inherit the trait.
    c. the trait is multifactorial.
    d. most people carry genes for the trait.

15. Some genetic diseases are recessive, so the child cannot inherit the condition unless both parents:
    a. have Kleinfelter syndrome.
    b. carry the same recessive gene.
    c. have XO chromosomes.
    d. have the disease.

Matching Items

Match each term with its corresponding description or definition.

Terms

_____ **1.** gametes
_____ **2.** chromosome
_____ **3.** genotype
_____ **4.** phenotype
_____ **5.** monozygotic
_____ **6.** dizygotic
_____ **7.** additive
_____ **8.** fragile X syndrome
_____ **9.** carrier
_____ **10.** zygote
_____ **11.** alleles
_____ **12.** XX
_____ **13.** XY

Descriptions or Definitions

a. chromosome pair inherited by genetic females
b. identical twins
c. sperm and ovum
d. the first cell of the developing person
e. a person who has a recessive gene in his or her genotype that is not expressed in the phenotype
f. fraternal twins
g. a pattern in which each gene in question makes an active contribution to the final outcome
h. a DNA molecule
i. the behavioral or physical expression of genetic potential
j. a chromosomal abnormality
k. alternate versions of a gene
l. chromosome pair inherited by genetic males
m. a person's entire genetic inheritance

Progress Test 2

Progress Test 2 should be completed during a final chapter review. Answer the following questions after you thoroughly understand the correct answers for the Chapter Review and Progress Test 1.

1. Which of the following provides the best broad description of the relationship between heredity and environment in determining height?
   a. Heredity is the primary influence, with environment affecting development only in severe situations.
   b. Heredity and environment contribute equally to development.
   c. Environment is the major influence on physical characteristics.
   d. Heredity directs the individual's potential and environment determines whether and to what degree the individual reaches that potential.

2. The recent increase in type 2 diabetes among children in the United States is the result of:
   a. unknown factors.
   b. genes acting alone.
   c. vitamin deficiencies among certain ethnic groups.
   d. genetic vulnerability coupled with increasing obesity.

3. Males with fragile X syndrome are:
   a. feminine in appearance.
   b. less severely affected than females.
   c. frequently retarded intellectually.
   d. likely to have fatty deposits around the breasts.

4. With the exception of sperm and egg cells, each human cell contains:
   a. 23 genes.   **c.** 46 genes.
   b. 23 chromosomes.   **d.** 46 chromosomes.

5. The disorder in which a genetic female inherits only one X chromosome (XO pattern) is called:
   a. trisomy 21.
   b. Down syndrome.
   c. Turner syndrome.
   d. Klinefelter syndrome.

6. Dizygotic twins result when:
   a. a single egg is fertilized by a sperm and then splits.
   b. a single egg is fertilized by two different sperm.
   c. two eggs are fertilized by two different sperm.
   d. either a single egg is fertilized by one sperm or two eggs are fertilized by two different sperm.

7. Molecules of DNA that in humans are organized into 23 complementary pairs are called:
   a. zygotes.   c. chromosomes.
   b. genes.   d. ova.

8. Shortly after the zygote is formed, it begins the processes of duplication and division. Each resulting new cell has:
   a. the same number of chromosomes as was contained in the zygote.
   b. half the number of chromosomes as was contained in the zygote.
   c. twice, then four times, then eight times the number of chromosomes as was contained in the zygote.
   d. all the chromosomes except those that determine sex.

9. If an ovum is fertilized by a sperm bearing a Y chromosome:
   a. a female will develop.
   b. cell division will result.
   c. a male will develop.
   d. spontaneous abortion will occur.

10. When the male cells in the testes and the female cells in the ovaries divide to produce gametes, the process differs from that in the production of all other cells. As a result of the different process, the gametes have:
   a. one rather than both members of each chromosome pair.
   b. 23 chromosome pairs.
   c. X but not Y chromosomes.
   d. chromosomes from both parents.

11. Most human traits are:
   a. polygenic.
   b. multifactorial.
   c. determined by dominant–recessive patterns.
   d. both a. and b.

12. Genotype is to phenotype as _____ is to _____ .
   a. genetic potential; physical expression
   b. physical expression; genetic potential
   c. sperm; ovum
   d. gamete; zygote

13. The genes that influence height and skin color interact according to the _____ pattern.
   a. dominant–recessive   c. additive
   b. X-linked   d. nonadditive

14. X-linked recessive genes explain why some traits seem to be passed from:
   a. father to son.
   b. father to daughter.
   c. mother to daughter.
   d. mother to son.

15. In vitro fertilization is a technique:
   a. in which sperm are mixed with ova that have been surgically removed from a woman's ovary.
   b. in which sperm from a donor are inserted into the woman's uterus via a syringe..
   c. for helping infertile couples conceive a pregnancy.
   d. for helping infertile couples sustain a pregnancy.

True or False Items

Write T (*true*) or F (*false*) on the line in front of each statement.

_____ 1. Most human characteristics are multifactorial, caused by the interaction of genetic and environmental factors.

_____ 2. Chromosomal abnormalities can occur only for genetic reasons.

_____ 3. Research suggests that susceptibility to alcoholism is at least partly the result of genetic inheritance.

_____ 4. The human reproductive cells (ova and sperm) are called gametes.

_____ 5. Only a very few human traits are polygenic.

_____ 6. The zygote contains all the biologically inherited information—the genes and chromosomes—that a person will have during his or her life.

_____ 7. A couple should probably seek genetic counseling if several earlier pregnancies ended in spontaneous abortion.

_____ 8. Many genetic conditions are recessive; thus, a child will have the condition even if only the mother carries the gene.

_____ 9. Two people who have the same phenotype may have a different genotype for a trait such as eye color.

_____ 10. When cells divide to produce reproductive cells (gametes), each sperm or ovum receives only 23 chromosomes, half as many as the original cell.

_____ 11. Most genes have only one function.

_____ 12. Psychopathologies such as depression and phobias are caused by environmental factors.

Thinking Critically About Chapter 3

Answer these questions the day before an exam as a final check on your understanding of the chapter's terms and concepts.

1. Randy's son was born with an XXY chromosomal pattern. It is likely that his son's condition will:
   a. go undetected until puberty.
   b. benefit from hormone supplements.
   c. develop some female sex characteristics at puberty.
   d. be characterized by all of the above.

2. Concluding her presentation on the hazards of multiple births, Kirsten notes that, "the more embryos that develop together, the":
   a. larger each is.
   b. less mature and more vulnerable each is.
   c. less vulnerable each is.
   d. larger and less vulnerable each is.

3. Which of the following is an inherited abnormality that quite possibly could develop into a recognizable syndrome?
   a. Just before dividing to form a sperm or ovum, corresponding gene segments of a chromosome pair break off and are exchanged.
   b. Just before conception, a chromosome pair splits imprecisely, resulting in a mixture of cells.
   c. A person inherits an X chromosome in which part of the chromosome is attached to the rest of it by a very slim string of molecules.
   d. A person inherits a recessive gene on his Y chromosome.

4. Some men are color-blind because they inherit a particular recessive gene from their mother. That recessive gene is carried on the:
   a. X chromosome.
   b. XX chromosome pair.
   c. Y chromosome.
   d. X or Y chromosome.

5. If your mother is much taller than your father, it is most likely that your height will be:
   a. about the same as your mother's, because the X chromosome determines height.
   b. about the same as your father's, because the Y chromosome determines height.
   c. somewhere between your mother's and father's heights because the genes for height are additive.
   d. greater than both your mother's and father's because of your grandfather's dominant gene.

6. If a dizygotic twin develops schizophrenia, the likelihood of the other twin experiencing serious mental illness is much lower than is the case with monozygotic twins. This suggests that:
   a. schizophrenia is caused by genes.
   b. schizophrenia is influenced by genes.
   c. environment is unimportant in the development of schizophrenia.
   d. monozygotic twins are especially vulnerable to schizophrenia.

7. A person's skin turns yellow-orange as a result of a carrot-juice diet regimen. This is an example of:
   a. an environmental influence.
   b. an alteration in genotype.
   c. polygenic inheritance.
   d. incomplete dominance.

8. Jason has an inherited, dominant disorder that causes him to exhibit uncontrollable tics and explosive outbursts. Jason most likely would be diagnosed with:
   a. Klinefelter syndrome.
   b. Huntington's disease.
   c. Fragile X syndrome.
   d. Tourette syndrome.

9. If a man carries the recessive gene for cystic fibrosis and his wife does not, the chances of their having a child with cystic fibrosis is:
   a. one in four.
   b. fifty-fifty.
   c. zero.
   d. dependent upon the wife's ethnic background.

10. One reason scientists are skeptical of research that attempts to distinguish genetic influences from environmental ones is that:
   a. genes elicit responses from other people that shape each child's development.
   b. there are too few monozygotic twins available for research studies.
   c. twin research is compromised by the fact that most environmental influences on children raised in the same household are shared.
   d. dizygotic twins raised together share both genes and environment.

11. Schizophrenia is most accurately described as a(n):
   a. genetic psychopathology.
   b. environmental psychopathology.
   c. multifactorial psychopathology
   d. psychopathology of unknown cause.

12. Laurie and Brad, who both have a history of alcoholism in their families, are concerned that the child they hope to have will inherit a genetic predisposition to alcoholism. Based on information presented in the text, what advice should you offer them?
    a. "Stop worrying, alcoholism is only weakly genetic."
    b. "It is almost certain that your child will become alcoholic."
    c. "Social influences, such as the family and peer environment, play a critical role in determining whether alcoholism is expressed."
    d. "Wait to have children until you are both middle aged, in order to see if the two of you become alcoholic."

13. Sixteen-year-old Joey experiences some mental slowness and hearing and heart problems, yet he is able to care for himself and is unusually sweet-tempered. Joey probably:
    a. has Tourette syndrome.
    b. has Alzheimer's disease.
    c. has Kleinfelter syndrome.
    d. has Down syndrome.

14. Genetically, Claude's potential height is 6'0. Because he did not receive a balanced diet, however, he grew to only 5'9". Claude's actual height is an example of a:
    a. recessive gene.
    b. dominant gene.
    c. genotype.
    d. phenotype.

15. Winona inherited a gene from her mother that, regardless of her father's contribution to her genotype, will be expressed in her phenotype. Evidently, the gene Winona received from her mother is a(n) _____ gene.
    a. polygenic   c. dominant
    b. recessive   d. X-linked

Key Terms

Writing Definitions

Using your own words, write on a separate piece of paper a brief definition or explanation of each of the following terms.

1. DNA
2. chromosome
3. gene
4. human genome
5. gamete
6. zygote
7. genotype
8. allele
9. 23rd pair
10. XX
11. XY
12. spontaneous abortion
13. phenotype
14. polygenic
15. multifactorial
16. Human Genome Project
17. additive gene
18. dominant—recessive pattern
19. X-linked
20. dizygotic (DZ) twins
21. monozygotic (MZ) twins
22. clone
23. infertility
24. assisted reproductive technology (ART)
25. in vitro fertilization
26. carrier
27. mosaic
28. Down syndrome
29. fragile X syndrome
30. genetic counseling

Cross-Check

After you have written the definitions of the key terms in this chapter, you should complete the crossword puzzle to ensure that you can reverse the process—recognize the term, given the definition.

ACROSS

2. Cluster of distinct characteristics that tend to occur together in a given disorder.
7. An organism's entire genetic inheritance.
9. The single cell formed from the fusing of an ovum and a sperm.
12. The stronger gene in an interacting pair of genes.
13. All of the genetic traits that are expressed in a person.
15. Genes that are on the X chromosome.
16. The sequence of chemical bases held within DNA molecules that directs development.
17. One of 46 in each normal human cell.
18. A disease that nearly always develops in middle age in people with Down syndrome.
19. The genes that affect height, hair curliness, and skin color are of this type.

DOWN

1. A genetic disorder in which part of the X chromosome is attached to the rest of it by a very slim string of molecules.
3. Fraternal twins.
4. All the nongenetic factors that can affect development.
5. The growth process in which cells begin to specialize, taking different forms and dividing at different rates.
6. The basic unit of genetic instruction.
8. A spontaneous abortion.
10. The international project to map the complete human genetic code.
11. Type of trait produced by the interaction of many genes (rather than by a single gene).
12. The most common extra-chromosome syndrome (also called trisomy-21).
14. The weaker gene in an interacting pair of genes.

ANSWERS
CHAPTER REVIEW

1. proteins; DNA; chromosome
2. 46; 23; genes; protein; amino acids; genome
3. gametes; sperm; ova
4. zygote
5. 23; 23
6. genotype
7. alleles
8. 23rd; X; XX; X; Y; XY
9. sperm; XY; spontaneous abortion
10. been roughly equal; abort female fetuses
11. phenotype
12. duplicate; divide; differentiate; on–off switching
13. polygenic; multifactorial
14. Human Genome Project; share
15. additive; height; skin color (or hair curliness)
16. nonadditive;   dominant–recessive;   dominant;   recessive;
17. X-linked; color blindness, many allergies, several diseases, and some learning disabilities; males
18. penetrate; temperature; stress
19. dizygotic; 50
20. 8; ethnicity
21. zygote; are

22. clone
23. death; disease; disabilities
24. infertility; assisted reproductive technology
25. drugs; artificial insemination; in vitro fertilization
  a. Genes affect every aspect of human behavior.
  b. Most environmental influences on children raised in the same household are not shared.
  c. Genes elicit responses from other people that shape each child's development.
26. carrier
27. psychopathologies; gene–gene; gene–environment; late winter; virus; a slow-acting virus, head injury, inadequate oxygen at birth; family interaction
28. addiction; personality; a quick temper, a readiness to take risks, and a high level of anxiety; polygenic; multifactorial; culture
29. nearsightedness; myopia; trauma; illness; nutrition; close study of books and papers
30. protective; genetically; body fat

They provide insight into the complexities of genetic interactions, knowledge about their origins suggests how to limit their harmful consequences, and misinformation and prejudice compound the problems of people who are affected by such abnormalities.

31. gametes
32. maternal age; mosaic
33. spontaneously aborted; 200; syndrome
34. Down Syndrome; trisomy-21; faster; Alzheimer's disease; communication

Most people with Down syndrome have certain facial characteristics—a thick tongue, round face, slanted eyes—as well as distinctive hands, feet, and fingerprints. Many also have hearing problems, heart abnormalities, muscle weakness, and short stature. Almost all experience some mental slowness, especially in language.

35. sex; Turner syndrome; X; Klinefelter syndrome; XXY
36. dominant; are not; rare; do not
37. Huntington's disease; Tourette syndrome
38. fragile X
39. cystic fibrosis, thalassemia, sickle-cell anemia
40. genetic counseling
41. Genetic counseling is recommended for (a) those who have a parent, sibling, or child with a serious genetic condition; (b) those who have a history of spontaneous abortions, stillbirths, or infertility; (c) couples who are from the same ethnic group or subgroup; and (d) women over age 35 and men age 40 or older.

PROGRESS TEST 1

Multiple-Choice Questions

1. **a.** is the answer. (p. 67)

   b. & c. The reproductive cells (sperm and ova), which are also called gametes, are individual entities.

   d. *Monozygote* refers to one member of a pair of identical twins.

2. **c.** is the answer. (p. 66)

   a. The zygote is the first cell of the developing person.

   b. Chromosomes are molecules of DNA that *carry* genes.

   d. DNA molecules contain genetic information.

3. **b.** is the answer. (p. 68)

4. **d.** is the answer. When the gametes are formed, one member of each chromosome pair splits off; because in females both are X chromosomes, each ovum must carry an X chromosome. (p. 68)

   a., b., & c. The zygote refers to the merged sperm and ovum that is the first new cell of the developing individual.

5. **b.** is the answer. *Mono* means "one." Thus, monozygotic twins develop from one zygote. (p. 76)

   a. & c. Dizygotic, or fraternal, twins develop from two (*di*) zygotes.

   d. A trizygotic birth would result in triplets (*tri*), rather than twins.

6. **d.** is the answer. (p. 81)

7. **a.** is the answer. (p. 90)

   c. & d. Most dominant disorders are neither seriously disabling nor sex-linked.

8. **c.** is the answer. (p. 71)

   a., b., & d. *Polygenic* means "many genes"; *multifactorial* means "many factors," which are not limited to either genetic or environmental factors.

9. **b.** is the answer. (p. 66)

   a. Genotype is a person's genetic potential.

   c. A karyotype is a picture of a person's chromosomes.

   d. Phenotype is the actual expression of a genotype.

10. **d.** is the answer. (p. 74)

11. **d.** is the answer. (p. 87)

a. & b. These chromosomal abnormalities affect females.

c. There is no such abnormality.

12. **c.** is the answer. (pp. 83–84)

a. Although nearsightedness is associated with rubella, there has not been an increase in rubella in these countries.

b. Vitamin A deficiencies may be a factor in the vision problems of children among certain African ethnic groups.

d. The rapid changes in the prevalence of myopia suggest that an environmental factor is the culprit.

13. **a.** is the answer. (p. 86)

14. **b.** is the answer. (p. 71)

15. **b.** is the answer. (p. 90)

a. & c. These abnormalities involve the sex chromosomes, not genes.

d. In order for an offspring to inherit a recessive condition, the parents need only be carriers of the recessive gene in their genotypes; they need not actually have the disease.

Matching Items

1. c (p. 67)	5. b (p. 76)	9. e (p. 78)
2. h (p. 65)	6. f (p. 75)	10. d (p. 67)
3. m (p. 67)	7. g (p. 72)	11. k (p. 68)
4. i (p. 70)	8. j (p. 76)	12. a (p. 68)
		13. l (p. 68)

PROGRESS TEST 2

Multiple-Choice Questions

1. **d.** is the answer. (pp. 79–80)

2. **d.** is the answer. (p. 85)

3. **c.** is the answer. (p. 90)

a. Physical appearance is usually normal in this syndrome.

b. Males are more frequently and more severely affected.

d. This is true of the XXY chromosomal abnormality, but not the fragile X syndrome.

4. **d.** is the answer. (p. 67)

a. & c. Human cells contain thousands of genes.

5. **c.** is the answer. (p. 87)

a. This syndrome involves inheriting an *extra* chromosome.

d. This syndrome involves inheriting three sex chromosomes in an XXY pattern.

6. **c.** is the answer. (p. 75)

a. This would result in monozygotic twins.

b. Only one sperm can fertilize an ovum.

d. A single egg fertilized by one sperm would produce a single offspring or monozygotic twins.

7. **c.** is the answer. (p. 65)

a. Zygotes are fertilized ova.

b. Genes are the smaller units of heredity that are organized into sequences on chromosomes.

d. Ova are female reproductive cells.

8. **a.** is the answer. (p. 70)

9. **c.** is the answer. The ovum will contain an X chromosome; with the sperm's Y chromosome, it will produce the male XY pattern. (p. 68)

a. Only if the ovum is fertilized by an X chromosome from the sperm will a female develop.

b. Cell division will occur regardless of whether the sperm contributes an X or a Y chromosome.

d. Spontaneous abortions are likely to occur when there are chromosomal or genetic abnormalities; the situation described is perfectly normal.

10. **a.** is the answer. (p. 67)

b. & d. These are true of all body cells *except* the gametes.

c. Gametes have either X or Y chromosomes.

11. **d.** is the answer. (p. 71)

12. **a.** is the answer. Genotype refers to the sum total of all the genes a person inherits; phenotype refers to the actual expression of the individual's characteristics. (pp. 67, 70)

13. **c.** is the answer. (p. 72)

14. **d.** is the answer. X-linked genes are located only on the X chromosome. Because males inherit only one X chromosome, they are more likely than females to have these characteristics in their phenotype. (p. 73)

15. **a.** is the answer. (p. 77)

b. This describes artificial insemination.

c. & d. These answers, which are too general, describe all forms of assisted reproductive technology.

True or False Items

1. T (p. 71)
2. F   Chromosomal abnormalities may be environmentally caused, as with parents' exposure to excessive radiation. (p. 86)
3. T (p. 82)
4. T (p. 67)
5. F   Most traits are polygenic. (p. 71)
6. T (p. 67)
7. T (p. 91)
8. F   A trait from a recessive gene will be part of the phenotype only when the person has two recessive genes for that trait. (p. 90)
9. T (p. 70)
10. T (p. 67)
11. F   Most genes have several functions. (p. 71)
12. F   These psychopathologies are partly genetic in origin. (p. 80)

THINKING CRITICALLY ABOUT CHAPTER 3

1. **d.** is the answer. (p. 87)
2. **b.** is the answer. (p. 77)
3. **c.** is the answer. This describes the fragile X syndrome. (p. 90)

   a. This phenomenon, which is called *crossing over*, merely contributes to genetic diversity.

   b. This is merely an example of a particular non-additive gene interaction pattern.

   d. For a recessive gene to be expressed, both parents must pass it on to the child.

4. **a.** is the answer. (p. 73)

   b. The male genotype is XY, not XX.

   c. & d. The mother contributes only an X chromosome.

5. **c.** is the answer. (p. 72)

   a., b., & d. It is unlikely that these factors account for height differences from one generation to the next.

6. **b.** is the answer. Because monozygotic twins are genetically identical, while dizygotic twins share only 50 percent of their genes, greater similarity of traits between monozygotic twins suggests that genes are an important influence. (p. 80)

   a. & c. Even though schizophrenia has a strong genetic component, it is not the case that if one twin has schizophrenia the other also automatically does. Therefore, the environment, too, is an important influence.

   d. This does not necessarily follow.

7. **a.** is the answer. (p. 79)

   b. Genotype is a person's genetic potential, established at conception.

   c. Polygenic inheritance refers to the influence of many genes on a particular trait.

   d. Incomplete dominance refers to the phenotype being influenced primarily, but not exclusively, by the dominant gene.

8. **d.** is the answer. (p. 90)
9. **c.** is the answer. Cystic fibrosis is a recessive gene disorder; therefore, in order for a child to inherit this disease, he or she must receive the recessive gene from both parents. (p. 90)
10. **a.** is the answer. (p. 79)

    b. Although identical twins are not common, there have been a number of studies of their traits.

    c. In fact, most environmental influences on children raised in the same household are not shared.

11. **c.** is the answer. (p. 81)
12. **c.** is the answer. (p. 82)

    a. Some people's inherited biochemistry makes them highly susceptible to alcoholism.

    b. Despite a strong genetic influence on alcoholism, the environment also plays a critical role.

    d. Not only is this advice unreasonable, but it might increase the likelihood of chromosomal abnormalities in the parents' sperm and ova.

13. **d.** is the answer. (pp. 86–87)
14. **d.** is the answer. (p. 70)

    a. & b. Genes are separate units of a chromosome.

    c. Genotype refers to genetic potential.

15. **c.** is the answer. (p. 72)

    a. There is no such thing as a "polygenic gene." *Polygenic* means "many genes."

    b. A recessive gene paired with a dominant gene will not be expressed in the phenotype.

    d. X-linked genes may be dominant or recessive.

KEY TERMS

Writing Definitions

1. **DNA (deoxyribonucleic acid)** is the molecule that contains the chemical instructions for cells to manufacture various proteins. (p. 65)
2. **Chromosomes** are molecules of DNA that contain the genes organized in precise sequences. (p. 65)

3. **Genes** are segments of a chromosome, which is a DNA molecule; they are the basic units for the transmission of hereditary instructions. (p. 66)

4. The **human genome** is the full set of 25,000 or so genes that are the instructions to make a human being. (p. 66)

5. **Gametes** are the human reproductive cells. (p. 67)

6. The **zygote** is the one-celled organism formed during conception by the union of sperm and ovum. (p. 67)

7. The total of all the genes a person inherits—his or her genetic potential—is called the **genotype.** (p. 67)

8. An **allele** is one of the normal versions of a gene that has several possible sequences of base pairs. (p. 68)

9. The **23rd pair** of chromosomes, in humans, determines the individual's sex. (p. 68)

10. **XX** is the twenty-third chromosome pair that, in humans, determines that the developing fetus will be female. (p. 68)

11. **XY** is the twenty-third chromosome pair that, in humans, determines that the developing fetus will be male. (p. 68)

12. Also known as a miscarriage, a **spontaneous abortion** is the natural termination of a pregnancy before the fetus is fully developed. (p. 69)

13. The actual physical or behavioral expression of a genotype, the result of the interaction of the genes with each other and with the environment, is called the **phenotype.** (p. 70)

14. Most human traits are **polygenic;** that is, they are affected by many genes. (p. 71)

15. Most human traits are also **multifactorial**—that is, influenced by many factors, including genetic and environmental factors. (p. 71)

    Memory aid: The roots of the words polygenic and multifactorial give their meaning: *poly* means "many" and genic means "of the genes"; *multi* means "several" and factorial obviously refers to factors.

16. **The Human Genome Project** is an international effort to map the complete human genetic code. (p. 71)

17. When a trait is determined by **additive genes,** the phenotype reflects the sum of the contributions of all the genes involved. The genes affecting height, for example, interact in this fashion. (p. 72)

18. The **dominant–recessive** pattern is the interaction of a gene's alleles in such a way that one, the dominant gene, has a stronger influence than the other, recessive gene. (p. 72)

19. **X-linked** genes are genes that are located only on the X chromosome. Since males have only one X chromosome, they are more likely than females to have the characteristics determined by these genes in their phenotype. (p. 73)

20. **Dizygotic (DZ) twins** develop from two separate ova fertilized by different sperm at roughly the same time, and therefore are no more genetically similar than ordinary siblings; also called **fraternal twins** (p. 75)

    Memory aid: A fraternity is a group of two (*di*) or more nonidentical individuals.

21. **Monozygotic (MZ) twins** develop from one zygote that splits apart, producing genetically identical zygotes; also called *identical twins.* (p. 76)

    Memory aid: Mono means "one"; **monozygotic twins** develop from one fertilized ovum.

22. A **clone** is an artificially created organism that has exactly the same genotype as another living organism. (p. 76)

23. **Infertility** is the inability to produce a baby after at least one year of trying. (p. 77)

24. **Assisted reproductive technology (ART)** refers to the various techniques available to help infertile couples conceive and sustain a pregnancy. (p. 77)

25. **In vitro fertilization (IVF)** is a form of ART in which ova surgically removed from a woman are mixed with sperm. If a zygote is produced, it is inserted in the woman's uterus after three duplications. (p. 77)

26. A person who has a recessive gene that is not expressed in his or her genotype but that can be passed on to the person's offspring is called a **carrier** of that gene. (p. 78)

27. **Mosaic** refers to the condition in which a person has a mixture of cells, some normal and some with too few or too many chromosomes. (p. 86)

28. **Down syndrome** (*trisomy-21*) is the most common extra-chromosome condition. People with Down syndrome age faster than others, often have usual facial features and heart abnormalities, and invariably develop Alzheimer's disease. (p. 86)

29. The **fragile X syndrome** is a single-gene disorder in which part of the X chromosome is attached by such a thin string of molecules that it seems about to break off. Although the characteristics associated with this syndrome are quite varied, some mental deficiency is relatively common. (p. 90)

30. Genetic counseling involves a variety of tests through which couples can learn more about their genes, and can thus make informed decisions about their childbearing and child-rearing future. (p. 91)

Cross-Check

ACROSS

2. syndrome
7. genotype
9. zygote
12. dominant
13. phenotype
15. X-linked
16. genetic code
17. chromosome
18. Alzheimer's
19. additive

DOWN

1. fragile X
3. dizygotic
4. environment
5. differentiation
6. gene
8. miscarriage
10. Human Genome
11. polygenic
12. Down syndrome
14. recessive

Chapter Four

Prenatal Development and Birth

Chapter Overview

Prenatal development is complex and startlingly rapid—more rapid than any other period of the life span. During prenatal development, the individual changes from a one-celled zygote to a complex human baby. This development is outlined in Chapter 4, along with some of the problems that can occur—among them prenatal exposure to disease, drugs, and other hazards—and the factors that moderate the risks of teratogenic exposure.

For the developing person, birth marks the most radical transition of the entire life span. No longer sheltered from the outside world, the fetus becomes a separate human being who begins life almost completely dependent upon his or her caregivers. Chapter 4 also examines the birth process and its possible variations and problems.

The chapter concludes with a discussion of the significance of the parent–infant bond, including factors that affect its development.

NOTE: Answer guidelines for all Chapter 4 questions begin on page 64.

Guided Study

The text chapter should be studied one section at a time. Before you read, preview each section by skimming it, noting headings and boldface items. Then read the appropriate section objectives from the following outline. Keep these objectives in mind and, as you read the chapter section, search for the information that will enable you to meet each objective. Once you have finished a section, write out answers for its objectives.

From Zygote to Newborn (pp. 97–104)

1. Describe the significant developments of the germinal period.

2. Describe the significant developments of the embryonic period.

3. Describe the significant developments of the fetal period, noting the importance of the age of viability.

Risk Reduction (pp. 104–117)

4. Explain the main goal of teratology, and discuss several factors that determine whether a specific teratogen will be harmful.

5. (Table 4.4) Identify at least five teratogens, and describe their possible effects on the developing embryo or fetus.

6. (Issues and Applications) Discuss AIDS and alcohol as teratogens, and describe the protective steps that may be taken to prevent their damaging effects.

7. (Table 4.6) Describe several methods of postconception testing to determine the health of the fetus.

8. Distinguish among low-birthweight (LBW), preterm, and small-for-gestational-age (SGA) infants, and identify the causes of low birthweight.

The Birth Process (pp. 117–126)

9. Describe the birth process in all its forms.

10. Describe the test used to assess the neonate's condition at birth.

11. Explain the causes of cerebral palsy, and discuss the special needs of high-risk infants.

12. Discuss the importance of a strong parental alliance and parent–infant bonding to a healthy start for the baby.

4. At the beginning of the period of the embryo, a thin line down the middle of the developing individual forms a structure that will become the _____ _____ , which becomes the _____ _____ and eventually will develop into the _____ _____ _____ .

Briefly describe the major features of development during the second month.

Chapter Review

When you have finished reading the chapter, work through the material that follows to review it. Complete the sentences and answer the questions. As you proceed, evaluate your performance for each section by consulting the answers on page 64. Do not continue with the next section until you understand each answer. If you need to, review or reread the appropriate section in the textbook before continuing.

From Zygote to Newborn (pp. 97–104)

1. Prenatal development is divided into _____ main periods. The first two weeks of development are called the _____ period; from the _____ week through the _____ week is known as the _____ period; and from this point until birth is the _____ period.

2. At about the _____-celled stage, clusters of cells begin to take on distinct traits. The first clear sign of this process, called _____ , occurs about _____ week(s) after conception, when the multiplying cells separate into outer cells that will become the _____ and inner cells that will become the _____ .

3. The next significant event is the burrowing of the zygote into the lining of the uterus, a process called _____ . This process _____ (is/is not) automatic.

5. Eight weeks after conception, the embryo weighs about _____ and is about _____ in length. The organism now becomes known as the _____ .

6. The genital organs are fully formed by week _____ . If the fetus has a(n) _____ chromosome, a gene on this chromosome sends a signal that triggers development of the _____ (male/female) sex organs. Without that gene, no signal is sent and the fetus begins to develop _____ (male/female) sex organs.

7. By the end of the _____ month, the fetus is fully formed, weighs approximately _____ , and is about _____ long. These figures _____ (vary/do not vary) from fetus to fetus.

8. During the fourth, fifth, and sixth months, the brain increases in size by a factor of _____ . This neurological maturation is essential to the regulation of such basic body functions as _____ and _____ . The brain develops new

neurons in a process called _____ and new connections between them in a process called _____ .

9. The age at which a fetus has at least some chance of surviving outside the uterus is called the _____ _____ _____ , which occurs _____ weeks after conception.

10. At about _____ weeks after conception, brain-wave patterns begin to resemble the _____–_____ cycles of a newborn.

11. A 28-week-old fetus typically weighs about _____ and has more than a _____ percent chance of survival.

12. Two crucial aspects of development in the last months of prenatal life are maturation of the _____ , _____ , and _____ systems.

13. By full term, brain growth is so extensive that the brain's advanced outer areas, called the _____ , must _____ _____ in order to fit into the skull.

14. Beginning at _____ (what week?), the fetus hears many sounds, including the mother's _____ and _____ .

15. (text and Table 4.3) The average newborn weighs _____ .

Risk Reduction (pp. 104–117)

16. The scientific study of birth defects is called _____ . Harmful agents that can cause birth defects, called _____ , include _____ _____ .

17. Substances that impair the child's action and intellect by harming the brain are called _____ _____ . Approximately _____ percent of all children are born with behavioral difficulties that could be connected to behavioral teratogens.

18. Teratology is a science of _____ _____ , which attempts to evaluate the factors that can make prenatal harm more or less likely to occur.

19. Three crucial factors that determine whether a specific teratogen will cause harm, and of what nature, are the _____ of exposure, the _____ of exposure, and the developing organism's _____ _____ to damage from the substance.

20. The time when a particular part of the body is most susceptible to teratogenic damage is called its _____ _____ . For physical structure and form, this is the entire period of the _____ . However, for _____ teratogens, the entire prenatal period is critical.

21. Some teratogens have a _____ effect—that is, the substances are harmless until exposure reaches a certain frequency or amount. However, the _____ of some teratogens when taken together may make them more harmful at lower dosage levels than when taken separately.

22. Genetic susceptibilities to the prenatal effects of alcohol and to certain birth disorders, such as cleft palate, may involve defective _____ .

23. When the mother-to-be's diet is deficient in _____ _____ , neural-tube defects such as _____ _____ or _____ may result. these defects occur more commonly in certain _____ groups.

24. Genetic vulnerability is also related to the sex of the developing organism. Generally, _____ (male/female) embryos and fetuses are more vulnerable to teratogens. This sex not only has more frequent _____ _____ and a higher rate of teratogenic birth defects, _____ _____ , and other behavioral problems.

25. (Issues and Applications) The most devastating viral teratogen is the _____ _____ _____ , which gradually overwhelms the body's _____ _____ and leads to _____ . Babies who are infected with this virus usually die by age _____ .

26. (Issues and Applications) Pregnant women who are HIV-positive can reduce the risk of transmitting the virus to their newborns by giving birth by _____ _____ , by not _____-_____ , and by taking _____ _____ .

27. (Issues and Applications) The most common teratogen in North America is _____ . High doses of this teratogen cause _____ _____ _____ , and less intense doses cause _____ _____ _____ . The damage is increased when alcohol is combined with other _____ _____ .

28. (Table 4.6) There are a number of tests to determine whether a pregnancy is problematic. Among them are the _____-_____ _____ , which tests for neural-tube defects, the _____ , which shows body malformations, and _____ , which shows

chromosomal abnormalities and other genetic and prenatal problems.

29. Newborns who weigh less than _____ are classified as _____-_____ babies. Below 3 pounds, they are called _____-_____-_____ babies; at less than 2 pounds they are _____-_____-_____ babies. Worldwide, rates of this condition _____ (vary/do not vary) from nation to nation.

30. Babies who are born 3 or more weeks early are called _____ .

31. Infants who weigh substantially less than they should, given how much time has passed since conception, are called _____ _____ _____ .

32. About 25 percent of all low-birthweight (LBW) births in the United States are linked to maternal use of _____ .

33. Two other common reasons for low birthweight are maternal _____ and _____ . In addition, _____ births are more likely to result in LBW. Consequently, the rate of LBW has increased dramatically with the use of _____ _____ _____ .

The Birth Process (pp. 117–126)

34. At about the 266th day, the fetal brain signals the release of certain _____ into the mother's bloodstream, which trigger her _____ _____ to contract and relax. The normal birth process begins when these contractions become regular. The average length of labor is _____ hours for first births and _____ hours for subsequent births.

35. The newborn is usually rated on the
_____ _____ , which
assigns a score of 0, 1, or 2 to each of the following five characteristics: _____
_____ . A
score below _____ indicates that the
newborn is in critical condition and requires
immediate attention; if the score is
_____ or better, all is well. This rat-
ing is made twice, at _____
minute(s) after birth and again at
_____ minutes.

36. The birth experience is influenced by several
factors, including _____
_____ .

37. In about 28 percent of U.S. births, a surgical
procedure called a _____
_____ is performed.

38. An increasing number of hospital deliveries occur
in the _____ _____ .
An even more family-oriented environment is the
_____ _____ . In addi-
tion, many North American mothers today use a
professional birth coach, or _____ , to
assist them.

39. The disorder _____
_____ , which affects motor centers
in the brain, often results from
_____ vulnerability, worsened by
exposure to _____ and a preterm
birth that involves _____ , a temporary lack of _____ during birth.

40. Because they are often confined to intensive-care
nurseries or hooked up to medical machinery,
low-birthweight infants may be deprived of normal kinds of stimulation such as
_____ .

41. Providing extra soothing stimulation to vulnerable infants in the hospital _____
(does/does not) aid weight gain and
_____ (does/does not) increase
overall alertness. One example of this is
_____ _____ , in
which mothers of low-birthweight infants spend
extra time holding their infants between their
breasts.

42. Among the minor developmental problems that
accompany preterm birth are being late to
_____ .
High-risk infants are often more
_____ , less _____ ,
and slower to _____ .

43. The deficits related to low birthweight usually
_____ (can/cannot) be
overcome.

44. The rate of LBW births among women born in
Mexico and now living in the United States is
_____ (higher/lower) than those of
other Americans. This difference has been attributed to _____ _____ .
Especially important is the role played by a supportive _____ , who can help _____
_____ .

45. A crucial factor in the birth experience is the formation of a strong _____
_____ between the prospective
parents.

46. Some new mothers experience a profound feeling
of sadness called _____
_____ .

47. The term used to describe the close relationship
that begins within the first hours after birth is the
_____-_____
_____ .

Progress Test 1

Multiple-Choice Questions

Circle your answers to the following questions and check them with the answers on page 65. If your answer is incorrect, read the explanation for why it is incorrect and then consult the appropriate pages of the text (in parentheses following the correct answer).

1. The third through the eighth week after conception is called the:
   a. embryonic period.
   b. ovum period.
   c. fetal period.
   d. germinal period.

2. The primitive streak develops into the:
   a. respiratory system.
   b. umbilical cord.
   c. brain and spinal column.
   d. circulatory system.

3. To say that a teratogen has a "threshold effect" means that it is:
   a. virtually harmless until exposure reaches a certain level.
   b. harmful only to low-birthweight infants.
   c. harmful to certain developing organs during periods when these organs are developing most rapidly.
   d. harmful only if the pregnant woman's weight does not increase by a certain minimum amount during her pregnancy.

4. By the eighth week after conception, the embryo has almost all the basic organs except the:
   a. skeleton.   c. sex organs.
   b. elbows and knees. d. fingers and toes.

5. The most critical factor in attaining the age of viability is development of the:
   a. placenta.   c. brain.
   b. eyes.   d. skeleton.

6. An important nutrient that many women do not get in adequate amounts from the typical diet is:
   a. vitamin A.   c. guanine.
   b. zinc.   d. folic acid.

7. An embryo begins to develop male sex organs if _____ , and female sex organs if _____ .
   a. genes on the *Y* chromosome send a signal; no signal is sent from an *X* chromosome
   b. genes on the *Y* chromosome send a signal; genes on the *X* chromosome send a signal

   c. genes on the *X* chromosome send a signal; no signal is sent from an *X* chromosome
   d. genes on the *X* chromosome send a signal; genes on the *Y* chromosome send a signal

8. A teratogen:
   a. cannot cross the placenta during the period of the embryo.
   b. is usually inherited from the mother.
   c. can be counteracted by good nutrition most of the time.
   d. may be a virus, a drug, a chemical, radiation, or environmental pollutants.

9. (Issues and Applications) Among the characteristics of babies born with fetal alcohol syndrome are:
   a. slowed physical growth and behavior problems.
   b. addiction to alcohol and methadone.
   c. deformed arms and legs.
   d. blindness.

10. The birth process begins:
    a. when the fetus moves into the right position.
    b. when the uterus begins to contract at regular intervals to push the fetus out.
    c. about eight hours (in the case of firstborns) after the uterus begins to contract at regular intervals.
    d. when the baby's head appears at the opening of the vagina.

11. The Apgar scale is administered:
    a. only if the newborn is in obvious distress.
    b. once, just after birth.
    c. twice, one minute and five minutes after birth.
    d. repeatedly during the newborn's first hours.

12. Most newborns weigh about:
    a. 5 pounds.   c. 7$\frac{1}{2}$ pounds.
    b. 6 pounds.   d. 8$\frac{1}{2}$ pounds.

13. Low-birthweight babies born near the due date but weighing substantially less than they should:
    a. are classified as preterm.
    b. are called small for gestational age.
    c. usually have no sex organs.
    d. show many signs of immaturity.

14. Approximately one out of every four low-birthweight births in the United States is caused by maternal use of:
    a. alcohol.   c. crack cocaine.
    b. tobacco.   d. household chemicals.

15. The idea of a parent–infant bond in humans arose from:

    a. observations in the delivery room.

    b. data on adopted infants.

    c. animal studies.

    d. studies of disturbed mother–infant pairs.

Matching Items

Match each definition or description with its corresponding term.

Terms

    _____   **1.** embryonic period

    _____   **2.** fetal period

    _____   **3.** placenta

    _____   **4.** preterm

    _____   **5.** teratogens

    _____   **6.** anoxia

    _____   **7.** HIV

    _____   **8.** critical period

    _____   **9.** primitive streak

    _____   **10.** fetal alcohol syndrome

    _____   **11.** germinal period

Definitions or Descriptions

    a. term for the period during which a developing baby's body parts are most susceptible to damage

    b. external agents and conditions that can damage the developing organism

    c. the age when viability is attained

    d. the precursor of the central nervous system

    e. lack of oxygen, which, if prolonged during the birth process, may lead to brain damage.

    f. characterized by abnormal facial characteristics, slowed growth, behavior problems, and mental retardation

    g. a virus that gradually overwhelms the body's immune responses

    h. the life-giving organ that nourishes the embryo and fetus

    i. when implantation occurs

    j. the prenatal period when all major body structures begin to form

    k. a baby born 3 or more weeks early

Progress Test 2

Progress Test 2 should be completed during a final chapter review. Answer the following questions after you thoroughly understand the correct answers for the Chapter Review and Progress Test 1.

Multiple-Choice Questions

1. A 35-year-old woman who is pregnant is most likely to undergo which type of test for the detection of prenatal chromosomal or genetic abnormalities?

    a. pre-implantation testing

    b. ultrasound

    c. amniocentesis

    d. alpha-fetoprotein assay

2. In order, the correct sequence of prenatal stages of development is:

    a. embryo; germinal; fetus

    b. germinal; fetus; embryo

    c. germinal; embryo; fetus

    d. ovum; fetus; embryo

3. Monika is preparing for the birth of her first child. If all proceeds normally, she can expect that her labor will last about:

    a. 7 hours.   **c.** 10 hours.

    b. 8 hours.   **d.** 12 hours.

4. (Table 4.5) Tetracycline and retinoic acid:
   a. can be harmful to the human fetus.
   b. have been proven safe for pregnant women after the embryonic period.
   c. will prevent spontaneous abortions.
   d. are safe when used before the fetal period.

5. (Table 4.4) The teratogen that, if not prevented by immunization, could cause deafness, blindness, and brain damage in the fetus is:
   a. rubella (German measles).
   b. anoxia.
   c. acquired immune deficiency syndrome (AIDS).
   d. neural-tube defect.

6. Kangaroo care refers to:
   a. the rigid attachment formed between mothers and offspring in the animal kingdom
   b. the fragmented care that the children of single parents often receive.
   c. a program of increased involvement by mothers of low-birthweight infants.
   d. none of the above.

7. Among the characteristics rated on the Apgar scale are:
   a. shape of the newborn's head and nose.
   b. presence of body hair.
   c. interactive behaviors.
   d. muscle tone and color.

8. A newborn is classified as low birthweight if he or she weighs less than:
   a. 7 pounds.
   b. 6 pounds.
   c. $5^1/_2$ pounds.
   d. 4 pounds.

9. A critical problem for preterm babies is:
   a. the immaturity of the sex organs—for example, undescended testicles.
   b. spitting up or hiccupping.
   c. infection from intravenous feeding.
   d. breathing difficulties.

10. (Issues and Applications) The most common teratogen in North America is:
    a. nicotine.
    b. alcohol.
    c. pesticide exposure.
    d. caffeine.

11. Neurogenesis refers to the process by which:
    a. the fetal brain develops new neurons.
    b. new connections between neurons develop.
    c. the neural tube forms during the middle trimester.
    d. the cortex folds into layers in order to fit into the skull.

12. Which Apgar score indicates that a newborn is in normal health?
    a. 4   c. 6
    b. 5   d. 7

13. Synaptogenesis refers to the process by which:
    a. the fetal brain develops new neurons.
    b. new connections between neurons develop.
    c. the neural tube forms during the middle trimester.
    d. the cortex folds into layers in order to fit into the skull.

14. When there is a strong parental alliance:
    a. mother and father cooperate because of their mutual commitment to their children.
    b. the parents agree to support each other in their shared parental roles.
    c. children are likely to thrive.
    d. all of the above are true.

15. The critical period for preventing physical defects appears to be the:
    a. zygote period.
    b. embryonic period.
    c. fetal period.
    d. entire pregnancy.

True or False Items

Write T (*true*) or F (*false*) on the line in front of each statement.

_____ 1. Newborns can recognize some of what they heard while in the womb.

_____ 2. Eight weeks after conception, the embryo has formed almost all the basic organs.

_____ 3. Only 1 percent of births in the United States take place in the home.

_____ 4. In general, behavioral teratogens have the greatest effect during the embryonic period.

_____ 5. The effects of cigarette smoking during pregnancy remain highly controversial.

_____ 6. The Apgar scale is used to measure vital signs such as heart rate, breathing, and reflexes.

_____ 7. Newborns usually cry on their own, moments after birth.

_____ 8. Research has shown that immediate mother–infant contact at birth is necessary for the normal emotional development of the child.

_____ 9. Low birthweight is often correlated with maternal malnutrition.

_____ 10. Cesarean sections are rarely performed in the United States today because of the resulting danger to the fetus.

Thinking Critically About Chapter 4

Answer these questions the day before an exam as a final check on your understanding of the chapter's terms and concepts.

1. (Table 4.5 and Issues and Applications) Babies born to mothers who are powerfully addicted to a psychoactive drug are *most* likely to suffer from:
   a. structural problems.
   b. behavioral problems.
   c. both a. and b.
   d. neither a. nor b.

2. I am about 1 inch long and 1 gram in weight. I have all of the basic organs (except sex organs) and features of a human being. What am I?
   a. a zygote   c. a fetus
   b. an embryo   d. ovum

3. Karen and Brad report to their neighbors that, 5 weeks after conception, a sonogram of their child-to-be revealed female sex organs. The neighbors are skeptical of their statement because:
   a. sonograms are never administered before the ninth week.
   b. sonograms only reveal the presence or absence of male sex organs.
   c. the fetus does not begin to develop female sex organs until about the eighth week.
   d. it is impossible to determine that a woman is pregnant until six weeks after conception.

4. Five-year-old Benjamin can't sit quietly and concentrate on a task for more than a minute at a time. Dr. Simmons, who is a teratologist, suspects that Benjamin may have been exposed to _____ during prenatal development.
   a. human immunodeficiency virus
   b. a behavioral teratogen
   c. rubella
   d. lead

5. Sylvia and Stan, who are of British descent, are hoping to have a child. Doctor Caruthers asks for a complete nutritional history and is particularly concerned when she discovers that Sylvia may have a deficiency of folic acid in her diet. Doctor Caruthers is probably worried about the risk of _____ in the couple's offspring.
   a. FAS   c. neural-tube defects
   b. brain damage   d. FAE

6. Three-year-old Kenny was born underweight and premature. Today, he is small for his age. His doctor suspects that:
   a. Kenny is a victim of fetal alcohol syndrome.
   b. Kenny suffers from fetal alcohol effects.
   c. Kenny's mother smoked heavily during her pregnancy.
   d. Kenny's mother used cocaine during her pregnancy.

7. Which of the following is an example of an interaction effect?
   a. Some teratogens are virtually harmless until exposure reaches a certain level.
   b. Maternal use of alcohol and tobacco together does more harm to the developing fetus than either teratogen would do alone.
   c. Some teratogens cause damage only on specific days during prenatal development.
   d. All of the above are examples of interaction effects.

8. Fetal alcohol syndrome is common in newborns whose mothers were heavy drinkers during pregnancy, whereas newborns whose mothers were moderate drinkers may suffer fetal alcohol effects. This finding shows that to assess and understand risk we must know:
   a. the kind of alcoholic beverage (for example, beer, wine, or whiskey).
   b. the level of exposure to the teratogen.
   c. whether the substance really is teratogenic.
   d. the timing of exposure to the teratogen.

9. Your sister and brother-in-law, who are about to adopt a 1-year-old, are worried that the child will never bond with them. What advice should you offer?
   a. Tell them that, unfortunately, this is true; they would be better off waiting for a younger child who has not yet bonded.
   b. Tell them that, although the first year is a biologically determined critical period for attachment, there is a fifty-fifty chance that the child will bond with them.

c. Tell them that bonding is a long-term process between parent and child that is determined by the nature of interaction throughout infancy, childhood, and beyond.

d. Tell them that if the child is female, there is a good chance that she will bond with them, even at this late stage.

10. Which of the following newborns would be most likely to have problems in body structure and functioning?
   a. Anton, whose Apgar score is 6
   b. Debora, whose Apgar score is 7
   c. Sheila, whose Apgar score is 3
   d. Simon, whose Apgar score is 5

11. At birth, Clarence was classified as small for gestational age. It is likely that Clarence:
   a. was born in a rural hospital.
   b. suffered several months of prenatal malnutrition.
   c. was born in a large city hospital.
   d. comes from a family with a history of such births.

12. Of the following, who is *most* likely to give birth to a low-birthweight child?
   a. 21-year-old Janice, who was herself a low-birthweight baby
   b. 25-year-old May Ling, who gained 25 pounds during her pregnancy
   c. 16-year-old Donna, who diets frequently despite being underweight
   d. 30-year-old Maria, who has already given birth to 4 children

13. An infant born 266 days after conception, weighing 4 pounds, would be designated a _____ infant.
   a. preterm
   b. low-birthweight
   c. small-for-gestational-age
   d. b. & c.

14. An infant who was born at 35 weeks, weighing 6 pounds, would be called a _____ infant.
   a. preterm
   b. low-birthweight
   c. small-for-gestational-age
   d. premature

15. The five characteristics evaluated by the Apgar scale are:
   a. heart rate, length, weight, muscle tone, and color.
   b. orientation, muscle tone, reflexes, interaction, and responses to stress.
   c. reflexes, breathing, muscle tone, heart rate, and color.
   d. pupillary response, heart rate, reflex irritability, alertness, and breathing.

Key Terms

Using your own words, write a brief definition or explanation of each of the following terms on a separate piece of paper.

1. germinal period
2. embryonic period
3. fetal period
4. implantation
5. embryo
6. fetus
7. age of viability
8. teratogens
9. behavioral teratogens
10. risk analysis
11. critical period
12. threshold effect
13. interaction effect
14. human immunodeficiency virus (HIV)
15. fetal alcohol syndrome (FAS)
16. low birthweight (LBW)
17. very low birthweight (VLBW)
18. extremely low birthweight (ELBW)
19. preterm birth
20. small for gestational age (SGA)
21. Apgar scale
22. cesarean section
23. doula
24. cerebral palsy
25. anoxia
26. kangaroo care

27. parental alliance
28. postpartum depression
29. parent–infant bond

ANSWERS
CHAPTER REVIEW

1. three; germinal; third; eighth; embryonic; fetal
2. eight; differentiation; one; placenta; embryo
3. implantation; is not
4. primitive streak; neural tube; central nervous system

The head begins to take shape as the eyes, ears, nose, and mouth start to form. A tiny blood vessel that will become the heart begins to pulsate. The upper arms, then the forearms, palms, and webbed fingers appear. Legs, feet, and webbed toes follow. At eight weeks, the embryo's head is more rounded, and the facial features are formed. The embryo has all the basic organs and body parts (except sex organs).

5. $^{1}/_{30}$ ounce (1 gram); 1 inch (2.5 centimeters); fetus
6. 12; Y; male; female
7. third; 3 ounces (87 grams); 3 inches (7.5 centimeters); vary
8. six; breathing; sucking; neurogenesis; synaptogenesis
9. age of viability; 22
10. 28; sleep–wake
11. 3 pounds (1.3 kilograms); 95
12. neurological; respiratory; cardiovascular
13. cortex; fold into layers
14. 28 weeks; heartbeat; voice
15. $7^{1}/_{2}$ pounds (3,400 grams)
16. teratology; teratogens; viruses, drugs, chemicals, pollutants, stressors, and malnutrition
17. behavioral teratogens; 20
18. risk analysis
19. timing; amount; genetic vulnerability
20. critical period; embryo; behavioral
21. threshold; interaction

22. enzymes
23. folic acid; spina bifida; anencephaly; ethnic
24. male; spontaneous abortions; learning disabilities
25. human immunodeficiency virus (HIV); immune system; AIDS; 5
26. cesarean section; breast-feeding; antiretroviral drugs
27. alcohol; fetal alcohol syndrome; fetal alcohol effects; psychoactive drugs
28. alpha-fetoprotein assay; sonogram; amniocentesis
29. 2,500 grams ($5^{1}/_{2}$ pounds); low-birthweight; very-low-birthweight; extremely-low-birthweight; vary
30. preterm
31. small for gestational age
32. tobacco
33. illness; malnutrition; multiple; assisted reproductive technology
34. hormones; uterine muscles; 12; 7
35. Apgar scale; heart rate, breathing, muscle tone, color, and reflexes; 4; 7; one; five
36. the parents' preparation for birth, the physical and emotional support provided by birth attendants, the position and size of the fetus, the customs of the culture
37. cesarean section
38. labor room; birthing center; doula
39. cerebral palsy; genetic; teratogens; anoxia; oxygen
40. rocking (or regular handling)
41. does; does; kangaroo care
42. smile, hold a bottle, and to communicate; distractible; obedient; talk
43. can
44. lower; social practices; father; ensure the future mother is healthy, well-nourished, and drug free
45. parental alliance
46. postpartum depression
47. parent–infant bond

PROGRESS TEST 1

Multiple-Choice Questions

1. **a.** is the answer. (p. 97)

   b. This term, which refers to the germinal period, is not used in the text.

   c. The fetal period is from the ninth week until birth.

   d. The germinal period covers the first two weeks.

2. **c.** is the answer. (p. 99)

3. **a.** is the answer. (p. 105)

   b., c., & d. Although low birthweight (b), critical periods of organ development (c), and maternal malnutrition (d) are all hazardous to the developing person during prenatal development, none is an example of a threshold effect.

4. **c.** is the answer. The sex organs do not begin to take shape until the fetal period. (p. 100)

5. **c.** is the answer. (p. 101)

6. **d.** is the answer. (p. 107)

7. **a.** is the answer. (p. 100)

8. **d.** is the answer. (p. 104)

   a. In general, teratogens can cross the placenta at any time.

   b. Teratogens are agents in the environment, not heritable genes (although *susceptibility* to individual teratogens has a genetic component).

   c. Although nutrition is an important factor in healthy prenatal development, the text does not suggest that nutrition alone can usually counteract the harmful effects of teratogens.

9. **a.** is the answer. (p. 110)

10. **b.** is the answer. (p. 117)

11. **c.** is the answer. (p. 118)

12. **c.** is the answer. (p. 104)

13. **b.** is the answer. (p. 115)

14. **b.** is the answer. (p. 116)

15. **c.** is the answer. (p. 125)

Matching Items

1. j (p. 97)	5. b (p. 104)	9. d (p. 99)
2. c (p. 97)	6. e (p. 122)	10. f (p. 110)
3. h (p. 98)	7. g (p. 110)	11. i (p. 97)
4. k (p. 115)	8. a (p. 105)	

PROGRESS TEST 2

Multiple-Choice Questions

1. **c.** is the answer. (p. 112)

2. **c.** is the answer. (p. 97)

3. **d.** is the answer. (p. 117)

   a. The average length of labor for subsequent births is 7 hours.

4. **a.** is the answer. (p. 109)

5. **a.** is the answer. (p. 108)

6. **c.** is the answer. (p. 122)

7. **d.** is the answer. (p. 118)

8. **c.** is the answer. (p. 115)

9. **d.** is the answer. (p. 103)

10. **b.** is the answer. (p. 110)

11. **a.** is the answer. (p. 101)

12. **d.** is the answer. (p. 118)

13. **b.** is the answer. (p. 101)

14. **d.** is the answer. (p. 125)

15. **b.** is the answer. (p. 105)

True or False Items

1. T (p. 103)

2. T (p. 100)

3. T (p. 121)

4. F   Behavioral teratogens can affect the fetus at any time during the prenatal period. (p. 105)

5. F   There is no controversy about the damaging effects of smoking during pregnancy. (p. 116)

6. T (p. 118)

7. T (p. 118)

8. F   Though highly desirable, mother–infant contact at birth is not necessary for the child's normal development or for a good parent–child relationship. Many opportunities for bonding occur throughout childhood. (p. 125)

9. T (p. 116)

10. F   About 28 percent of births in the United States are now cesarean. (p. 119)

THINKING CRITICALLY ABOUT CHAPTER 4

1. c. is the answer. (pp. 109, 110–111)

2. b. is the answer. (p. 100)

    a. The zygote is the fertilized ovum.

    c. The developing organism is designated a fetus starting at the ninth week.

    d. The ovum is the female egg that is fertilized by the sperm.

3. c. is the answer. (p. 100)

4. b. is the answer. (p. 105)

    a. This is the virus that causes AIDS.

    c. Rubella may cause blindness, deafness, and brain damage.

    d. In small doses, it may be harmless; large doses may produce brain damage in the fetus.

5. c. is the answer. (p. 107)

    a. FAS is caused in infants by the mother-to-be drinking high doses of alcohol during pregnancy.

    b. Brain damage is caused by the use of social drugs during pregnancy.

    d. FAE is caused in infants by less intense drinking by the mother-to-be.

6. c. is the answer. (p. 116)

7. b. is the answer. (p. 106)

8. b. is the answer. (pp. 105, 110)

9. c. is the answer. (pp. 125, 126)

    a. & b. Bonding in humans is not a biologically determined event limited to a critical period, as it is in many other animal species.

    d. There is no evidence of any gender differences in the formation of the parent–infant bond.

10. c. is the answer. If a neonate's Apgar score is below 4, the infant is in critical condition and needs immediate medical attention. (pp. 118–119)

11. b. is the answer. (p. 116)

    a., c., & d. Prenatal malnutrition is the most common cause of a small-for-dates baby.

12. c. is the answer. Donna's risk factor for having an LBW baby is her weight (teens tend not to eat well and so to be undernourished). (p. 116)

    a. & d. Neither of these has been linked to increased risk of having LBW babies.

    b. In fact, based only on her age and normal weight gain, May Ling's baby would *not* be expected to be LBW.

13. d. is the answer. (p. 115)

    a. & c. At 266 days, this infant is full term.

14. a. is the answer. (p. 115)

    b. Low birthweight is defined as weighing less than $5^{1}/_{2}$ pounds.

    c. Although an infant can be both preterm and small for gestational age, this baby's weight is within the normal range of healthy babies.

    d. This term is no longer used to describe early births.

15. c. is the answer. (p. 118)

KEY TERMS

1. The first two weeks of development after conception, characterized by rapid cell division and the beginning of cell differentiation, are called the **germinal period.** (p. 97)

    Memory aid: A *germ cell* is one from which a new organism can develop. The **germinal period** is the first stage in the development of the new organism.

2. The **embryonic period** is approximately the third through the eighth week of prenatal development, when the basic forms of all body structures develop. (p. 97)

3. From the ninth week after conception until birth is the **fetal period,** when the organs grow in size and mature in functioning. (p. 97)

4. Implantation is the process by which the zygote burrows into the uterine lining, where it can be nourished and protected during growth. (p. 98)

5. Embryo is the name given to the developing organism from the third through the eighth week after conception. (p. 99)

6. Fetus is the name for the developing organism from eight weeks after conception until birth. (p. 100)

7. About 22 weeks after conception, the fetus attains the **age of viability,** at which point it has at least some slight chance of survival outside the uterus if specialized medical care is available. (p. 101)

8. Teratogens are external agents and conditions, such as viruses, drugs, chemicals, stressors, and malnutrition, that can impair prenatal development and lead to birth defects and even death. (p. 104)

9. **Behavioral teratogens** tend to damage the brain, impairing the future child's intellectual and emotional functioning. (p. 105)

10. The science of teratology is a science of **risk analysis**, meaning that it attempts to evaluate what factors make prenatal harm more or less likely to occur. (p. 105)

11. In prenatal development, a **critical period** is the time when a particular organ or other body part is most susceptible to teratogenic damage. (p. 105)

12. A **threshold effect** is the harmful effect of a substance that occurs when exposure to it reaches a certain level. (p. 105)

13. An **interaction effect** occurs when one teratogen intensifies the harmful effects of another. (p. 106)

14. **Human immunodeficiency virus (HIV)** is the most devastating viral teratogen. HIV gradually overwhelms the body's immune system, making the individual vulnerable to the host of diseases and infections that constitute AIDS. (p. 110)

15. Prenatal alcohol exposure may cause **fetal alcohol syndrome (FAS)**, which includes abnormal facial characteristics, slow physical growth, behavior problems, and mental retardation. Likely victims are those who are genetically vulnerable and whose mothers drink three or more drinks daily during pregnancy. (p. 110)

16. A birthweight of less than 5¹/₂ pounds (2.5 kilograms) is called **low birthweight (LBW).** Low-birthweight infants are at risk for many immediate and long-term problems. (p. 115)

17. A birthweight of less than 3 pounds (1.3 kilograms) is called **very low birthweight (VLBW).** (p. 115)

18. A birthweight of less than 2 pounds (1 kilogram) is called **extremely low birthweight (ELBW).** (p. 115)

19. When an infant is born three or more weeks before the due date, it is said to be a **preterm birth.** (p. 115)

20. Infants who weigh substantially less than they should, given how much time has passed since conception, are called **small for gestational age (SGA),** or small-for-dates. (p. 115)

21. Newborns are rated at one and then at five minutes after birth according to the **Apgar scale.** This scale assigns a score of 0, 1, or 2 to each of five characteristics: heart rate, breathing, muscle tone, color, and reflexes. A score of 7 or better indicates that all is well. (p. 118)

22. In a **cesarean section**, the fetus is removed from the mother surgically. (p. 119)

23. A **doula** is a woman who works alongside medical staff to assist a woman through labor and delivery. (p.121)

24. **Cerebral palsy** is a muscular control disorder caused by damage to the brain's motor centers during or before birth. (p. 121)

25. **Anoxia** is a temporary lack of fetal oxygen during the birth process that, if prolonged, can cause brain damage or even death. (p. 122)

26. **Kangaroo care** occurs when the mother of a low-birthweight infant spends at least one hour a day holding her infant between her breasts. (p. 122)

27. **Parental alliance** refers to the cooperation and mutual support between mother and father because of their commitment to their children. (p. 125)

28. **Postpartum depression** is a profound feeling of sadness, inadequacy, and hopelessness sometimes experienced by new mothers. (p. 125)

29. The term **parent–infant bond** describes the strong feelings of attachment between parent and child in the early moments of their relationship together. (p. 125)

Chapter Five

The First Two Years: Biosocial Development

Chapter Overview

Chapter 5 is the first of a three-chapter unit that describes the developing person from birth to age 2 in terms of biosocial, cognitive, and psychosocial development. Physical development is the first to be examined.

The chapter begins with observations on the overall growth and health of infants, including information on infant sleep patterns. Following is a discussion of brain growth and development and the importance of experience in brain development. The chapter then turns to a discussion of sensory, perceptual, and motor abilities and the ages at which the average infant acquires them. Preventive medicine, the importance of immunizations during the first two years, and the possible causes of sudden infant death syndrome (SIDS) are discussed next. The final section explains the importance of nutrition during the first two years and the consequences of severe malnutrition and undernutrition.

NOTE: Answer guidelines for all Chapter 5 questions begin on page 80.

Guided Study

The text chapter should be studied one section at a time. Before you read, preview each section by skimming it, noting headings and boldface items. Then read the appropriate section objectives from the following outline. Keep these objectives in mind and, as you read the chapter section, search for the information that will enable you to meet each objective. Once you have finished a section, write out answers for its objectives.

Body Changes (pp. 131–138)

1. Describe the infant's height and weight, including how they change during the first two years.

2. Describe the infant's changing sleep patterns.

3. Discuss the attitudes of different cultures about where infants sleep.

Brain Development (pp. 138–145)

4. Describe the ways in which the brain changes or matures during infancy.

5. (text and Thinking Like a Scientist) Discuss the role of experience in brain development.

The Senses and Motor Skills (pp. 146–154)

6. Distinguish among sensation, perception, and cognition.

7. Describe the development of an infant's sensory and perceptual abilities in terms of the senses of hearing, vision, taste, smell, and touch.

8. Describe the basic reflexes of the newborn, and distinguish between gross motor skills and fine motor skills.

9. Describe the basic pattern of motor-skill development, and discuss variations in the timing of motor-skill acquisition.

Public Health Measures (pp. 154–161)

10. Identify key factors in the worldwide decline in childhood mortality over the past century, and discuss the importance of childhood immunizations.

11. Identify risk factors for sudden infant death syndrome, and discuss possible explanations for ethnic group variations in the incidence of this situation.

12. Describe the nutritional needs of infants.

13. Discuss the causes and effects of malnutrition in the first years.

Chapter Review

When you have finished reading the chapter, work through the material that follows to review it. Complete the sentences and answer the questions. As you proceed, evaluate your performance for each section by consulting the answers on page 80. Do not continue with the next section until you understand each answer. If you need to, review or reread the appropriate section in the textbook before continuing.

Body Changes (pp. 131–138)

1. The average North American newborn measures _____ and weighs about _____ .

2. The phenomenon in which inadequate nutrition causes the body to stop growing but not the brain is called _____-_____ .

3. A standard, or average, of physical development that is derived for a specific group or population is a _____ .

4. By age 2, the typical child weighs about _____ and measures _____ . The typical 2-year-old is almost _____ (what percent?) of his or her adult weight and _____ (what percent?) of his or her adult height.

5. (text and A Case to Study) To compare a child's growth to that of other children, we determine a _____ , a point on a ranking scale of _____ (what number?) to _____ (what number?). A child who stops growing, or who loses weight despite appearing healthy, is said to be displaying a _____ _____ _____ .

6. Throughout childhood, regular and ample _____ correlates with _____ maturation, _____ , _____ regulation, and _____ adjustment in school and within the family. Approximately _____ percent of 1-year-olds sleep through the night.

7. Over the first months of life, the relative amount of time spent in the different _____ of sleep changes. The stage of sleep characterized by flickering eyes behind closed lids and _____ is called _____ _____ . During this stage of sleep brain waves are fairly _____ (slow/rapid). This stage of sleep _____ (increases/decreases) over the first months, as does the dozing stage called _____ _____ . Slow-wave sleep, also called _____ _____ , increases markedly at about _____ months of age.

8. In most North American and European cultures, children _____ (do/do not) sleep with their parents. Westerners connect sexual abuse with _____ sleeping, whereas Easterners view _____ sleeping as child neglect. A type of farming commune that was once common in Israel, in which infants sleep apart from adults, is called a _____ .

Brain Development (pp. 138–145)

9. At birth, the brain has attained about _____ percent of its adult weight; by age 2 the brain is about _____ percent of its adult weight. In comparison, body weight at age 2 is about _____ percent of what it will be in adulthood.

10. The brain's communication system consists primarily of nerve cells called _____ connected by intricate networks of nerve fibers, called _____ and _____ . About _____ percent of these cells are in the brain's outer layer called the _____ . This area takes up about _____ percent of human brain material and is the site of _____ , _____ , and _____ .

11. Each neuron has many _____ but only a single _____ .

12. Neurons communicate with one another at intersections called _____ . After traveling down the length of the _____ , electrical impulses excite chemicals called _____ that carry information across the _____ _____ to the _____ of a "receiving" neuron. Most of the nerve cells _____ (are/are not) present at birth, whereas the fiber networks _____ (are/are not) rudimentary.

13. During the first months of life, brain development is most noticeable in the _____ .

14. From birth until age 2, the density of dendrites in the cortex _____ (increases/ decreases) by a factor of _____ . The phenomenal increase in neural connections over the first two years has been called _____ _____ . Following this growth process, neurons in some areas of the brain wither in the process called _____ , because _____ does not activate those brain areas. The importance of early experience is seen in the brain's production of stress hormones such as _____ .

15. Brain functions that require basic common experiences in order to develop are called _____-_____ brain functions; those that depend on particular, and variable, experiences in order to develop are called _____-_____ brain functions. The last part of the brain to mature is the _____ _____ , which is the area for _____ , _____ , and _____ _____ .

16. An important implication of brain development for caregivers is that early brain growth is _____ and reflects _____ . Another is that each part of the brain has its own _____ for _____ ,

_____ , and _____ . The inborn drive to remedy any deficit that may occur in development is called _____ .

17. (Thinking Like a Scientist) Neuroscientists once believed that brains were entirely formed by _____ and _____ ; today, most believe in _____ , which is the concept that personality, intellect, habits, and emotions change throughout life for _____ (one/a combination of) reason(s). Specific times when particular kinds of development are primed to occur are called _____ _____ . Marion Diamond, William Greenough, and colleagues discovered that the brains of rats who were raised in stimulating environments were better developed, with more _____ branching, than the brains of rats raised in barren environments. Orphaned Romanian children who were isolated and deprived of stimulation showed signs of _____ damage. Placed in healthier environments, these children _____ (improved/did not improve); years later, persistent deficits in these children _____ (were/were not) found.

The Senses and Motor Skills (pp. 146–154)

18. The process by which the visual, auditory, and other sensory systems detect stimuli is called _____ ; _____ occurs when the brain tries to make sense out of a stimulus so that the individual becomes aware of it. At birth, only _____ is apparent; _____ requires experience. In the process called _____ , a person thinks about and interprets what he or she has perceived. This process _____ (can/ cannot) occur without either sensation or perception.

19. Generally speaking, newborns' hearing _____ (is/is not) very acute at birth. Newborns _____ (can/cannot) perceive differences in voices, rhythms, and language. The brain is especially good at

detecting differences in sound that are

_____ .

20. The least mature of the senses at birth is

_____ . Newborns' visual focusing

is best for objects between _____

and _____ inches away.

21. Increasing maturation of the visual cortex
accounts for improvements in other visual abilities, such as the infant's ability to _____
on an object and _____ to its critical
areas. The ability to use both eyes in a coordinated manner to focus on one object, which is called
_____ _____ , devel-
ops at about _____ of age.

22. Taste, smell, and touch _____ (func-
tion/do not function) at birth. The ability to be
comforted by the human _____ is a
skill tested in the _____ Neonatal
Behavioral Assessment Scale.

23. The infant's early sensory abilities seem organized for two goals: _____
_____ and _____ .

24. The most visible and dramatic body changes of
infancy involve _____
_____ . The sequence of development of motor skills is _____ –
_____ , or from _____
to _____ , and _____ –
_____ , or from _____
to _____ .

25. An involuntary response to a stimulus is called a

_____ .

26. The involuntary response that causes the newborn to take the first breath even before the
umbilical cord is cut, is called the

_____ _____ . Because
breathing is irregular during the first few days,
other reflexive behaviors, such as

_____ , _____ ,

and _____ , are common.

27. Shivering, crying, and tucking the legs close to
the body are examples of reflexes that help to

maintain _____

_____ _____ .

28. A third set of reflexes manages _____ .
One of these is the tendency of the newborn to
suck anything that touches the lips; this is the
_____ reflex. Another is the tenden-
cy of newborns to turn their heads and start to
suck when something brushes against their
cheek; this is the _____ reflex.

Identify each reflex by filling in the missing information in the chart below.

Name of reflex	Description
a. _____	toes fan upward when infants' feet are stroked
b. _____	infants move their legs as if to walk when they are held upright and their feet touch a flat surface
c. _____	infants stretch out their arms and legs when they are held on their stomachs
d. _____	infants grip things that touch their palms
e. _____	infants fling their arms outward and then clutch them against their chests in response to a loud noise

29. Large movements such as running and climbing
are called _____
_____ skills.

30. Most infants are able to crawl on all fours (sometimes called creeping) between _____
and _____ months of age. Three factors in the development of walking are

_____ _____ ,

_____ , and _____

_____ .

List the major hallmarks in children's mastery of
walking.

31. Abilities that require more precise, small movements, such as picking up a coin, are called _____ _____ skills. By _____ of age, most babies can reach for, grab, and hold onto almost any object of the right size. By _____ months, most infants can transfer objects from one hand to the other.

32. Although the _____ in which motor skills are mastered is the same in all healthy infants, the _____ of acquisition of skills varies greatly.

33. The average ages, or _____ , at which most infants master major motor skills are based on a large sample of infants drawn from _____ (a single/many) ethnic group(s).

34. Motor skill norms vary from one _____ group to another.

35. Motor skill acquisition in identical twins _____ (is/is not) more similar than in fraternal twins, suggesting that genes _____ (do/do not) play an important role. Another influential factor is the _____ .

Public Health Measures (pp. 136–143)

36. In 1900, about 1 in _____ (how many?) children died before age 5. This childhood death rate _____ (varied from one nation to another/was the same throughout the world). Today, in the healthiest nations such as _____ , _____ , and _____ , about _____ percent of babies who survive birth die before age 5.

37. A key factor in reducing the childhood death rate was the development of _____—a process that stimulates the body's _____ system to defend against contagious diseases.

38. Another reason for lower infant mortality worldwide is a decrease in _____ _____ _____ .

_____ , in which seemingly healthy infants die unexpectedly in their _____ .

39. A key factor in SIDS is _____ background. In ethnically diverse nations, babies of _____ descent are less likely, to succumb to SIDS than are babies of _____ descent. In ethnic groups with a low incidence of SIDS, babies are put to sleep _____ (in what position?).

Identify several other practices that may explain why certain ethnic groups have a low incidence of SIDS.

40. The ideal infant food is _____ , beginning with the thick, high-calorie fluid called _____ . The only situations in which formula may be healthier for the infant than breast milk are when _____ _____ .

State several advantages of breast milk over cow's milk for the developing infant.

41. The most serious nutritional problem of infancy is _____-_____ _____ .

42. Chronically malnourished infants suffer in three ways: Their _____ may not develop normally; they may have no _____ _____ to protect them against disease, and they may develop the diseases _____ or _____ .

43. Severe protein-calorie deficiency in early infancy causes _____ . If malnutrition begins after age 1, protein-calorie deficiency is more likely to cause the disease called _____ , which involves swelling or bloating of the face, legs, and abdomen.

Progress Test 1

Multiple-Choice Questions

Circle your answers to the following questions and check them with the answers on page 81. If your answer is incorrect, read the explanation for why it is incorrect and then consult the appropriate pages of the text (in parentheses following the correct answer).

1. The average North American newborn:
   a. weighs approximately 6 pounds.
   b. weighs approximately 7 pounds.
   c. is "overweight" because of the diet of the mother.
   d. weighs 10 percent less than what is desirable.

2. Compared to the first year, growth during the second year:
   a. proceeds at a slower rate.
   b. continues at about the same rate.
   c. includes more insulating fat.
   d. includes more bone and muscle.

3. The major motor skill most likely to be mastered by an infant before the age of 6 months is:
   a. rolling over.
   b. sitting without support.
   c. turning the head in search of a nipple.
   d. grabbing an object with thumb and forefinger.

4. Norms suggest that the earliest walkers in the world are infants from:
   a. Western Europe.   c. Uganda.
   b. the United States.   d. Denver.

5. Head-sparing is the phenomenon in which:
   a. the brain continues to grow even though the body stops growing as a result of malnutrition.
   b. the infant's body grows more rapidly during the second year.
   c. axons develop more rapidly than dendrites.
   d. dendrites develop more rapidly than axons.

6. Dreaming is characteristic of:
   a. slow-wave sleep.
   b. transitional sleep.
   c. REM sleep.
   d. quiet sleep.

7. For a pediatrician, the most important factor in assessing a child's healthy growth is:
   a. height in inches.
   b. weight in pounds.
   c. body fat percentage.
   d. the percentile rank of a child's height or weight.

8. Brain functions that depend on babies' having things to see and hear, and people to feed and carry them, are called:
   a. experience-dependent.
   b. experience-expectant.
   c. pruning functions.
   d. transient exuberance.

9. Compared with formula-fed infants, breast-fed infants tend to have:
   a. greater weight gain.
   b. fewer allergies and digestive upsets.
   c. less frequent feedings during the first few months.
   d. more social approval.

10. Marasmus and kwashiorkor are caused by:
    a. bloating.
    b. protein-calorie deficiency.
    c. living in a developing country.
    d. poor family food habits.

11. The infant's first "motor skills" are:
    a. fine motor skills.   c. reflexes.
    b. gross motor skills.   d. unpredictable.

12. Which of the following is said to have had the greatest impact on human mortality reduction and population growth?
    a. improvements in infant nutrition
    b. oral rehydration therapy
    c. medical advances in newborn care
    d. childhood immunization

13. Which of the following is true of motor-skill development in healthy infants?

    a. It follows the same basic sequence the world over.

    b. It occurs at different rates from individual to individual.

    c. It follows norms that vary from one ethnic group to another.

    d. All of the above are true.

14. All the nerve cells a human brain will ever need are present:

    a. at conception.

    b. about 1 month following conception.

    c. at birth.

    d. at age 5 or 6.

15. Chronically malnourished children suffer in which of the following ways?

    a. They have no body reserves to protect them.

    b. Their brains may not develop normally.

    c. They may die from marasmus.

    d. All of the above are true of malnourished children.

Matching Items

Match each definition or description with its corresponding term.

Terms

_____ 1. neurons

_____ 2. dendrites

_____ 3. kwashiorkor

_____ 4. marasmus

_____ 5. gross motor skill

_____ 6. fine motor skill

_____ 7. reflex

_____ 8. protein-calorie malnutrition

_____ 9. transient exuberance

_____ 10. prefrontal cortex

_____ 11. self-righting

Definitions or Descriptions

a. protein deficiency during the first year in which growth stops and body tissues waste away

b. picking up an object

c. the most common serious nutrition problem of infancy

d. protein deficiency during toddlerhood

e. communication networks among nerve cells

f. running or climbing

g. an involuntary response

h. the phenomenal increase in neural connections over the first 2 years

i. nerve cells

j. the brain area that specializes in anticipation, planning, and impulse control

k. the inborn drive to correct a developmental deficit

Progress Test 2

Progress Test 2 should be completed during a final chapter review. Answer the following questions after you thoroughly understand the correct answers for the Chapter Review and Progress Test 1.

Multiple-Choice Questions

1. Dendrite is to axon as neural _____ is to neural _____ .
   a. input; output
   b. output; input
   c. myelin; synapse
   d. synapse; myelin

2. A reflex is best defined as a(n):
   a. fine motor skill.
   b. motor ability mastered at a specific age.
   c. involuntary response to a given stimulus.
   d. gross motor skill.

3. A norm is:
   a. a standard, or average, that is derived for a specific group or population.
   b. a point on a ranking scale of 1 to 99.
   c. a milestone of development that all children reach at the same age.
   d. all of the above.

4. Most babies can reach for, grasp, and hold onto an object by about the _____ month.
   a. second
   b. sixth
   c. ninth
   d. fourteenth

5. Regarding the brain's cortex, which of the following is not true?
   a. The cortex houses about 70 percent of the brain's neurons.
   b. The cortex is the brain's outer layer.
   c. The cortex is the location of most thinking, feeling, and sensing.
   d. Only primates have a cortex.

6. During the first weeks of life, babies seem to focus reasonably well on:
   a. little in their environment.
   b. objects at a distance of 4 to 30 inches.
   c. objects at a distance of 1 to 3 inches.
   d. objects several feet away.

7. Which sleep stage increases markedly at about 3 or 4 months?
   a. REM
   b. transitional
   c. fast-wave
   d. slow-wave

8. An advantage of breast milk over formula is that it:
   a. is always sterile and at body temperature.
   b. contains traces of medications ingested by the mother.
   c. can be given without involving the father.
   d. contains more protein and vitamin D than does formula.

9. Synapses are:
   a. nerve fibers that receive electrical impulses from other neurons.
   b. nerve fibers that transmit electrical impulses to other neurons.
   c. intersections between the axon of one neuron and the dendrites of other neurons.
   d. chemical signals that transmit information from one neuron to another.

10. Transient exuberance and pruning demonstrate that:
    a. the pace of acquisition of motor skills varies markedly from child to child.
    b. Newborns sleep more than older children because their immature nervous systems cannot handle the higher, waking level of sensory stimulation.
    c. The specifics of brain structure and growth depend partly on the infant's experience.
    d. Good nutrition is essential to healthy biosocial development.

11. Climbing is to using a crayon as _____ is to _____ .
    a. fine motor skill; gross motor skill
    b. gross motor skill; fine motor skill
    c. reflex; fine motor skill
    d. reflex; gross motor skill

12. Some infant reflexes are critical for survival. Hiccups and sneezes help the infant maintain the _____ and leg tucking maintains _____ .
    a. feeding; oxygen supply
    b. feeding; a constant body temperature
    c. oxygen supply; feeding
    d. oxygen supply; a constant body temperature

13. (Thinking Like a Scientist) Compared to the brains of laboratory rats that were raised in barren cages, those of rats raised in stimulating, toy-filled cages:
    a. were better developed and had more dendritic branching.
    b. had fewer synaptic connections.
    c. showed less transient exuberance.
    d. displayed all of the above characteristics.

14. In determining a healthy child's growth, a pediatrician focuses on
    a. the child's past growth.
    b. the growth of the child's brothers and sisters.
    c. the stature of other children.
    d. all of the above.

15. Infant sensory and perceptual abilities appear to be especially organized for:
    a. obtaining adequate nutrition and comfort.
    b. comfort and social interaction.
    c. looking.
    d. touching and smelling.

True or False Items

Write T (*true*) or F (*false*) on the line in front of each statement.

_____ 1. Imaging studies have identified a specific area of the brain that specializes in recognizing faces.

_____ 2. Putting babies to sleep on their stomachs increases the risk of SIDS.

_____ 3. Reflexive hiccups, sneezes, and thrashing are signs that the infant's reflexes are not functioning properly.

_____ 4. Infants of all ethnic backgrounds develop the same motor skills at approximately the same age.

_____ 5. The typical 2-year-old is almost one-fifth its adult weight and one-half its adult height.

_____ 6. Vision is better developed than hearing in most newborns.

_____ 7. Today, most infants in industrialized nations are breast-fed up to 6 months.

_____ 8. Certain basic sensory experiences seem necessary to ensure full brain development in the human infant.

_____ 9. Dendrite growth is the major reason that brain weight increases so dramatically in the first two years.

_____ 10. The only motor skills apparent at birth are reflexes.

_____ 11. The prefrontal cortex is one of the first brain areas to mature.

Thinking Critically About Chapter 5

Answer these questions the day before an exam as a final check on your understanding of the chapter's terms and concepts.

1. Newborns cry, shiver, and tuck their legs close to their bodies. This set of reflexes helps them:
   a. ensure proper muscle tone.
   b. learn how to signal distress.
   c. maintain constant body temperature.
   d. communicate serious hunger pangs.

2. I am a chemical that carries information between nerve cells in the brain. What am I?
   a. a synapse.
   b. a dendrite
   c. a neurotransmitter
   d. a neuron

3. (Thinking Like a Scientist) Research studies of the more than 100,000 Romanian children orphaned and severely deprived in infancy reported all of the following *except*:
   a. all of the children were overburdened with stress.
   b. after adoption, the children gained weight quickly.
   c. during early childhood, many still showed signs of emotional damage.
   d. most of the children placed in healthy adoptive homes eventually recovered.

4. The Farbers, who are first-time parents, are wondering whether they should be concerned because their 12-month-old daughter, who weighs 22 pounds and measures 30 inches, is not growing quite as fast as she did during her first year. You should tell them that:
   a. any slowdown in growth during the second year is a cause for immediate concern.
   b. their daughter's weight and height are well below average for her age.
   c. growth patterns for a first child are often erratic.
   d. physical growth is somewhat slower in the second year.

5. Regarding body size, a child generally is said to be average if he or she is:
   a. at the 25th percentile.
   b. between the 25th and 40th percentiles.
   c. at the 50th percentile.
   d. at the 75th percentile or greater.

6. Concluding her presentation on sleep, Lakshmi notes each of the following *except:*
   a. dreaming occurs during REM sleep.
   b. quiet sleep increases markedly at about 3 or 4 months.
   c. the dreaming brain is characterized by slow brain waves.
   d. regular and ample sleep is an important factor in a child's emotional regulation.

7. Michael can focus on objects between 4 and 30 inches from him and is able to discriminate subtle sound differences. Michael most likely:
   a. is a preterm infant.
   b. has brain damage in the visual processing areas of the cortex.
   c. is a newborn.
   d. is slow-to-mature.

8. A baby turns her head and starts to suck when her receiving blanket is brushed against her cheek. The baby is displaying the:
   a. sucking reflex.   c. thrashing reflex.
   b. rooting reflex.   d. tucking reflex.

9. The pediatrician notices that Freddy seems indifferent to everything. Knowing that Freddy was abused as an infant, she suspects that:
   a. because of pruning, his brain's neuronal reactions has lost the capacity to react normally to stress.
   b. Freddy has a learning disability.
   c. Freddy has developed a personality disorder.
   d. as a result of the early abuse, Freddy is now mentally retarded.

10. Sensation is to perception as _____ is to _____ .
    a. hearing; seeing
    b. detecting a stimulus; making sense of a stimulus
    c. making sense of a stimulus; detecting a stimulus
    d. tasting; smelling

11. Sharetta's pediatrician informs her parents that Sharetta's 1-year-old brain is exhibiting transient exuberance. In response to this news, Sharetta's parents:
    a. smile, because they know their daughter's brain is developing new neural connections.
    b. worry, because this may indicate increased vulnerability to a later learning disability.
    c. know that this process, in which axons become coated, is normal.

d. are alarmed, since this news indicates that the frontal area of Sharetta's cortex is immature.

12. (Thinking Like a Scientist) To say that most developmentalists are multidisciplinary and believe in plasticity means they believe personality, intellect, and emotions:
    a. change throughout life as a result of biological maturation.
    b. change throughout life for a combination of reasons.
    c. remain stable throughout life.
    d. More strongly reveal the impact of genes as people get older.

13. Like all newborns, Serena is able to:
    a. differentiate one sound from another.
    b. see objects more than 30 inches from her face quite clearly.
    c. use her mouth to recognize objects by taste and touch.
    d. do all of the above.

14. Three-week-old Nathan should have the *least* difficulty focusing on the sight of:
    a. stuffed animals on a bookshelf across the room from his crib.
    b. his mother's face as she holds him in her arms.
    c. the checkerboard pattern in the wallpaper covering the ceiling of his room.
    d. the family dog as it dashes into the nursery.

15. Trying to impress his professor, Erik notes that the reason humans have a critical period for learning certain skills might be due to the fact that the brain cannot form new synapses after age 13. Should the professor be impressed with Erik's knowledge of biosocial development?
    a. Yes, although each neuron may have already formed as many as 15,000 connections with other neurons.
    b. Yes, although the branching of dendrites and axons does continue through young adulthood.
    c. No. Although Erik is correct about neural development, the brain attains adult size by about age 7.
    d. No. Synapses form throughout life.

Key Terms

Using your own words, write a brief definition or explanation of each of the following terms on a separate piece of paper.

1. head-sparing
2. norm
3. percentile
4. failure to thrive
5. REM sleep
6. neuron
7. cortex
8. axon
9. dendrite
10. synapse
11. transient exuberance
12. experience-expectant
13. experience-dependent
14. prefrontal cortex
15. self-righting
16. sensitive period
17. sensation
18. perception
19. binocular vision
20. motor skill
21. reflex
22. gross motor skills
23. fine motor skills
24. immunization
25. sudden infant death syndrome (SIDS)
26. protein-calorie malnutrition
27. marasmus
28. kwashiorkor

ANSWERS

CHAPTER REVIEW

1. 20 inches (51 centimeters); 7 pounds (3.2 kilograms)
2. head-sparing
3. norm
4. 30 pounds (13 kilograms); between 32 and 36 inches inches (81–91 centimeters); one-fifth; half

5. percentile; 1; 99; failure to thrive
6. sleep; brain; learning, emotional, psychological; 80
7. stages; dreaming; REM sleep; rapid; decreases; transitional sleep; quiet sleep; 3 or 4
8. do not; communal; isolated; kibbutz
9. 25; 75; 20
10. neurons; axons; dendrites; 70; cortex; thinking; feeling; sensing
11. dendrites; axon
12. synapses; axon; neurotransmitters; synaptic gap; dendrite; are; are
13. cortex
14. increases; five; transient exuberance; pruning; experience; cortisol
15. experience-expectant; experience-dependent; prefrontal cortex; anticipation; planning; impulse control
16. rapid; experience; sequence; growth; connecting; pruning; self-righting
17. genes; prenatal influences; plasticity; a combination of; sensitive periods; dendritic; emotional; improved; were
18. sensation; perception; sensation; perception; cognition; can
19. is; can; meaningful
20. vision; 4; 30
21. focus; scan; binocular vision; 14 weeks
22. function; touch; Brazelton
23. social interaction; comfort
24. motor skills; proximal-distal; near; far; cephalo-caudal; head; tail
25. reflex
26. breathing reflex; hiccups; sneezes; thrashing
27. constant body temperature
28. feeding; sucking; rooting
    a. Babinski reflex
    b. stepping reflex
    c. swimming reflex
    d. Palmar grasping reflex
    e. Moro reflex
29. gross motor
30. 8; 10; muscle strength; practice; brain maturation within the motor cortex

On average, a child can walk while holding a hand at

9 months, can stand alone momentarily at 10 months, and can walk well, unassisted, at 12 months.

31. fine motor; 6 months; 6 months

32. sequence; age

33. norms; many

34. ethnic

35. is; do; pattern of infant care

36. 3; was the same throughout the world; Japan; the Netherlands; France; 0.1

37. immunization; immune

38. sudden infant death syndrome (SIDS); sleep

39. ethnic; Asian; European; on their backs

Chinese parents tend to their babies periodically as they sleep, which makes them less likely to fall into a deep, nonbreathing sleep. Bangladeshi infants are usually surrounded by many family members in a rich sensory environment, making them less likely to sleep deeply for very long.

40. breast milk; colostrum; the mother is HIV-positive, using toxic drugs, or has some other serious condition that makes her milk unhealthy

Breast milk is always sterile and at body temperature; it contains more iron, vitamin C, and vitamin A; it contains antibodies that provide the infant some protection against disease; it is more digestible than any formula; and it decreases the frequency of almost every infant illness and allergy.

41. protein-calorie malnutrition

42. brains; body reserves; marasmus; kwashiorkor

43. marasmus; kwashiorkor

PROGRESS TEST 1

Multiple-Choice Questions

1. **b.** is the answer. (p. 131)

2. **a.** is the answer. (p. 131)

3. **a.** is the answer. (p. 152)

   b. The age norm for this skill is 7.8 months.

   c. This is a reflex, not an acquired motor skill.

   d. This skill is acquired between 9 and 14 months.

4. **c.** is the answer. (p. 152)

5. **a.** is the answer. (p. 132)

6. **c.** is the answer. (p. 134)

7. **d.** is the answer. (p. 132)

8. **b.** is the answer. (p. 142)

   a. Experience-dependent functions depend on

particular, and variable, experiences in order to develop.

   c. Pruning refers to the process by which some neurons wither because experience does not activate them.

   d. This refers to the great increase in the number of neurons, dendrites, and synapses that occurs in an infant's brain over the first two years of life.

9. **b.** is the answer. This is because breast milk is more digestible than cow's milk or formula. (p. 159)

   a., c., & d. Breast- and bottle-fed babies do not differ in these attributes.

10. **b.** is the answer. (pp. 160–161)

11. **c.** is the answer. (p. 149)

   a. & b. These motor skills do not emerge until somewhat later; reflexes are present at birth.

   d. On the contrary, reflexes are quite predictable.

12. **d.** is the answer. (p. 155)

13. **d.** is the answer. (p. 152)

14. **c.** is the answer. (p. 140)

15. **d.** is the answer. (p. 160)

Matching Items

1. i (p. 138)	6. b (p. 151)	11. k (p. 143)
2. e (p. 139)	7. g (p. 149)	
3. d (p. 161)	8. c (p. 160)	
4. a (p. 160)	9. h (p. 140)	
5. f (p. 150)	10. j (p. 143)	

PROGRESS TEST 2

Multiple-Choice Questions

1. **a.** is the answer. (p. 139)

2. **c.** is the answer. (p. 149)

   a., b., & d. Each of these refers to voluntary responses that are acquired only after a certain amount of practice; reflexes are involuntary responses that are present at birth and require no practice.

3. **a.** is the answer. (p. 132)

   b. This defines percentile.

4. **b.** is the answer. (p. 151)

5. **d.** is the answer. All mammals have a cortex. (p. 138)

6. **b.** is the answer. (p. 147)

   a. Although focusing ability seems to be limited to a certain range, babies do focus on many objects in this range.

   c. This is not within the range at which babies *can*

focus.

d. Babies have very poor distance vision.

7. **d.** is the answer. (p. 134)

8. **a.** is the answer. (p. 159)

b. If anything, this is a potential *disadvantage* of breast milk over formula.

c. So can formula.

d. Breast milk contains more iron, vitamin C, and vitamin A than cow's milk; it does not contain more protein and vitamin D, however.

9. **c.** is the answer. (p. 139)

a. These are dendrites.

b. These are axons.

d. These are neurotransmitters.

10. **c.** is the answer. (pp. 140–141)

11. **b.** is the answer. (pp. 150, 151)

c. & d. Reflexes are involuntary responses; climbing and using a crayon are both voluntary responses.

12. **d.** is the answer. (pp. 149–150)

13. **a.** is the answer. (p. 144)

14. **d.** is the answer. (p. 132)

15. **b.** is the answer. (p. 148)

True or False Items

1. T (p. 139)

2. T (p. 158)

3. F Hiccups, sneezes, and thrashing are common during the first few days, and they are entirely normal reflexes. (pp. 149–150)

4. F   Although all healthy infants develop the same motor skills in the same sequence, the age at which these skills are acquired can vary greatly from infant to infant. (p. 152)

5. T (p. 131)

6. F   Vision is relatively poorly developed at birth, whereas hearing is well developed. (p. 147)

7. F Only one-third of all babies are breast-fed up to 6 months. (p. 160)

8. T (p. 142)

9. T (p. 140)

10. T (p. 149)

11. F   In fact, the prefrontal cortex is probably the last area of the brain to attain maturity. (p. 143)

THINKING CRITICALLY ABOUT CHAPTER 5

1. **c.** is the answer. (p. 150)

2. **c.** is the answer. (p. 139)

a. A synapse is the intersection between the axon of one neuron and the dendrites of other neurons.

b. Dendrites are nerve fibers that receive electrical impulses transmitted from other neurons.

d. Neurons are nerve cells.

3. **d.** is the answer. Although all of the children improved, persistent deficits remained in many of them. (p. 144)

4. **d.** is the answer. (p. 131)

a. & b. Although slowdowns in growth during infancy are often a cause for concern, their daughter's weight and height are typical of 1-year-old babies.

c. Growth patterns are no more erratic for first children than for later children.

5. **c.** is the answer. (p. 132)

6. **c.** is the answer. The dreaming brain is characterized by rapid brain waves. (p. 134)

7. **c.** is the answer. (p. 147)

8. **b.** is the answer. (p. 150)

a. This is the reflexive sucking of newborns in response to anything that touches their *lips.*

c. This is the response that infants make when their feet are stroked.

d. This is part of the reflex when the infant is cold.

9. **a.** is the answer. (p. 141)

b., c., & d. Freddy's indifference and history point to an abnormal capacity to react to stress, not a learning disability, personality disorder, or mental retardation.

10. **b.** is the answer. (p. 146)

a. & d. Sensation and perception operate in all of these sensory modalities.

11. **a.** is the answer. Transient exuberance results in a proliferation of neural connections during infancy, some of which will disappear because they are not used; that is, they are not needed to process information. (p. 140)

b. & d. Transient exuberance is a normal developmental process that occurs in all healthy infants.

c. This describes the coating of axons with myelin, which speeds neural transmission.

12. **b.** is the answer. (p. 144)

13. **a.** is the answer. (p. 147)

    b. Objects at this distance are out of focus for newborns.

    c. This ability does not emerge until about one month of age.

14. **b.** is the answer. This is true because, at birth, focusing is best for objects between 4 and 30 inches away. (p. 147)

    a., c., & d. Newborns have very poor distance vision; each of these situations involves a distance greater than the optimal focus range.

15. **d.** is the answer. (pp. 140)

KEY TERMS

1. **Head-sparing** is the phenomenon by which the brain continues to grow even though the body stops growing in a malnourished child. (p. 132)

2. A **norm** is an average, or standard, developed for a specific population. (p. 132)

3. A **percentile** is any point on a ranking scale of 1 to 99; percentiles are often used to compare a child's development to group norms and to his or her own prior development. (p. 132)

4. **Failure to thrive** is the situation in which a seemingly healthy infant stops growing or loses weight. (p. 133)

5. **REM sleep,** or rapid eye movement sleep, is a stage of sleep characterized by flickering eyes behind closed eyelids, dreaming, and rapid brain waves. (p. 134)

6. A **neuron,** or nerve cell, is the main component of the central nervous system. (p. 138)

7. The **cortex** is the outer layers of the brain that is involved in most thinking, feeling, and sensing. (p. 138)

    Memory aid: Cortex in Latin means "bark." As bark covers a tree, the cortex is the "bark of the brain."

8. An **axon** is the nerve fiber that sends electrical impulses from one neuron to the dendrites of other neurons. (p. 139)

9. A **dendrite** is a nerve fiber that receives the electrical impulses transmitted from other neurons via their axons. (p. 139)

10. A **synapse** is the point at which the axon of a sending neuron meets the dendrites of a receiving neuron. (p. 139)

11. **Transient exuberance** is the dramatic increase in the number of dendrites that occurs in an infant's brain over the first two years of life. (p. 140)

12. **Experience-expectant** brain functions are those that require basic common experiences (such as having things to see and hear) in order to develop. (p. 142)

13. **Experience-dependent** brain functions are those that depend on particular, and variable, experiences (such as experiencing language) in order to develop. (p. 142)

14. The **prefrontal cortex** is the brain area that specializes in anticipation, planning, and impulse control. (p. 143)

15. **Self-righting** is the inborn drive to correct a deficit in development. (p. 143)

16. A **sensitive period** is a time when a specific kind of development is most likely to take place. (p. 144)

17. **Sensation** is the process by which a sensory system detects a particular stimulus. (p. 146)

18. **Perception** is the process by which the brain tries to make sense of a stimulus such that the individual becomes aware of it. (p. 146)

19. **Binocular vision** is the ability to use both eyes in a coordinated fashion in order to see one image. (p. 148)

    Memory aid: Bi- indicates "two"; ocular means something pertaining to the eye. Binocular vision is vision for "two eyes."

20. **Motor skills** are learned abilities to move specific parts of the body. (p. 149)

21. A **reflex** is an involuntary physical response to a specific stimulus. (p. 149)

22. **Gross motor skills** are physical abilities that demand large body movements, such as climbing, jumping, or running. (p. 150)

23. **Fine motor skills** are physical abilities that require precise, small movements, such as picking up a coin. (p. 151)

24. **Immunization** is the process through which the body's immune system is stimulated (as by a vaccine) to defend against attack by a particular contagious disease. (p. 155)

25. **Sudden infant death syndrome (SIDS)** is a set of circumstances in which a seemingly healthy infant, at least 2 months of age, dies unexpectedly in his or her sleep. (p. 157)

26. **Protein-calorie malnutrition** results when a person does not consume enough food to thrive. (p. 160)

27. **Marasmus** is a disease caused by severe protein-calorie deficiency during the first year of life. Growth stops, body tissues waste away, and the infant dies. (p. 160)

28. **Kwashiorkor** is a disease caused by protein-calorie deficiency during childhood. The child's face, legs, and abdomen swell with water, sometimes making the child appear well fed; the child becomes more vulnerable to other diseases. Other body parts are degraded, including the hair, which becomes thin, brittle, and colorless. (p. 161)

Chapter Six

The First Two Years: Cognitive Development

Chapter Overview

Chapter 6 explores the ways in which the infant comes to learn about, think about, and adapt to his or her surroundings. It focuses on the various ways in which infant intelligence is revealed: through sensorimotor intelligence, perception, memory, and language development. The chapter begins with a description of Jean Piaget's theory of sensorimotor intelligence, which maintains that infants think exclusively with their senses and motor skills. Piaget's six stages of sensorimotor intelligence are examined.

The second section discusses the information-processing theory, which compares cognition to the ways in which computers analyze data. Eleanor and James Gibson's influential theory is also described. Central to this theory is the idea that infants gain cognitive understanding of their world through the affordances of objects, that is, the activities they can do with them.

The text also discusses the key cognitive elements needed by the infant to structure the environment discovered through his or her newfound perceptual abilities. Using the habituation procedure, researchers have found that the speed with which infants recognize familiarity and seek something novel is related to later cognitive skill. It points out the importance of memory to cognitive development.

Finally, the chapter turns to the most remarkable cognitive achievement of the first two years, the acquisition of language. Beginning with a description of the infant's first attempts at language, the chapter follows the sequence of events that leads to the child's ability to utter two-word sentences. The chapter concludes with an examination of three classic theories of language acquisition and a fourth, hybrid theory that combines aspects of each.

NOTE: Answer guidelines for all Chapter 6 questions begin on page 95.

Guided Study

The text chapter should be studied one section at a time. Before you read, preview each section by skimming it, noting headings and boldface items. Then read the appropriate section objectives from the following outline. Keep these objectives in mind and, as you read the chapter section, search for the information that will enable you to meet each objective. Once you have finished a section, write out answers for its objectives.

Sensorimotor Intelligence (pp. 165–172)

1. Identify and describe Piaget's first two stages of sensorimotor intelligence.

2. Identify and describe stages 3 and 4 of Piaget's theory of sensorimotor intelligence.

3. (text and Thinking Like A Scientist) Explain what object permanence is, how it is tested in infancy, and what these tests reveal.

4. Identify and describe stages 5 and 6 of Piaget's theory of sensorimotor intelligence.

5. Describe some major advances in the scientific investigation of infant cognition.

Information Processing (pp. 172–178)

6. Explain the information-processing theory of cognition.

7. Discuss the Gibsons' contextual view of perception, focusing on the idea of affordances and giving examples of the affordances perceived by infants.

8. Discuss research findings on infant memory.

Language: What Develops in Two Years? (pp. 178–187)

9. Identify the main features of child-directed speech, and explain its importance.

10. Describe language development during infancy, and identify its major hallmarks.

11. Differentiate three theories of language learning, and explain current views on language learning.

Chapter Review

When you have finished reading the chapter, work through the material that follows to review it. Complete the sentences and answer the questions. As you proceed, evaluate your performance for each section by consulting the answers beginning on page 95. Do not continue with the next section until you understand each answer. If you need to, review or reread the appropriate section in the textbook before continuing.

Sensorimotor Intelligence (pp. 165–172)

1. Cognition involves _____
_____ .

   The first major theorist to realize that infants are active learners was _____ .

2. At every stage, people _____ their thinking to their _____ . This is revealed in two ways: by _____ of new information into previously developed

mental categories, or _____ ; and by _____ of previous mental categories to incorporate new information.

3. When infants begin to explore the environment through sensory and motor skills, they are displaying what Piaget called _____ intelligence. In number, Piaget described _____ stages of development of this type of intelligence.

4. The first two stages of sensorimotor intelligence are examples of _____ _____ _____ . Stage one begins with newborns' reflexes, such as _____ and _____ , and also the _____ , which are very responsive at birth. It lasts from birth to _____ of age.

5. Stage two begins when newborns show signs of _____ of their _____ and senses to the specifics of the environment.

Describe the development of the sucking reflex during stages one and two.

6. In stages three and four, development switches to _____ _____ _____ , involving the baby with an object or with another person. During stage three, which occurs between _____ and _____ months of age, infants repeat a specific action that has just elicited a pleasing response.

Describe a typical stage-three behavior.

7. In stage four, which lasts from _____ to _____ months of age, infants can better _____ events. At this stage, babies also engage in purposeful actions, or _____-_____ behavior.

8. (text and Thinking Like a Scientist) A major cognitive accomplishment of infancy is the ability to understand that objects exist even when they are _____ . This awareness is called _____ _____ . To test for this awareness, Piaget devised a procedure to observe whether an infant will _____ for a hidden object. Using this test, Piaget concluded that this awareness does not develop until about _____ of age.

9. During stage five, which lasts from _____ to _____ months, infants begin experimenting in thought and deed. They do so through _____ _____ _____ , which involve taking in experiences and trying to make sense of them.

Explain what Piaget meant when he described the stage-five infant as a little scientist.

10. Stage six, which lasts from _____ to _____ months, is the stage of achieving new means by using _____ _____ .

11. One sign that children have reached stage six is _____ _____ , which is their emerging ability to imitate behaviors they noticed earlier.

12. Two research tools that have become available since Piaget's time are _____ studies and _____ , which reveals brain activity as cognition occurs.

Information Processing (pp. 172–178)

13. A perspective on human cognition that is modeled on how computers analyze data is the _____-_____ theory. Two aspects of this theory as applied to human development are _____ , which concern perception and so are analogous to

computer input, and _____ , which involves storage and retrieval of ideas, or output.

14. Much of the current research in perception and cognition has been inspired by the work of the Gibsons, who stress that perception is a(n) _____ (active/passive/automatic) cognitive phenomenon.

15. According to the Gibsons, any object in the environment offers diverse opportunities for interaction; this property of an object is called an _____ .

16. Which of these an individual perceives in an object depends on the individual's _____ _____ and _____ _____ , on his or her _____ _____ , and on his or her _____ _____ of what the object might be used for.

17. A firm surface that appears to drop off is called a _____ _____ .

    Although perception of this drop off was once linked to _____ maturity, later research found that infants as young as _____ are able to perceive the drop off, as evidenced by changes in their _____ _____ and their wide open eyes.

18. Perception that is primed to focus on movement and change is called _____ _____ . Another universal principle of infant perception is _____ _____ , which may have evolved because humans _____ by learning to attend to, and rely on, one another.

19. Babies have great difficulty storing new memories in their first _____ (how long?).

20. Research has shown, however, that babies can show that they remember when three conditions are met:

    (a) _____

    (b) _____

    (c) _____

21. When these conditions are met, infants as young as _____ months "remembered" events from two weeks earlier if they experienced a _____ _____ prior to retesting.

22. After about _____ months, infants become capable of retaining information for longer periods of time, with less reminding.

23. Most researchers believe there _____ (is one type of memory/are many types of memory). Memory for routines that remains hidden until a stimulus triggers it is called _____ _____ .

    Memories that can be recalled on demand are referred to as _____ _____ .

Language: What Develops in Two Years? (pp. 158–167)

24. Children the world over _____ (follow/do not follow) the same sequence of early language development. The timing of this sequence and depth of ability _____ (varies/does not vary).

25. Newborns show a preference for hearing _____ over other sounds, including the high-pitched, simplified adult speech called _____-_____ speech, which is sometimes called _____ _____ .

26. By 4 months of age, most babies' verbal repertoire consists of _____ _____ .

27. Between _____ and _____ months of age, babies begin to repeat certain syllables, a phenomenon referred to as _____ .

28. Deaf babies begin oral babbling _____ (earlier/later) than hearing babies do. Deaf babies may also babble _____ , with this behavior emerging _____ (earlier than/at the same

time as/later than) hearing infants begin oral babbling.

29. The average baby speaks a few words at about _____ of age. When vocabulary reaches approximately 50 words, it suddenly begins to build rapidly, at a rate of _____ or more words a month. This language spurt is called the _____ _____ , because toddlers learn a disproportionate number of _____ .

30. Language acquisition may be shaped by our _____ , as revealed by the fact that English-speaking infants learn more _____ than Chinese or Korean infants, who learn more _____ . Alternatively, the entire _____ _____ may determine language acquisition.

31. Another characteristic is the use of the _____ , in which a single word expresses a complete thought.

32. Children begin to produce their first two-word sentences at about _____ months, showing a clearly emerging understanding of _____ , which refers to all the methods that languages use to communicate meaning, apart from the words themselves.

33. Reinforcement and other conditioning processes account for language development, according to the learning theory of _____ . Support for this theory comes from the fact that there are wide variations in language _____ , especially when children from different cultures are compared. One study that followed mother–infant pairs over time found that the frequency of early _____ _____ predicted the child's rate of language acquisition many months later.

34. The theorist who stressed that language is too complex to be mastered so early and easily through conditioning is _____ . This theorist maintained that all children are born with a LAD, or _____ _____ _____ , that enables children to quickly derive the rules of grammar from the speech they hear.

35. According to this theory, words are _____-_____ by a LAD in the developing brain.

Summarize the research support for theory two.

36. A third, _____-_____ theory of language proposes that _____ _____ foster infant language.

37. A new hybrid theory, based on a model called an _____ _____ , combines aspects of several theories. A fundamental aspect of this theory is that _____ _____ .

Progress Test 1

Multiple-Choice Questions

Circle your answers to the following questions and check them with the answers beginning on page 96. If your answer is incorrect, read the explanation for why it is incorrect and then consult the appropriate pages of the text (in parentheses following the correct answer).

1. In general terms, the Gibsons' concept of affordances emphasizes the idea that the individual perceives an object in terms of its:
   a. economic importance.
   b. physical qualities.
   c. function or use to the individual.
   d. role in the larger culture or environment.

2. According to Piaget, when a baby repeats an action that has just triggered a pleasing response from his or her caregiver, a stage _____ behavior has occurred.
   a. one   c. three
   b. two   d. six

3. Sensorimotor intelligence begins with a baby's first:
   a. attempt to crawl.
   b. reflex actions.
   c. auditory perception.
   d. adaptation of a reflex.

4. Piaget and the Gibsons would most likely agree that:
   a. perception is largely automatic.
   b. language development is biologically predisposed in children.
   c. learning and perception are active cognitive processes.
   d. it is unwise to "push" children too hard academically.

5. By the end of the first year, infants usually learn how to:
   a. accomplish simple goals.
   b. manipulate various symbols.
   c. solve complex problems.
   d. pretend.

6. When an infant begins to understand that objects exist even when they are out of sight, she or he has begun to understand the concept of object:
   a. displacement.   c. permanence.
   b. importance.   d. location.

7. Today, most cognitive psychologists view language acquisition as:
   a. primarily the result of imitation of adult speech.
   b. a behavior that is determined primarily by biological maturation.
   c. a behavior determined entirely by learning.
   d. determined by both biological maturation and learning.

8. Despite cultural differences, children all over the world attain very similar language skills:
   a. according to ethnically specific timetables.
   b. in the same sequence according to a variable timetable.
   c. according to culturally specific timetables.
   d. according to timetables that vary from child to child.

9. The average baby speaks a few words at about:
   a. 6 months.   c. 12 months.
   b. 9 months.   d. 24 months.

10. A single word used by toddlers to express a complete thought is:
    a. a holophrase.
    b. child-directed speech.
    c. babbling.
    d. an affordance.

11. A distinctive form of language, with a particular pitch, structure, etc., that adults use in talking to infants is called:
    a. a holophrase.
    b. the LAD.
    c. child-directed speech.
    d. conversation.

12. Habituation studies reveal that most infants detect the difference between a pah sound and a bah sound at:
    a. birth.   c. 3 months.
    b. 1 month.   d. 6 months.

13. The imaging technique in which the brain's magnetic properties indicate activation in various parts of the brain is called a(n):
    a. PET scan.   c. fMRI.
    b. EEG.   d. CAT scan.

14. A toddler who taps on the computer's keyboard after observing her mother sending e-mail the day before is demonstrating:
    a. assimilation.   c. deferred imitation.
    b. accommodation.   d. dynamic perception.

15. In Piaget's theory of sensorimotor intelligence, reflexes that involve the infant's own body are examples of:
    a. primary circular reactions
    b. secondary circular reactions.
    c. tertiary circular reactions.
    d. none of the above.

Matching Items

Match each definition or description with its corresponding term.

Terms

_____ 1. people preference
_____ 2. affordances
_____ 3. object permanence
_____ 4. Noam Chomsky
_____ 5. B. F. Skinner
_____ 6. sensorimotor intelligence
_____ 7. babbling
_____ 8. holophrase
_____ 9. adaptation
_____ 10. deferred imitation
_____ 11. dynamic perception

Definitions or Descriptions

a. cognitive process by which new information is taken in and responded to
b. repetitive utterance of certain syllables
c. perception that focuses on movement and change
d. the ability to witness, remember, and later copy a behavior
e. the realization that something that is out of sight continues to exist
f. the innate attraction of human babies to humans.
g. opportunities for interaction that an object offers
h. theorist who believed that verbal behavior is conditioned
i. a single word used to express a complete thought
j. theorist who believed that language ability is innate
k. thinking through the senses and motor skills

Progress Test 2

Progress Test 2 should be completed during a final chapter review. Answer the following questions after you thoroughly understand the correct answers for the Chapter Review and Progress Test 1.

Multiple-Choice Questions

1. Stage five (12 to 18 months) of sensorimotor intelligence is best described as:
   a. first acquired adaptations.
   b. the period of the little scientist.
   c. procedures for making interesting sights last.
   d. new means through symbolization.

2. Which of the following is *not* evidence of dynamic perception during infancy?
   a. Babies prefer to look at things in motion.
   b. Babies form simple expectations of the path that a moving object will follow.
   c. Babies use movement cues to discern the boundaries of objects.
   d. Babies quickly grasp that even though objects look different when seen from different viewpoints, they are the same objects.

3. (text and Thinking Like a Scientist) Research suggests that the concept of object permanence:
   a. fades after a few months.
   b. is a skill some children never acquire.
   c. may occur earlier and more gradually than Piaget recognized.
   d. involves pretending as well as mental combinations.

4. Which of the following is an example of a secondary circular reaction?
   a. 1-month-old infant staring at a mobile suspended over her crib
   b. a 2-month-old infant sucking a pacifier
   c. realizing that rattles make noise, a 4-month-old infant laughs with delight when his mother puts a rattle in his hand
   d. a 12-month-old toddler licks a bar of soap to learn what it tastes like

5. Eighteen-month-old Colin puts a collar on his stuffed dog, then pretends to take it for a walk. Colin's behavior is an example of a:
   a. primary circular reaction.
   b. secondary circular reaction.
   c. tertiary circular reaction.
   d. first acquired adaptation.

6. According to Piaget, assimilation and accommodation are two ways in which:
   a. infants adapt their thinking to the specifics of the environment.
   b. goal-directed behavior occurs.
   c. infants form mental combinations.
   d. language begins to emerge.

7. For Noam Chomsky, the language acquisition device refers to:
   a. the human predisposition to acquire language.
   b. the portion of the human brain that processes speech.
   c. the vocabulary of the language the child is exposed to.
   d. all of the above.

8. The first stage of sensorimotor intelligence lasts until:
   a. infants can anticipate events that will fulfill their needs.
   b. infants begin to adapt their reflexes to the environment.
   c. infants interact with objects to produce exciting experiences.
   d. infants are capable of thinking about past and future events.

9. Whether or not an infant perceives certain characteristics of objects, such as "suckability" or "graspability," seems to depend on:
   a. his or her prior experiences.
   b. his or her needs.
   c. his or her sensory awareness.
   d. all of the above.

10. (Thinking Like a Scientist) Piaget was *incorrect* in his belief that infants do not have:
    a. object permanence.
    b. intelligence.
    c. goal-directed behavior.
    d. all of the above.

11. The purposeful actions that begin to develop in sensorimotor stage four are called:
    a. reflexes.
    b. affordances.
    c. goal-directed behaviors.
    d. mental combinations.

12. What is the correct sequence of stages of language development?
    a. crying, babbling, cooing, first word
    b. crying, cooing, babbling, first word
    c. crying, babbling, first word, cooing
    d. crying, cooing, first word, babbling

13. Compared with hearing babies, deaf babies:
    a. are less likely to babble.
    b. are more likely to babble.
    c. begin to babble vocally at about the same age.
    d. begin to babble manually at about the same age as hearing babies begin to babble vocally.

14. According to Skinner, children acquire language:
    a. as a result of an inborn ability to use the basic structure of language.
    b. through reinforcement and other aspects of conditioning.
    c. mostly because of biological maturation.
    d. in a fixed sequence of predictable stages.

15. A fundamental idea of the emergentist coalition model of language acquisition is that:
    a. all humans are born with an innate language acquisition device.
    b. some aspects of language are best learned in one way at one age, others in another way at another age.
    c. language development occurs too rapidly and easily to be entirely the product of conditioning.
    d. imitation and reinforcement are crucial to the development of language.

Matching Items
Match each definition or description with its corresponding term.

Terms

_____ 1. goal-directed behavior
_____ 2. visual cliff
_____ 3. primary circular reaction
_____ 4. child-directed speech
_____ 5. assimilation
_____ 6. little scientist
_____ 7. accommodation
_____ 8. secondary circular reaction
_____ 9. tertiary circular reaction
_____ 10. LAD
_____ 11. grammar

Definitions or Descriptions

a. a device for studying depth perception
b. incorporating new information into an existing schema
c. readjusting an existing schema to incorporate new information
d. a feedback loop involving the infant's own body
e. a feedback loop involving people and objects
f. a hypothetical device that facilitates language development
g. also called baby talk
h. Piaget's term for the stage-five toddler
i. purposeful actions
j. a feedback loop involving active exploration and experimentation
k. all the methods used by a language to communicate meaning

Thinking Critically About Chapter 6

Answer these questions the day before an exam as a final check on your understanding of the chapter's terms and concepts.

1. A 9-month-old repeatedly reaches for his sister's doll, even though he has been told "no" many times. This is an example of:
   a. primary circular reactions.
   b. habituation.
   c. delayed imitation.
   d. goal-directed behavior.

2. If a baby sucks harder on a nipple, evidences a change in heart rate, or stares longer at one image than at another when presented with a change of stimulus, the indication is that the baby:
   a. is annoyed by the change.
   b. is both hungry and angry.
   c. has become habituated to the new stimulus.
   d. perceives some differences between stimuli.

3. As an advocate of the social-pragmatic theory, Professor Robinson believes that:
   a. infants communicate in every way they can because they are social beings.
   b. biological maturation is a dominant force in language development.
   c. infants' language abilities mirror those of their primary caregivers.

   d. language develops in many ways for many reasons.

4. According to Skinner's theory, an infant who learns to delight his father by saying "da-da" is probably benefiting from:
   a. social reinforcers, such as smiles and hugs.
   b. modeling.
   c. learning by imitation.
   d. an innate ability to use language.

5. When 18-month-old Jessica sees a hairless dog, she does not know what to call it. After her mother says, "See Jessie, not all dogs have fur," Jessica proudly calls "doggie!" Jessica's manipulation of her doggie schema to incorporate this experience is an example of:
   a. assimilation.
   b. accommodation.
   c. adaptation.
   d. a primary circular reaction.

6. At about 21 months, the typical child will:
   a. have a vocabulary of between 250 and 350 words.
   b. begin to speak in holophrases.
   c. put words together to form rudimentary sentences.
   d. do all of the above.

7. A 20-month-old girl who is able to try out various actions mentally without having to actually perform them is learning to solve simple problems by using:
   a. dynamic perception.
   b. object permanence.
   c. affordances.
   d. mental combinations.

8. A baby who attempts to interact with a smiling parent is demonstrating an ability that typically occurs in which stage of sensorimotor development?
   a. one   c. three
   b. two   d. four

9. Piaget referred to the shift in an infant's behavior from reflexes to deliberate actions as the shift from:
   a. secondary circular reactions to primary circular reactions.
   b. first acquired adaptations to secondary circular reactions.
   c. primary circular reactions to tertiary circular reactions.
   d. stage one primary circular reactions to stage two primary circular reactions.

10. A baby who realizes that a rubber duck that has fallen out of the tub must be somewhere on the floor has achieved:
   a. object permanence.
   b. deferred imitation.
   c. mental combinations.
   d. goal-directed behavior.

11. As soon as her babysitter arrives, 21-month-old Christine holds on to her mother's legs and, in a questioning manner, says "bye-bye." Because Christine clearly is "asking" her mother not to leave, her utterance can be classified as:
   a. babbling.
   b. a noun.
   c. a holophrase.
   d. subject-predicate order.

12. The 6-month-old infant's continual repetition of sound combinations such as "ba-ba-ba" is called:
   a. cooing.   c. a holophrase.
   b. babbling.   d. crooning.

13. Nine-month-old Akshay, who looks out of his crib for a toy that has fallen, is clearly demonstrating:
   a. object permanence.
   b. goal-directed behavior.
   c. a secondary circular reaction.
   d. all of the above.

14. Monica firmly believes that her infant daughter "taught" herself language because of the seemingly effortless manner in which she has mastered new words and phrases. Monica is evidently a proponent of the theory proposed by:
   a. B. F. Skinner.
   b. Noam Chomsky.
   c. social pragmatic theorists.
   d. the emergentist coalition.

15. Like most Korean toddlers, Noriko has acquired a greater number of _____ in her vocabulary than her North American counterparts, who tend to acquire more _____ .
   a. verbs; nouns
   b. nouns; verbs
   c. adjectives; verbs
   d. adjectives; nouns

Key Terms

Writing Definitions

Using your own words, write a brief definition or explanation of each of the following terms on a separate piece of paper.

1. adaptation
2. sensorimotor intelligence
3. primary circular reactions
4. secondary circular reactions
5. object permanence
6. tertiary circular reactions
7. little scientist
8. deferred imitation
9. habituation
10. fMRI
11. information-processing theory
12. affordance
13. visual cliff
14. dynamic perception

15. people preference
16. reminder session
17. child-directed speech
18. babbling

19. naming explosion
20. holophrase
21. grammar
22. language acquisition device (LAD)

Cross-Check
After you have written the definitions of the key terms in this chapter, you should complete the crossword puzzle to ensure that you can reverse the process—recognize the term, given the definition.

ACROSS

1. the methods used by languages to communicate meaning
7. a brain-imaging technique
8. a circular reaction involving the infant's own body
9. a circular reaction involving people and objects
10. a type of perception primed to focus on movement
12. the process of getting used to an object
13. child-directed speech
15. a sudden increase in an infant's vocabulary

DOWN

2. the cognitive process by which new information is taken in
3. a type of circular reaction that involves active exploration
4. a single word used to express a complete thought
5. Piaget's term for the stage-five toddler
6. an opportunity for perception
10. imitation of something that occurred earlier
11. extended repetition of syllables
14. Chomsky's term for a brain structure that enables language

ANSWERS
CHAPTER REVIEW

1. intelligence, learning, memory, and language; Piaget

2. adapt; experiences; assimilation; schemas; accommodation

3. sensorimotor; six

4. primary circular reactions; sucking; grasping; senses; 1 month

5. adaptation; reflexes

Stage-one infants suck everything that touches their lips. At about 1 month, they start to adapt their sucking to specific objects. After several months, they have organized the world into objects to be sucked for nourishment, objects to be sucked for pleasure, and objects not to be sucked at all.

6. secondary circular reactions; 4; 8

A stage-three infant may squeeze a duck, hear a quack, and squeeze the duck again.

7. 8; 12; anticipate; goal-directed

8. no longer in sight; object permanence; search; 8 months

9. 12; 18; tertiary circular reactions

Having discovered some action or set of actions that is possible with a given object, stage-five little scientists seem to ask, "What else can I do with this?"

10. 18; 24; mental combinations

11. deferred imitation

12. habituation; fMRI

13. information-processing; affordances; memory

14. active

15. affordance

16. past experiences; current development; immediate motivation; sensory awareness

17. visual cliff; visual; 3 months; heart rate

18. dynamic perception; people preference; evolved

19. year

20. (a) experimental conditions are similar to real life; (b) motivation is high; (c) special measures aid memory retrieval

21. 3 months; reminder session

22. 6

23. are many types of memory; implicit memory; explicit memory

24. follow; varies

25. speech; child-directed; baby talk

26. squeals, growls, gurgles, grunts, croons, and yells, as well as some speechlike sounds

27. 6; 9; babbling

28. later; manually; at the same time as

29. 1 year; 50 to 100; naming explosion; nouns

30. culture; nouns; verbs; social context

31. holophrase

32. 21; grammar

33. B. F. Skinner; fluency; maternal responsiveness

34. Noam Chomsky; language acquisition device

35. experience-expectant

Support for this theory comes from the fact that all babies babble ma-ma and da-da sounds at about 6 to 9 months. No reinforcement is needed. All they need is for dendrites to grow, mouth muscles to strengthen, neurons to connect, and speech to be heard.

36. social-pragmatic; social impulses

37. emergentist coalition; some aspects of language are best learned in one way at one age, others in another way at another age

PROGRESS TEST 1

Multiple-Choice Questions

1. **c.** is the answer. (p. 173)

2. **c.** is the answer. (p. 167)

3. **b.** is the answer. This was Piaget's most basic contribution to the study of infant cognition—that intelligence is revealed in behavior at every age. (p. 166)

4. **c.** is the answer. (pp. 165, 173)

   b. This is Chomsky's position.

   d. This issue was not discussed in the text.

5. **a.** is the answer. (p. 168)

   b. & c. These abilities are not acquired until children are much older.

   d. Pretending is associated with stage six (18 to 24 months).

6. **c.** is the answer. (p. 168)

7. **d.** is the answer. (pp. 185–186)

8. **b.** is the answer. (p. 178)

   a., c., & d. Children the world over follow the same sequence, but the timing of their accomplishments may vary considerably.

9. **c.** is the answer. (p. 180)

10. **a.** is the answer. (p. 181)

    b. Baby talk is the speech adults use with infants.

    c. Babbling refers to the first syllables a baby utters.

    d. An affordance is an opportunity for perception and interaction.

11. **c.** is the answer. (p. 178)

    a. A holophrase is a single word uttered by a toddler to express a complete thought.

    b. According to Noam Chomsky, the LAD, or language acquisition device, is an innate ability in humans to acquire language.

    d. These characteristic differences in pitch and structure are precisely what distinguish child-directed speech from regular conversation.

12. **b.** is the answer. (p. 170)

13. **c.** is the answer. (p. 171)

14. **c.** is the answer (p. 170)

    a. & b. In Piaget's theory, these refer to processes by which mental concepts incorporate new experiences (assimilation) or are modified in response to new experiences (accommodation).

    d. Dynamic perception is perception that is primed to focus on movement and change.

15. **a.** is the answer. (p. 166)

    b. Secondary circular reactions involve the baby with an object or with another person.

c. Tertiary circular reactions involve active exploration and experimentation, rather than mere reflexive action.

Matching Items

1. f (p. 174)	**5.** h (p. 182)	**9.** a (p. 165)
2. g (p. 173)	**6.** k (p. 166)	**10.** d (pp. 170)
3. e (p. 168)	**7.** b (p. 179)	**11.** c (p. 174)
4. j (p. 184)	**8.** i (p. 181)	

PROGRESS TEST 2

Multiple-Choice Questions

1. **b.** is the answer. (p. 170)

   a. & c. These are stages two and three.

   d. This is not one of Piaget's stages of sensorimotor intelligence.

2. **d.** is the answer. This is an example of perceptual constancy. (p. 174)

3. **c.** is the answer. (pp. 168–169)

4. **c.** is the answer. (p. 167)

   a. & b. These are examples of primary circular reactions.

   d. This is an example of a tertiary circular reaction.

5. **c.** is the answer. (pp. 169–170)

6. **a.** is the answer. (p. 165)

   b. Assimilation and accommodation are cognitive processes, not behaviors.

   c. Mental combinations are sequences of actions that are carried out mentally.

   d. Assimilation and accommodation do not directly pertain to language use.

7. **a.** is the answer. Chomsky believed that this device is innate. (p. 184)

8. **b.** is the answer. (p. 166)

   a. & c. Both of these occur later than stage one.

   d. This is a hallmark of stage six.

9. **d.** is the answer. (p. 173)

10. **a.** is the answer. (pp. 168–169)

11. **c.** is the answer. (p. 168)

   a. Reflexes are involuntary (and therefore unintentional) responses.

   b. Affordances are perceived opportunities for interaction with objects.

   d. Mental combinations are actions that are carried out mentally, rather than behaviorally. Moreover, mental combinations do not develop until a later age, during sensorimotor stage six.

12. **b.** is the answer. (pp. 179–180)

13. **d.** is the answer. (p. 179)

   a. & b. Hearing and deaf babies do not differ in the overall likelihood that they will babble.

   c. Deaf babies begin to babble vocally several months later than hearing babies do.

14. **b.** is the answer. (p. 182)

   a., c., & d. These views on language acquisition describe the theory offered by Noam Chomsky.

15. **b.** is the answer. (p. 185)

   a. & c. These ideas are consistent with Noam Chomsky's theory.

   d. This is the central idea of B. F. Skinner's theory.

Matching Items

1. i (p. 168)	**5.** b (p. 165)	**9.** j (p. 169)
2. a (p. 174)	**6.** h (p. 170)	**10.** f (p. 184)
3. d (p. 166)	**7.** c (p. 165)	**11.** k (p. 181)
4. g (p. 178)	**8.** e (p. 167)	

THINKING CRITICALLY ABOUT CHAPTER 6

1. **d.** is the answer. The baby is clearly behaving purposefully, the hallmark of goal-directed behavior. (p. 168)

   a. This is a stage-four behavior, not stages one or two.

   b. He is clearly not getting used to the stimulus.

   c. Delayed imitation is the ability to imitate actions seen in the past.

2. **d.** is the answer. (p. 170)

   a. & b. These changes in behavior indicate that the newborn has perceived an unfamiliar stimulus, not that he or she is hungry, annoyed, or angry.

   c. Habituation refers to a *decrease* in physiological responsiveness to a familiar stimulus.

3. **a.** is the answer. (pp. 184–185)

   b. This idea is more consistent with Noam Chomsky's theory.

   c. This idea is more consistent with B. F. Skinner's theory.

   d. This expresses the emergentist coalition theory.

4. **a.** is the answer. The father's expression of delight is a reinforcer in that it has increased the likelihood of the infant's vocalization. (pp. 182–183)

b. & c. Modeling, or learning by imitation, would be implicated if the father attempted to increase the infant's vocalizations by repeatedly saying "da-da" himself, in the infant's presence.

d. This is Chomsky's viewpoint; Skinner maintained that language is acquired through learning.

5. **b.** is the answer. (p. 165)

    a. This answer would have been correct had Jessica initially recognized the hairless animal as a dog.

    c. This answer is too general. Adaptation occurs in two very different ways.

    d. Primary circular reactions are behaviors that involve the infant's body.

6. **c.** is the answer. (p. 182)

    a. At 21 months of age, most children have much smaller vocabularies.

    b. Speaking in holophrases is typical of younger infants.

7. **d.** is the answer. (p. 170)

    a. Dynamic perception is perception primed to focus on movement and change.

    b. Object permanence is the awareness that objects do not cease to exist when they are out of sight.

    c. Affordances are the opportunities for perception and interaction that an object or place offers to any individual.

8. **c.** is the answer. (p. 167)

9. **d.** is the answer. (p. 166)

10. **a.** is the answer. Before object permanence is attained, an object that disappears from sight ceases to exist for the infant. (p. 168)

    b. Deferred imitation is the ability to witness, remember, and later copy a particular behavior.

    c. Mental combinations are actions that are carried out mentally.

    d. Goal-directed behavior refers to purposeful actions initiated by infants in anticipation of events that will fulfill their needs and wishes.

11. **c.** is the answer. (p. 181)

    a. Because Christine is expressing a complete thought, her speech is much more than babbling.

    b. "Bye-bye" is not a noun.

    d. The ability to understand subject-predicate order emerges later, when children begin forming 2-word sentences.

12. **b.** is the answer. (p. 179)

    a. & d. Cooing and crooning are the pleasant-sounding utterances of the infant by about 4 months.

    c. The holophrase occurs later and refers to the toddler's use of a single word to express a complete thought.

13. **d.** is the answer. (p. 168)

14. **b.** is the answer. (p. 184)

15. **a.** is the answer. (p. 181)

KEY TERMS

1. A key element of Piaget's theory, **adaptation** is the cognitive process by which information is taken in and responded to. (p. 165)

2. Piaget's stages of **sensorimotor intelligence** (from birth to about 2 years old) are based on his theory that infants think exclusively with their senses and motor skills. (p. 166)

3. In Piaget's theory, **primary circular reactions** are a type of feedback loop involving the infant's own body, in which infants take in experiences (such as sucking and grasping) and try to make sense of them. (p. 166)

4. **Secondary circular reactions** are a type of feedback loop involving the infant's responses to objects and other people. (p. 167)

5. **Object permanence** is the understanding that objects continue to exist even when they cannot be seen, touched, or heard. (p. 168)

6. In Piaget's theory, **tertiary circular reactions** are the most sophisticated type of infant feedback loop, involving active exploration and experimentation. (p. 169)

7. **Little scientist** is Piaget's term for the stage-five toddler who learns about the properties of objects in his or her world through active experimentation. (p. 170)

8. **Deferred imitation** is the ability of infants to witness, remember, and later copy a behavior they noticed hours or days earlier. (p. 170)

9. **Habituation** is the process of getting used to an object or event through repeated exposure to it. (p. 170)

10. **fMRI** (functional magnetic resonance imaging) is an imaging technique in which the brain's magnetic properties are measured to reveal changes in activity levels in various parts of the brain. (p. 171)

11. **Information-processing theory** is a theory of human cognition that compares thinking to the ways in which a computer analyzes data, through the processes of sensory input, connections, stored memories, and output. (p. 172)

12. **Affordances** are perceived opportunities for interacting with people, objects, or places in the environment. Infants perceive sucking, grasping, noisemaking, and many other affordances of objects at an early age. (p. 173)

13. A **visual cliff** is an experimental apparatus that provides the illusion of a drop between one surface and another. (p. 174)

14. **Dynamic perception,** a universal principle of infant perception, is perception that is primed to focus on movement and change. (p. 174)

15. **People preference,** a universal principle of infant perception, is the innate attraction that human babies have to other humans. (p. 174)

16. A **reminder session** any perceptual experience of some aspect of an event that triggers the entire memory of the event. (p. 176)

17. **Child-directed speech** is a form of speech used by adults when talking to infants. It is simplified, it has a higher pitch, and it is repetitive; also called *baby talk* or *motherese*. (p. 178)

18. **Babbling,** which begins at about 6 or 7 months, is characterized by the extended repetition of certain syllables (such as "ma-ma"). (p. 179)

19. The **naming explosion** refers to the dramatic increase in the infant's vocabulary that begins at about 18 months of age. (p. 180)

20. Another characteristic of infant speech is the use of the **holophrase,** in which a single word is used to convey a complete thought. (p. 181)

21. The **grammar** of a language includes rules of word order, verb forms, and all other methods used to communicate meaning apart from words themselves. (p. 181)

22. According to Chomsky, children possess an innate **language acquisition device (LAD),** a hypothesized brain structure that enables them to acquire language, including the basic aspects of grammar. (p. 184)

Cross-Check

ACROSS	DOWN
1. grammar	2. adaptation
7. fMRI	3. tertiary
8. primary	4. holophrase
9. secondary	5. little scientist
10. dynamic	6. affordance
12. habituation	10. deferred
13. baby talk	11. babbling
15. naming explosion	14. LAD

Chapter Seven

The First Two Years: Psychosocial Development

Chapter Overview

Chapter 7 describes the emotional and social life of the developing person during the first two years. It begins with a description of the infant's emerging emotions and how they reflect mobility and social awareness. Two emotions, contentment and distress, are apparent at birth and are soon joined by anger and fear. As self-awareness develops, many new emotions emerge, including embarrassment, shame, guilt, and pride.

The second section explores the psychoanalytic theories of Freud and Erikson along with behaviorist, cognitive, epigenetic systems, and sociocultural theories, which help us understand how the infant's emotional and behavioral responses begin to take on the various patterns that form personality. Temperament, which affects later personality and is primarily inborn, is influenced by the individual's interactions with the environment.

The third section explores the social context in which emotions develop. By referencing their caregivers' signals, infants learn when and how to express their emotions. Emotions and relationships are then examined from a different perspective—that of parent–infant interaction. Videotaped studies of parents and infants, combined with laboratory studies of attachment, have greatly expanded our understanding of psychosocial development. This section concludes by exploring the impact of day care on infants.

NOTE: Answer guidelines for all Chapter 7 questions begin on page 111.

Guided Study

The text chapter should be studied one section at a time. Before you read, preview each section by skimming it, noting headings and boldface items. Then read the appropriate section objectives from the following outline. Keep these objectives in mind and, as you read the chapter section, search for the information that will enable you to meet each objective. Once you have finished a section, write out answers for its objectives.

Emotional Development (pp. 192–196)

1. Describe the basic emotions expressed by infants during the first days and months.

2. Describe the main developments in the emotional life of the child between 6 months and 2 years.

3. Discuss the links between the infant's emerging self-awareness and his or her continuing emotional development.

Theories About Early Psychosocial Development
(pp. 196–203)

4. Describe Freud's psychosexual stages of infant development.

5. Describe Erikson's psychosocial stages of infant development.

6. Contrast the perspectives of behaviorism and cognitive theory regarding psychosocial development in the first two years of life.

7. Discuss the epigenetic theory explanation of the origins, characteristics, and role of temperament in the child's psychosocial development.

8. Discuss the sociocultural view regarding the influence of culture on development, focusing on the different parenting practices.

The Development of Social Bonds (pp. 203–215)

9. (text and Thinking Like a Scientist) Describe the synchrony of parent–infant interaction during the first year and the still-face technique for measuring it, and discuss the significance of synchrony for the developing person.

10. Define attachment, explain how it is measured and how it is influenced by context, and identify factors that predict secure or insecure attachment.

11. Discuss the concept of social referencing, noting the difference in how the infant interacts with mother and father.

12. Discuss the impact of nonrelative care on young children, and identify the factors that define high-quality day care.

Conclusions in Theory and Practice (pp. 215–217)

13. State several conclusions that can be drawn from research on early psychosocial development.

Chapter Review

When you have finished reading the chapter, work through the material that follows to review it. Complete the sentences and answer the questions. As you proceed, evaluate your performance for each section by consulting the answers on page 111. Do not continue with the next section until you understand each answer. If you need to, review or reread the appropriate section in the textbook before continuing.

Introduction and Emotional Development
(pp. 192–196)

1. Psychosocial development includes _____ development and _____ development.

2. The first emotions that can be reliably discerned in infants are _____ and _____ . Other early infant emotions include _____ , _____ , and _____ . Infants' pleasure in seeing faces is first expressed by the _____ _____ , which appears at about _____ weeks.

3. Fully formed fear emerges at about _____ . One expression of this new emotion is _____ _____ , which becomes full-blown by _____ months; another is _____ _____ , or fear of abandonment, which is normal at age _____ year(s) and intensifies by age _____ year(s). During the second year, anger and fear typically _____ (increase/decrease) and become more _____ toward specific things.

4. Toward the end of the second year, the new emotions of _____ , _____ , _____ , and _____ become apparent. These emotions require an awareness of _____ _____ .

5. An important foundation for emotional growth is _____ ; very young infants have no sense of _____ . This emerging sense of "me" and "mine" leads to a new _____ of others.

Briefly describe the nature and findings of the classic rouge-and-mirror experiment on self-awareness in infants.

6. Pride and shame are strongly linked with _____ . Important in this development is children's ability to form their own positive _____ . The best way to build self-esteem is not to _____ young children but to allow them to _____ .

Theories About Early Psychosocial Development
(pp. 196–203)

7. In Freud's theory, development begins with the _____ stage, so named because the _____ is the infant's prime source of gratification and pleasure.

8. According to Freud, in the second year the prime focus of gratification comes from stimulation and control of the bowels. Freud referred to this period as the _____ stage.

Describe Freud's ideas on the importance of early oral experiences to later personality development.

9. The theorist who believed that development occurs through a series of psychosocial crises is _____ . According to his theory, the crisis of infancy is one of

   _____ ,

   whereas the crisis of toddlerhood is one of

   _____ .

10. According to the perspective of _____ , personality is molded through the processes of _____ and _____ of the child's spontaneous behaviors. A strong proponent of this position was _____ .

11. Later theorists incorporated the role of _____ learning, that is, infants' tendency to observe and _____ the personality traits of their parents. The theorist most closely associated with this type of learning is

    _____ .

12. According to cognitive theory, a person's

    _____ , _____ ,

    _____ and _____

    determine his or her perspective on the world. More specifically, infants use their early relationships to build a _____

    _____ that becomes a frame of reference for organizing perceptions and experiences.

13. According to _____ theory, each infant is born with a _____ predisposition to develop certain emotional traits. Among these are the traits of _____ .

14. These traits are similar to _____ . Although these traits are not learned, their expression is influenced by the _____ .

15. The classic long-term study of children's temperament is the _____ . The study found that by 2 to 3 months, infants can be clustered into one of four types: _____ ,

    _____ , _____ ,

    and _____ .

16. The "Big Five" personality traits include

    _____ , _____ ,

    _____ , _____ , and

    _____ .

17. An important factor in healthy psychosocial development is _____

    _____ _____ between the developing child and the caregiving context.

18. According to _____ theory, the entire _____ context can have a major impact on infant–caregiver relationships and the infant's development. An _____ is a theory of child rearing that is specific to a culture or _____ group. As an example, researchers have found that physically close, _____ parenting predicts toddlers who later are more _____ and _____ , in comparison to phyiscally far, _____ parenting, which produces children with the opposite traits.

The Development of Social Bonds (pp. 203–215)

19. The coordinated interaction of response between infant and caregiver is called _____ . Partly through this interaction, infants learn to _____ _____ and to develop some of the basic skills of _____ _____ . It also helps infants express their own _____ . A crucial aspect of this interaction is _____

    _____ .

20. (Thinking Like a Scientist) To study the importance of synchrony to development, researchers use an experimental device, called the _____-_____ technique, in which the caregiver _____ (does/does not) respond to the infant's movements.

21. The emotional bond that develops between slightly older infants and their caregivers is called _____ .

22. Approaching, following, and climbing onto the caregiver's lap are signs of _____-_____ behaviors, while snuggling and holding are signs of _____ -_____ behaviors.

23. An infant who derives comfort and confidence from the secure base provided by the caregiver is displaying _____ _____ (type B). In this type of relationship, the caregiver acts as a _____ _____ _____ from which the child is willing to venture forth.

24. By contrast, _____ _____ is characterized by an infant's fear, anger, or seeming indifference to the caregiver. Two extremes of this type of relationship are _____-_____ (type A) and _____-_____ /_____ (type C).

(text and Table 7.3) Briefly describe three types of insecure attachment.

25. The procedure developed by Mary Ainsworth to measure attachment is called the _____ _____ .

Approximately _____ (what proportion?) of all normal infants tested with this procedure demonstrate secure attachment. When infant–caregiver interactions are inconsistent, infants are classified as _____ .

26. The most troubled infants may be those who are type _____ . Attachment status _____ (can/cannot) change.

State several conditions that promote secure attachment.

State several conditions that promote insecure attachment.

27. The search for information about another person's feelings is called _____ _____ . For infants, this phenomenon is particularly noticeable at _____ .

28. Although early research on psychosocial development focused on _____– _____ relationships, it is clear that other relatives and unrelated people are crucial to the child's development.

29. The social information from fathers tends to be more _____ than that from mothers, who are more _____ and _____ . Fathers are more _____ (proximal/distal) in their parenting than mothers are.

30. Infant day care programs include _____ day care, in which children of various ages are card for in a paid caregiver's home, and _____ day care , in which several paid providers care for children in a designated place. Of the two, _____ day care may be the best option, because these centers are _____ and _____ .

31. Regarding the impact of nonmaternal care on young children, recent research studies have generally found that children _____ _____ .

32. The best predictor of a kindergartner's social skills is _____ .

33. One benefit of day care is the opportunity for toddlers to learn to _____ _____ .

34. (Table 7.5) Researchers have identified five factors that seem essential to high-quality day care:

a. _____

b. _____

c. _____

d. _____

e. _____

35. Early day care may be detrimental when the mother is _____ and the infant spends more than _____ (how many?) hours each week in a poor-quality program.

Conclusions in Theory and Practice (pp. 189–191)

36. Regarding the major theories of development, _____ _____ theory stands out as the best interpretation. Although the first two years are important, early _____ and _____ development is influenced by the _____ behavior, the support provided by the _____ , the quality of _____ _____ , patterns within the child's _____ , and traits that are _____ .

Progress Test 1

Multiple-Choice Questions

Circle your answers to the following questions and check them with the answers on page 112. If your answer is incorrect, read the explanation for why it is incorrect and then consult the appropriate pages of the text (in parentheses following the correct answer).

1. Newborns have two identifiable emotions:
   a. shame and distress.
   b. distress and contentment.
   c. anger and joy.
   d. pride and guilt.

2. Synchrony begins to appear at about what age?
   a. 6 weeks
   b. 2 months
   c. 3 months
   d. 4 months

3. An infant's fear of being left by the mother or other caregiver, called _____ , is most obvious at about _____ .
   a. separation anxiety; 2 to 4 months
   b. stranger wariness; 2 to 4 months
   c. separation anxiety; 9 to 14 months
   d. stranger wariness; 9 to 14 months

4. Social referencing refers to:
   a. parenting skills that change over time.
   b. changes in community values regarding, for example, the acceptability of using physical punishment with small children.
   c. the support network for new parents provided by extended family members.
   d. the infant response of looking to trusted adults for emotional cues in uncertain situations.

5. A key difference between temperament and personality is that:
   a. temperamental traits are learned.
   b. personality includes traits that are primarily learned.
   c. personality is more stable than temperament.
   d. personality does not begin to form until much later, when self-awareness emerges.

6. The concept of a working model is most consistent with:
   a. psychoanalytic theory.
   b. behaviorism.
   c. cognitive theory.
   d. sociocultural theory.

7. Freud's oral stage corresponds to Erikson's crisis of:
   a. orality versus anality.
   b. trust versus mistrust.
   c. autonomy versus shame and doubt.
   d. secure versus insecure attachment.

8. Erikson felt that the development of a sense of trust in early infancy depends on:
   a. the quality of the infant's food.
   b. the child's genetic inheritance.
   c. consistency, continuity, and sameness of experience.
   d. the introduction of toilet training.

9. Keisha is concerned that her 15-month-old daughter, who no longer seems to enjoy face-to-face play, is showing signs of insecure attachment. You tell her:
   a. not to worry; face-to-face play almost disappears toward the end of the first year.
   b. she may be right to worry, because face-to-face play typically increases throughout infancy.
   c. not to worry; attachment behaviors are unreliable until toddlerhood.
   d. that her child is typical of children who spend more than 20 hours in day care each week.

10. "Easy," "slow to warm up," and "difficult" are descriptions of different:
    a. forms of attachment.
    b. types of temperament.
    c. types of parenting.
    d. toddler responses to the Strange Situation.

11. The more physical play of fathers has been described as:
    a. proximal parenting.
    b. distal parenting.
    c. disorganized parenting.
    d. insecure parenting.

12. *Synchrony* is a term that describes:
    a. the carefully coordinated interaction between caregiver and infant.
    b. a mismatch of the temperaments of caregiver and infant.
    c. a research technique involving videotapes.
    d. the concurrent evolution of different species.

13. The emotional tie that develops between an infant and his or her primary caregiver is called:
    a. self-awareness.   c. affiliation.
    b. synchrony.   d. attachment.

14. Research studies using the still-face technique have demonstrated that:
    a. a parent's responsiveness to an infant aids development.
    b. babies become more upset when a parent leaves the room than when the parent's facial expression is not synchonized with the infant's.
    c. beginning at about 2 months, babies become very upset by a still-faced caregiver.
    d. beginning at about 10 months, babies become very upset by a still-faced caregiver.

15. Interest in people, as evidenced by the social smile, appears for the first time when an infant is _____ weeks old.
    a. 3   c. 9
    b. 6   d. 12

True or False Items

Write T (*true*) or F (*false*) on the line in front of each statement.

_____ 1. The major developmental theories all agree that maternal care is better for children than nonmaternal care.

_____ 2. Approximately 25 percent of infants display secure attachment.

_____ 3. A baby at 11 months is likely to display both stranger wariness and separation anxiety.

_____ 4. Emotional development is affected by maturation of conscious awareness.

_____ 5. A securely attached toddler is most likely to stay close to his or her mother even in a familiar environment.

_____ 6. Current research shows that the majority of infants in day care are slow to develop cognitive and social skills.

_____ 7. Infants use their fathers for social referencing when they look for encouragement.

_____ 8. Temperament is genetically determined and is unaffected by environmental factors.

_____ 9. Self-awareness enables toddlers to feel pride as well as guilt.

_____ 10. The expression of genetic tendencies in temperament are influenced by the environment throughout life.

Progress Test 2

Progress Test 2 should be completed during a final chapter review. Answer the following questions after you thoroughly understand the correct answers for the Chapter Review and Progress Test 1.

Multiple-Choice Questions

1. Infant–caregiver interactions that are marked by inconsistency are usually classified as:
   a. disorganized.
   b. insecure-avoidant.
   c. insecure-resistant.
   d. insecure-ambivalent.

2. Freud's anal stage corresponds to Erikson's crisis of:
   a. autonomy versus shame and doubt.
   b. trust versus mistrust.
   c. orality versus anality.
   d. identity versus role confusion.

3. Not until the sense of self begins to emerge do babies realize that they are seeing their own faces in the mirror. This realization usually occurs:
   a. shortly before 3 months.
   b. at about 6 months.
   c. between 15 and 24 months.
   d. after 24 months.

4. When there is goodness of fit, the parents of a slow-to-warm-up boy will:
   a. give him extra time to adjust to new situations.
   b. encourage independence in their son by frequently leaving him for short periods of time.
   c. put their son in regular day care so other children's temperaments will "rub off" on him.
   d. do all of the above.

5. Emotions such as shame, guilt, embarrassment, and pride emerge at the same time that:
   a. the social smile appears.
   b. aspects of the infant's temperament can first be discerned.
   c. self-awareness begins to emerge.
   d. parents initiate toilet training.

6. Research by the NYLS on temperamental characteristics indicates that:
   a. temperament is probably innate.
   b. the interaction of parent and child determines later personality.
   c. parents pass their temperaments on to their children through modeling.
   d. self-awareness contributes to the development of temperament.

7. In the second six months, stranger wariness is a:
   a. result of insecure attachment.
   b. result of social isolation.
   c. normal emotional response.
   d. setback in emotional development.

8. The caregiving environment can affect a child's temperament through:
   a. the child's temperamental pattern and the demands of the home environment.
   b. parental expectations.
   c. both a. and b.
   d. neither a. nor b.

9. While observing mothers playing with their infants in a playroom, you notice one mother who often teases her son, ignores him when he falls down, and tells him to "hush" when he cries. Mothers who display these behaviors usually have infants who exhibit which type of attachment?
   a. secure
   b. insecure-avoidant
   c. insecure-resistant
   d. disorganized

10. The later consequences of secure attachment and insecure attachment for children are:
    a. balanced by the child's current rearing circumstances.
    b. irreversible, regardless of the child's current rearing circumstances.
    c. more significant in girls than in boys.
    d. more significant in boys than in girls.

11. The attachment pattern marked by anxiety and uncertainty is:
    a. insecure-avoidant.
    b. insecure-resistant/ambivalent.
    c. disorganized.
    d. type B.

12. Compared with mothers, fathers are more likely to:
    a. engage in noisier, more boisterous play.
    b. encourage intellectual development in their children.
    c. encourage social development in their children.
    d. read to their toddlers.

13. Like Freud, Erikson believed that:
    a. problems arising in early infancy last a lifetime.
    b. inability to resolve a conflict in infancy may result in later fixation.
    c. human development can be viewed in terms of psychosexual stages.
    d. all of the above are true.

14. Which of the following is an example of social learning?
    a. Sue discovers that a playmate will share a favorite toy if she asks politely.
    b. Jon learns that other children are afraid of him when he raises his voice.
    c. Zach develops a hot temper after seeing his father regularly display anger and in turn receive respect from others.
    d. All of these are examples of social learning.

15. Which of the following is *not* true regarding synchrony?
    a. There are wide variations in the frequency of synchrony from baby to baby.
    b. Synchrony appears to be uninfluenced by cultural differences.
    c. The frequency of mother–infant synchrony has varied over historical time.
    d. Parents and infants spend about one hour a day in face-to-face play.

Matching Items

Match each theorist, term, or concept with its corresponding description or definition.

Theorists, Terms, or Concepts

_____ 1. temperament
_____ 2. Erikson
_____ 3. the Strange Situation
_____ 4. synchrony
_____ 5. trust versus mistrust
_____ 6. Freud
_____ 7. social referencing
_____ 8. autonomy versus shame and doubt
_____ 9. self-awareness
_____ 10. Ainsworth
_____ 11. proximity-seeking behaviors
_____ 12. contact-maintaining behaviors

Descriptions or Definitions

a. looking to caregivers for emotional cues
b. the crisis of infancy
c. the crisis of toddlerhood
d. approaching, following, and climbing
e. theorist who described psychosexual stages of development
f. researcher who devised a laboratory procedure for studying attachment
g. laboratory procedure for studying attachment
h. the relatively consistent, basic dispositions inherent in a person
i. clinging and resisting being put down
j. coordinated interaction between parent and infant
k. theorist who described psychosocial stages of development
l. a person's sense of being distinct from others

Thinking Critically About Chapter 7

Answer these questions the day before an exam as a final check on your understanding of the chapter's terms and concepts.

1. In laboratory tests of attachment, when the mother returns to the playroom after a short absence, a securely attached infant is most likely to:
   a. cry and protest the mother's return.
   b. climb into the mother's arms, then leave to resume play.
   c. climb into the mother's arms and stay there.
   d. continue playing without acknowledging the mother.

2. After a scary fall, 18-month-old Miguel looks to his mother to see if he should cry or laugh. Miguel's behavior is an example of:
   a. proximity-seeking behavior.
   b. social referencing.
   c. insecure attachment.
   d. the crisis of trust versus mistrust.

3. Which of the following is a clear sign of an infant's attachment to a particular person?
   a. The infant turns to that person when distressed.
   b. The infant protests when that person leaves a room.
   c. The infant may cry when strangers appear.
   d. They are all signs of infant attachment.

4. If you had to predict a newborn baby's personality "type" solely on the basis of probability, which classification would be the most likely?
   a. easy
   b. slow-to-warm-up
   c. difficult
   d. hard to classify.

5. Professor Kipketer believes that infants' emotions are molded as their parents reinforce or punish their behaviors. Professor Kipketer evidently is a proponent of:
   a. cognitive theory.
   c. epigenetic theory.
   b. behaviorism.
   d. sociocultural theory.

6. Monica, who recently read a newspaper headline stating that "low-income infants are more likely to be insecurely attached to their mothers," is concerned that her own state of poverty will adversely influence any children she might have. You wisely tell her that:
   a. attachment status is determined by a mother's overt responses to an infant's attempts at synchrony and attachment.
   b. the correlation between income and attachment is due to the fact that most low-income mothers are clinically depressed.
   c. insecure attachment has not been shown to adversely influence a child's later development.
   d. all of the above are true.

7. Concluding her report on the impact of day care on young children, Deborah notes that infants are likely to become insecurely attached if:
   a. their own mothers are insensitive caregivers.
   b. the quality of day care is poor.
   c. more than 20 hours per week are spent in day care.
   d. all of the above are true.

8. Mashiyat, who advocates epigenetic theory in explaining the origins of personality, points to research evidence that:
   a. infants are born with definite and distinct temperaments that can change.
   b. early temperamental traits almost never change.
   c. an infant's temperament does not begin to clearly emerge until 2 years of age.
   d. temperament appears to be almost completely unaffected by the social context.

9. Kalil's mother left him alone in the room for a few minutes. When she returned, Kalil seemed indifferent to her presence. According to Mary Ainsworth's research with children in the Strange Situation, Kalil is probably:
   a. a normal, independent infant.
   b. an abused child.
   c. insecurely attached.
   d. securely attached.

10. Connie and Lev, who are first-time parents, are concerned because their 1-month-old baby is difficult to care for and hard to soothe. They are worried that they are doing something wrong. You inform them that their child is probably that way because:
    a. they are reinforcing the child's tantrum behaviors.
    b. they are not meeting some biological need of the child's.
    c. of his or her inherited temperament.
    d. at 1 month of age all children are difficult to care for and hard to soothe.

11. Two-year-old Anita and her mother visit a day care center. Seeing an interesting toy, Anita runs a few steps toward it, then stops and looks back to see if her mother is coming. Anita's behavior illustrates:
    a. the crisis of autonomy versus shame and doubt.
    b. synchrony.
    c. dyssynchrony.
    d. social referencing.

12. Felix has a biting, sarcastic manner. Freud would probably say that Felix is:
    a. anally expulsive.
    b. anally retentive.
    c. fixated in the oral stage.
    d. experiencing the crisis of trust versus mistrust.

13. A researcher at the child development center places a dot on an infant's nose and watches to see if the infant reacts to her image in a mirror by touching her nose. Evidently, the researcher is testing the child's:
    a. attachment.
    c. self-awareness.
    b. temperament.
    d. social referencing.

14. Four-month-old Carl and his 13-month-old sister Carla are left in the care of a babysitter. As their parents are leaving, it is to be expected that:
    a. Both Carl and Carla will become very upet as their parents leave.
    b. Carl will become more upset over his parents' departure than will Carla.
    c. Carla will become more upset over her parents' departure than will Carl.
    d. Neither Carl nor Carla will become very upset as their parents leave.

15. Dr. Hidalgo believes that infants use their early relationships to develop a set of assumptions that become a frame of reference for later experiences. Dr. Hidalgo evidently is a proponent of:

a. cognitive theory.
c. epigenetic theory.
b. behaviorism.
d. sociocultural theory.

Key Terms

Using your own words, write a brief definition or explanation of each of the following terms on a separate piece of paper.

1. social smile
2. stranger wariness
3. separation anxiety
4. self-awareness
5. trust versus mistrust
6. autonomy versus shame and doubt
7. social learning
8. working model
9. temperament
10. goodness of fit
11. ethnotheory
12. proximal parenting
13. distal parenting
14. synchrony
15. still-face technique
16. attachment
17. secure attachment
18. insecure-avoidant attachment
19. insecure-resistant/ambivalent attachment
20. Strange Situation
21. disorganized attachment
22. social referencing
23. family day care
24. center day care

ANSWERS
CHAPTER REVIEW

1. emotional; social
2. distress; contentment; curiosity; pleasure; anger; social smile; 6

3. 9 months; stranger wariness; 1; 2; separation anxiety; 1; 2; decrease; targeted
4. pride, shame, embarrassment, guilt; other people
5. self-awareness; self; consciousness

In the classic self-awareness experiment, babies look in a mirror after a dot of rouge is put on their nose. If the babies react to the mirror image by touching their nose, it is clear they know they are seeing their own face. Most babies demonstrate this self-awareness between 15 and 24 months of age.

6. self-concept; self-evaluations; praise; accomplish things that make them feel proud
7. oral; mouth
8. anal

Freud believed that the oral and anal stages are fraught with potential conflict that can have long-term consequences for the infant. If nursing is a hurried or tense event, for example, the child may become fixated at the oral stage, excessively eating, drinking, chewing, biting, or talking in quest of oral satisfaction. Similarly, if toilet training is overly strict or begins too soon, the child may become fixated and, as an adult, have an unusually strong need for self-control and regularity.

9. Erikson; trust versus mistrust; autonomy versus shame and doubt
10. behaviorism; reinforcement; punishment; John Watson
11. social; imitate; Albert Bandura
12. beliefs; thoughts; perceptions; memories; working model
13. epigenetic; genetic; temperament
14. personality; environment
15. New York Longitudinal Study (NYLS); easy; difficult; slow to warm up; hard to classify
16. openness; conscientiousness; extroversion; agreeableness; neuroticism
17. goodness of fit
18. sociocultural; social; ethnotheory; ethnic; proximal; self-aware; compliant; distal
19. synchrony; read other people's emotions; social interaction; feelings; reciprocal imitation
20. still-face; does not
21. attachment
22. proximity-seeking; contact-maintaining
23. secure attachment; base for exploration

24. insecure attachment; insecure-avoidant; insecure-resistant/ambivalent

Some infants are avoidant: They engage in little interaction with their mother before and after her departure. Others are anxious and resistant: They cling nervously to their mother, are unwilling to explore, cry loudly when she leaves, and refuse to be comforted when she returns. Others are disorganized: They show an inconsistent mixture of behavior toward the mother.

25. Strange Situation; two-thirds; disorganized

26. D; can

Secure attachment is more likely if the parent is sensitive and responsive to the infant's needs, the relationship is high in synchrony, the infant has an "easy" temperament, the parents are not highly stressed, and the parents have a "working model" of secure attachment from their own parents.

Insecure attachment is more likely if the child is mistreated or has a "difficult" or "slow-to-warm-up" temperament; the mother is mentally ill; the parents are highly stressed, intrusive, controlling, or actively alcoholic.

27. social referencing; mealtime

28. mother–infant

29. encouraging; cautious; protective; proximal

30. family; center; center; licensed; inspected

31. are not harmed by, and sometimes benefit from, professional day care

32. the mother's warmth and sensitivity

33. express emotions

34. (a) adequate attention to each child; (b) encouragement of sensorimotor and language development; (c) attention to health and safety; (d) well-trained and professional caregivers; (e) warm and reponsive caregivers

35. insensitive; 20

36. no single; emotional; social; mothers'; father; day care; culture; inborn

PROGRESS TEST 1

Multiple-Choice Questions

1. **b.** is the answer. (p. 192)

   a., c., & d. These emotions emerge later in infancy, at about the same time as self-awareness emerges.

2. **c.** is the answer. (pp. 203–204)

3. **c.** is the answer. (p. 193)

4. **d.** is the answer. (p. 210)

5. **b.** is the answer. (p. 198)

6. **c.** is the answer. (p. 198)

7. **b.** is the answer. (pp. 196, 197)

   a. Orality and anality refer to personality traits that result from fixation in the oral and anal stages, respectively.

   c. According to Erikson, this is the crisis of toddlerhood, which corresponds to Freud's anal stage.

   d. This is not a developmental crisis in Erikson's theory.

8. **c.** is the answer. (p. 197)

9. **a.** is the answer. (p. 206)

   c. Attachment behaviors are reliably found during infancy.

   d. There is no indication that the child attends day care.

10. **a.** is the answer. Another type is "hard to classify." (p. 199)

    b. "Secure" and "insecure" are different forms of attachment.

    c. The chapter does not describe different types of parenting.

    d. The Strange Situation is a test of attachment rather than of temperament.

11. **a.** is the answer. (p. 202)

    c. & d. These terms were not used to describe parenting styles.

12. **a.** is the answer. (p. 204)

13. **d.** is the answer. (p. 206)

    a. Self-awareness refers to the infant's developing sense of "me and mine."

    b. Synchrony describes the coordinated interaction between infant and caregiver.

    c. Affiliation describes the tendency of people at any age to seek the companionship of others.

14. **b.** is the answer. In fact just the opposite is true. (p. 205)

    c. & d. Not usually at 2 months, but clearly at 6 months, babies become very upset by a still-faced caregiver.

15. **b.** is the answer. (p. 193)

True or False Items

1. F   Sociocultural theorists contend that the entire social context can have an impact on the infant's development. (p. 200)

2. F   Almost two-thirds of infants display secure attachment. (p. 208)

3. T (p. 193)

4. T (p. 194)

5. F   A securely attached toddler is most likely to explore the environment, the mother's presence being enough to give him or her the courage to do so. (pp. 207–208)

6. F   Researchers believe that high-quality day care is not likely to harm the child. In fact, it is thought to be beneficial to the development of cognitive and social skills. (pp. 212–213)

7. T (p. 211)

8. F   Temperament is a product of both nature and nurture. (p. 198)

9. T (p. 194)

10. T (p. 198)

PROGRESS TEST 2

Multiple-Choice Questions

1. **a.** is the answer. (p. 208)

2. **a.** is the answer. (pp. 196, 197)

3. **c.** is the answer. (pp. 194–195)

4. **a.** is the answer. (p. 200)

5. **c.** is the answer. (p. 194)

   a. & b. The social smile, as well as temperamental characteristics, emerge well before the first signs of self-awareness.

   d. Contemporary developmentalists link these emotions to self-consciousness, rather than any specific environmental event such as toilet training.

6. **a.** is the answer. (p. 199)

   b. & c. Although environment, especially parents, affects temperamental tendencies, the study noted that temperament was established within 3 months of birth.

   d. Self-awareness is not a temperamental characteristic.

7. **c.** is the answer. (p. 193)

8. **c.** is the answer. (p. 200)

9. **d.** is the answer. (p. 208)

10. **a.** is the answer. (pp. 208–209)

    c. & d. The text does not suggest that the consequences of secure and insecure attachment differ in boys and girls.

11. **b.** is the answer. (p. 207)

    a. Insecure-avoidant attachment is marked by behaviors that indicate an infant is uninterested in a caregiver's presence or departure.

    c. Disorganized attachment is marked only by the inconsistency of infant–caregiver behaviors.

    d. Type B, or secure attachment, is marked by behaviors that indicate an infant is using a caregiver as a base from which to explore the environment.

12. **a.** is the answer. (p. 212)

13. **a.** is the answer. (p. 197)

    b. & c. Freud alone would have agreed with these statements.

14. **c.** is the answer. (p. 197)

    a. & b. Social learning involves learning by observing others. In these examples, the children are learning directly from the consequences of their own behavior.

15. **b.** is the answer. (p. 205)

Matching Items

1. h (p. 198)	5. b (p. 197)	9. l (p. 194)
2. k (p. 197)	6. e (p. 196)	10. f (p. 206)
3. g (p. 207)	7. a (p. 210)	11. d (p. 206)
4. j (p. 204)	8. c (p 197)	12. i (p. 206)

THINKING CRITICALLY ABOUT CHAPTER 7

1. **b.** is the answer. (pp. 207–208)

   a., c., & d. These responses are more typical of insecurely attached infants.

2. **b.** is the answer. (p. 210)

3. **d.** is the answer. (pp. 207–208)

4. **a.** is the answer. About 40 percent of young infants can be described as "easy." (p. 199)

   b. About 15 percent of infants are described as "slow to warm up."

   c. About 10 percent of infants are described as "difficult."

   d. About 35 percent are described as "hard to classify."

5. **b.** is the answer. (p. 197)

   a. Cognitive theorists focus on a person's thoughts and values.

b. Epigenetic theory explores the relative effects of nature and nurture on behavior.

d. Sociocultural theory explores the entire social context.

6. **a.** is the answer. (pp. 208–209)

7. **d.** is the answer. (pp. 213–214)

8. **a.** is the answer. (p. 198)

   b. Although temperament is genetic in origin, early temperamental traits *can* change.

   c. Temperament is apparent shortly after birth.

   d. As the person develops, the social context exerts a strong effect on temperament.

9. **c.** is the answer. (pp. 207, 208)

   a. & d. When their mothers return following an absence, securely attached infants usually re-establish social contact (with a smile or by climbing into their laps) and then resume playing.

   b. There is no evidence in this example that Kalil is an abused child.

10. **c.** is the answer. (p. 199)

    a. & b. There is no evidence in the question that the parents are reinforcing tantrum behavior or failing to meet some biological need of the child's.

    d. On the contrary, about 50 percent of infants are "easy" in temperamental style.

11. **d.** is the answer. (p. 210)

    a. According to Erikson, this is the crisis of toddlerhood.

    b. This describes a moment of coordinated and mutually responsive interaction between a parent and an infant.

    c. Dyssynchrony occurs when the coordinated pace and timing of a synchronous interaction are temporarily lost.

12. **c.** is the answer. (p. 196)

    a. & b. In Freud's theory, a person who is fixated in the anal stage exhibits messiness and disorganization or compulsive neatness.

    d. Erikson, rather than Freud, proposed crises of development.

13. **c.** is the answer. (pp. 194–195)

14. **b.** is the answer. The fear of being left by a caregiver (separation anxiety) is most obvious at 9 to 14 months. For this reason, 4-month-old Carl can be expected to become less upset than his older sister. (p. 178)

15. **a.** is the answer. (p. 198)

KEY TERMS

1. A **social smile** occurs when an infant smiles in response to a human face. (p. 193)

2. A common early fear, **stranger wariness** (also called fear of strangers) is first noticeable at about 6 months. (p. 193)

3. **Separation anxiety**, which is the infant's fear of being left by the mother or other caregiver, is usually strongest at 9 to 14 months. (p. 193)

4. **Self-awareness** refers to a person's realization that he or she is a distinct individual whose body, mind, and actions are separate from other people. Self-awareness makes possible many new self-conscious emotions, including shame, guilt, embarrassment, and pride. (p. 194)

5. In Erikson's theory, the crisis of infancy is one of **trust versus mistrust,** in which the infant learns whether the world is essentially a secure place in which basic needs will be met. (p. 197)

6. In Erikson's theory, the crisis of toddlerhood is one of **autonomy versus shame and doubt,** in which toddlers strive to rule their own actions and bodies. (p. 197)

7. **Social learning** is learning by observing others. (p. 197)

8. According to cognitive theory, infants use social relationships to develop a set of assumptions called a **working model** that organizes their perceptions and experiences. (p. 198)

9. **Temperament** refers to the "constitutionally based individual differences" in emotions, activity, and self-control. (p. 198)

10. **Goodness of fit** is the pattern of smooth interaction between the individual and the social context. (p. 200)

11. An **ethnotheory** is a theory of child rearing that reflects a specific ethnic group or culture. (p. 201)

12. **Proximal parenting** practices involve close physical contact between child and parent. (p. 202)

13. **Distal parenting** practices focus more on intellectual development than on physical development. (p. 202)

14. **Synchrony** refers to the coordinated, rapid, and smooth interaction between caregiver and infant that helps infants learn to express and read emotions. (p. 204)

15. The **still-face technique** is an experimental device in which an adult keeps his or her face unmoving and without expression in face-to-face interaction with an infant. (p. 205)

16. According to Mary Ainsworth, **attachment** is the enduring emotional tie that a person forms with another. (p. 206)

17. A **secure attachment** is one in which the infant derives comfort and confidence from the base of exploration provided by a caregiver. (p. 207)

18. **Insecure-avoidant attachment** is the pattern of attachment in which the infant seems uninterested in the caregiver's presence or departure. (p. 207)

19. **Insecure-resistant/ambivalent attachment** is the pattern of attachment in which an infant resists active exploration, becomes very upset when the caregiver leaves, and both resists and seeks contact when the caregiver returns. (p. 207)

20. The **Strange Situation** is a laboratory procedure developed by Mary Ainsworth for assessing attachment. Infants are observed in a playroom, in several successive episodes, while the caregiver (usually the mother) and a stranger move in and out of the room. (p. 207)

21. **Disorganized attachment** is the pattern of attachment that is neither secure nor insecure and is marked by inconsistent infant–caregiver interactions. (p. 208)

22. When infants engage in **social referencing,** they are looking to trusted adults for emotional cues on how to interpret uncertain situations. (p. 210)

23. **Family day care** is regular care provided for six or fewer children in a paid caregiver's home. (p. 212)

24. **Center day care** is regular care provided for children by several paid caregivers in a place designed for that purpose. (p. 212)

Chapter Eight

The Play Years: Biosocial Development

Chapter Overview

Chapter 8 introduces the developing person between the ages of 2 and 6. This period is called the play years, emphasizing the central importance of play to the biosocial, cognitive, and psychosocial development of preschoolers.

The chapter begins by outlining growth rates and the changes in shape that occur from ages 2 through 6. This is followed by a look at brain growth and development and its role in the development of physical and cognitive abilities. The developing limbic system is also described, along with its role in the expression and regulation of emotions during the play years. A description of the acquisition of gross and fine motor skills follows, noting that mastery of such skills develops steadily during the play years along with intellectual growth. The section concludes with a discussion of the important issues of injury control and accidents, the major cause of childhood death except in times of famine.

The last section is an in-depth exploration of child maltreatment, including its prevalence, contributing factors, consequences for future development, treatment, and prevention.

NOTE: Answer guidelines for all Chapter 8 questions begin on page 127.

Guided Study

The text chapter should be studied one section at a time. Before you read, preview each section by skimming it, noting headings and boldface items. Then read the appropriate section objectives from the following outline. Keep these objectives in mind and, as you read the chapter section, search for the information that will enable you to meet each objective. Once you have finished a section, write out answers for its objectives.

Body Changes (pp. 223–227)

1. Describe normal physical growth during the play years, and account for variations in height and weight.

2. Describe changes in eating habits during the preschool years.

Brain Development (pp. 227–234)

3. Discuss the processes of myelination and lateralization and their effect on development during the play years.

4. Describe the development of the prefrontal cortex during the play years and its role in impulse control, appropriate focus, and emotional balance.

8. Discuss the significance of artistic expression and drawing during the play years.

5. Describe the development of the limbic system during the play years and its role in emotional expression and regulation.

9. Identify several factors that contribute to variation in the risk of accidental injury among children.

6. Discuss factors that can lead to brain damage in the young child.

10. Explain what is meant by *injury control,* and differentiate three levels of prevention that have significantly reduced accidental death rates for children.

Motor Skills and Hazards (pp. 234–241)

7. Distinguish between gross and fine motor skills, and discuss the development of each during the play years.

Child Maltreatment (pp. 241–250)

11. Identify the various categories of child maltreatment, and discuss several factors that contribute to its occurrence.

12. Describe warnings signs of child maltreatment.

13. Discuss the consequences of child maltreatment.

14. Discuss foster care, kinship care, and adoption as intervention options in cases of child maltreatment.

Chapter Review

When you have finished reading the chapter, work through the material that follows to review it. Complete the sentences and answer the questions. As you proceed, evaluate your performance for each section by consulting the answers on page 127. Do not continue with the next section until you understand each answer. If you need to, review or reread the appropriate section in the textbook before continuing.

Body Changes (pp. 223–227)

1. During the preschool years, from age _____ to _____, children add almost _____ in height and gain about _____ in weight per year. By age 6, the average child in a developed nation weighs about _____ and measures _____ in height. In numbers, _____ are more useful than _____ in monitoring growth.

2. The range of normal physical development is quite _____ (narrow/broad).

3. In multiethnic countries, children of _____ descent tend to be tallest, followed by _____, then _____, and then _____. The impact of _____ patterns on physical development can be seen in families in South Asia and India, where _____ (which gender?) are better fed and cared for than the other sex.

4. Household _____ also affects physical growth. In Brazil, for instance, whereas low income once correlated with _____, today it also correlates with more _____. Other factors in physical growth include _____ _____, _____, _____, and _____.

5. During the preschool years, children need _____ (fewer/more) calories per pound than they did as infants.

6. The most prevalent nutritional problem in early childhood is an insufficient intake of _____, _____, and _____. An additional problem for American children is that they consume too many _____.

7. Young children generally insist that a particular experience occur in an exact sequence and manner, a phenomenon called _____ _____. By age _____, this rigidity fades.

Brain Development (pp. 227–234)

8. By age 2, most pruning of the brain's _____ has occurred and the brain weighs _____ percent of its adult weight. By age 5, the brain has attained about _____ percent of its adult weight;

by age 7 it is almost _____ percent.

9. Part of the brain's increase in size during childhood is due to the continued proliferation of _____ pathways and the ongoing process of _____ . This process, which is influenced by _____ , is essential for communication that is _____ and _____ . During the play years, this process proceeds most rapidly in brain areas dedicated to _____ and _____ .

10. The band of nerve fibers that connects the right and left sides of the brain, called the _____ _____ , grows and _____ rapidly during the play years. This helps children better coordinate functions that involve _____ _____ .

11. The two sides of the body and brain _____ (are/are not) identical. The specialization of the two sides of the body and brain is called _____ . Throughout the world, societies are organized to favor _____-handedness.

12. The left hemisphere of the brain controls the _____ side of the body and contains areas dedicated to _____ , _____ , and _____ . The right hemisphere controls the _____ side of the body and contains brains areas dedicated to _____ and _____ impulses.

13. The corpus callosum _____ (is/is not) fully developed in young children, which partly explains why their behaviors sometimes are _____ .

14. Training one side of the body is easier _____ (before/after) the process of _____ is complete. Thus, damage to the left side of the brain, where most _____ functions are located, is more serious in _____ than in _____ .

15. The final part of the brain to reach maturity is the _____ _____ . Development of this brain area increases throughout _____ .

16. Two signs of an undeveloped prefrontal cortex are _____ and _____ , which is the tendency to stick to a thought or action even after it has become inappropriate.

17. The part of the brain that plays a crucial role in the expression and regulation of emotions is the _____ _____ . Within this system is the _____ , which registers emotions, particularly _____ and _____ . Next to this area is the _____ , which is a central processor of _____ , especially of _____ . Another structure in this brain region is the_____ , which produces _____ that activate other parts of the brain and body.

18. The amygdala's reaction to stress during the preschool years is guided by three other parts of the brain: the _____ , the _____ , and the _____ _____ .

19. The life-threatening condition that occurs when an infant his held by the shoulders and quickly shaken back and forth is called _____ _____ _____ . The preschooler's developing brain can also be adversely affected by mothers who are clinically _____ and unable to provide normal encouragement and emotional guidance. A third problem occurs in children who are in group residential homes; the emotions and brain activity of these children are _____ .

Motor Skills and Hazards (pp. 234–241)

20. Large body movements such as running, climbing, jumping, and throwing are called _____ _____ skills. These skills, which improve dramatically during the preschool years, require guided

_____ , as well as a certain level of _____ _____ and _____ .

21. Most children learn these skills from _____ (other children/parents).

22. Skills that involve small body movements, such as pouring liquids and cutting food, are called _____ _____ skills. Preschoolers have greater difficulty with these skills primarily because they have not developed the _____ control, patience, or _____ needed—in part because the _____ of the central nervous system is not complete.

23. Fine motor skills are useful in almost all forms of _____ _____ , yet such skills are far from perfect. Fortunately, young children tend not to be _____ . The pictures children draw often reveal their unique _____ and _____ .

24. Except in famine, the leading cause of childhood death is _____ _____ , and the rate is _____ (higher/lower) for boys than for girls.

25. Not until age _____ does any disease become a greater cause of mortality.

26. Instead of "accident prevention," many experts speak of _____ _____ (or _____ _____), an approach based on the belief that most accidents _____ (are/are not) preventable.

27. Preventive community actions that reduce everyone's chance of injury are called

_____ _____ .

Preventive actions that avert harm in the immediate situation constitute _____ _____ . Actions aimed at minimizing the impact of an adverse event that has already occurred constitute _____ _____ .

28. The first strategy that most people advocate to prevent injury to young children is _____ _____ . However, public research finds that _____ that apply to everyone are more effective. One risk factor in accident rates is _____ , with children in the _____ countries being more likely than other children to die from _____ or an _____ .

Child Maltreatment (pp. 241–250)

29. Until about 1960, the concept of child maltreatment was mostly limited to rare and _____ outbursts of a mentally disturbed stranger. Today, it is known that most perpetrators of maltreatment are the child's

_____ .

30. Intentional harm to, or avoidable endangerment of, someone under age 18 defines child _____ . Actions that are deliberately harmful to a child's well-being are classified as _____ . A failure to act appropriately to meet a child's basic needs is classified as

_____ .

31. Since 1993, the ratio of the number of cases of _____ _____ , in which authorities have been officially notified, to cases of _____ _____ , which have been reported, investigated, and verified, has been about _____ (what ratio?).

32. One sign of maltreatment is called _____ _____ , in which an infant or young child gains little or no _____ , despite apparently normal health. Another sign is _____ , in which an older child seems too nervous to concentrate on anything. These phenomena are symptoms of _____ _____ _____ _____ , which was first described in combat victims. Children can also suffer from _____ neglect or from _____ neglect.

33. Abused and neglected children are more often _____ , _____ , and _____ .

Describe other deficits of children who have been maltreated.

34. Public policy measures and other efforts designed to prevent maltreatment from ever occurring are called _____ _____ .
An approach that focuses on spotting and treating the first symptoms of maltreatment is called _____ _____ . Last-ditch measures such as removing a child from an abusive home, jailing the perpetrator, and so forth constitute _____

_____ .

35. Once maltreatment has been substantiated, the first priority is _____

_____ for the child's long-term care.

36. Some children are officially removed from their parents and placed in a _____

_____ arrangement with another adult or family who is paid to nurture them.

37. In another type of foster care, called

_____ _____ , a relative of the maltreated child becomes the approved caregiver. A final option is

_____ .

Progress Test 1

Multiple-Choice Questions

Circle your answers to the following questions and check them with the answers beginning on page 127. If your answer is incorrect, read the explanation for why it is incorrect and then consult the appropriate pages of the text (in parentheses following the correct answer).

1. During the preschool years, the most common nutritional problem in developed countries is:
a. serious malnutrition.
b. excessive intake of sweets.
c. insufficient intake of iron, zinc, and calcium.
d. excessive caloric intake.

2. The brain center for speech is usually located in the:
a. right hemisphere.
b. left hemisphere.
c. corpus callosum.
d. space just below the right ear.

3. Which of the following is an example of tertiary prevention of child maltreatment?
a. removing a child from an abusive home
b. home visitation of families with infants by a social worker
c. new laws establishing stiff penalties for child maltreatment
d. public policy measures aimed at creating stable neighborhoods

4. The brain area that registers emotions is the:
a. hippocampus.
b. hypothalamus.
c. amygdala.
d. prefrontal cortex.

5. Children tend to have too much _____ in their diet, which contributes to _____ .
a. iron; anemia
b. sugar; tooth decay
c. fat; delayed development of fine motor skills
d. carbohydrate; delayed development of gross motor skills

6. Skills that involve large body movements, such as running and jumping, are called:
a. activity-level skills.
b. fine motor skills.
c. gross motor skills.
d. left-brain skills.

7. The brain's ongoing myelination during childhood helps children:
a. control their actions more precisely.
b. react more quickly to stimuli.
c. control their emotions.
d. do all of the above.

8. The leading cause of death in childhood is:
a. accidents.
b. untreated diabetes.
c. malnutrition.
d. iron deficiency anemia.

9. Regarding lateralization, which of the following is *not* true?
a. Some cognitive skills require only one side of the brain.
b. Brain centers for generalized emotional impulses can be found in the right hemisphere.

c. The left hemisphere contains brain areas dedicated to spatial reasoning.

d. The right side of the brain controls the left side of the body.

10. In some countries in Asia and Africa, children are notably shorter than their genetic peers in more affluent nations, primarily as a result of:

a. overfeeding.

b. underfeeding.

c. birth order.

d. regional diseases.

11. The area of the brain that directs and controls the other areas is the:

a. corpus callosum.

b. myelin sheath.

c. prefrontal cortex.

d. temporal lobe.

12. The relationship between accident rate and income can be described as:

a. a positive correlation.

b. a negative correlation.

c. curvilinear.

d. no correlation.

13. Which of the following is true of the corpus callosum?

a. It enables short-term memory.

b. It connects the two halves of the brain.

c. It must be fully myelinated before gross motor skills can be acquired.

d. All of the above are correct.

14. The improvements in eye–hand coordination that allow preschoolers to catch and then throw a ball occur, in part, because:

a. the brain areas associated with this ability become more fully myelinated.

b. the corpus callosum begins to function.

c. fine motor skills have matured by age 2.

d. gross motor skills have matured by age 2.

15. During the school years, inadequate lateralization of the brain and immaturity of the prefrontal cortex may contribute to deficiencies in:

a. cognition.

b. peer relationships.

c. emotional control.

d. all of the above.

True or False Items

Write T (*true*) or F (*false*) on the line in front of each statement.

_____ 1. Growth between ages 2 and 6 results in body proportions more similar to those of an adult.

_____ 2. During childhood, the legs develop faster than any other part of the body.

_____ 3. For most people, the brain center for speech is located in the left hemisphere.

_____ 4. Cultural patterns and household income influence growth.

_____ 5. Memories of when, where, and how a certain fact was learned are quite inaccurate in preschoolers.

_____ 6. Fine motor skills are usually easier for preschoolers to master than are gross motor skills.

_____ 7. Most serious childhood injuries truly are "accidents."

_____ 8. Children often fare as well in kinship care as they do in conventional foster care.

_____ 9. Most child maltreatment does not involve serious physical abuse.

_____ 10. Myelination is essential for basic communication between neurons.

_____ 11. In most developed nations, girls are more vulnerable than boys to serious illness.

Progress Test 2

Progress Test 2 should be completed during a final chapter review. Answer the following questions after you thoroughly understand the correct answers for the Chapter Review and Progress Test 1.

Multiple-Choice Questions

1. Each year from ages 2 to 6, the average child gains and grows, respectively:

a. 2 pounds and 1 inch.

b. 3 pounds and 2 inches.

c. 4½ pounds and 3 inches.

d. 6 pounds and 6 inches.

2. The center for perceiving various types of visual configurations is usually located in the brain's:

a. right hemisphere.

b. left hemisphere.

c. right or left hemisphere.

d. corpus callosum.

3. Regarding handedness, which of the following is *not* true?
   a. Sleeping newborns show a preference for turning their heads rightward or leftward.
   b. Some societies favor left-handed people.
   c. Experience can influence hand development.
   d. Language, customs, tools, and taboos, all illustrate social biases toward right-handedness.

4. The most prevalent disease or condition of young children in developed nations is:
   a. obesity.
   b. tooth decay.
   c. measles.
   d. muscular dystrophy.

5. Seeing her toddler reach for a brightly glowing burner on the stove, Sheila grabs his hand and says, "No, that's very hot." Sheila's behavior is an example of:
   a. primary prevention.
   b. secondary prevention.
   c. tertiary prevention.
   d. none of the above.

6. When parents or caregivers do not provide adequate food, shelter, attention, or supervision, it is referred to as:
   a. abuse.
   b. neglect.
   c. endangering.
   d. maltreatment.

7. Which of the following is true of a developed nation in which many ethnic groups live together?
   a. Ethnic variations in height and weight disappear.
   b. Ethnic variations in stature persist, but are substantially smaller.
   c. Children of African descent tend to be tallest, followed by Europeans, Asians, and Latinos.
   d. Cultural patterns exert a stronger-than-normal impact on growth patterns.

8. Which of the following is an example of perseveration?
   a. 2-year-old Jason sings the same song over and over
   b. 3-year-old Kwame falls down when attempting to kick a soccer ball
   c. 4-year-old Kara pours water very slowly from a pitcher into a glass
   d. None of the above is an example.

9. Which of the following is an example of a fine motor skill?
   a. kicking a ball
   b. running
   c. drawing with a pencil
   d. jumping

10. Children who have been maltreated often:
    a. regard other children and adults as hostile and exploitative.
    b. are less friendly and more aggressive.
    c. are more isolated than other children.
    d. are all of the above.

11. The left half of the brain contains areas dedicated to all of the following *except*:
    a. language.
    b. logic.
    c. analysis.
    d. creative impulses.

12. Most gross motor skills can be learned by healthy children by about age:
    a. 2.   c. 5.
    b. 3.   d. 7.

13. Andrea is concerned because her three-year-old daughter has been having nightmares. Her pediatrician tells her:
    a. not to worry, because nightmares are often caused by increased activity in the amygdala, which is normal during early childhood.
    b. nightmares are a possible sign of an overdeveloped prefrontal cortex.
    c. to monitor her daughter's diet, because nightmares are often caused by too much sugar.
    d. to consult a neurologist, because nightmares are never a sign of healthy development.

14. The brain area that is a central processor for memory is the:
    a. hippocampus.
    b. amygdala.
    c. hypothalamus.
    d. prefrontal cortex.

15. During the play years, children's appetites seem _____ they were in the first two years of life.
    a. larger than
    b. smaller than
    c. about the same as
    d. erratic, sometimes smaller and sometimes larger than

Matching Items

Match each term or concept with its corresponding description or definition.

Terms or Concepts

_____ 1. corpus callosum
_____ 2. gross motor skills
_____ 3. fine motor skills
_____ 4. kinship care
_____ 5. foster care
_____ 6. injury control
_____ 7. right hemisphere
_____ 8. left hemisphere
_____ 9. child abuse
_____ 10. child neglect
_____ 11. primary prevention
_____ 12. secondary prevention
_____ 13. tertiary prevention

Descriptions or Definitions

a. brain area that is primarily responsible for processing language
b. brain area that is primarily responsible for recognizing visual shapes
c. legal placement of a child in the care of someone other than his or her biological parents
d. a form of care in which a relative of a maltreated child takes over from the biological parents
e. procedures to prevent unwanted events or circumstances from ever occurring
f. running and jumping
g. actions that are deliberately harmful to a child's well-being
h. actions for averting harm in the immediate situation
i. painting a picture or tying shoelaces
j. failure to appropriately meet a child's basic needs
k. an approach emphasizing accident prevention
l. actions aimed at reducing the harm that has occurred
m. band of nerve fibers connecting the right and left hemispheres of the brain

Thinking Critically About Chapter 8

Answer these questions the day before an exam as a final check on your understanding of the chapter's terms and concepts.

1. Although 4-year-old Winston otherwise appears to be healthy, he has not gained any weight over the past year. Winston's physical condition is probably best described as:
   a. failure to thrive.
   b. hypervigilance.
   c. shaken baby syndrome.
   d. perseveration.

2. Two-year-old Carrie is hyperactive, often confused between fantasy and reality, and jumps at any sudden noise. Her pediatrician suspects that she is suffering from:
   a. shaken baby syndrome.
   b. failure to thrive.
   c. post-traumatic stress disorder.
   d. child neglect.

3. Following an automobile accident, Amira developed severe problems with her speech. Her doctor believes that the accident injured the _____ of her brain.
   a. left side
   b. right side
   c. communication pathways
   d. corpus callosum

4. Two-year-old Ali is quite clumsy, falls down frequently, and often bumps into stationary objects. Ali most likely:
   a. has a neuromuscular disorder.
   b. has an underdeveloped right hemisphere of the brain.
   c. is suffering from an iron deficiency.
   d. is a normal 2-year-old whose gross motor skills will improve dramatically during the preschool years.

5. Climbing a fence is an example of a:
   a. fine motor skill.   c. circular reaction.
   b. gross motor skill.   d. launching event.

6. To prevent accidental death in childhood, some experts urge forethought and planning for safety and measures to limit the damage of such accidents as do occur. This approach is called:
   a. protective analysis.   c. injury control.
   b. safety education.   d. childproofing.

7. After his daughter scraped her knee, Ben gently cleansed the wound and bandaged it. Ben's behavior is an example of:
   a. primary prevention.
   b. secondary prevention.
   c. tertiary prevention.
   d. none of the above.

8. Which of the following activities would probably be the most difficult for a 5-year-old child?
   a. climbing a ladder
   b. catching a ball
   c. throwing a ball
   d. pouring juice from a pitcher without spilling it

9. Of the following children, the child with the greatest risk of accidental injury is:
   a. 6-year-old Brandon, whose family lives below the poverty line.
   b. 6-year-old Stacey, whose family lives below the poverty line.
   c. 3-year-old Daniel, who comes from an affluent family.
   d. 3-year-old Bonita, who comes from an affluent family.

10. Most child maltreatment:
    a. does not involve serious physical abuse.
    b. involves a rare outburst from the perpetrator.
    c. involves a mentally ill perpetrator.
    d. can be predicted from the victim's personality characteristics.

11. A mayoral candidate is calling for sweeping policy changes to help ensure the well-being of children by promoting home ownership, high-quality community centers, and more stable neighborhoods. If these measures are effective in reducing child maltreatment, they would be classified as:
    a. primary prevention.
    b. secondary prevention.
    c. tertiary prevention.
    d. differential response.

12. A factor that would figure very little into the development of fine motor skills, such as drawing and writing, is:
    a. strength.   c. judgment.
    b. muscular control. d. short, fat fingers.

13. Jason is a 3-year-old child, whose hyperactivity and hypervigilance may be symptoms of:
    a. post-traumatic stress disorder.
    b. an immature corpus callosum.
    c. an immature prefrontal cortex.
    d. normal development.

14. Which aspect of brain development during the play years contributes *most* to enhancing communication among the brain's various specialized areas?
    a. increasing brain weight
    b. proliferation of dendrite networks
    c. myelination
    d. increasing specialization of brain areas

15. Three-year-old Kyle's parents are concerned because Kyle, who generally seems healthy, doesn't seem to have the hefty appetite he had as an infant. Should they be worried?
    a. Yes, because appetite normally increases throughout the preschool years.
    b. Yes, because appetite remains as good during the preschool years as it was earlier.
    c. No, because caloric need is less during the preschool years than during infancy.
    d. There is not enough information to determine whether Kyle is developing normally.

Key Terms

Using your own words, write a brief definition or explanation of each of the following terms on a separate piece of paper.

1. myelination
2. corpus callosum
3. lateralization
4. perseveration
5. amygdala
6. hippocampus
7. hypothalamus
8. shaken baby syndrome
9. injury control/harm reduction
10. primary prevention
11. secondary prevention
12. tertiary prevention
13. child maltreatment
14. child abuse
15. child neglect
16. reported maltreatment
17. substantiated maltreatment

18. failure to thrive
19. post-traumatic stress disorder
20. permanency planning
21. foster care
22. kinship care

ANSWERS
CHAPTER REVIEW

1. 2; 6; 3 inches (about 7 centimeters); 4½ pounds (2 kilograms); 46 pounds (21 kilograms); 46 inches (117 centimeters); percentiles; norms
2. broad
3. African; Europeans; Asians; Latinos; cultural; boys
4. income; underweight; overweight; birth order; sex; disease; region
5. fewer
6. iron; zinc; calcium; sweetened cereals and drinks
7. just right (just so); 6
8. dendrites; 75; 90; 100
9. communication; myelination; experience; fast; complex; memory; reflection
10. corpus callosum; myelinates; both sides of the brain and body
11. are not; lateralization; right
12. right; logic; analysis; language; left; emotional; creative
13. is not; clumsy, wobbly, and slow
14. before; lateralization; language; adults; children
15. prefrontal cortex; adolescence
16. impulsiveness; perseveration
17. limbic system; amygdala; fear; anxiety; hippocampus; memory; locations; hypothalamus; hormones
18. hippocampus; hypothalamus; prefrontal cortex
19. shaken baby syndrome; depressed; flatter
20. gross motor; practice; brain maturation; motivation
21. other children
22. fine motor; muscular; judgment; myelination
23. artistic expression; self-critical; perception; cognition
24. accidental injury; higher
25. 40

26. injury control; harm reduction; are
27. primary prevention; secondary prevention; tertiary prevention
28. parental education; laws; income; poorest; disease; accident
29. sudden; own parents or immediate relatives
30. maltreatment; abuse; neglect
31. reported maltreatment; substantiated maltreatment; 3-to-1
32. failure to thrive; weight; hypervigilance; post-traumatic stress disorder; medical; educational
33. injured; sick; hospitalized

Maltreated children tend to regard other people as hostile and exploitative, and hence are less friendly, more aggressive, and more isolated than other children. As adolescents and adults they often use drugs or alcohol, choose unsupportive relationships, become victims or aggressors, sabotage their own careers, eat too much or too little, and generally engage in self-destructive behavior.

34. primary prevention; secondary prevention; tertiary prevention
35. permanency planning
36. foster care
37. kinship care; adoption

PROGRESS TEST 1
Multiple-Choice Questions

1. **c.** is the answer. (p. 225)

   a. Serious malnutrition is much more likely to occur in infancy or in adolescence than in early childhood.

   b. Although an important health problem, eating too much candy or other sweets is not as serious a problem as this.

   d. Because growth is slower during the preschool years, children need fewer calories per pound during this period.

2. **b.** is the answer. (pp. 228–229)

   a. & d. The right brain is the location of areas associated with generalized emotional and creative impulses.

   c. The corpus callosum helps integrate the functioning of the two halves of the brain; it does not contain areas specialized for particular skills.

3. **a.** is the answer. (p. 248)

   b. This is an example of secondary prevention.

c. & d. These are examples of primary prevention.

4. **c.** is the answer. (p. 231)

   a. The hippocampus is a central processor of memory.

   b. The hypothalamus produces hormones that activate other parts of the brain and body.

   c. The prefrontal cortex is responsible for regulating attention, among other things. It makes formal education more possible in children.

5. **b.** is the answer. (p. 225)

6. **c.** is the answer. (p. 234)

7. **d.** is the answer. (pp. 227–230)

8. **a.** is the answer. (p. 237)

9. **a.** is the answer. (p. 229)

10. **b.** is the answer. (p. 224)

    c. & d. Although birth order and disease are factors in ethnic and cultural differences in growth, in poorer countries they are overshadowed in importance by underfeeding.

11. **c.** is the answer. (p. 229)

    a. The corpus callosum is the band of fibers that link the two halves of the brain.

    b. The myelin sheath is the fatty insulation that surrounds some neurons in the brain.

    d. The temporal lobes of the brain contain the primary centers for hearing.

12. **b.** is the answer. Children with *lower* SES have *higher* accident rates. (p. 241)

13. **b.** is the answer. (p. 228)

    a. The corpus callosum is not directly involved in memory.

    c. Myelination of the central nervous system is important to the mastery of *fine* motor skills.

14. **a.** is the answer. (p. 227)

    b. The corpus callosum begins to function long before the play years.

    c. & d. Neither fine nor gross motor skills have fully matured by age 2.

15. **d.** is the answer. (p. 230)

True or False Items

1. T (p. 223)

2. F   During childhood, the brain develops faster than any other part of the body. (p. 227)

3. T (pp. 228–229)

4. T (p. 224)

5. T (pp. 231–232)

6. F Fine motor skills are more difficult for preschoolers to master than are gross motor skills. (p. 235)

7. F   Most serious accidents involve someone's lack of forethought. (p. 238)

8. T (p. 249)

9. T (p. 243)

10. F   Although myelination is not essential for basic communication between neurons, it is essential for fast and complex communication (p. 227)

11. F   Just the opposite is true. (p. 224)

PROGRESS TEST 2

Multiple-Choice Questions

1. **c.** is the answer. (pp. 223–224)

2. **a.** is the answer. (p. 229)

   b. & c. The left hemisphere of the brain contains areas associated with language development.

   d. The corpus callosum does not contain areas for specific behaviors.

3. **b.** is the answer. All societies favor right-handed people. (p. 228)

4. **b.** is the answer. (p. 225)

5. **b.** is the answer. (pp. 238–239)

6. **b.** is the answer. (p. 242)

   a. Abuse is deliberate, harsh injury to the body.

   c. Endangerment was not discussed.

   d. Maltreatment is too broad a term.

7. **c.** is the answer. (p. 224)

8. **a.** is the answer. (p. 230)

   b. Kicking a ball is a gross motor skill.

   c. Pouring is a fine motor skill.

9. **c.** is the answer. (p. 235)

   a., b., & d. These are gross motor skills.

10. **d.** is the answer. (p. 246)

11. **d.** is the answer. Brain areas that control generalized creative and emotional impulses are found in the right hemisphere. (pp. 228–229)

12. **c.** is the answer. (p. 234)

13. **a.** is the answer. (p. 231)

    b. Nightmares generally occur when activity in the amygdala overwhelms the slowly developing prefrontal cortex.

    c. There is no indication that nightmares are caused by diet.

d. Increased activity in the amygdala is normal during early childhood, as are the nightmares that some children experience.

14. a. is the answer. (p. 231)

b. The amygdala is responsible for registering emotions.

c. The hypothalamus produces hormones that activate other parts of the brain and body.

d. The prefrontal cortex is involved in planning and goal-directed behavior.

15. b. is the answer. (p. 225)

Matching Items

1. m (p. 228)	**6.** k (p. 238)	**11.** e (p. 238)
2. f (p. 234)	**7.** b (p. 228)	**12.** h (p. 238)
3. i (p. 235)	**8.** a (p. 228)	**13.** l (p. 238)
4. d (p. 249)	**9.** g (p. 242)	
5. c (p. 249)	**10.** j (p. 242)	

THINKING CRITICALLY ABOUT CHAPTER 8

1. a. is the answer. (p. 243)

b. Hypervigilance is a condition in which an older child seems too nervous to concentrate on anything.

c. This life-threatening syndrome is generally not accompanied by a failure to gain weight.

d. Perseveration is a child's tendency to stick to a thought or action even after it has become inappropriate.

2. c. is the answer. (p. 244)

a. Shaken baby syndrome is a consequence of maltreatment associated with memory impairment and delays in logical thinking.

b. Failure to thrive is associated with little or no weight gain, despite apparent good health.

d. Child neglect simply refers to failure to meet a child's basic needs. Carrie's specific symptoms may be caused by neglect or maltreatment, but they are most directly signs of PTSD.

3. a. is the answer. In most people, the left hemisphere of the brain contains centers for language, including speech. (pp. 228–229)

4. d. is the answer. (p. 234)

5. b. is the answer. (p. 234)

a. Fine motor skills involve small body movements, such as the hand movements used in painting.

c. & d. These events were not discussed in this chapter.

6. c. is the answer. (p. 238)

7. c. is the answer. (p. 238)

8. d. is the answer. (p. 235)

a., b., & c. Preschoolers find these gross motor skills easier to perform than fine motor skills such as that described in d.

9. a. Impoverished parents care about their children, but their children are much more likely to be seriously injured. (p. 241)

b. & d. Boys, as a group, suffer more injuries than girls do.

10. a. is the answer. (p. 243)

11. a. is the answer. (p. 247)

b. Had the candidate called for measures to spot the early warning signs of maltreatment, this answer would be true.

c. Had the candidate called for jailing those who maltreat children or providing greater counseling and health care for victims, this answer would be true.

d. Differential response is not discussed in the chapter; however, it refers to separate reporting procedures for high- and low-risk families.

12. a. is the answer. Strength is a more important factor in the development of gross motor skills. (pp. 234–235)

13. a. is the answer. (p. 244)

14. b. is the answer. (p. 227)

15. c. is the answer. (p. 225)

KEY TERMS

1. **Myelination** is the process by which axons become coated with myelin, which speeds up the transmission of nerve impulses between neurons. (p. 227)

2. The **corpus callosum** is a long band of nerve fibers that connects the right and left hemispheres of the brain. (p. 228)

3. **Lateralization** refers to the differentiation of the two sides of the brain so that each serves specific, specialized functions. (p. 228)

4. **Perseveration** is the tendency to stick to thoughts or actions, even after they have become useless or inappropriate. In young children, perseveration is a normal product of immature brain functions. (p. 230)

Memory Aid: To *persevere* is to continue, or persist, at something.

5. A part of the brain's limbic system, the **amygdala** registers emotions, particularly fear and anxiety. (p. 231)

6. The **hippocampus** is the part of the brain's limbic system that is a central processor of memory. (p. 231)

7. The **hypothalamus** is the brain structure that produces hormones that activate other parts of the brain and body. (p. 232)

8. A serious condition caused by sharply and quickly shaking an infant to stop his or her crying, **shaken baby syndrome** is associated with severe brain damage that results from internal hemorrhaging and broken neural connections. (p. 233)

9. **Injury control/harm reduction** is the practice of limiting the extent of injuries by anticipating, controlling, and preventing dangerous activities. (p. 238)

10. **Primary prevention** refers to actions that change overall background conditions to prevent some unwanted event or circumstance. (p. 238)

11. **Secondary prevention** involves actions that avert harm in the immediate situation. (p. 238)

12. **Tertiary prevention** involves actions taken after an adverse event occurs, aimed at reducing the harm or preventing disability. (p. 238)

13. **Child maltreatment** is intentional harm to, or avoidable endangerment of, anyone under age 18. (p. 242)

14. **Child abuse** refers to deliberate actions that are harmful to a child's physical, emotional, or sexual well-being. (p. 242)

15. **Child neglect** refers to failure to appropriately meet a child's basic physical, educational, or emotional needs. (p. 242)

16. Child maltreatment that has been officially reported to the police or other authorities is called **reported maltreatment**. (p. 242)

17. Child maltreatment that has been officially reported to authorities, investigated, and verified is called **substantiated maltreatment**. (p. 242)

18. A sign of possible child neglect, **failure to thrive** occurs when an otherwise healthy infant or child gains little or no weight. (p. 243)

19. **Post-traumatic stress disorder (PTSD)** is a syndrome triggered by exposure to an extreme traumatic stressor. In maltreated children, symptoms of PTSD include hyperactivity and hypervigilance, sleeplessness, sudden terror or anxiety, and confusion between fantasy and reality. (p. 244)

20. **Permanency planning** is planning for the long-term care of a child who has experienced substantiated maltreatment. (p. 248)

21. **Foster care** is a legally sanctioned, publicly supported arrangement in which children are removed from their biological parents and temporarily given to another adult to nurture. (p. 249)

22. **Kinship care** is a form of foster care in which a relative of a maltreated child becomes the child's approved caregiver. (p. 249)

Chapter Nine

The Play Years: Cognitive Development

Chapter Overview

In countless everyday instances, as well as in the findings of numerous research studies, young children reveal themselves to be remarkably thoughtful, insightful, and perceptive thinkers whose grasp of the causes of everyday events, memory of the past, and mastery of language are sometimes astonishing. Chapter 9 begins with Piaget's and Vygotsky's views of cognitive development at this age. According to Piaget, young children's thought is prelogical: Between the ages of 2 and 6, they are unable to perform many logical operations and are limited by irreversible, centered, and static thinking. Lev Vygotsky, a contemporary of Piaget's, saw learning as a social activity more than as a matter of individual discovery. Vygotsky focused on the child's "zone of proximal development" and the relationship between language and thought.

The next section focuses on what preschoolers can do, including their emerging abilities to theorize about the world. This leads into a section on language development during the play years. Although young children demonstrate rapid improvement in vocabulary and grammar, they have difficulty with abstractions, metaphorical speech, and certain rules of grammar. A discussion of whether bilingualism in young children is useful concludes the section on language.

The chapter ends with a discussion of preschool education, including a description of "quality" preschool programs and an evaluation of their impact on children.

NOTE: Answer guidelines for all Chapter 9 questions begin on page 141.

Guided Study

The text chapter should be studied one section at a time. Before you read, preview each section by skimming it, noting headings and boldface items. Then read the appropriate section objectives from the following outline. Keep these objectives in mind and, as you read the chapter section, search for the information that will enable you to meet each objective. Once you have finished a section, write out answers for its objectives.

Piaget: Children as Thinkers (pp. 254–257)

1. Describe and discuss the major characteristics of preoperational thought, according to Piaget.

2. Identify the major limitations of Piaget's theory.

Vygotsky: Children as Learners (pp. 257–261)

3. Discuss Vygotsky's views on cognitive development, focusing on the concept of guided participation.

4. Explain the significance of the zone of proximal development and scaffolding in promoting cognitive growth.

5. Describe Vygotsky's view of the role of language in cognitive growth.

Children's Theories (pp. 261–266)

6. Describe how theory-theory supports the idea that children are active learners.

7. Explain the typical young child's theory of mind, noting how it is affected by cultural context.

Language (pp. 266–275)

8. (text and In Person) Describe the development of vocabulary in children, and explain the role of fast-mapping in this process.

9. Describe the development of grammar during the play years, noting limitations in the young child's language abilities.

10. Discuss the advantages and disadvantages of bilingualism at a young age.

Early-Childhood Education (pp. 275–282)

11. Describe variations in early-childhood education programs.

12. Identify the characteristics of a high-quality preschool intervention program, and briefly discuss the benefits of preschool education.

Chapter Review

When you have finished reading the chapter, work through the material that follows to review it. Complete the sentences and answer the questions. As you proceed, evaluate your performance for each section by consulting the answers beginning on page 141. Do not continue with the next section until you understand each answer. If you need to, review or reread the appropriate section in the textbook before continuing.

1. As a result of their experiences with others, young children acquire a _____ _____ _____ that reflects their understanding of how minds work.

Piaget: Children as Thinkers (pp. 254–257)

2. Piaget referred to cognitive development between the ages of 2 and 6 as _____ thought. In his theory, a _____ _____ involves organizing and evaluating ideas and using them to come to some conclusion.

3. Young children's tendency to contemplate the world exclusively from their personal perspective is referred to as _____ . Their tendency think about one aspect of a situation at a time is called _____ . This tendency _____ (is/is not) equated with selfishness. Children also tend to focus on _____ to the exclusion of other attributes of objects and people.

4. Preschoolers' understanding of the world tends to focus on _____ (static/dynamic) reasoning, which means that they tend to think of their world as _____ . A closely related characteristic is _____ —the inability to recognize that reversing a process will restore the original conditions from which the process began.

5. The idea that amount is unaffected by changes in appearance is called _____ . In the case of _____ _____ _____ , preschoolers who are shown pairs of checkers in two even rows and who then observe one row being spaced out will say that the spaced-out row has more checkers.

6. Researchers now believe that Piaget _____ (overestimated/underestimated) conceptual ability during early childhood.

Vygotsky: Children as Learners (pp. 257–261)

7. Much of the research from the sociocultural perspective on the young child's emerging cognition is inspired by the Russian psychologist _____ . According to this perspective, a child is an _____ _____ _____ , whose intellectual growth is stimulated by more skilled members of society.

8. Vygotsky believed that adults can most effectively help a child solve a problem by presenting _____ , by offering _____ for their successes, by maintaining _____ , and by providing _____ . This emphasizes that children's intellectual growth is stimulated by their _____ _____ in _____ experiences of their environment. The critical element in this process is that the mentor and the child _____ to accomplish a task.

9. Vygotsky suggested that for each developing individual there is a _____ _____ _____ _____ , a range of skills that the person can exercise with assistance but is not yet able to perform independently.

10. How and when new skills are developed depends, in part, on the willingness of tutors to _____ the child's participation in learning encounters.

11. Vygotsky believed that language is essential to the advancement of thinking in two crucial ways. The first is through the internal dialogue in which a person talks to himself or herself, called _____ _____ . In preschoolers, this dialogue is likely to be _____ (expressed silently/uttered aloud).

12. According to Vygotsky, another way language advances thinking is as the _____ of the social interaction.

Children's Theories (pp. 261–266)

13. The term _____-_____
    highlights the idea that children attempt to construct theories to explain everything they see and hear.

14. As a result of their experiences with others, young children acquire a _____
    _____ _____
    that reflects their developing concepts about human mental processes.

Describe the theory of mind of children between the ages of 3 and 6.

15. Most 3-year-olds _____ (have/do not have) difficulty realizing that a belief can be false.

16. Research studies reveal that theory-of-mind development depends depends partly on _____ maturation, particularly of the brain's _____
    _____ . General _____ ability is also important in strengthening preschoolers' theory of mind. A third helpful factor is having at least one
    _____ .
    Finally, _____ may be a factor.

Language (pp. 266–275)

17. Two aspects of development that make ages 2 to 6 the prime time for learning language are _____ and _____ in the language areas of the brain.

18. Although early childhood does not appear to be a _____ period for language develop-

ment, it does seem to be a _____ period for the learning of vocabulary, grammar, and pronunciation.

19. During the preschool years, a dramatic increase in language occurs, with _____ increasing exponentially.

20. Through the process called _____-
    _____ , preschoolers often learn words after only one or two hearings. A closely related process is _____
    _____ , by which children are able to apply newly learned words to other objects in the same category.

21. Abstract nouns and metaphors are _____ (more/no more) difficult for preschoolers to understand.

22. Because preschool children tend to think in absolute terms, they have difficulty with words that express _____ , as well as words expressing relationships of _____ and _____ .

23. The structures, techniques, and rules that a language uses to communicate meaning define its _____ . A distinction is often made between _____ _____ , which is what a person says, and _____ _____ , which is what a person _____ . By age _____ , children typically demonstrate extensive understanding of this aspect of language.

24. Two factors that affect how well 3- to 5-year-olds use language are _____ input and encouragement and _____ .

25. Preschoolers' tendency to apply rules of grammar when they should not is called
    _____ .

Give several examples of this tendency.

26. Most developmentalists agree that bilingualism _____ (is/is not necessarily) an asset to children in today's world. Even so, language-minority children are at a _____ (advantage/disadvantage) in most ways.

27. Children who speak two languages by age 5 often are less _____ in their understanding of language and more advanced in their _____ _____ _____ . Advocates of monolingualism point out that bilingual proficiency comes at the expense of _____ in one or both languages, slowing down the development of _____ and other linguistic skills.

28. Some immigrant parents are saddened when their children make a _____ _____ and become more fluent in their new language than that of their home culture. The best solution is for children to become _____ _____ , who are fluent in both languages. This is easiest for children when their parents _____ _____ .

29. Language learning provides a crucial foundation for _____ _____ . Another correlate for the development of reading is _____ _____ in early childhood.

Early-Childhood Education (pp. 275–282)

30. Current research _____ (supports/refutes) the long-held belief that school should not begin until age 7.

31. A century ago, _____ _____ opened the first structured nursery schools for poor children in Rome. Many new programs use an educational model inspired by _____ that allows children to _____ . Many programs are also influenced by _____ , who believed that children

learn a great deal by _____ under the watchful guidance of adults.

32. The new early-childhood curriculum called _____ _____ encourages children to master skills not usually seen until about age _____ .

33. Other preschool programs explicitly teach basic _____ skills, including _____ , _____ , and _____ , typically using _____ _____ by a teacher.

34. In 1965, _____ _____ _____ was inaugurated to give low-income children some form of compensatory education during the preschool years. Longitudinal research found that graduates of similar but more intensive, well-evaluated programs scored _____ (higher/no higher) on achievement tests and were more likely to attend college and less likely to go to jail.

List several characteristics of high-quality early childhood education.

Progress Test 1

Multiple-Choice Questions

Circle your answers to the following questions and check them with the answers on beginning on page 141. If your answer is incorrect, read the explanation for why it is incorrect and then consult the appropriate pages of the text (in parentheses following the correct answer).

1. Piaget believed that children are in the preoperational stage from ages:
   a. 6 months to 1 year.   c. 2 to 6 years.
   b. 1 to 3 years.   d. 5 to 11 years.

2. Which of the following is *not* a characteristic of preoperational thinking?

   a. focus on appearance
   b. static reasoning
   c. abstract thinking
   d. centration

3. Which of the following provides evidence that early childhood is a sensitive period, rather than a critical period, for language learning?

   a. People can and do master their native language after early childhood.
   b. Vocabulary, grammar, and pronunciation are acquired especially easily during early childhood.
   c. Neurological characteristics of the young child's developing brain facilitate language acquisition.
   d. a. and b.
   e. a., b., and c.

4. Emergent literacy refers to the:

   a. skills needed to learn to read.
   b. "teachability" of pre-K children.
   c. best time for learning a second or third language.
   d. learning experiences provided to children by skilled tutors.

5. Reggio Emilia is:

   a. the educator who first opened nursery schools for poor children in Rome.
   b. the early-childhood curriculum that allows children to discover ideas at their own pace.
   c. a new form of early-childhood education that encourages children to master skills not usually seen until age 7 or so.
   d. the Canadian system for promoting bilingualism in young children.

6. The vocabulary of preschool children consists primarily of:

   a. metaphors.
   b. self-created words.
   c. abstract nouns.
   d. verbs and concrete nouns.

7. Preschoolers sometimes apply the rules of grammar even when they shouldn't. This tendency is called:

   a. overregularization.   **c.** practical usage.
   b. literal language.   **d.** single-mindedness.

8. The Russian psychologist Vygotsky emphasized that:

   a. language helps children form ideas.
   b. children form concepts first, then find words to express them.
   c. language and other cognitive developments are unrelated at this stage.
   d. preschoolers learn language only for egocentric purposes.

9. Private speech can be described as:

   a. a way of formulating ideas to oneself.
   b. fantasy.
   c. an early learning difficulty.
   d. the beginnings of deception.

10. The child who has not yet grasped the principle of conservation is likely to:

   a. insist that a tall, narrow glass contains more liquid than a short, wide glass, even though both glasses actually contain the same amount.
   b. be incapable of egocentric thought.
   c. be unable to reverse an event.
   d. do all of the above.

11. In later life, High/Scope graduates showed:

   a. better report cards, but more behavioral problems.
   b. significantly higher IQ scores.
   c. higher scores on math and reading achievement tests.
   d. alienation from their original neighborhoods and families.

12. The best preschool programs are generally those that provide the most:

   a. behavioral control.
   b. positive social interactions among children and adults.
   c. instruction in conservation and other logical principles.
   d. demonstration of toys by professionals.

13. Many newer preschool programs that are inspired by Piaget stress _____ , in contrast to alternative programs that stress _____ .

   a. academics; readiness
   b. readiness; academics
   c. child development; readiness
   d. academics; child development

14. Preschoolers can succeed at tests of conservation when:
   a. they are allowed to work cooperatively with other children.
   b. the test is presented as a competition.
   c. they are informed that they are being observed by their parents.
   d. the test is presented in a simple, nonverbal, and gamelike way.

15. Through the process called fast mapping, children:
   a. immediately assimilate new words by connecting them through their assumed meaning to categories of words they have already mastered.
   b. acquire the concept of conservation at an earlier age than Piaget believed.
   c. are able to move beyond egocentric thinking.
   d. become skilled in the practical use of language.

True or False Items

Write T (*true*) or F (*false*) on the line in front of each statement.

_____ 1. Early childhood is a prime learning period for every child.

_____ 2. In conservation problems, many preschoolers are unable to understand the transformation because they focus exclusively on appearances.

_____ 3. Preschoolers use private speech more selectively than older children.

_____ 4. Children typically develop a theory of mind at about age 7.

_____ 5. Preoperational children tend to focus on one aspect of a situation to the exclusion of all others.

_____ 6. Piaget focused on what children cannot do rather than what they can do.

_____ 7. With the beginning of preoperational thought, most preschoolers can understand abstract words.

_____ 8. A preschooler who says "You comed up and hurted me" is demonstrating a lack of understanding of English grammar.

_____ 9. Successful preschool programs generally have a low adult/child ratio.

_____ 10. Vygotsky believed that cognitive growth is largely a social activity.

_____ 11. *Theory-theory* refers to the tendency of young children to see the world as an unchanging reflection of their current construction of reality.

Progress Test 2

Progress Test 2 should be completed during a final chapter review. Answer the following questions after you thoroughly understand the correct answers for the Chapter Review and Progress Test 1.

Multiple-Choice Questions

1. Children who speak two languages by age 5:
   a. are less egocentric in their understanding of language.
   b. are more advanced in their theory of mind.
   c. have somewhat slower vocabulary development in one or both languages.
   d. are characterized by all of the above.

2. Piaget believed that preoperational children fail conservation of liquid tests because of their tendency to:
   a. focus on appearance.
   b. fast map.
   c. overregularize.
   d. do all of the above.

3. A preschooler who focuses his or her attention on only one feature of a situation is demonstrating a characteristic of preoperational thought called:
   a. centration.   c. reversibility.
   b. overregularization.   d. egocentrism.

4. One characteristic of preoperational thought is:
   a. the ability to categorize objects.
   b. the ability to count in multiples of 5.
   c. the inability to perform logical operations.
   d. difficulty adjusting to changes in routine.

5. The zone of proximal development represents the:
   a. skills or knowledge that are within the potential of the learner but are not yet mastered.
   b. influence of a child's peers on cognitive development.
   c. explosive period of language development during the play years.
   d. normal variations in children's language proficiency.

6. According to Vygotsky, language advances thinking through private speech, and by:
   a. helping children to privately review what they know.
   b. helping children explain events to themselves.
   c. serving as a mediator of the social interaction that is a vital part of learning.
   d. facilitating the process of fast-mapping.

7. Irreversibility refers to the:
   a. inability to understand that other people view the world from a different perspective than one's own.
   b. inability to think about more than one idea at a time.
   c. failure to understand that changing the arrangement of a group of objects doesn't change their number.
   d. failure to understand that undoing a process will restore the original conditions.

8. According to Piaget:
   a. it is impossible for preoperational children to grasp the concept of conservation, no matter how carefully it is explained.
   b. preschoolers fail to solve conservation problems because they center their attention on the transformation that has occurred and ignore the changed appearances of the objects.
   c. with special training, even preoperational children are able to grasp some aspects of conservation.
   d. preschoolers fail to solve conservation problems because they have no theory of mind.

9. Scaffolding of a child's cognitive skills can be provided by:
   a. a mentor.
   b. the objects or experiences of a culture.
   c. the child's past learning.
   d. all of the above.

10. Which theorist would be most likely to agree with the statement, "Adults should focus on helping children learn rather than on what they cannot do"?
    a. Piaget
    b. Vygotsky
    c. both a. and b.
    d. neither a. nor b.

11. Children first demonstrate some understanding of grammar:
    a. as soon as the first words are produced.
    b. once they begin to use language for practical purposes.
    c. through the process called fast-mapping.
    d. in their earliest sentences.

12. Balanced bilingualism is easiest for children to attain when:
    a. the parents themselves speak two languages.
    b. the second language is not taught until the child is fluent in the first.
    c. fast-mapping is avoided.
    d. overregularization is discouraged.

13. Most 5-year-olds have difficulty understanding metaphors because:
    a. they have not yet begun to develop grammar.
    b. the literal nature of the fast-mapping process allows only one meaning per word.
    c. of their limited vocabulary.
    d. of their tendency to overregularize.

14. Overregularization indicates that a child:
    a. is clearly applying rules of grammar.
    b. persists in egocentric thinking.
    c. has not yet mastered the principle of conservation.
    d. does not yet have a theory of mind.

15. Regarding the value of preschool education, most developmentalists believe that:
    a. most disadvantaged children will not benefit from an early preschool education.
    b. most disadvantaged children will benefit from an early preschool education.
    c. the early benefits of preschool education are likely to disappear by grade 3.
    d. the relatively small benefits of antipoverty measures such as Head Start do not justify their huge costs.

Matching Items

Match each term or concept with its corresponding description or definition.

Terms or Concepts

_____ 1. emergent literacy
_____ 2. scaffold
_____ 3. theory of mind
_____ 4. zone of proximal development
_____ 5. overregularization
_____ 6. fast-mapping
_____ 7. irreversibility
_____ 8. centration
_____ 9. conservation
_____ 10. private speech
_____ 11. guided participation
_____ 12. static reasoning

Descriptions or Definitions

a. the idea that amount is unaffected by changes in shape or placement
b. the tendency to see the world as an unchanging place
c. the cognitive distance between a child's actual and potential levels of development
d. the tendency to think about one aspect of a situation at a time
e. the process whereby the child learns through social interaction with a mentor
f. our understanding of mental processes in ourselves and others
g. the process by which words are learned after only one hearing
h. an inappropriate application of rules of grammar
i. the internal use of language to form ideas
j. the inability to understand that original conditions are restored by the undoing of some process
k. to structure a child's participation in learning encounters
l. the skills needed to learn to read.

Thinking Critically About Chapter 9

Answer these questions the day before an exam as a final check on your understanding of the chapter's terms and concepts.

1. An experimenter first shows a child two rows of checkers that each have the same number of checkers. Then, with the child watching, the experimenter elongates one row and asks the child if each of the two rows still has an equal number of checkers. This experiment tests the child's understanding of:

   a. reversibility.
   b. conservation of matter.
   c. conservation of number.
   d. centration.

2. A preschooler believes that a "party" is the one and only attribute of a birthday. She says that Daddy doesn't have a birthday because he never has a party. This thinking demonstrates the tendency Piaget called:

   a. egocentrism.   c. conservation of events.
   b. centration.   d. mental representation.

3. A child who understands that 6 + 3 = 9 means that 9 − 6 = 3 has had to master the concept of:

   a. reversibility.   c. conservation.
   b. number.   d. egocentrism.

4. A 4-year-old tells the teacher that a clown should not be allowed to visit the class because "Pat is 'fraid of clowns." The 4-year-old thus shows that he can anticipate how another will feel. This is evidence of the beginnings of:

   a. egocentrism.
   b. deception.
   c. a theory of mind.
   d. conservation.

5. Asked "Where do dreams come from?," a 5-year-old child is likely to answer:

   a. "from God."
   b. "from the sky."
   c. "from my pillow."
   d. "from inside my head."

6. A nursery school teacher is given the job of selecting holiday entertainment for a group of preschool children. If the teacher agrees with the ideas of Vygotsky, she is most likely to select:
   a. a simple TV show that every child can understand.
   b. a hands-on experience that requires little adult supervision.
   c. brief, action-oriented play activities that the children and teachers will perform together.
   d. holiday puzzles for children to work on individually.

7. Which of the following terms does *not* belong with the others?
   a. focus on appearances
   b. static reasoning
   c. reversibility
   d. centration

8. That a child produces sentences that follow such rules of word order as "the initiator of an action precedes the verb, the receiver of an action follows it" demonstrates a knowledge of:
   a. grammar.   c. pragmatics.
   b. semantics.   d. phrase structure.

9. The 2-year-old child who says, "We goed to the store," is making a grammatical:
   a. centration.   c. extension.
   b. overregularization. d. fast map.

10. An experimenter who makes two balls of clay of equal amount, then rolls one into a long, skinny rope and asks the child if the amounts are still the same, is testing the child's understanding of:
    a. conservation.   c. perspective-taking.
    b. reversibility.   d. centration.

11. Dr. Jones, who believes that children's language growth greatly contributes to their cognitive growth, evidently is a proponent of the ideas of:
    a. Piaget.   c. Flavell.
    b. Chomsky.   d. Vygotsky.

12. Comparing the views of Piaget with those of Vygotsky, active learning is to guided participation as egocentrism is to:
    a. apprenticeship.   c. scaffold.
    b. structure.   d. fast-mapping.

13. In describing the limited logical reasoning of preschoolers, a developmentalist is *least* likely to emphasize:
    a. irreversibility.   c. its action-bound nature.
    b. centration.   d. its static nature.

14. A preschooler fails to put together a difficult puzzle on her own, so her mother encourages her to try again, this time guiding her by asking questions such as, "For this space do we need a big piece or a little piece?" With Mom's help, the child successfully completes the puzzle. Lev Vygotsky would attribute the child's success to:
    a. additional practice with the puzzle pieces.
    b. imitation of her mother's behavior.
    c. the social interaction with her mother that restructured the task to make its solution more attainable.
    d. modeling and reinforcement.

15. Mark is answering an essay question that asks him to "discuss the positions of major developmental theorists regarding the relationship between language and cognitive development." To help organize his answer, Mark jots down a reminder that _____ contended that language is essential to the advancement of thinking, as private speech, and as a _____ of social interactions.
    a. Piaget; mediator   c. Piaget; theory
    b. Vygotsky; mediator   d. Vygotsky; theory

Key Terms

Using your own words, write a brief definition or explanation of each of the following terms on a separate piece of paper.

1. preoperational thought
2. cognitive operation
3. egocentrism
4. centration
5. focus on appearance
6. static reasoning
7. irreversibility
8. conservation
9. apprentice in thinking
10. guided participation
11. zone of proximal development
12. scaffolding
13. private speech
14. social mediation
15. theory-theory
16. theory of mind
17. critical period
18. sensitive period

19. fast-mapping

20. overregularization

21. balanced bilingual

22. emergent literacy

ANSWERS
CHAPTER REVIEW

1. theory of mind

2. preoperational; cognitive operation

3. egocentrism; centration; is not; appearances

4. static; unchanging; irreversibility

5. conservation; conservation of number

6. underestimated

7. Lev Vygotsky; apprentice in thinking

8. challenges; assistance; praise; enthusiasm; instruction; guided participation; social; interact

9. zone of proximal development

10. scaffold

11. private speech; uttered aloud

12. mediator

13. theory-theory

14. theory of mind

Between the ages of 3 and 6, young children come to realize that mental phenomena may not reflect reality and that individuals can believe various things and, therefore, can be deliberately deceived or fooled.

15. have

16. neurological; prefrontal cortex; language; brother or sister; culture

17. maturation; myelination

18. critical; sensitive

19. vocabulary

20. fast-mapping; logical extension

21. more

22. comparisons; time; place

23. grammar; expressive language; receptive language; understands; 3

24. parental; genes

25. overregularization

Many preschoolers overapply the rule of adding "s" to form the plural, as well as the rule of adding "ed" to form the past tense. Thus, preschoolers are likely to say "foots" and "snows" and that someone "broked" a toy.

26. is; disadvantage

27. egocentric; theories of mind; fluency; reading

28. language shift; balanced bilinguals; speak two languages themselves

29. emergent literacy; symbolic play

30. refutes

31. Maria Montessori; Piaget; discover ideas at their own pace; Vygotsky; playing

32. Reggio Emilia; 7

33. school; reading; writing; arithmetic; direct instruction

34. Project Head Start; higher

In Chapter 6, high-quality preschools were described as being characterized by (a) a low adult/child ratio, (b) a trained staff (or educated parents) who are unlikely to leave the program, (c) positive social interactions among children and adults, (d) adequate space and equipment, and (e) safety. Continuity also helps, and curriculum is important.

PROGRESS TEST 1

Multiple-Choice Questions

1. **c.** is the answer. (p. 254)

2. **c.** is the answer. Preoperational children have great difficulty understanding abstract concepts. (pp. 254–255, 269)

3. **e.** is the answer. (p. 266)

4. **a.** is the answer. (p. 274)

5. **c.** is the answer. (p. 277)

   a. This describes Maria Montessori.

   b. This refers to Piaget's approach.

   d. The program originated in Italy.

6. **d.** is the answer. (p. 267)

   a. & c. Preschoolers generally have great difficulty understanding, and therefore using, metaphors and abstract nouns.

   b. Other than the grammatical errors of overregularization, the text does not indicate that preschoolers use a significant number of self-created words.

7. **a.** is the answer. (p. 270)

   b. & d. These terms are not identified in the text and do not apply to the use of grammar.

c. Practical usage, which also is not discussed in the text, refers to communication between one person and another in terms of the overall context in which language is used.

8. a. is the answer. (p. 259)

b. This expresses the views of Piaget.

c. Because he believed that language facilitates thinking, Vygotsky obviously felt that language and other cognitive developments are intimately related.

d. Vygotsky did not hold this view.

9. a. is the answer. (p. 260)

10. a. is the answer. (pp. 255–256)

b., c., & d. Failure to conserve is the result of thinking that is centered on appearances. Egocentrism and irreversibility are also examples of centered thinking.

11. c. is the answer. (pp. 279–280)

b. This is not discussed in the text.

a. & d. There was no indication of greater behavioral problems or alienation in graduates of this program.

12. b. is the answer. (p. 281)

13. c. is the answer. (pp. 276, 278)

14. d. is the answer. (pp. 256–257)

15. a. is the answer. (p. 267)

True or False Items

1. T (p. 253)

2. T (p. 256)

3. F   In fact, just the opposite is true. (p. 260)

4. F   Children develop a theory of mind between the ages of 3 and 6. (p. 264)

5. T (p. 254)

6. T (p. 254)

7. F   Preschoolers have difficulty understanding abstract words; their vocabulary consists mainly of concrete nouns and verbs. (p. 269)

8. F   In adding "ed" to form a past tense, the child has indicated an understanding of the grammatical rule for making past tenses in English, even though the construction in these two cases is incorrect. (p. 270)

9. T (p. 281)

10. T (p. 258)

11. F   This describes static reasoning; theory-theory is the idea that children attempt to construct a theory to explain all their experiences. (p. 262)

PROGRESS TEST 2

Multiple-Choice Questions

1. d. is the answer. (p. 272)

2. a. is the answer. (pp. 255–256)

b. & c. Fast-mapping and overregularization are characteristics of language development during the play years; they have nothing to do with reasoning about volume.

3. a. is the answer. (p. 254)

b. Overregularization is the child's tendency to apply grammatical rules even when he or she shouldn't.

c. Reversibility is the concept that reversing an operation, such as addition, will restore the original conditions.

d. This term is used to refer to the young child's belief that people think as he or she does.

4. c. is the answer. This is why the stage is called *pre*operational. (p. 254)

5. a. is the answer. (p. 259)

6. c. is the answer. (p. 260)

a. & b. These are both advantages of private speech.

d. Fast-mapping is the process by which new words are acquired, often after only one hearing.

7. d. is the answer. (p. 255)

a. This describes egocentrism.

b. This is the opposite of centration.

c. This defines conservation of number.

8. a. is the answer. (p. 255)

b. According to Piaget, preschoolers fail to solve conservation problems because they focus on the *appearance* of objects and ignore the transformation that has occurred.

d. Piaget did not relate conservation to a theory of mind.

9. d. is the answer. (p. 259)

10. b. is the answer. (p. 257)

a. Piaget focused on what children cannot do.

11. d. is the answer. Preschoolers almost always put subject before verb in their two-word sentences. (p. 270)

12. a. is the answer. (pp. 273)

b. Although there are many different approaches to promoting bilingualism, the text does not suggest that children should master one language before being exposed to another.

c. & d. Fast-mapping and overregularization are normal aspects of language development that stimulate the development of vocabulary and grammar.

13. **b.** is the answer. (p. 268)

   a. By the time children are 3 years old, their grammar is quite impressive.

   c. On the contrary, vocabulary develops so rapidly that, by age 5, children seem to be able to understand and use almost any term they hear.

   d. This tendency to make language more logical by overapplying certain grammatical rules has nothing to do with understanding the *meaning* of metaphors.

14. **a.** is the answer. (p. 270)

   b., c., & d. Overregularization is a *linguistic* phenomenon rather than a characteristic type of thinking (b. and d.), or a logical principle (c.).

15. **b.** is the answer. (p. 279)

Matching Items

1. l (p. 274)	**5.** h (p. 270)	**9.** a (p. 255)
2. k (p. 259)	**6.** g (p. 267)	**10.** i (p. 260)
3. f (p. 263)	**7.** j (p. 255)	**11.** e (p. 258)
4. c (p. 259)	**8.** d (p. 254)	**12.** b (p. 255)

THINKING CRITICALLY ABOUT CHAPTER 9

1. **c.** is the answer. (p. 256)

   a. A test of reversibility would ask a child to perform an operation, such as adding 4 to 3, and then reverse the process (subtract 3 from 7) to determine whether the child understood that the original condition (the number 4) was restored.

   b. A test of conservation of matter would transform the appearance of an object, such as a ball of clay, to determine whether the child understood that the object remained the same.

   d. A test of centration would involve the child's ability to see various aspects of a situation.

2. **b.** is the answer. (p. 254)

   a. Egocentrism is thinking that is self-centered.

   c. This is not a concept in Piaget's theory.

   d. Mental representation is an example of symbolic thought.

3. **a.** is the answer. (p. 255)

4. **c.** is the answer. (p. 263)

   a. Egocentrism is self-centered thinking.

   b. Although deception provides evidence of a theory of mind, the child in this example is not deceiving anyone.

   d. Conservation is the understanding that the amount of a substance is unchanged by changes in its shape or placement.

5. **d.** is the answer. (p. 264)

   a., b., & c. These answers are typical of younger children, who have not yet developed a theory of mind.

6. **c.** is the answer. In Vygotsky's view, learning is a social activity. Thus, social interaction that provides motivation and focuses attention facilitates learning. (pp. 258–259)

   a., b., & d. These situations either provide no opportunity for social interaction (b. & d.) or do not challenge the children (a.).

7. **c.** is the answer. (pp. 254–255)

   a., b., & d. These are all characteristics of preoperational thinking.

8. **a.** is the answer. (p. 270)

   b. & d. The text does not discuss these aspects of language.

   c. Pragmatics, which is not mentioned in the text, refers to the practical use of language in varying social contexts.

9. **b.** is the answer. (p. 270)

10. **a.** is the answer. (p. 255)

11. **d.** is the answer. (p. 259)

   a. Piaget believed that cognitive growth precedes language development.

   b. & c. Chomsky focused on the *acquisition* of language, and Flavell emphasizes cognition.

12. **a.** is the answer. Piaget emphasized the preschooler's egocentric tendency to perceive everything from his or her own perspective; Vygotsky emphasized the preschooler's tendency to look to others for insight and guidance. (pp. 254, 258)

13. **c.** is the answer. This is typical of cognition during the first two years, when infants think exclusively with their senses and motor skills. (pp. 254–255)

14. **c.** is the answer. (pp. 258–259)

15. **b.** is the answer. (p. 260)

KEY TERMS

1. According to Piaget, thinking between ages 2 and 6 is characterized by **preoperational thought,** meaning that children cannot yet perform logical operations; that is, they cannot use logical principles. (p. 254)

2. **Cognitive operations** involve the organization and evaluation of ideas in order to reach some conclusion. Preoperational children, who lack this ability, are "before" this developmental milestone. (p. 254)

3. **Egocentrism** is Piaget's term for a type of centration in which the preoperational child views the world exclusively from his or her own perspective. (p. 254)

4. **Centration** is the tendency of preoperational children to focus only on a single aspect of a situation or object. (p. 254)

5. **Focus on appearance** refers to the preoperational child's tendency to focus only on apparent attributes and ignore all others. (p. 255)

6. Preoperational thinking is characterized by **static reasoning,** in which the young child sees the world as unchanging. (p. 255)

7. **Irreversibility** is the characteristic of preoperational thought in which the young child fails to recognize that a process can be reversed to restore the original conditions of a situation. (p. 255)

8. **Conservation** is the understanding that the amount or quantity of a substance or object is unaffected by changes in its appearance. (p. 255)

9. According to Vygotsky, a young child is an **apprentice in thinking,** whose intellectual growth is stimulated and directed by more skilled members of society. (p. 258)

10. According to Vygotsky, **guided participation** is the process by which young children learn to think by having social experiences and by exploring their universe. As mentors, parents, siblings, and peers present challenging tasks, offer assistance (not taking over), maintain enthusiasm, provide instructions, and support the child's interest and motivation. (p. 258)

11. According to Vygotsky, for each individual there is a **zone of proximal development (ZPD),** which represents the skills that are within the potential of the learner but cannot be performed independently. (p. 259)

12. Tutors who utilize **scaffolding** structure children's learning experiences in order to foster their emerging capabilities. (p. 259)

13. **Private speech** is Vygotsky's term for the internal dialogue in which a person talks to himself or herself. Private speech, which often is uttered aloud, helps preschoolers to think, review what they know, and decide what to do. (p. 260)

14. In Vygotsky's theory, **social mediation** is a function of speech by which a person's cognitive skills are refined and extended through both formal instruction and casual conversation (p. 260)

15. **Theory-theory** is Gopnik's term for the tendency of young children to attempt to construct theories to explain everything they experience. (p. 262)

16. A **theory of mind** is an understanding of human mental processes, that is, of one's own or another's emotions, beliefs, intentions, motives, and thoughts. (p. 263)

17. A **critical period** is a time when a specific type of development must happen if the individual is to develop normally. (p. 266)

18. A **sensitive period** is a time when a specific type of development is most likely to happen, and when it happens most easily. (p. 266)

19. **Fast-mapping** is the not very precise process by which children rapidly learn new words by quickly connecting them to words and categories that they already understand. (p. 267)

20. **Overregularization** occurs when children apply rules of grammar when they should not. It is seen in English, for example, when children add "s" to form the plural even in irregular cases that form the plural in a different way. (p. 270)

21. A **balanced bilingual** is a person who is equally fluent in two languages. (p. 273)

22. **Emergent literacy** refers to the skills needed to learn to read. (p. 274)

Chapter Ten

The Play Years: Psychosocial Development

Chapter Overview

Chapter 10 explores the ways in which young children begin to relate to others in an ever-widening social environment. The chapter begins where social understanding begins, with emotional development and the emergence of the sense of self. With their increasing social awareness, children become more concerned with how others evaluate them and better able to regulate their emotions. This section also explores the origins of helpful, prosocial behaviors in young children, as well as antisocial behaviors such as the different forms of aggressive behavior. The child's social skills reflect many influences, including learning from playmates through various types of play.

The next section discusses Baumrind's parenting patterns and their effects on the developing child. The usefulness of the different forms of punishment is also explored.

The chapter concludes with a description of children's emerging awareness of male–female differences and gender identity. Five major theories of gender-role development are considered.

NOTE: Answer guidelines for all Chapter 10 questions begin on page 156.

Guided Study

The text chapter should be studied one section at a time. Before you read, preview each section by skimming it, noting headings and boldface items. Then read the appropriate section objectives from the following outline. Keep these objectives in mind and, as you read the chapter section, search for the information that will enable you to meet each objective. Once you have finished a section, write out answers for its objectives.

Emotional Development (pp. 285–295)

1. Explain the relationship between Erik Erikson's third stage and the development of the self-concept.

2. Discuss the development during early childhood of emotional regulation, focusing on how it is determined by both nature and nurture.

3. Explain the views of Daniel Goleman regarding emotional development in young children.

4. Explain how and why children develop empathy or antipathy, and describe the behaviors they produce.

Play (pp. 295–300)

5. Differentiate five types of play.

6. Discuss the nature and significance of rough-and-tumble and sociodramatic play during the play years.

7. Differentiate four types of aggression during the play years, and explain why certain types of aggression are more troubling to developmentalists.

Parents (pp. 300–311)

8. Compare and contrast three classic patterns of parenting and their effect on children.

9. Discuss the pros and cons of punishment, and describe the most effective method for disciplining a child.

10. Discuss how watching television and playing video games contribute to the development of aggression and other antisocial behaviors.

Becoming Boys and Girls (pp. 311–319)

11. Describe the developmental progression of gender awareness in young children.

12. Summarize five theories of gender-role development during the play years, noting important contributions of each.

Chapter Review

When you have finished reading the chapter, work through the material that follows to review it. Complete the sentences and answer the questions. As you proceed, evaluate your performance for each section by consulting the answers on page 156. Do not continue with the next section until you understand each answer. If you need to, review or reread the appropriate section in the textbook before continuing.

Emotional Development (pp. 285–295)

1. Between 3 and 6 years of age, according to Erikson, children are in the stage of

   _____ _____

   _____ . As they acquire skills and

   competencies, children develop

_____ , a belief in their own ability. In the process, they develop a positive _____ and feelings of _____ in their accomplishments.

2. Unlike the earlier stage of _____ _____ _____ , children in this stage want to begin *and* _____ something. Children also develop a longer _____ span that enables concentration, greater _____ , and a willingness to _____ .

3. Erikson also believed that during this stage children begin to feel _____ when their efforts result in failure or criticism. Many people believe that _____ is a more mature emotion than _____ , because the former emotion is _____ .

4. For the most part, preschool children enjoy learning, playing, and practicing for their own joy; that is, they are _____ _____ .

5. The ability to inhibit, enhance, direct, or modify one's feelings is called _____ _____ . This ability begins with the control of _____ . Children who have _____ problems and lash out at other people or things are said to be "_____" (overcontrolled/undercontrolled). Children who have _____ problems tend to be inhibited, fearful, and withdrawn.

6. In the early years, aspects of neurological maturation are affected by the child's unique _____ , depending on the _____ rules regarding emotional display.

7. Genetic influences _____ (are/are not) a source of variation in emotional regulation in young children. One research study found that fearful children had greater activity in the _____ _____ _____ of their brains, while those who were less withdrawn had greater activity in

their _____ _____ _____ .

8. Girls generally have _____ (more/less) trouble with emotional regulation than boys do.

9. Repeated exposure to extreme stress can kill _____ and make some children physiologically unable to regulate their emotions. Extreme stress can also affect the release of stress hormones such as _____ . One study found _____ (higher-than-normal/lower-than-normal) levels of this hormone in abused children.

10. Another set of influences on emotional regulation is the child's early and current _____ _____ . Neglect or abuse in the first two years of life is likely to cause later _____ problems.

11. According to _____ , the ability to modulate and direct emotions is crucial to the development of _____ _____ .

12. The ability to truly understand the emotions of another, called _____ , often leads to sharing, helping, and other examples of _____ _____ . In contrast, dislike for others, or _____ , may lead to actions that are destructive or deliberately hurtful. Such actions are called _____ _____ .

13. By age _____ , most children can be deliberately prosocial or antisocial. This occurs as a result of _____ maturation, _____ regulation, _____ _____ _____ , and interactions with _____ .

14. Preschool children are capable of identifying with and being proud of their own group without being _____ against other groups.

Play (pp. 295–300)

15. Play is both _____ and _____ by culture, gender, and age.

16. The developmentalist who distinguished five kinds of play is _____ . These include _____ play, in which a child plays alone; _____ play, in which a child watches other children play; _____ play, in which children play together without interacting; _____ play, in which child interact, but their play is not yet mutual and reciprocal; and _____ play, in which children play together and take turns.

17. The type of physical play that mimics aggression is called _____-_____-_____ play. A distinctive feature of this form of play, which _____ (occurs only in some cultures/is universal), is the positive facial expression that characterizes the "_____ _____ ." Age differences are evident, because this type of play relies on the child's _____ _____ . Gender differences _____ (are/are not) evident in rough-and-tumble play.

18. In _____ play, children act out various roles and themes in stories of their own creation. _____ (Girls/Boys) tend to engage in this type of play more often than do _____ (girls/boys).

19. The most antisocial behavior of all is active _____ . Developmentalists distinguish four types of physical aggression: _____ , used to obtain or retain an object or privilege; _____ , used in angry retaliation against an intentional or accidental act committed by a peer; _____ , which takes the form of insults or social rejection; and _____ , used in an unprovoked attack on a peer.

20. (Table 10.1) The form of aggression that is most likely to increase from age 2 to 6 is _____ _____ . Of greater concern are _____ _____ , because it can indicate a lack of _____

_____ , and _____

_____ , which is most worrisome overall.

Parents (pp. 300–311)

21. A significant influence on early psychosocial growth is the style of _____ that characterizes a child's family life.

22 The early research on parenting styles, which was conducted by _____ , found that parents varied in four dimensions: their expressions of _____ ; their strategies for _____ ; their _____ ; and their expectations for _____ .

23. Parents who adopt the _____ style demand unquestioning obedience from their children. In this style of parenting, nurturance tends to be _____ (low/high), maturity demands are _____ (low/high), and parent–child communication tends to be _____ (low/high).

24. Parents who adopt the _____ style make few demands on their children and are lax in discipline. Such parents _____ (are/are not very) nurturant, communicate _____ (well/poorly), and make _____ (few/extensive) maturity demands.

25. Parents who adopt the _____ style set limits and enforce rules but also listen to their children. Such parents make _____ (high/low) maturity demands, communicate _____ (well/poorly), and _____ (are/are not) nurturant. Two other styles of parenting that have been identified are _____ parenting, in which parents don't seem to care at all about their children, and _____ parenting, in which parents give in to a child's every whim.

26. Follow-up studies indicate that children raised by _____ parents are likely to be obedient but unhappy and those raised by _____ parents are likely to lack self-control. Those raised by _____ parents are more likely to be successful, happy with themselves,

and generous with others; these advantages _____ (grow stronger/weaken) over time.

27. An important factor in the effectiveness of parenting style is the child's _____ . In addition, _____ and _____ _____ influence the child's perception of the quality of parenting. The crucial factors in how children perceive their parents are _____ _____ , _____ , and _____ for the child. All parents _____ (do/do not) neatly fit into one of Baumrind's three major categories of parenting.

28. Culture _____ (exerts/does not exert) a strong influence on disciplinary techniques. Japanese mothers tend to use _____ as disciplinary techniques more often than do North American mothers and to blame themselves for their child's misbehavior; European and European American mothers _____ (blame themselves/blame others). A disciplinary technique in which a child is required to stop all activity and sit quietly for a few minutes is the _____-_____ . This technique is widely used in _____ _____ .

(Table 10.4) State four specific recommendations for the use of punishment that are derived from developmental research findings.

a. _____

b. _____

c. _____

d. _____

29. Six major organizations concerned with the well-being of children urge parents to avoid exposing their children to _____ _____ . Those who advocate the opposite viewpoint contend that the media are merely reflecting _____ .

30. Most young children in the United States spend more than _____ (how many?) hours each day using some sort of media.

31. Longitudinal research demonstrates that children who watched educational programs as young children became teenagers who had _____ . This finding was especially true for _____ (boys/girls). Teenagers who, as children watched violent television programs, had _____ , especially if they were _____ (boys/girls).

32. Children who watch violence on television _____ (do/do not) become more violent themselves.

33. In comparison to broadcast television programs, video games are more _____ , _____ , and _____

Becoming Boys and Girls (pp. 311–319)

34. Social scientists distinguish between biological, or _____ , differences between males and females, and cultural, or _____ , differences in the _____ and behavior of males and females.

35. True sex differences are _____ (more/less) apparent in childhood than in adulthood; _____ differentiation seems more significant to children than to adults.

36. By age _____ , children can consistently apply gender labels and have a rudimentary understanding of the permanence of their own gender. By age _____ , children are convinced that certain toys and roles are appropriate for one gender but not the other. Awareness that sex is a fixed biological characteristic does not become solid until about age _____ .

37. Freud called the period from age 3 to 6 the _____ _____ . According to his view, boys in this stage develop sexual feelings about their _____ and become jealous of their _____ . Freud called this phenomenon the _____ _____ .

38. In Freud's theory, preschool boys resolve their guilty feelings defensively through _____ with their father. Boys also develop, again in self-defense, a powerful conscience called the _____ .

39. During the phallic stage little girls may experience the _____ _____ , in which they want to get rid of their mother and become intimate with their father. Alternatively, they may become jealous of boys because they have a penis; this emotion Freud called _____ _____ .

40. According to behaviorism, preschool children develop gender-role ideas by being _____ for behaviors deemed appropriate for their sex and _____ for behaviors deemed inappropriate.

41. Behaviorists also maintain that children learn gender-appropriate behavior not only through direct reinforcement but also by _____ .

42. Cognitive theorists focus on children's _____ of male–female differences.

43. Gender education varies by region, socioeconomic status, and historical period, according to the _____ theory. Gender distinctions are emphasized in many _____ cultures. This theory points out that children can maintain a balance of male and female characteristics, or _____ , only if their culture promotes that idea.

44. According to _____ theory, gender attitudes and roles are the result of interaction between _____ and _____ _____ .

45. The idea that is supported by recent research is that some gender differences are _____ based because of differences between male and female _____ .

46. These differences probably result from the differing _____ _____ that influence brain development. However, the theory maintains that the manifestations of biological origins are shaped, enhanced, or halted by _____ _____ . One example of such a factor is that prehistorically, female brains apparently favored _____ , which may have created a genetically inclined tendency for girls to _____ earlier than boys.

Progress Test 1

Multiple-Choice Questions

Circle your answers to the following questions and check them with the answers beginning on page 157. If your answer is incorrect, read the explanation for why it is incorrect and then consult the appropriate pages of the text (in parentheses following the correct answer).

1. Preschool children have a clear (but not necessarily accurate) concept of self. Typically, the preschooler believes that she or he:
   a. owns all objects in sight.
   b. is great at almost everything.
   c. is much less competent than peers and older children.
   d. is more powerful than her or his parents.

2. According to Freud, the third stage of psychosexual development, during which the penis is the focus of psychological concern and pleasure, is the:
   a. oral stage.   **c.** phallic stage.
   b. anal stage.   **d.** latency period.

3. Because it helps children rehearse social roles, work out fears and fantasies, and learn cooperation, an important form of social play is:
   a. sociodramatic play.
   b. mastery play.
   c. rough-and-tumble play.
   d. sensorimotor play.

4. The three *basic* patterns of parenting described by Diana Baumrind are:
   a. hostile, loving, and harsh.
   b. authoritarian, permissive, and authoritative.
   c. positive, negative, and punishing.
   d. indulgent, neglecting, and traditional.

5. Authoritative parents are receptive and loving, but they also normally:
   a. set limits and enforce rules.
   b. have difficulty communicating.
   c. withhold praise and affection.
   d. encourage aggressive behavior.

6. Children who watch a lot of violent television or play violent video games:
   a. are more likely to be violent.
   b. do less reading.
   c. tend to have lower grades in school.
   d. have all of the above characteristics.

7. (Table 10.1) Between 2 and 6 years of age, the form of aggression that is most likely to increase is:
   a. reactive
   b. instrumental
   c. relational
   d. bullying

8. During the play years, a child's self-concept is defined largely by his or her:
   a. expanding range of skills and competencies.
   b. physical appearance.
   c. gender.
   d. relationship with family members.

9. Behaviorists emphasize the importance of _____ in the development of the preschool child.
   a. identification
   b. praise and blame
   c. initiative
   d. a theory of mind

10. Children apply gender labels and have definite ideas about how boys and girls behave as early as age:
    a. 2.
    b. 4.
    c. 5.
    d. 7.

11. Psychologist Daniel Goleman believes that emotional regulation is especially crucial to the preschooler's developing:
    a. a sense of self.
    b. social awareness.
    c. emotional intelligence.
    d. a sense of gender.

12. Six-year-old Leonardo has superior verbal ability rivaling that of most girls his age. Dr. Laurent believes this is due to the fact that although his sex is predisposed to slower language development, Leonardo's upbringing in a linguistically rich home enhanced his biological capabilities. Dr. Laurent is evidently a proponent of:
    a. cognitive theory.
    b. psychoanalytic theory.
    c. sociocultural theory.
    d. epigenetic theory.

13. Three-year-old Jake, who lashes out at the family pet in anger, is displaying signs of _____ problems, which suggests that he is emotionally _____ .
    a. internalizing; overcontrolled
    b. internalizing; undercontrolled
    c. externalizing; overcontrolled
    d. externalizing; undercontrolled

14. Compared to Japanese mothers, North American mothers are more likely to:
    a. use reasoning to control their preschoolers' social behavior.
    b. use expressions of disappointment to control their preschoolers' social behavior.
    c. blame others for their child's misbehavior.
    d. do all of the above.

15. When her friend hurts her feelings, Maya shouts that she is a "mean old stinker!" Maya's behavior is an example of:
    a. instrumental aggression.
    b. reactive aggression.
    c. bullying aggression.
    d. relational aggression.

True or False Items

Write T *(true)* or F *(false)* on the line in front of each statement.

_____ 1. According to Diana Baumrind, only authoritarian parents make maturity demands on their children.

_____ 2. Children of authoritative parents tend to be successful, happy with themselves, and generous with others.

_____ 3. True sex differences are more apparent in childhood than in adulthood.

_____ 4. Usually, as children grow older their play becomes more social.

_____ 5. Many gender differences are genetically based.

_____ 6. Children can be truly androgynous only if their culture promotes such ideas and practices.

_____ 7. Developmentalists do not agree about how children acquire gender roles.

_____ 8. By age 4, most children have definite ideas about what constitutes appropriate masculine and feminine roles.

_____ 9. Identification was defined by Freud as a means of defending one's self-concept by taking on the attitudes and behaviors of another person.

_____ **10.** Sociodramatic play allows children free expression of their emotions.

Progress Test 2

Progress Test 2 should be completed during a final chapter review. Answer the following questions after you thoroughly understand the correct answers for the Chapter Review and Progress Test 1.

Multiple-Choice Questions

1. Children of permissive parents are *most* likely to lack:
   a. social skills.
   b. self-control.
   c. initiative and guilt.
   d. care and concern.

2. Children learn how to manage conflict through the use of humor most readily from their interaction with:
   a. their mothers.
   b. their fathers.
   c. friends.
   d. others of the same sex.

3. The initial advantages of parenting style:
   a. do not persist past middle childhood.
   b. remain apparent through adolescence.
   c. are likely to be even stronger over time.
   d. have an unpredictable impact later in children's lives.

4. When they are given a choice of playmates, 2- to 5-year-old children:
   a. play with children of their own sex.
   b. play equally with girls and boys.
   c. segregate by gender in cultures characterized by traditional gender roles.
   d. prefer to play alone.

5. Which of the following best summarizes the current view of developmentalists regarding gender differences?
   a. Developmentalists disagree on the proportion of gender differences that are biological in origin.
   b. Most gender differences are biological in origin.
   c. Nearly all gender differences are cultural in origin.
   d. There is no consensus among developmentalists regarding the origin of gender differences.

6. According to Freud, a young boy's jealousy of his father's relationship with his mother, and the guilt feelings that result, are part of the:
   a. Electra complex.
   b. Oedipus complex.
   c. phallic complex.
   d. penis envy complex.

7. The style of parenting in which the parents make few demands on children, the discipline is lax, and the parents are nurturant and accepting is:
   a. authoritarian.
   b. authoritative.
   c. permissive.
   d. traditional.

8. Cooperating with a playmate is to _____ as insulting a playmate is to _____ .
   a. antisocial behavior; prosocial behavior
   b. prosocial behavior; antisocial behavior
   c. emotional regulation; antisocial behavior
   d. prosocial behavior; emotional regulation

9. Antipathy refers to a person's:
   a. understanding of the emotions of another person.
   b. self-understanding.
   c. feelings of anger or dislike toward another person.
   d. tendency to internalize emotions or inhibit their expression.

10. Which of the following theories advocates the development of gender identification as a means of avoiding guilt over feelings for the opposite-sex parent?
    a. behaviorism
    b. sociocultural
    c. psychoanalytic
    d. social learning

11. A parent who wishes to use a time-out to discipline her son for behaving aggressively on the playground would be advised to:
    a. have the child sit quietly indoors for a few minutes.
    b. tell her son that he will be punished later at home.
    c. tell the child that he will not be allowed to play outdoors for the rest of the week.
    d. choose a different disciplinary technique since time-outs are ineffective.

12. The preschooler's readiness to learn new tasks and play activities reflects his or her:
    a. emerging competency and self-awareness.
    b. theory of mind.
    c. relationship with parents.
    d. growing identification with others.

13. Emotional regulation is in part related to maturation of a specific part of the brain in the:
    a. prefrontal cortex.
    b. parietal cortex.
    c. temporal lobe.
    d. occipital lobe.

14. In which style of parenting is the parents' word law and misbehavior strictly punished?
    a. permissive
    b. authoritative
    c. authoritarian
    d. traditional

15. Erikson noted that preschoolers eagerly begin many new activities but are vulnerable to criticism and feelings of failure; they experience the crisis of:
    a. identity versus role confusion.
    b. initiative versus guilt.
    c. basic trust versus mistrust.
    d. efficacy versus helplessness.

Matching Items

Match each term or concept with its corresponding description or definition.

Terms or Concepts

_____ 1. rough-and-tumble play
_____ 2. androgyny
_____ 3. sociodramatic play
_____ 4. prosocial behavior
_____ 5. antisocial behavior
_____ 6. Electra complex
_____ 7. Oedipus complex
_____ 8. authoritative
_____ 9. authoritarian
_____ 10. identification
_____ 11. instrumental aggression

Descriptions or Definitions

a. forceful behavior whose purpose is to obtain an object desired by another
b. Freudian theory that every daughter secretly wishes to replace her mother
c. parenting style associated with high maturity demands and low parent–child communication
d. an action performed for the benefit of another person without the expectation of reward
e. Freudian theory that every son secretly wishes to replace his father
f. parenting style associated with high maturity demands and high parent–child communication
g. two children wrestle without serious hostility
h. an action that is intended to harm someone else
i. two children act out roles in a story of their own creation
j. a defense mechanism through which children cope with their feelings of guilt during the phallic stage
k. a balance of traditional male and female characteristics in an individual

Thinking Critically About Chapter 10

Answer these questions the day before an exam as a final check on your understanding of the chapter's terms and concepts.

1. Bonita eventually copes with the fear and anger she feels over her hatred of her mother and love of her father by:
   a. identifying with her mother.
   b. copying her brother's behavior.
   c. adopting her father's moral code.
   d. competing with her brother for her father's attention.

2. A little girl who says she wants her mother to go on vacation so that she can marry her father is voicing a fantasy consistent with the _____ described by Freud.
   a. Oedipus complex
   b. Electra complex
   c. theory of mind
   d. crisis of initiative versus guilt

3. According to Erikson, before the preschool years children are incapable of feeling guilt because:
   a. guilt depends on a sense of self, which is not sufficiently established in preschoolers.
   b. they do not yet understand that they are male or female for life.
   c. this emotion is unlikely to have been reinforced at such an early age.
   d. guilt is associated with the resolution of the Oedipus complex, which occurs later in life.

4. Parents who are strict and aloof are *most* likely to make their children:
   a. cooperative and trusting.
   b. obedient but unhappy.
   c. violent.
   d. withdrawn and anxious.

5. When 4-year-old Seema grabs for Vincenzo's Beanie Baby, Vincenzo slaps her hand away, displaying an example of:
   a. bullying aggression.
   b. reactive aggression.
   c. instrumental aggression.
   d. relational aggression.

6. The belief that almost all sexual patterns are learned rather than inborn would find its strongest adherents among:
   a. cognitive theorists.
   b. behaviorists.
   c. psychoanalytic theorists.
   d. epigenetic theorists.

7. In explaining the origins of gender distinctions, Dr. Christie notes that every society teaches its children its values and attitudes regarding preferred behavior for men and women. Dr. Christie is evidently a proponent of:
   a. behaviorism.
   b. sociocultural theory.
   c. epigenetic theory.
   d. psychoanalytic theory.

8. Three-year-old Ali, who is fearful and withdrawn, is displaying signs of _____ problems, which suggests that he is emotionally _____ .
   a. internalizing; overcontrolled
   b. internalizing; undercontrolled
   c. externalizing; overcontrolled
   d. externalizing; undercontrolled

9. Summarizing her report on neurological aspects of emotional regulation, Alycia notes that young children who have internalizing problems tend to have greater activity in the:
   a. right temporal lobe.
   b. left temporal lobe.
   c. right prefrontal cortex.
   d. left prefrontal cortex.

10. Concerning children's concept of gender, which of the following statements is true?
    a. By age 3, children have a rudimentary understanding that sex distinctions are lifelong.
    b. Children as young as 1 year have a clear understanding of the physical differences between girls and boys and can consistently apply gender labels.
    c. Not until age 5 or 6 do children show a clear preference for gender-typed toys.
    d. All of the above are true.

11. Which of the following is *not* a feature of parenting used by Baumrind to differentiate authoritarian, permissive, and authoritative parents?
    a. maturity demands for the child's conduct
    b. efforts to control the child's actions
    c. nurturance
    d. adherence to stereotypic gender roles

12. Seeking to discipline her 3-year-old son for snatching a playmate's toy, Cassandra gently says, "How would you feel if Juwan grabbed your car?" Developmentalists would probably say that Cassandra's approach:
    a. is too permissive and would therefore be ineffective in the long run.
    b. would probably be more effective with a girl.
    c. will be effective in increasing prosocial behavior because it promotes empathy.
    d. will backfire and threaten her son's self-confidence.

13. Five-year-old Curtis, who is above average in height and weight, often picks on children who are smaller than he is. Curtis' behavior is an example of:
    a. bullying aggression.
    b. reactive aggression.
    c. instrumental aggression.
    d. relational aggression.

14. Although Juvaria and Brittany are sharing drawing materials and watching each other, their play is not yet mutual or reciprocal. Mildred Parten would probably classify this type of play as:
    a. onlooker.
    b. parallel.
    c. associative.
    d. cooperative.

15. Aldo and Jack are wrestling and hitting each other. Although this rough-and-tumble play mimics negative, aggressive behavior, it serves a useful purpose, which is to:
    a. rehearse social roles.
    b. develop interactive skills.
    c. improve fine motor skills.
    d. do both b. and c.

Key Terms

Writing Definitions

Using your own words, write a brief definition or explanation of each of the following terms on a separate piece of paper.

1. initiative versus guilt
2. self-esteem
3. self-concept
4. intrinsic motivation
5. emotional regulation
6. externalizing problems
7. internalizing problems
8. emotional intelligence
9. empathy
10. antipathy
11. prosocial behavior
12. antisocial behavior
13. rough-and-tumble play
14. sociodramatic play
15. instrumental aggression
16. reactive aggression
17. relational aggression
18. bullying aggression
19. authoritarian parenting
20. permissive parenting
21. authoritative parenting
22. time-out
23. sex differences
24. gender differences
25. phallic stage
26. Oedipus complex
27. identification
28. superego
29. Electra complex
30. androgyny

Cross-Check

Cross-Check
After you have written the definitions of the key terms in this chapter, you should complete the crossword puzzle to ensure that you can reverse the process—recognize the term, given the definition.

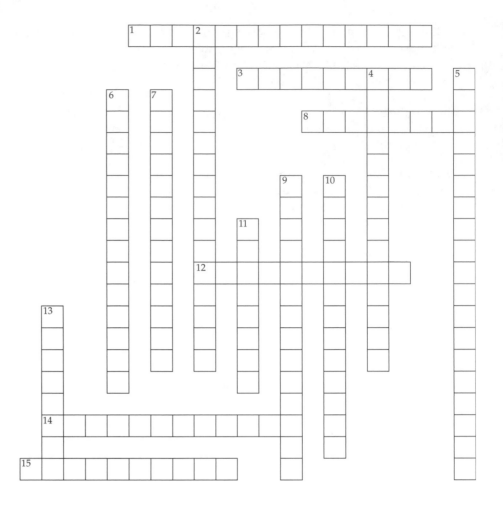

ACROSS

1. Physical play that often mimics aggression but involves no intent to harm.
3. A behavior, such as cooperating or sharing, performed to benefit another person without the expectation of a reward.
8. In psychoanalytic theory, the self-critical and judgmental part of personality that internalizes the moral standards set by parents and society.
12. Behavior that takes the form of insults or social rejection is called _____ aggression.
14. Act intended to obtain or retain an object desired by another is called _____ aggression.
15. Style of parenting in which parents make few demands on their children yet are nurturant and accepting and communicate well with their children.

DOWN

2. Cultural differences in the roles and behaviors of males and females.
4. Defense mechanism through which a person takes on the role and attitudes of a person more powerful than himself or herself.
5. Ability to manage and modify one's feelings, particularly feelings of fear, frustration, and anger.
6. In Freud's phallic stage of psychosexual development, a boy's sexual attraction toward the mother and resentment of the father.
7. Style of child-rearing in which the parents show little affection or nurturance for their children, maturity

demands are high, and parent–child communication is low.
9. In Freud's phallic stage of psychosexual development, a girl's sexual attraction toward the father and resentment of the mother.
10. Style of parenting in which the parents set limits and enforce rules but do so more democratically than do authoritarian parents.
11. Form of aggression involving an unprovoked attack on another child.
13. Aggressive behavior that is an angry retaliation for some intentional or incidental act by another person.

ANSWERS

CHAPTER REVIEW

1. initiative versus guilt; self-esteem; self-concept; pride
2. autonomy versus shame; complete; attention; persistence; try new experiences
3. guilt; guilt; shame; internalized
4. intrinsically motivated
5. emotional regulation; impulses; externalizing; undercontrolled; internalizing
6. experiences; culture
7. are; right prefrontal cortex; left prefrontal cortex
8. less
9. neurons; cortisol; lower-than-normal
10. care experiences; internalizing or externalizing
11. Daniel Goleman; emotional intelligence

12. empathy; prosocial behaviors; antipathy; antisocial behavior

13. 4 or 5; brain; emotional; theory of mind; caregivers

14. prejudiced

15. universal; adaptable

16. Mildred Parten; solitary; onlooker; parallel; associative; cooperative

17. rough-and-tumble; is universal; play face; social experience; are

18. sociodramatic; Girls; boys

19. aggression; instrumental; reactive; relational; bullying

20. instrumental aggression; reactive aggression; emotional regulation; bullying aggression

21. parenting

22. Diana Baumrind; warmth; discipline; communicate; maturity

23. authoritarian; low; high; low

24. permissive; are; well; few

25. authoritative; high; well; are; neglectful; indulgent

26. authoritarian; permissive; authoritative; grow stronger

27. temperament; community; cultural differences; parental warmth; support; concern; do not

28. exerts; reasoning; emotional; blame others; time-out; North America

a. Remember theory of mind.

b. Remember emerging self-concept.

c. Remember the language explosion and fast-mapping.

d. Remember that young children are not yet logical.

29. video violence; reality

30. 3

31. higher grades; boys; lower grades; girls

32. do

33. violent; sexist; racist

34. sex; gender; roles

35. less; gender

36. 2; 4; 8

37. phallic stage; mothers; fathers; Oedipus complex

38. identification; superego

39. Electra complex; penis envy

40. reinforced; punished

41. modeling

42. understanding

43. sociocultural; traditional; androgyny

44. epigenetic; genes; early experience

45. biologically; brains

46. sex hormones; environmental factors; language; speak

PROGRESS TEST 1

Multiple-Choice Questions

1. **b.** is the answer. (p. 286)

2. **c.** is the answer. (p. 312)

   a. & b. In Freud's theory, the oral and anal stages are associated with infant and early childhood development, respectively.

   d. In Freud's theory, the latency period is associated with development during the school years.

3. **a.** is the answer. (p. 297)

   b. & d. These two types of play are not discussed in this chapter. Mastery play is play that helps children develop new physical and intellectual skills. Sensorimotor play captures the pleasures of using the senses and motor skills.

   c. Rough-and-tumble play is physical play that mimics aggression.

4. **b.** is the answer. (p. 302)

   d. Traditional is a variation of the basic styles uncovered by later research. Indulgent and neglecting are abusive styles and clearly harmful, unlike the styles initially identified by Baumrind.

5. **a.** is the answer. (p. 302)

   b. & c. Authoritative parents communicate very well and are quite affectionate.

   d. This is not typical of authoritative parents.

6. **d.** is the answer. (p. 309)

7. **b.** is the answer. (p. 300)

8. **a.** is the answer. (p. 286)

9. **b.** is the answer. (p. 314)

   a. This is the focus of Freud's phallic stage.

   c. This is the focus of Erikson's psychosocial theory.

   d. This is the focus of cognitive theorists.

10. **a.** is the answer. (p. 311)

11. **c.** is the answer. (p. 292)

12. **d.** is the answer. In accounting for Leonardo's verbal ability, Dr. Laurent alludes to both genetic and environmental factors, a giveaway for epigenetic theory. (pp. 317–318)

    a., b., & c. These theories do not address biological or genetic influences on development.

13. **d.** is the answer. (p. 289)

    a. & b. Children who display internalizing problems are withdrawn and bottle up their emotions.

    c. Jake is displaying an inability to control his negative emotions.

14. **c.** is the answer. (pp. 305–306)

    a. & b. These strategies are more typical of Japanese mothers.

15. **d.** is the answer. (p. 299)

True or False Items

1. F   All parents make some maturity demands on their children; maturity demands are high in both the authoritarian and authoritative parenting styles. (p. 302)

2. T (p. 302)

3. F   Just the opposite is true. (p. 311)

4. T (p. 295)

5. T (p. 317)

6. T (p. 317)

7. T (pp. 312–318)

8. T (p. 311)

9. T (p. 313)

10. F   The reverse is true; it provides a way for children to learn emotional regulation. (p. 297)

PROGRESS TEST 2

Multiple-Choice Questions

1. **b.** is the answer. (p. 302)

2. **c.** is the answer. (p. 295)

    a. & b. Parents, especially mothers, are more understanding and self-sacrificing than playmates and so less able to teach this lesson.

    d. The text does not indicate that same-sex friends are more important in learning these than friends of the other sex.

3. **c.** is the answer. (p. 302)

4. **a.** is the answer. (p. 312)

    c. & d. The preference for same-sex playmates is universal.

5. **a.** is the answer. (p. 312)

6. **b.** is the answer. (p. 312)

    a. & d. These are Freud's versions of phallic-stage development in little girls.

    c. There is no such thing as the "phallic complex."

7. **c.** is the answer. (p. 302)

    a. & b. Both authoritarian and authoritative parents make high demands on their children.

    d. This is not one of the three parenting styles. Traditional parents could be any one of these types.

8. **b.** is the answer. (p. 293)

9. **c.** is the answer. (p. 293)

    a. This describes empathy.

    b. This describes self-concept.

    d. This describes an internalizing problem.

10. **c.** is the answer. (p. 313)

    a. & d. Behaviorism, which includes social learning theory, emphasizes that children learn about gender by rewards and punishments and by observing others.

    b. Sociocultural theory focuses on the impact of the environment on gender identification.

11. **a.** is the answer. (p. 306)

    b. & c. Time-outs involve removing a child from a situation in which misbehavior has occurred. Moreover, these threats of future punishment would likely be less effective because of the delay between the behavior and the consequence.

    d. Although developmentalists stress the need to prevent misdeeds instead of punishing them and warn that time-outs may have unintended consequences, they nevertheless can be an effective form of discipline.

12. **a.** is the answer. (pp. 285–286)

    b. This viewpoint is associated only with cognitive theory.

    c. Although parent–child relationships are important to social development, they do not determine readiness.

    d. Identification is a Freudian defense mechanism.

13. **a.** is the answer. (p. 290)

14. **c.** is the answer. (p. 302)

15. **b.** is the answer. (p. 286)

    a. & c. According to Erikson, these are the crises of adolescence and infancy, respectively.

    d. This is not a crisis described by Erikson.

Matching Items

1. g (p. 296)	**5.** h (p. 293)	**9.** c (p. 302)
2. k (p. 317)	**6.** b (p. 313)	**10.** j (p. 313)
3. i (p. 297)	**7.** e (p. 312)	**11.** a (p. 299)
4. d (p. 293)	**8.** f (p. 302)	

THINKING CRITICALLY ABOUT CHAPTER 10

1. a. is the answer. (p. 313)

2. b. is the answer. (p. 313)

a. According to Freud, the Oedipus complex refers to the male's sexual feelings toward his mother and resentment toward his father.

c. & d. These are concepts introduced by cognitive theorists and Erik Erikson, respectively.

3. a. is the answer. (pp. 286–287)

b. Erikson did not equate gender constancy with the emergence of guilt.

c. & d. These reflect the viewpoints of learning theory and Freud, respectively.

4. b. is the answer. (p. 302)

5. c. is the answer. The purpose of Vincenzo's action is clearly to retain the Beanie Baby, rather than to retaliate (b) or bully Seema (a). (p. 299)

d. Relational aggression takes the form of a verbal insult.

6. b. is the answer. (p. 314)

7. b. is the answer. (p. 316)

8. a. is the answer. (p. 289)

9. c. is the answer. (p. 290)

a. & b. The temporal lobes are involved in speech and hearing rather than emotional regulation.

d. Children who have externalizing problems tend to have greater activity in this area.

10. a. is the answer. (p. 311)

b. Not until about age 2 can children consistently apply gender labels.

c. By age 4, children prefer gender-typed toys.

11. d. is the answer. (p. 301)

12. c. is the answer. (p. 293)

13. a. is the answer. (p. 299)

14. c. is the answer. (p. 296)

a. & b. In onlooker and parallel play, children merely watch one another (onlooker) or play with similar toys (parallel) and do not interact.

d. Because Juvaria and Brittany are not creating or elaborating their drawings together, their play is not cooperative.

15. b. is the answer. (p. 296)

KEY TERMS

Writing Definitions

1. According to Erikson, the crisis of the preschool years is **initiative versus guilt**. In this crisis, young children eagerly take on new tasks and play activities and feel guilty when their efforts result in failure or criticism. (p. 286)

2. **Self-esteem** is the belief in one's own ability. (p. 286)

3. **Self-concept** refers to people's understanding of who they are. (p. 286)

4. **Intrinsic motivation** is the internal goals or drives to accomplish something for the joy of doing it. (p. 288)

5. **Emotional regulation** is the ability to inhibit, enhance, direct, and modulate emotions. (p. 288)

6. Young children who have **externalizing problems** tend to experience emotions outside themselves and uncontrollably lash out at other people or things. (p. 289)

7. Children who have **internalizing problems** tend to be fearful and withdrawn as a consequence of their tendencies to keep their emotions bottled up inside themselves. (p. 289)

8. **Emotional intelligence** is Goleman's term for a person's understanding of how to interpret and express emotions. (p. 292)

9. **Empathy** is a person's true understanding of the emotions of another person. (p. 293)

10. **Antipathy** is a person's feelings of anger, distrust, dislike, or even hatred toward another person. (p. 293)

11. **Prosocial behavior** is an action, such as helping or sharing, that is performed for another person without any obvious benefit. (p. 293)

12. **Antisocial behavior** is an action, such as hitting or insulting, that is deliberately hurtful or destructive. (p. 293)

13. **Rough-and-tumble play** is physical play that often mimics aggression but involves no intent to harm. (p. 296)

14. In **sociodramatic play**, children act out roles and themes in stories of their own creation, allowing them to develop a self-concept in a nonthreatening context. (p. 297)

15. **Instrumental aggression** is hurtful behavior whose purpose is to obtain or retain an object or privilege that is also desired by another. (p. 299)

16. **Reactive aggression** is impulsive retaliation for some intentional or accidental act, verbal or physical, by another person. (p. 299)

Memory aid: Instrumental aggression is behavior that is *instrumental* in allowing a child to retain a favorite toy. **Reactive aggression** is a *reaction* to another child's behavior.

17. Hurtful behavior that takes the form of verbal insults or social rejection is called **relational aggression**. (p. 299)

18. An unprovoked, repeated physical or verbal attack on another person is an example of **bullying aggression**. (p. 299)

19. **Authoritarian parenting** is Baumrind's term for a style of child rearing in which the parents show little affection or nurturance for their children; maturity demands are high and parent–child communication is low. (p. 302)

    Memory aid: Someone who is an **authoritarian** demands unquestioning obedience and acts in a dictatorial way.

20. **Permissive parenting** is Baumrind's term for a style of child rearing in which the parents make few demands on their children, yet are nurturant and accepting and communicate well with their children. (p. 302)

21. **Authoritative parenting** is Baumrind's term for a style of child rearing in which the parents set limits and enforce rules but are willing to listen to the child's ideas and to make compromises. (p. 302)

    Memory aid: **Authoritative parents** act as *authorities* do on a subject—by discussing and explaining why certain family rules are in place.

22. A **time-out** is a form of discipline in which a child is required to stop all activity and sit quietly apart from other people for a few minutes. (p. 306)

23. **Sex differences** are biological differences between females and males. (p. 311)

24. **Gender differences** are cultural differences in the roles and behavior of males and females. (p. 311)

25. In psychoanalytic theory, the **phallic stage** is the third stage of psychosexual development, in which the penis becomes the focus of concern and pleasure. (p. 312)

26. According to Freud, boys in the phallic stage of psychosexual development develop a collection of feelings, known as the **Oedipus complex**, that center on sexual attraction to the mother and resentment of the father. (p. 312)

27. In Freud's theory, **identification** is a means of defending one's self-concept by taking on the roles and attitudes of another person. (p. 313)

28. In psychoanalytic theory, the **superego** is the self-critical and judgmental part of personality that internalizes the moral standards of the parents. (p. 313)

29. Girls in Freud's phallic stage may develop a collection of feelings, known as the **Electra complex**, that center on sexual attraction to the father and resentment of the mother. (p. 313)

30. **Androgyny** is a balance of traditionally female and male psychological characteristics in a person. (p. 317)

Cross-Check

ACROSS

1. rough-and-tumble
3. prosocial
8. superego
12. relational
14. instrumental
15. permissive

DOWN

2. gender difference
4. identification
5. emotional regulation
6. Oedipus complex
7. authoritarian
9. Electra complex
10. authoritative
11. bullying
13. reactive

Chapter Eleven

The School Years: Biosocial Development

Chapter Overview

This chapter introduces middle childhood, the years from 7 to 11. Changes in physical size and shape are described, and the problem of obesity is addressed. The discussion then turns to the continuing development of motor and intellectual skills during the school years, culminating in an evaluation of intelligence testing. A final section examines the experiences of children with special needs, such as autistic children, those with learning disabilities, and those diagnosed as having an attention-deficit disorder. The causes of and treatments for these problems are discussed, with emphasis placed on insights arising from the new developmental psychopathology perspective. This perspective makes it clear that the manifestations of any special childhood problem will change as the child grows older and that treatment must often focus on all three domains of development.

NOTE: Answer guidelines for all Chapter 11 questions begin on page 171.

Guided Study

The text chapter should be studied one section at a time. Before you read, preview each section by skimming it, noting headings and boldface items. Then read the appropriate section objectives from the following outline. Keep these objectives in mind and, as you read the chapter section, search for the information that will enable you to meet each objective. Once you have finished a section, write out answers for its objectives.

A Healthy Time (pp. 327–333)

1. Describe normal physical growth and development during middle childhood, and account for the usual variations among children.

2. Discuss the problems of obese children in middle childhood, and describe possible causes.

3. Discuss the physical and psychological impact of chronic illness, especially asthma, during middle childhood.

Brain Development (pp. 333–342)

4. Discuss the role of brain maturation in motor and cognitive development during middle childhood.

5. Describe motor-skill development during the school years, focusing on variations due to culture, practice, motivation, and genetics.

6. (Issues and Applications) Discuss the benefits and hazards of play activity and physical exercise of 6- to 11-year-olds.

7. Explain how achievement and aptitude tests are used in evaluating individual differences in cognitive growth, and discuss why use of such tests is controversial.

8. Describe Sternberg's and Gardner's theories of multiple intelligences, and explain the significance of these theories.

Children with Special Needs (pp. 343–354)

9. Explain the new developmental psychopathology perspective, and discuss its value in treating children with special needs.

10. Identify the symptoms and possible causes of autism, and describe its most effective treatment.

11. Discuss the characteristics of learning disabilities.

12. Describe the symptoms and possible causes of ADD (attention-deficit disorder) and ADHD (attention-deficit/hyperactivity disorder).

13. Discuss the types of treatment available for children with attention-deficit disorders.

14. Describe techniques that have been tried in efforts to educate children with special needs.

Chapter Review

When you have finished reading the chapter, work through the material that follows to review it. Complete the sentences and answer the questions. As you proceed, evaluate your performance for each section by consulting the answers on page 171. Do not continue with the next section until you understand each answer. If you need to, review or reread the appropriate section in the textbook before continuing.

1. The biggest influence on development from age 7 to 11 is the changing _____ context.

A Healthy Time (pp. 327–333)

2. Compared with biosocial development during other periods of the life span, biosocial development during this time, known as _____ _____ , is _____ (relatively smooth/often fraught with problems). For example, disease and death during these years are _____ (more common/rarer) than during any other period.

3. Children grow at a _____ (faster/ slower) rate during middle childhood than they did earlier. The typical child gains about _____ pounds and at least _____ inches per year.

Describe several other features of physical development during the school years.

4. Variations in growth rate during middle childhood are caused by differences in _____ , _____ , and _____ .

5. Children are said to be overweight when their body mass index is in the top _____ (what number?) percentile of the growth chart for their age. Obesity is defined as having a BMI in the top _____ (what number?) percentile.

6. Childhood obesity, which is _____ (increasing/decreasing) in the United States, is hazardous to children's health because it reduces _____ and increases _____ _____ , both of which are associated with serious health problems in middle adulthood. School achievement and self-esteem _____ (increase/decrease) as weight increases.

7. Adopted children are more often overweight when their _____ (adoptive/biological) parents are obese. However, _____ factors are the main reasons for the recent increase in childhood obesity. The most significant of these is lack of _____ . Children of immigrants are often _____ (overfed/underfed) by their parents.

8. Overweight children are likely to experience puberty _____ (earlier/later) than their underweight peers. Historically, puberty began, on average, at age _____ , primarily because children had not accumulated enough _____ for brain _____ to trigger the process. Today, the more typical age of onset is _____ .

9. Compared to the past, middle childhood is now a healthier time _____ (in every nation of the world/only in developed nations).

10. During middle childhood, children are _____ (more/less) aware of one another's, or their own, physical imperfections.

11. A chronic inflammatory disorder of the airways is called _____ . This disorder is _____ (more common/less common) today than in the past.

12. The causes or triggers of asthma include _____ , _____ , and exposure to _____ such as pet hair.

13. The use of injections, inhalers, and pills to treat asthma is an example of _____ prevention. Less than _____ (how many?) of all asthmatic children in the United States benefit from this type of treatment. The best approach to treating childhood diseases is _____ _____ , which in the case of asthma includes proper _____ of homes and schools, decreased _____ , eradication of cockroaches, and safe outdoor _____ _____ .

Brain Development (pp. 333–342)

14. The brain reaches adult size at about age _____ . Advances in brain development during early childhood enable emerging _____ regulation and _____ _____ . Left-right coordination emerges in middle childhood as the _____ _____ strengthens connections between the brain's two _____ . The executive functions of the brain also develop, along with maturation of the _____ _____ . Increasing myelination in the cerebral cortex and cerebellum enables greater control over _____ _____ , _____ , _____ , and _____ _____ . Brain maturation also allows children to analyze the possible _____ of their behaviors before engaging in them.

15. Two other advances in brain function at this time include the ability to _____ _____ , called

_____ _____ , and the _____ of thoughts and actions that are repeated in sequence.

16. The most obvious evidence of neurological maturation is a child's _____ skills.

17. The length of time it takes a person to respond to a particular stimulus is called _____ _____ .

18. Other important abilities that continue to develop during the school years are _____– _____ _____ , balance, and judgment of _____ .

19. Animal research demonstrates that brain development is stimulated through _____ . In addition, _____-_____-_____ play may help boys overcome their genetic tendencies toward _____ and _____ _____ because it helps with regulation and coordination in the _____ _____ of the brain.

20. Along with brain maturation, _____ , _____ , and _____ are important factors in the development of motor skills. Early brain damage and _____ differences also affect motor skills. Approximately _____ percent of all children have a motor coordination disability serious enough to interfere with school achievement.

21. The potential to learn a particular skill or body of knowledge is a person's _____ . The most commonly used tests of this type are _____ _____ . In the original version of the most commonly used test of this type, a person's score was calculated as a _____ (the child's _____ _____ divided by the child's _____ _____ and multiplied by 100 to determine his or her _____).

22. Tests that are designed to measure what a child has learned are called _____ tests.

Tests that are designed to measure learning potential are called _____ tests.

23. Two highly regarded IQ tests are the

_____ _____

_____ _____

_____ and the

_____-_____ .

24. To be classified as _____

_____ , children must have IQs

below _____ and be unusually low

in _____ .

25. The average IQ scores of nations have

_____ (increased/decreased), a

phenomenon called the _____

_____ .

26. IQ tests are quite accurate at predicting

_____ achievement and somewhat

reliable in predicting adult success.

27. IQ testing is controversial in part because no test

can measure _____ without also

measuring _____ or without reflect-

ing the _____ . Another reason is

that a child's intellectual potential

_____ (changes/does not change)

over time.

28. Robert Sternberg believes that there are three dis-

tinct types of intelligence:_____ ,

_____ , and _____ .

Similarly, Howard Gardner describes

_____ (how many?) distinct

intelligences.

Children with Special Needs (pp. 343–354)

29. Among the conditions that give rise to "special

needs" are _____

_____

_____

_____ .

30. Down syndrome and other conditions that give

rise to "special needs" begin with a

_____ anomaly.

31. The field of study that is concerned with child-

hood psychological disorders is

_____ _____ . This

perspective has provided several lessons that

apply to all children. Three of these are that

_____ is normal; disability

_____ (changes/does not change)

over time; and adolescence and adulthood may

be _____ .

32. This perspective also has made diagnosticians

much more aware of the _____

_____ of childhood problems. This

awareness is reflected in the official diagnostic

guide of the American Psychiatric Association,

which is the _____

_____ .

33. The most severe disturbance of early childhood is

_____ , which is used to describe

children who are _____ . Autism is

an example of a _____ _____

_____ .

34. In early childhood autism, severe deficiencies

appear in three areas: _____ ability,

_____ _____ , and

_____ .

35. Children who have autistic symptoms that are

less severe than those in the classic syndrome are

sometimes diagnosed with _____

_____ , also called

_____-_____

_____ .

36. Although _____ make some

embryos vulnerable to autism, another possibility

is that some _____ harms their

developing brains. Among the possible toxins are

_____ , _____ ,

_____ , or _____ . One

suspected toxin is the antiseptic

_____ , which is used in childhood

_____ .

37. Children who have difficulty acquiring a particu-

lar skill that others acquire easily are said to have

a _____ _____ . The

crucial factor is a _____

_____ between expected learning

and actual accomplishment.

38. A disability in reading is called

    _____ . Other specific academic sub-
    jects that may show a learning disability are

    _____ , _____ , and

    _____ .

39. A condition that manifests itself in a difficulty in
    concentrating for more than a few moments is

    called _____-_____

    _____ . Children with this disorder

    may have an underdeveloped _____

    _____ , an overactive

    _____ _____ , or an

    imbalance of _____ .

40. The most common type of this disorder, which
    includes a need to be active, often accompanied
    by excitability and impulsivity, is called

    _____-_____/

    _____ _____ .

    Children suffering from this disorder can be

    _____ , _____ , and

    _____ .

41. Researchers have identified several factors that
    may contribute to ADHD. These include

    _____ _____ , prenatal

    damage from _____ , and postnatal

    damage, such as from _____

    _____ , and simply being at the

    extreme end of a normal distribution.

42. In childhood, the most effective forms of treat-
    ment for ADHD are _____ ,

    _____ therapy, and _____

    for parents and teachers.

43. Certain drugs that stimulate adults, such as

    _____ and _____ ,

    have a reverse effect on many hyperactive chil-
    dren.

44. In response to a 1975 act requiring that children
    with special needs be taught in the

    _____ _____

    _____ , the strategy of not separat-
    ing special-needs children into special classes,

called _____ , emerged. More
recently, some schools have developed a

_____ _____ , in

which such children spend part of each day with
a teaching specialist. In the most recent approach,

called _____ , learning-disabled
children receive targeted help within the setting
of a regular classroom.

45. The process of formally identifying a child with
    special needs usual begins with a teacher

    _____ , which may ultimately lead

    to agreement on an _____

    _____ _____ for the

    child.

Progress Test 1

Multiple-Choice Questions

Circle your answers to the following questions and
check them with the answers on page 172. If your
answer is incorrect, read the explanation for why it is
incorrect and then consult the appropriate pages of
the text (in parentheses following the correct answer).

1. As children move into middle childhood:
   a. the rate of accidental death increases.
   b. sexual urges intensify.
   c. the rate of weight gain increases.
   d. biological growth slows and steadies.

2. Ongoing maturation of which brain area contributes most to left–right coordination?
   a. corpus callosum
   b. prefrontal cortex
   c. brainstem
   d. temporal lobe

3. A factor that is *not* primary in the development of
   motor skills during middle childhood is:
   a. practice.   c. brain maturation.
   b. gender.   d. heredity.

4. Dyslexia is a learning disability that affects the
   ability to:
   a. do math.   c. write.
   b. read.   d. speak.

5. The developmental psychopathology perspective is characterized by its:
   a. contextual approach.
   b. emphasis on the unchanging nature of developmental disorders.
   c. emphasis on the cognitive domain of development.
   d. concern with all of the above.

6. The time—usually measured in fractions of a second—it takes for a person to respond to a particular stimulus is called:
   a. the interstimulus interval.
   b. reaction time.
   c. the stimulus-response interval.
   d. response latency.

7. The underlying problem in attention-deficit/hyperactivity disorder appears to be:
   a. low overall intelligence.
   b. a neurological difficulty in paying attention.
   c. a learning disability in a specific academic skill.
   d. the existence of a conduct disorder.

8. Most of the variation in children's growth rates can be attributed to:
   a. gender.
   b. nutrition.
   c. genes.
   d. the interaction of the above factors.

9. Autistic children generally have severe deficiencies in all but which of the following?
   a. social skills
   b. imaginative play
   c. echolalia
   d. communication ability

10. Although asthma has genetic origins, several environmental factors contribute to its onset, including:
    a. urbanization.
    b. airtight windows.
    c. dogs and cats living inside the house.
    d. all of the above.

11. Psychoactive drugs are most effective in treating attention-deficit/hyperactivity disorder when they are administered:
    a. before the diagnosis becomes certain.
    b. for several years after the basic problem has abated.
    c. as part of the labeling process.
    d. with psychological therapy and training of parents and teachers.

12. Tests that measure a child's potential to learn a new subject are called _____ tests.
    a. aptitude
    b. achievement
    c. vocational
    d. intelligence

13. In the earliest aptitude tests, a child's score was calculated by dividing the child's _____ age by his or her _____ age to find the _____ quotient.
    a. mental; chronological; intelligence
    b. chronological; mental; intelligence
    c. intelligence; chronological; mental
    d. intelligence; mental; chronological

14. Selective attention refers to the ability to:
    a. choose which of many stimuli to concentrate on.
    b. control emotional outbursts.
    c. persist at a task.
    d. perform a familiar action without much conscious thought.

15. Ongoing maturation of which brain area enables schoolchildren to more effectively analyze the potential consequences of their actions?
    a. corpus callosum
    b. cerebral cortex
    c. brainstem
    d. temporal lobe

True or False Items

Write *T* (*true*) or *F* (*false*) on the line in front of each statement.

_____ 1. Variations in children's growth are usually caused by diet rather than heredity.

_____ 2. Genes and hereditary differences in taste preferences are the most important factors in promoting childhood obesity.

_____ 3. Childhood obesity increases the risk for serious health problems in adulthood.

_____ 4. The quick reaction time that is crucial in some sports can be readily achieved with practice.

_____ 5. The intellectual performance of children with Asperger syndrome is poor in all areas.

_____ 6. The incidence of children with autistic characteristics is decreasing.

_____ 7. Despite the efforts of teachers and parents, most children with learning disabilities can expect their disabilities to persist and even worsen as they enter adulthood.

_____ 8. Stressful living conditions are an important consideration in diagnosing a learning disability.

_____ 9. The drugs sometimes given to children to reduce hyperactive behaviors have a reverse effect on adults.

_____ 10. Mainstreaming is the most effective educational method for children with special needs.

Progress Test 2

Progress Test 2 should be completed during a final chapter review. Answer the following questions after you thoroughly understand the correct answers for the Chapter Review and Progress Test 1.

Multiple-Choice Questions

1. During the years from 7 to 11, the average child:
   a. becomes slimmer.
   b. gains about 12 pounds a year.
   c. has decreased lung capacity.
   d. is more likely to become obese than at any other period in the life span.

2. Among the factors that are known to contribute to obesity are body type, quantity and types of food eaten, and:
   a. metabolism.
   b. activity level.
   c. TV watching.
   d. all of the above.

3. A specific learning disability that becomes apparent when a child experiences unusual difficulty in learning to read is:
   a. dyslexia.   c. ADHD.
   b. dyscalcula.   d. ADD.

4. Problems in learning to write, read, and do math are collectively referred to as:
   a. learning disabilities.
   b. attention-deficit/hyperactivity disorder.
   c. hyperactivity.
   d. dyscalcula.

5. Aptitude and achievement testing are controversial in part because:
   a. most tests are unreliable with respect to the individual scores they yield.
   b. a child's intellectual potential often changes over time.
   c. they often fail to identify serious learning problems.
   d. of all of the above reasons.

6. The most effective form of help for children with ADHD is:
   a. medication.
   b. psychological therapy.
   c. training parents and teachers.
   d. a combination of some or all of the above.

7. A key factor in reaction time is:
   a. whether the child is male or female.
   b. brain maturation.
   c. whether the stimulus to be reacted to is an auditory or visual one.
   d. all of the above.

8. The first noticeable symptom of autism is usually:
   a. the lack of spoken language.
   b. abnormal social responsiveness.
   c. both a. and b.
   d. unpredictable.

9. Which of the following is true of children with a diagnosed learning disability?
   a. They are, in most cases, average in intelligence.
   b. They often have a specific physical handicap, such as hearing loss.
   c. They often lack basic educational experiences.
   d. All of the above are true.

10. Which of the following is a key factor in the automatization of children's thoughts and actions?
    a. the continuing myelination of neurons
    b. diet
    c. activity level
    d. All of the above are key factors.

11. Which approach to education may best meet the needs of learning-disabled children in terms of both skill remediation and social interaction with other children?
    a. mainstreaming
    b. special education
    c. inclusion
    d. resource rooms

12. Asperger syndrome is a disorder in which:
    a. body weight fluctuates dramatically over short periods of time.
    b. verbal skills seem normal, but social perceptions and skills are abnormal.
    c. an autistic child is extremely aggressive.
    d. a child of normal intelligence has difficulty mastering a specific cognitive skill.

13. Which of the following is *not* a contributing factor in most cases of ADHD?

   a. genetic inheritance
   b. dietary sugar and caffeine
   c. prenatal damage
   d. postnatal damage

14. Tests that measure what a child has already learned are called _____ tests.

   a. aptitude
   b. vocational
   c. achievement
   d. intelligence

15. Which of the following is *not* a type of intelligence identified in Robert Sternberg's theory?

   a. academic
   b. practical
   c. achievement
   d. creative

Matching Items

Match each term or concept with its corresponding description or definition.

Terms or Concepts

_____ **1.** dyslexia
_____ **2.** automatization
_____ **3.** Asperger syndrome
_____ **4.** attention-deficit/hyperactivity disorder
_____ **5.** asthma
_____ **6.** Flynn Effect
_____ **7.** autism
_____ **8.** developmental psychopathology
_____ **9.** *DSM-IV-R*
_____ **10.** learning disability
_____ **11.** mainstreaming

Descriptions or Definitions

a. set of symptoms in which a child has impaired social skills despite having normal speech and intelligence
b. the rise in IQ score averages that has occurred in many nations
c. the diagnostic guide of the American Psychiatric Association
d. process by which thoughts and actions become routine and no longer require much thought
e. system in which learning-disabled children are taught in general education classrooms
f. disorder characterized by self-absorption
g. chronic inflammation of the airways
h. behavior problem involving difficulty in concentrating, as well as excitability and impulsivity
i. applies insights from studies of normal development to the study of childhood disorders
j. an unexpected difficulty with one or more academic skills
k. difficulty in reading

Thinking Critically About Chapter 11

Answer these questions the day before an exam as a final check on your understanding of the chapter's terms and concepts.

1. According to developmentalists, the best game for a typical group of 8-year-olds would be:

   a. football or baseball.
   b. basketball.
   c. one in which reaction time is not crucial.
   d. a game involving one-on-one competition.

2. Dr. Rutter, who believes that knowledge about normal development can be applied to the study and treatment of psychological disorders, evidently is working from which of the following perspectives?

   a. clinical psychology
   b. developmental psychopathology
   c. behaviorism
   d. psychoanalysis

3. Twelve-year-old Angela, who just began puberty, is surprised to learn that her grandmother was 15 when she began puberty. You tell her the difference is likely due to the fact that children today:

   a. experience more stress-related hormonal changes than did children in earlier generations.

   b. accumulate enough body fat for hormones in the brain to kick off the process at a younger age.

   c. are much more variable in the ages at which they begin puberty.

   d. are not as well nourished.

4. Angela was born in 1984. In 1992, she scored 125 on an intelligence test. Using the original formula, what was Angela's mental age when she took the test?

   a. 6   c. 10
   b. 8   d. 12

5. Ten-year-old Clarence is quick-tempered, easily frustrated, and is often disruptive in the classroom. Clarence may be suffering from:

   a. dyslexia.

   b. Asperger syndrome.

   c. attention-deficit disorder.

   d. attention-deficit/hyperactivity disorder.

6. Because 11-year-old Wayne is obese, he runs a greater risk of developing:

   a. heart problems.

   b. diabetes.

   c. psychological problems.

   d. all of the above.

7. Of the following individuals, who is likely to have the fastest reaction time?

   a. a 7-year-old   c. an 11-year-old
   b. a 9-year-old   d. an adult

8. Harold weighs about 20 pounds more than his friend Jay. During school recess, Jay can usually be found playing soccer with his classmates, while Harold sits on the sidelines by himself. Harold's rejection is likely due to his:

   a. being physically different.

   b. being dyslexic.

   c. intimidation of his schoolmates.

   d. being hyperactive.

9. In determining whether an 8-year-old has a learning disability, a teacher looks primarily for:

   a. exceptional performance in a subject area.

   b. the exclusion of other explanations.

   c. a family history of the learning disability.

   d. both a. and b.

10. Although 9-year-old Carl has severely impaired social skills, his intelligence and speech are normal. Carl is evidently displaying symptoms of:

   a. autism.

   b. ADD.

   c. ADHD.

   d. Asperger syndrome.

11. Concluding his presentation on the Flynn Effect, Kwame notes that the reasons for this trend include all of the following except:

   a. better health.

   b. genetic vulnerability.

   c. more schooling.

   d. smaller families.

12. Jennifer has been diagnosed as having a pervasive developmental disorder. As an infant, her brain grew too rapidly, especially in the limbic area. It is likely that suffers from:

   a. autism.

   b. Rett syndrome.

   c. dyslexia.

   d. dyscalcula.

13. Danny has been diagnosed as having attention-deficit/hyperactivity disorder. Every day his parents make sure that he takes the proper dose of Ritalin. His parents should:

   a. continue this behavior until Danny is an adult.

   b. try different medications when Danny seems to be reverting to his normal overactive behavior.

   c. make sure that Danny also has psychotherapy.

   d. not worry about Danny's condition; he will outgrow it.

14. Concluding her presentation on "Asthma During Middle Childhood," Amanda mentions each of the following except that:

   a. asthma is much more common today than 20 years ago.

   b. genetic vulnerability is rarely a factor in a child's susceptibility to developing asthma.

   c. the incidence of asthma continues to increase.

   d. carpeted floors, airtight windows, and less outdoor play increase the risk of asthma attacks.

15. Howard Gardner and Robert Sternberg would probably be most critical of traditional aptitude and achievement tests because they:
    a. inadvertently reflect certain nonacademic competencies.
    b. do not reflect knowledge of cultural ideas.
    c. measure only a limited set of abilities.
    d. underestimate the intellectual potential of disadvantaged children.

Key Terms

Using your own words, write a brief definition or explanation of each of the following terms on a separate piece of paper.

1. middle childhood
2. overweight
3. obesity
4. asthma
5. selective attention
6. automatization
7. reaction time
8. aptitude
9. IQ test
10. achievement test
11. Wechsler Intelligence Scale for Children (WISC)
12. mental retardation
13. Flynn Effect
14. child with special needs
15. developmental psychopathology
16. *Diagnostic and Statistical Manual of Mental Disorders (DSM-IV-R)*
17. pervasive developmental disorders
18. autism
19. learning disability
20. dyslexia
21. attention-deficit disorder (ADD)
22. attention-deficit/hyperactivity disorder (ADHD)
23. least restrictive environment (LRE)
24. mainstreaming
25. resource room
26. inclusion
27. individual education plan (IEP)

ANSWERS
CHAPTER REVIEW

1. social
2. middle childhood; relatively smooth; rarer
3. slower; 5 to 7; 2

During the school years, children generally become slimmer, muscles become stronger, and lung capacity increases.

4. genes; gender; nutrition
5. 15; 5
6. increasing; exercise; blood pressure; decrease
7. biological; environmental; exercise; overfed
8. earlier; 14; body fat; hormones; 11 or 12
9. in every nation of the world
10. more
11. asthma; more common
12. genes; infections; allergens
13. tertiary; half; primary prevention; ventilation; pollution; play spaces
14. 7; emotional; theory of mind; corpus callosum; hemispheres; prefrontal cortex; emotional outbursts; perseveration, inattention, the insistence on routines; consequences
15. pay special heed to one source of information among many; selective attention; automatization
16. motor
17. reaction time
18. eye–hand coordination; movement
19. play; rough-and-tumble; hyperactivity; learning disabilities; frontal lobes
20. culture, practice, motivation; heredity; 6
21. aptitude; IQ tests; quotient; mental age; chronological age; IQ
22. achievement; aptitude
23. Wechsler Intelligence Scale for Children (WISC); Stanford-Binet
24. mentally retarded; 70; adaptation to daily life
25. increased; Flynn Effect
26. school
27. aptitude; achievement; culture; changes
28. academic; creative; practical; eight
29. anxiety disorder, autism, conduct disorder, clinical depression, developmental delay, learning disability, Down syndrome, attachment disorder, attention-deficit disorder, bipolar disorder, and Asperger syndrome
30. biological

31. developmental psychopathology; abnormality; changes; better or worse

32. social context; *Diagnostic and Statistical Manual of Mental Disorders* (DSM-IV-R)

33. autism; self-absorbed; pervasive developmental disorder

34. language; social interaction; play

35. Asperger syndrome; high-functioning autism

36. genes; teratogen; viruses; infections; pesticides; drugs; thimerosal; immunizations

37. learning disability; measured discrepancy

38. dyslexia; math; spelling; handwriting

39. attention-deficit disorder; prefrontal cortex; limbic system; neurotransmitters

40. attention deficit/hyperactivity disorder; inattentive; impulsive; overactive

41. genetic vulnerability; teratogens; lead poisoning

42. medication; psychological; training

43. amphetamines; methylphenidate (Ritalin)

44. least restrictive environment (LRE); mainstreaming; resource room; inclusion

45. referral; individual education plan (IEP)

PROGRESS TEST 1

Multiple-Choice Questions

1. **d.** is the answer. (p. 327)

2. **a.** is the answer. (p. 333)

3. **b.** Gender is not mentioned as a factor in the development of motor skills. (pp. 335, 338)

4. **b.** is the answer. (p. 348)

   a. Though not defined in the text, this is called dyscalcula.

   c. & d. The text does not give labels for learning disabilities in writing or speaking.

5. **a.** is the answer. (p. 344)

   b. & c. Because of its contextual approach, developmental psychopathology emphasizes *all* domains of development. Also, it points out that behaviors change over time.

6. **b.** is the answer. (p. 338)

7. **b.** is the answer. (p. 349)

8. **d.** is the answer. (p. 328)

9. **c.** is the answer. Echolalia *is* a type of communication difficulty, a characteristic form of speech of many autistic children. (pp. 345–346)

10. **d.** is the answer. (p. 332)

11. **d.** is the answer. (p. 349)

12. **a.** is the answer. (p. 339)

   b. Achievement tests measure what has already been learned.

   c. Vocational tests, which, as their name implies, measure what a person has learned about a particular trade, are achievement tests.

   d. Intelligence tests measure general aptitude, rather than aptitude for a specific subject.

13. **a.** is the answer. (p. 339)

14. **a.** is the answer. (p. 334)

   b. This is emotional regulation.

   d. This is automatization.

15. **b.** is the answer. (pp. 333–334)

   a. Maturation of the corpus callosum contributes to left–right coordination.

   c. & d. These brain areas, which were not discussed in this chapter, play important roles in regulating sleep–waking cycles (brainstem) and hearing and language abilities (temporal lobe).

True or False Items

1. F   Variations in children's growth are caused by heredity and gender as well as nutrition. (p. 328)

2. F   Environmental factors are more important in promoting obesity during middle childhood. (p. 329)

3. T   (p. 329)

4. F   Reaction time depends on brain maturation and is not readily affected by practice. (p. 338)

5. F   Children with Asperger syndrome show isolated areas of remarkable skill. (p. 345)

6. T (p. 346)

7. F   Some children find ways to compensate for their deficiencies, and others are taught effective strategies for learning. (p. 348)

8. F   Stressful living conditions must be excluded before diagnosing a learning disability. (p. 347)

9. T (pp. 349–350)

10. F   Mainstreaming did not meet all children's educational needs. (p. 351)

PROGRESS TEST 2

Multiple-Choice Questions

1. **a.** is the answer. (p. 328)

   b. & c. During this period children gain 5 to 7 pounds per year and experience increased lung capacity.

d. Although childhood obesity is a common problem, the text does not indicate that a person is more likely to become obese at this age than at any other.

2. **d.** is the answer. (pp. 329–330)

3. **a.** is the answer. (p. 348)

b. Although not discussed in the text, this learning disability involves math rather than reading.

c. & d. These disorders do not manifest themselves in a particular academic skill but instead appear in psychological processes that affect learning in general.

4. **a.** is the answer. (p. 347)

b. & c. ADHD is a disorder that usually does not manifest itself in specific subject areas. Hyperactivity is a facet of this disorder.

d. Dyslexia is a learning disability in reading only.

5. **b.** is the answer. (p. 341)

6. **d.** is the answer. (p. 349)

7. **b.** is the answer. (p. 338)

8. **c.** is the answer. (p. 345)

9. **a.** is the answer. (p. 347)

10. **a.** is the answer. (p. 334)

11. **c.** is the answer. (p. 351)

a. Many general education teachers are unable to cope with the special needs of some children.

b. & d. These approaches undermined the social integration of children with special needs.

12. **b.** is the answer. (p. 345)

13. **b.** is the answer. (p. 349)

14. **c.** is the answer. (p. 339)

15. **c.** is the answer. (p. 342)

Matching Items

1. k (p. 348)	**5.** g (p. 331)	**9.** c (p. 344)
2. d (p. 334)	**6.** b (p. 341)	**10.** j (p. 347)
3. a (p. 345)	**7.** f (p. 345)	**11.** e (p. 351)
4. h (p. 349)	**8.** i (p. 344)	

THINKING CRITICALLY ABOUT CHAPTER 11

1. **c.** is the answer. (p. 338)

a. & b. Each of these games involves skills that are hardest for schoolchildren to master.

d. Because one-on-one sports are likely to accentuate individual differences in ability, they may be especially discouraging to some children.

2. **b.** is the answer. (p. 344)

3. **b.** is the answer. (p. 330)

4. **c.** is the answer. At the time she took the test, Angela's chronological age was 8. Knowing that her IQ was 125, we can solve the equation to yield a mental age value of 10. (p. 340)

5. **d.** is the answer. (p. 349)

6. **d.** is the answer. (p. 329)

7. **d.** is the answer. (p. 338)

8. **a.** is the answer. (p. 329)

b., c., & d. Obese children are no more likely to be dyslexic, physically intimidating, or hyperactive than other children.

9. **d.** is the answer. (p. 347)

10. **d.** is the answer. (p. 345)

11. **b.** is the answer. (p. 341)

12. **a.** is the answer. (p. 345)

b. In Rett syndrome, the brain does not grow and development is slow.

c. & d. Dyslexia and dyscalcula are learning disabilities.

13. **c.** is the answer. Medication alone cannot ameliorate all the problems of ADHD. (p. 349)

14. **b.** is the answer. Genes typically *do* play a role in a child's susceptibility to asthma. (p. 331)

15. **c.** is the answer. Both Sternberg and Gardner believe that there are multiple intelligences rather than the narrowly defined abilities measured by traditional aptitude and achievement tests. (p. 342)

a., b., & d. Although these criticisms are certainly valid, they are not specifically associated with Sternberg or Gardner.

KEY TERMS

1. **Middle childhood** is the period from roughly age 6 or 7 to 10 or 11. (p. 327)

2. A person whose body mass index (BMI) falls in the top 15th percentile for people of a specific age and height is designated as **overweight.** (p. 328)

3. **Obesity** is a body mass index (BMI) in the top 5th percentile for people of a specific age and height. (p. 328)

4. **Asthma** is a disorder in which the airways are chronically inflamed. (p. 331)

5. **Selective attention** is the ability to concentrate on one stimulus while ignoring others. (p. 334)

6. **Automatization** is the process by which thoughts and actions that are repeated often enough to become routine no longer require much conscious thought. (p. 334)

7. **Reaction time** is the length of time it takes a person to respond to a particular stimulus. (p. 338)

8. **Aptitude** is the potential to learn a particular skill or body of knowledge. (p. 339)

9. **IQ tests** are aptitude tests, which were originally designed to yield a measure of intelligence and calculated as mental age divided by chronological age, multiplied by 100. (p. 339)

10. **Achievement tests** are tests that measure what a child has already learned in a particular academic subject or subjects. (p. 339)

11. The **Wechsler Intelligence Scale for Children (WISC)** is a widely used IQ test for school-age children that assesses vocabulary, general knowledge, memory, and spatial comprehension. (p. 340)

12. People are considered **mentally retarded** if their IQs fall below 70 and they are unusually low in adaptation to daily life. (p. 340)

13. The **Flynn Effect** refers to the increases in average IQ scores that has occurred recently in many nations. (p. 341)

14. A **child with special needs** is one who, because of physical or mental disability, requires extra help in order to learn. (p. 344)

15. **Developmental psychopathology** is a field that applies the insights from studies of normal development to the study and treatment of childhood disorders, and vice versa. (p. 344)

16. The fourth edition of the *Diagnostic and Statistical Manual of Mental Disorders (DSM-IV-R)*, developed by the American Psychiatric Association, is the leading means of diagnosing mental disorders. (p. 344)

17. **Pervasive developmental disorders,** such as autism, are disorders that affect numerous aspects of the psychological growth of a child under age 6. (p. 345)

18. **Autism** is a severe disturbance of early childhood characterized by an inability to communicate with others in an ordinary way, by extreme self-absorption, and by an inability to learn normal speech. (p. 345)

19. A **learning disability is** a difficulty in a particular area of learning that is not attributable to overall intellectual slowness, a physical handicap, or a severely stressful living condition. (p. 347)

20. **Dyslexia is** a learning disability in reading. (p. 348)

21. **Attention-deficit disorder (ADD)** is a condition in which a child has great difficulty concentrating but is not impulsive or overactive. (p. 349)

22. A form of ADD, **attention-deficit/hyperactivity disorder (ADHD)** is a behavior problem in which the individual has great difficulty concentrating and is often inattentive, impulsive, and overactive. (p. 349)

23. A **least restrictive environment (LRE)** is a legally required school setting that offers special-needs children as much freedom as possible to benefit from the instruction available to other children, often in a mainstreamed classroom. (p. 351)

24. **Mainstreaming** is an educational approach in which children with special needs are included in regular classrooms. (p. 351)

25. A **resource room** is a classroom equipped with special material, in which children with special needs spend part of their day working with a trained specialist in order to learn basic skills. (p. 351)

26. **Inclusion** is an educational approach in which children with special needs receive individualized instruction within a regular classroom setting. (p. 351)

27. An **individual education plan (IEP)** is a legal document that specifies a set of educational goals and plans for a child with special needs. (p. 351)

Chapter Twelve

The School Years: Cognitive Development

Chapter Overview

Chapter 12 examines the development of cognitive abilities in children from ages 7 to 11. The first section discusses the views of Piaget and Vygotsky regarding the child's cognitive development, which involves a growing ability to use logic and reasoning (as emphasized by Piaget) and to benefit from social interactions with skilled mentors (as emphasized by Vygotsky). Because the school years are also a time of expanding moral reasoning, this section also examines Kohlberg's stage theory of moral development as well as current evaluations of his theory.

The second section focuses on changes in the child's processing speed and capacity, control processes, knowledge base, and metacognition. It also looks at language development during middle childhood. During this time, children develop a more analytic understanding of words and show a marked improvement in their language skills.

The last section covers educational and environmental conditions that are conducive to learning by schoolchildren, including how reading, math, and science are best taught, and fluency in a second language.

NOTE: Answer guidelines for all Chapter 12 questions begin on page 187.

Guided Study

The text chapter should be studied one section at a time. Before you read, preview each section by skimming it, noting headings and boldface items. Then read the appropriate section objectives from the following outline. Keep these objectives in mind and, as you read the chapter section, search for the information that will enable you to meet each objective. Once you have finished a section, write out answers for its objectives.

Building on Piaget and Vygotsky (pp. 357–366)

1. Identify and discuss the logical operations of concrete operational thought, and give examples of how these operations are demonstrated by schoolchildren.

2. Discuss Vygotsky's views regarding the influence of the sociocultural context on learning during middle childhood.

3. Outline Kohlberg's stage theory of moral development.

4. Identify and evaluate several criticisms of Kohlberg's theory, and discuss sociocultural effects on moral development.

Information Processing (pp. 366–374)

5. Describe the components of the information-processing system, noting how they interact.

6. Explain how processing speed increases in middle childhood as the result of advances in myelination and brain connections and a larger knowledge base.

7. Discuss advances in the control processes, especially selective attention and metacognition, during middle childhood.

8. Describe the development of language during the school years, noting changing abilities in vocabulary and pragmatics.

9. Discuss the relationship between language development and socioeconomic status.

Teaching and Learning (pp. 374–391)

10. Describe the concept of a hidden curriculum.

11. Discuss different approaches to the objective assessment of what children have learned, and describe differences between the American and Japanese educational systems.

12. Differentiate several approaches to teaching reading and math, and discuss evidence regarding the effectiveness of these methods.

13. Discuss the merits of small class size.

14. Identify several conditions that foster the learning of a second language, and describe the best approaches to bilingual education.

Chapter Review

When you have finished reading the chapter, work through the material that follows to review it. Complete the sentences and answer the questions. As you proceed, evaluate your performance for each section by consulting the answers beginning on page 187. Do not continue with the next section until you understand each answer. If you need to, review or reread the appropriate section in the textbook before continuing.

1. In 2001, Congress passed legislation to improve public education in the United States. This was the _____ _____ _____ _____ Act.

Building on Piaget and Vygotsky (pp. 357–366)

2. According to Piaget, between ages 7 and 11, children are in the stage of _____ _____ _____ . Unlike Piaget, Vygotsky regarded instruction by _____ as crucial to cognitive development.

3. The concept that objects can be organized into categories according to some common property is _____ .
The logical principle that certain characteristics of an object remain the same even when other characteristics change is _____ . The idea that a transformation process can be reversed to restore the original condition is _____ . The logical principle that two things can change in opposite ways to balance each other out is _____ .

4. Neurological research demonstrates that learning is both _____ and _____ . This supports the theories of both _____ and _____ .

5. Cross-cultural studies of classification and other logical processes demonstrate that these principles _____ (apply/do not apply) throughout the world.

6. The theorist who has extensively studied moral development by presenting subjects with stories that pose ethical dilemmas is _____ .

According to his theory, the three levels of moral reasoning are _____ , _____ , and _____ .

7. (Table 12.1) In preconventional reasoning, emphasis is on getting _____ and avoiding _____ . "Might makes right" describes stage _____ (1/2), whereas "look out for number one" describes stage _____ (1/2).

8. (Table 12.1) In conventional reasoning, emphasis is on _____ _____ , such as being a dutiful citizen, in stage _____ (3/4), or winning approval from others, in stage _____ (3/4).

9. (Table 12.1) In postconventional reasoning, emphasis is on _____ _____ , such as _____ _____ (stage 5) and _____ _____ _____ (stage 6).

10. During middle childhood, children's moral reasoning generally falls at the _____ and _____ levels.

11. One criticism of Kohlberg's theory is that the later stages reflect values associated with liberal, _____ intellectual values. Another is that Kohlberg ignored the moral development of _____ .

12. Also, Kohlberg may have _____ (underestimated/overestimated) the potential of school-age children. It is now well established that different cultures _____ (have/do not have) distinctive morals and values.

13. Carol Gilligan believes that females develop a _____ _____ _____ , based on concern for the well-being of others, more than a _____ _____ _____ , based on depersonalized standards of right and wrong. Research testing Gilligan's theory _____ (finds/does not find) a male–female difference in moral thought.

Information Processing (pp. 366–374)

14. The idea that the advances in thinking that accompany middle childhood occur because of basic changes in how children take in, store, and process data is central to the _____-_____ theory.

15. Incoming stimulus information is held for a split second in the _____ _____ , after which most of it is lost.

16. Meaningful material is transferred into _____ _____ , which is sometimes called _____-_____ _____ . This part of memory handles mental activity that is _____ .

17. The part of memory that stores information for days, months, or years is _____-_____ _____ . Crucial in this component of the system is not only storage of the material but also its _____ .

18. The ability to remember the origin of information, called _____ _____ , is particularly inadequate in middle childhood, partly because of the immaturity of the _____ _____ . Adults may confuse a child's tendency to imagine things that never happened, called _____ , with lying.

19. Children in the school years are better learners and problem solvers than younger children are, because they have faster _____ _____ , and they have a larger mental _____ .

20. One reason for the cognitive advances of middle childhood is _____ maturation, especially the _____ of neural axons and the development of the _____ _____ .

21. Processing capacity also becomes more efficient through _____ , as familiar mental activities become routine.

22. Memory ability improves during middle childhood in part because of the child's expanded _____ _____ .

23. The knowledge base also depends on _____ and _____ .

24. The mechanisms of the information-processing system that regulate the analysis and flow of information are the _____ _____ . These include _____ _____ , _____ , and _____ _____ .

25. The area of the brain called the _____ _____ is sometimes called the _____ _____ , because it controls other parts of the brain.

26. The ability to use _____ _____—to screen out distractors and concentrate on relevant information— improves steadily during the school years and beyond.

27. The ability to evaluate a cognitive task to determine what to do—and to monitor and adjust one's performance—is called _____ . This ability becomes evident by age _____ .

28. The practical application of linguistic knowledge is called the _____ of language.

29. During middle childhood, some children learn as many as _____ new words a day. Unlike the vocabulary explosion of the play years, this language growth is distinguished by _____ , _____ , _____ , and the ability to make connections between one bit of knowledge and another and later vocabulary performance in school.

30. Children's ability to change from proper speech, or a _____ _____ , to a colloquial form, or _____ _____ , with their peers is called _____-_____ .

31. Language development and socioeconomic status _____ (are strongly correlated/are not correlated). Children from families that are low in _____ _____ tend to fall behind in _____ and then in _____ and other subjects.

32. Two crucial factors that affect language development are _____ _____ and _____ .

33. Schoolchildren's love of words is evident in their _____ , secret _____ , the _____ they use, the puns they enjoy, and the _____ that they tell.

Teaching and Learning (pp. 374–391)

34. In middle childhood, instruction is best if it is _____ and _____ . There _____ (is/is not) universal agreement on how best to educate schoolchildren.

35. Every culture creates its own _____ _____ , the unofficial rules and priorities that influence every aspect of school learning. These rules are taught by the way schools are _____ , by the _____ of schools, by the school's _____ , and by the _____ _____ of the school.

36. Two international approaches to objective assessment of children's school achievement are the _____ and the _____ .

37. Some researchers distinguish among the _____ curriculum, which refers to the content endorsed by _____ _____ ; the _____ curriculum, which refers

to what is actually offered; and the
_____ curriculum, which is what
the students actually learn.

Describe several differences between the educational
systems in Japan and the United States.

38. Japanese children _____ (score
about the same as/outscore) U.S. children on
most tests of academic achievement. The recent
shift toward greater federal involvement in education in the United States was triggered by pas-
sage of the _____ _____
_____ _____ Act.

39. Two distinct approaches to teaching reading are
the _____ approach, in which chil-
dren learn the sounds of letters first, and the
_____-_____
approach, in which children are encouraged to
develop all their language skills at the same time.
Most developmentalists believe that
_____(both approaches/neither
approach/only the phonics approach/only the
whole-language approach) make(s) sense.

40. In the United States, math was traditionally
taught through _____ . A more
recent approach replaces this type of learning by
emphasizing _____ ,
_____ _____ , and
estimating _____ . Recommended
techniques stress _____
_____ .

41. Cross-cultural research reveals that North
American teachers present math at a lower level
with more _____ but less
_____ to other learning. In contrast,
teachers in Japan work more _____
to build children's knowledge.

42. Most people assume that children learn best
when class size is _____ . Research
studies demonstrate that the relationship
between class size and student performance is
_____ (clear-cut/complex).

43. Children who speak a minority language and are
learning to speak English are called
_____-_____
_____ . The best time to learn a second language by listening and talking is during
_____ _____ , and the
best time to teach a second language is during
_____ _____ .

44. The approach to bilingual education in which the
child's instruction occurs entirely in the second
language is called _____
_____ . In _____
_____ programs, teachers instruct
children in both their native language as well as
in English. Some programs offer
_____ _____ classes
that allow children to connect with their culture
while learning academic subjects in the dominant
language.

45. (Table 12.4) In ESL, or _____
_____
programs, children must master the basics of
English before joining regular classes with other
children.

46. Immersion programs were successful in
_____ , when English-speaking chil-
dren were initially placed in French-only classrooms. Immersion tends to fail if the child feels
_____ , _____ ,
or _____ _____ .

47. The crucial difference between success and failure in second-language learning rests with
_____
_____ . When
both languages are valued, _____
_____ is likely to occur. When
second-language learning fails and neither language is learned well, a child is said to be
_____ .

Progress Test 1

Multiple-Choice Questions

Circle your answers to the following questions and check them with the answers on beginning on page 187. If your answer is incorrect, read the explanation for why it is incorrect and then consult the appropriate pages of the text (in parentheses following the correct answer).

1. According to Piaget, the stage of cognitive development in which a person understands specific logical ideas and can apply them to concrete problems is called:
   a. preoperational thought.
   b. operational thought.
   c. concrete operational thought.
   d. formal operational thought.

2. Japanese children outscore children in the United States in math. This difference has been attributed to which of the following?
   a. U.S. teachers present math at a lower level.
   b. Japanese teachers encourage more social interaction among groups of children.
   c. Japanese teachers are more collaborative in their teaching.
   d. Each of the above has been offered as an explanation of national differences in math scores.

3. The idea that an object that has been transformed in some way can be restored to its original form by undoing the process is:
   a. identity.   c. reciprocity.
   b. reversibility.   d. automatization.

4. Information-processing theorists contend that major advances in cognitive development occur during the school years because:
   a. the child's mind becomes more like a computer as he or she matures.
   b. children become better able to process and analyze information.
   c. most mental activities become automatic by the time a child is about 13 years old.
   d. the major improvements in reasoning that occur during the school years involve increased long-term memory capacity.

5. The ability to filter out distractions and concentrate on relevant details is called:
   a. metacognition.
   b. information processing.
   c. selective attention.
   d. decentering.

6. Concrete operational thought is Piaget's term for the school-age child's ability to:
   a. reason logically about things and events he or she perceives.
   b. think about thinking.
   c. understand that certain characteristics of an object remain the same when other characteristics are changed.
   d. understand that moral principles may supersede the standards of society.

7. The term for the ability to monitor and adjust one's cognitive performance—to think about thinking—is:
   a. pragmatics.
   b. information processing.
   c. selective attention.
   d. metacognition.

8. Long-term memory is _____ permanent and _____ limited than working memory.
   a. more; less   c. more; more
   b. less; more   d. less; less

9. In making moral choices, according to Gilligan, females are more likely than males to:
   a. score at a higher level in Kohlberg's system.
   b. emphasize the needs of others.
   c. judge right and wrong in absolute terms.
   d. formulate abstract principles.

10. Compared to more advantaged children, children from low-income families show deficits in their development of:
    a. vocabulary.   c. sentence length.
    b. grammar.   d. all the above.

11. A 7-year-old's ability to remember the origin of information, called _____ , is likely to be poor because of the immaturity of the _____ .
    a. long-term memory; corpus callosum
    b. source memory; prefrontal cortex
    c. focal memory; hippocampus
    d. short-term memory; amygdala

12. Eight-year-old Cho, who recently emigrated from Mayanmar, attends a school in Canada in which all subjects are taught in English. Cho's school is using which strategy to teach English-language learners?

    a. bilingual education
    b. heritage language classes
    c. total immersion
    d. ESL

13. The idea that two things can change in opposite directions, yet balance each other out is:

    a. identity.
    b. reversibility.
    c. reciprocity.
    d. automatization.

14. Between 9 and 11 years of age, children are most likely to demonstrate moral reasoning at which of Kohlberg's stages?

    a. preconventional
    b. conventional
    c. postconventional
    d. It is impossible to predict based only on a child's age.

15. Of the following, which was not identified as an important factor in the difference between success and failure in second-language learning?

    a. the age of the child
    b. the attitudes of the parents
    c. community values regarding second language learning
    d. the difficulty of the language

True or False Items

Write T (*true*) or F (*false*) on the line in front of each statement.

_____ 1. A major objection to Piaget's theory is that he underestimated the influence of context, instruction, and culture.

_____ 2. Total immersion is the best strategy for teaching English-language learners.

_____ 3. During middle childhood, children are passionately concerned with issues of right and wrong.

_____ 4. As a group, Japanese and Korean children outscore children in the United States and Canada in math and science.

_____ 5. The process of telling a joke involves remembering the right words and their sequence, a skill usually not mastered before middle childhood.

_____ 6. Research evidence consistently demonstrates that children learn best with fewer students in each classroom.

_____ 7. The best time to learn a second language by listening and talking is during middle childhood.

_____ 8. Most information that comes into the sensory memory is lost or discarded.

_____ 9. Information-processing theorists believe that advances in the thinking of school-age children occur primarily because of changes in long-term memory.

_____ 10. New standards of math education in many nations emphasize problem-solving skills rather than simple memorization of formulas.

Progress Test 2

Progress Test 2 should be completed during a final chapter review. Answer the following questions after you thoroughly understand the correct answers for the Chapter Review and Progress Test 1.

Multiple-Choice Questions

1. According to Piaget, 8- and 9-year-olds can reason only about concrete things in their lives. "Concrete" means:

    a. logical.
    b. abstract.
    c. tangible or specific.
    d. mathematical or classifiable.

2. Research regarding Piaget's theory has found that:

    a. cognitive development seems to be considerably less affected by sociocultural factors than Piaget's descriptions imply.
    b. the movement to a new level of thinking is much more erratic than Piaget predicted.
    c. there is no dramatic shift in the thinking of children when they reach the age of 5.
    d. all of the above are true.

3. The increase in processing speed that occurs during middle childhood is partly the result of:

    a. ongoing myelination of axons.
    b. neurological development in the limbic system.
    c. the streamlining of the knowledge base.
    d. all of the above.

4. When psychologists look at the ability of children to receive, store, and organize information, they are examining cognitive development from a view based on:
   a. the observations of Piaget.
   b. information processing.
   c. behaviorism.
   d. the idea that the key to thinking is the sensory register.

5. Kohlberg's stage theory of moral development is based on his research on a group of boys and on:
   a. psychoanalytic ideas.
   b. Piaget's theory of cognitive development.
   c. Carol Gilligan's research on moral dilemmas.
   d. questionnaires distributed to a nationwide sample of high school seniors.

6. The logical operations of concrete operational thought are particularly important to an understanding of the elementary-school subject(s) of:
   a. spelling.   c. math and science.
   b. reading.   d. social studies.

7. Although older school-age children are generally at the conventional level of moral reasoning, *when* they reach a particular level depends on:
   a. the specific context and the child's opportunity to discuss moral issues.
   b. the level of moral reasoning reached by their parents.
   c. how strongly their peers influence their thinking.
   d. whether they are male or female.

8. Which of the following ideas is *not* widely accepted by developmentalists today?
   a. The thinking of school-age children is characterized by a more comprehensive logic than that of preschoolers.
   b. Children are active learners.
   c. How children think is as important as what they know.
   d. Boys and girls develop very different styles of moral reasoning.

9. Processing capacity refers to:
   a. the ability to selectively attend to more than one thought.
   b. the amount of information that a person is able to hold in working memory.
   c. the size of the child's knowledge base.
   d. all of the above.

10. The retention of new information is called:
    a. retrieval.   c. automatization.
    b. storage.   d. metacognition.

11. According to Kohlberg, a person who is a dutiful citizen and obeys the laws set down by society would be at which level of moral reasoning?
    a. preconventional stage one
    b. preconventional stage two
    c. conventional
    d. postconventional

12. Which aspect of the information-processing system assumes an executive role in regulating the analysis and transfer of information?
    a. sensory register   c. long-term memory
    b. working memory   d. control processes

13. An example of schoolchildren's growth in metacognition is their understanding that:
    a. transformed objects can be returned to their original state.
    b. rehearsal is a good strategy for memorizing, but outlining is better for understanding.
    c. objects may belong to more than one class.
    d. they can use different language styles in different situations.

14. Which of the following most accurately states the relative merits of the phonics approach and the whole-language approach to teaching reading?
    a. The phonics approach is more effective.
    b. The whole-language approach is the more effective approach.
    c. Both approaches have merit.
    d. Both approaches have been discarded in favor of newer, more interactive methods of instruction.

15. Juan attends a school that offers instruction in both English and Spanish. This strategy for teaching English-language learners is called:
    a. bilingual education.
    b. total immersion.
    c. heritage language instruction.
    d. ESL.

Matching Items

Match each term or concept with its corresponding description or definition.

Terms or Concepts

_____ 1. automatization
_____ 2. reversibility
_____ 3. conventional
_____ 4. identity
_____ 5. information processing
_____ 6. selective attention
_____ 7. retrieval
_____ 8. storage
_____ 9. metacognition
_____ 10. total immersion
_____ 11. postconventional
_____ 12. preconventional

Descriptions or Definitions

a. the ability to screen out distractions and concentrate on relevant information

b. the idea that a transformation process can be undone to restore the original conditions

c. the idea that certain characteristics of an object remain the same even when other characteristics change

d. developmental perspective that conceives of cognitive development as the result of changes in the processing and analysis of information

e. moral reasoning in which the individual focuses on his or her own welfare

f. moral reasoning in which the individual follows principles that supersede the standards of society

g. an educational technique in which instruction occurs entirely in the second language

h. accessing previously learned information

i. holding information in memory

j. moral reasoning in which the individual considers social standards and laws to be primary

k. process by which familiar mental activities become routine

l. the ability to evaluate a cognitive task and to monitor one's performance on it

Thinking Critically About Chapter 12

Answer these questions the day before an exam as a final check on your understanding of the chapter's terms and concepts.

1. Of the following statements made by children, which best exemplifies the logical principle of identity?

   a. "You can't leave first base until the ball is hit!"
   b. "See how the jello springs back into shape after I poke my finger into it?"
   c. "I know it's still a banana, even though it's mashed down in my sandwich."
   d. "You're my friend, so I don't have to use polite speech like I do with adults."

2. Which of the following statements is the clearest indication that the child has grasped the principle of reversibility?

   a. "See, the lemonade is the same in both our glasses; even though your glass is taller than mine, it's narrower."

   b. "Even though your dog looks funny, I know it's still a dog."
   c. "I have one sister and no brothers. My parents have two children."
   d. "I don't cheat because I don't want to be punished."

3. After moving to a new country, a child's parents are struck by the greater tendency of math teachers in their new homeland to work collaboratively and to emphasize social interaction in the learning process. To which country have these parents probably moved?

   a. the United States   c. Japan
   b. Germany   d. Australia

4. Dr. Larsen believes that the cognitive advances of middle childhood occur because of basic changes in children's thinking speed, knowledge base, and memory retrieval skills. Dr. Larsen evidently is working from the _____ perspective.
   a. Piagetian
   b. Vygotskian
   c. information-processing
   d. psychoanalytic

5. Some researchers believe that cognitive processing speed and capacity increase during middle childhood because of:
   a. the myelination of neural axons.
   b. the maturation of the prefrontal cortex.
   c. better use of cognitive resources.
   d. all of the above.

6. Mei-Chin is able to sort her Legos into groups according to size. Clearly, she has an understanding of the principle of:
   a. classification.   c. reversibility.
   b. identity.   d. reciprocity.

7. For a 10-year-old, some mental activities have become so familiar or routine as to require little mental work. This development is called:
   a. selective attention.   c. metacognition.
   b. identity.   d. automatization.

8. Lana is 4 years old and her brother Roger is 7. The fact that Roger remembers what their mother just told them about playing in the street while Lana is more interested in the children playing across the street is due to improvements in Roger's:
   a. selective attention.   c. control processes.
   b. automatization.   d. long-term memory.

9. Which of the following statements is the best example of Kohlberg's concept of stage 1 preconventional moral reasoning?
   a. "Might makes right."
   b. "Law and order."
   c. "Nice boys do what is expected of them."
   d. "Look out for number one."

10. According to Carol Gilligan, a girl responding to the hypothetical question of whether an impoverished child should steal food to feed her starving dog is most likely to:
    a. respond according to a depersonalized standard of right and wrong.

    b. hesitate to take a definitive position based on the abstract moral premise of "right and wrong.""
    c. immediately respond that the child was justified in stealing the food.
    d. respond unpredictably, based on her own personal experiences.

11. Four-year-old Tasha, who is learning to read by sounding out the letters of words, evidently is being taught using which approach?
    a. phonics
    b. whole-word
    c. total immersion
    d. reverse immersion

12. The study of street children in Brazil revealed that:
    a. many never attended school.
    b. many scored poorly on standardized math tests.
    c. many were quite adept at using math practically to sell fruit, candy, and other products to earn their living.
    d. all of the above were true.

13. During the school board meeting a knowledgeable parent proclaimed that the board's position on achievement testing and class size was an example of the district's "hidden curriculum." The parent was referring to:
    a. the unofficial and unstated educational priorities of the school district.
    b. the political agendas of individual members of the school board.
    c. the legal mandates for testing and class size established by the state board of education.
    d. none of the above.

14. Critics of Kohlberg's theory of moral development argue that it:
    a. places too much emphasis on sociocultural factors.
    b. places too much emphasis on traditional, religious beliefs.
    c. is biased toward liberal, Western intellectual values.
    d. can't be tested.

15. Andy understands that a ball of clay that is flattened and rolled into a rope hasn't changed in size. Andy's awareness demonstrates an understanding of the logical principle of:
    a. classification.   c. reversibility.
    b. identity.   d. reciprocity.

Key Terms

Writing Definitions

Using your own words, write a brief definition or explanation of each of the following terms on a separate piece of paper.

1. No Child Left Behind Act
2. concrete operational thought
3. classification
4. identity
5. reversibility
6. reciprocity
7. preconventional moral reasoning
8. conventional moral reasoning
9. postconventional moral reasoning
10. morality of care
11. morality of justice
12. information-processing theory
13. sensory memory
14. working memory
15. long-term memory
16. knowledge base
17. control processes
18. metacognition
19. code-switching
20. hidden curriculum
21. Trends in Math and Science Study (TIMSS)
22. phonics approach
23. whole-language approach
24. English-language learner (ELL)
25. total immersion
26. ESL (English as a second language)

Cross-Check

After you have written the definitions of the key terms in this chapter, you should complete the crossword puzzle to ensure that you can reverse the process—recognize the term, given the definition.

ACROSS

3. Processes that regulate the analysis and flow of information in memory.
7. According to Gilligan, men develop a morality of _____ .
9. The part of memory that stores unlimited amounts of information for days, months, or years.
10. English as a second language.
12. According to the theorist in 17 across, cognitive development occurs in _____ .
16. Moral reasoning in which the individual considers social standards and laws to be primary.
17. Psychologist who developed an influential theory of cognitive development.

DOWN

1. The body of knowledge that has been learned about a particular area.
2. The part of memory that handles current, conscious mental activity.

3. According to Gilligan, females develop a morality of _____ .

4. The ability to evaluate a cognitive task in order to determine what to do.

5. Process by which familiar mental activities become routine.

6. Ongoing neural process that speeds up neural processing.

8. An approach to teaching a second language in which the teacher instructs the children in school subjects using their native language as well as the second language.

11. Neurological development in the _____ cortex during middle childhood helps speed neural processing.

13. One of Kohlberg's harshest critics.

14. The main characteristic of concrete operational thinking is the ability to use _____ .

15. According to Piaget, the type of cognitive operations that occur during middle childhood.

ANSWERS

CHAPTER REVIEW

1. No Child Left Behind
2. concrete operational thought; others (or peers and teachers)
3. classification; identity; reversibility; reciprocity
4. developmental; sociocultural; Piaget; Vygotsky
5. apply
6. Kohlberg; preconventional; conventional; postconventional
7. rewards; punishments; 1; 2
8. social rules; 4; 3
9. moral principles; social contracts; universal ethical principles
10. preconventional; conventional
11. Western; women
12. underestimated; have
13. morality of care; morality of justice; does not find
14. information-processing
15. sensory memory (register)
16. working memory; short-term memory; conscious
17. long-term memory; retrieval
18. source memory; prefrontal cortex; confabulation
19. processing speed; capacity
20. neurological; myelination; prefrontal cortex
21. automatization
22. knowledge base
23. opportunity; motivation
24. control processes; selective attention; metacognition; emotional regulation
25. prefrontal cortex; executive function
26. selective attention
27. metacognition; 8 or 9
28. pragmatics
29. 20; logic; memory; speed

30. formal code; informal code; code-switching
31. are strongly correlated; socioeconomic status; talking; reading
32. parental expectations; exposure to language
33. poems; languages; slang; jokes
34. concrete; straightforward; is not
35. hidden curriculum; organized; segregation; schedules; physical condition
36. Trends in Math and Science Study (TIMSS); Progress in International Reading Literacy Study (PIRLS)
37. intended; educational leaders; implemented; attained

Children in Japan study more than U.S. children and are more likely to believe that effort is crucial to success. The school day and year are both longer in Japan, and teachers are given more respect. Virtually all children attend public schools, and the curriculum is universal. Most Japanese children also attend private schools (juko) for at least a few years between grades 1 and 8.

38. outscore; No Child Left Behind
39. phonics; whole-language; both approaches
40. rote; concepts; problem solving; probability; social interaction
41. definitions; connection; collaboratively
42. small; complex
43. English-language learners (ELLs); early childhood; middle childhood
44. total immersion; bilingual education; heritage language
45. English as a second language
46. Canada; shy; stupid; socially isolated
47. the larger society's attitudes and adult choices; additive bilingualism; semilingual

PROGRESS TEST 1

Multiple-Choice Questions

1. **c.** is the answer. (p. 357)

   a. Preoperational thought is "pre-logical" thinking.

   b. There is no such stage in Piaget's theory.

   d. Formal operational thought extends logical reasoning to abstract problems.

2. **d.** is the answer. (p. 384)

3. **b.** is the answer. (p. 359)

   a. This is the concept that certain characteristics of an object remain the same even when other characteristics change.

   c. This is the concept that two things can change in opposite directions to balance each other out.

   d. This is the process by which familiar mental activities become routine and automatic.

4. **b.** is the answer. (pp. 366–367)

   a. Information-processing theorists use the mind–computer metaphor at every age.

   c. Although increasing automatization is an important aspect of development, the information-processing perspective does not suggest that most mental activities become automatic by age 13.

   d. Most of the important changes in reasoning that occur during the school years are due to the improved processing capacity of the person's *working memory.*

5. **c.** is the answer. (p. 369)

   a. This is the ability to evaluate a cognitive task and to monitor and adjust one's performance on it.

   b. Information processing is a perspective on cognitive development that focuses on how the mind analyzes, stores, retrieves, and reasons about information.

   d. Decentering, which refers to the school-age child's ability to consider more than one aspect of a problem simultaneously, is not discussed in this chapter.

6. **a.** is the answer. (p. 357)

   b. This refers to metacognition.

   c. This refers to Piaget's concept of identity.

   d. This is characteristic of Kohlberg's postconventional moral reasoning.

7. **d.** is the answer. (p. 370)

   a. Pragmatics refers to the practical use of language to communicate with others.

   b. The information-processing perspective views the mind as being like a computer.

   c. This is the ability to screen out distractions in order to focus on important information.

8. **a.** is the answer. (p. 367)

9. **b.** is the answer. (p. 365)

10. **d.** is the answer. (p. 372)

11. **b.** is the answer. (p. 367)

    a. The corpus callosum plays no role in memory; it is the band of fibers that links the two cerebral hemispheres.

    c. "Focal memory" is not a term used in the text.

    d. The amygdala plays an important role in emotions, not in memory.

12. **c.** is the answer. (p. 387)

    a. In bilingual education, instruction occurs in both languages.

    b. Heritage language classes are usually supplemental classes that are held after school.

    d. ESL children are taught intensively in English for a few months to prepare them for regular classes. It is not clear that Mei-chin received this type of preparatory instruction.

13. **c.** is the answer. (p. 359)

14. **b.** is the answer. (p. 364)

15. **d.** is the answer. (pp. 387–388)

True or False Items

1. T (pp. 360–361)

2. F No single approach to teaching a second language is best for all children in all contexts. (pp. 387–388)

3. T (pp. 363–364)

4. T (p. 384)

5. T (p. 374)

6. F Research support for this popular assumption is weak. (p. 385)

7. F   The best time to learn a second language by listening and talking is during *early* childhood. (p. 387)

8. T (p. 367)

9. F   They believe that the changes are due to basic changes in control processes. (p. 369)

10. T (p. 383)

PROGRESS TEST 2

Multiple-Choice Questions

1. **c.** is the answer. (p. 357)

2. **b.** is the answer. (pp. 360–361)

3. **a.** is the answer. (p. 368)

   b. Neurological development in the frontal cortex facilitates processing speed during middle childhood. The limbic system, which was not discussed in this chapter, is concerned with emotions.

   c. Processing speed is facilitated by *growth*, rather than streamlining, of the knowledge base.

4. **b.** is the answer. (pp. 366–367)

5. **b.** is the answer. (p. 363)

6. **c.** is the answer. (p. 360)

7. **a.** is the answer. (p. 364)

   b., c., & d. Although these may be factors, they don't necessarily determine the child's level of moral reasoning.

8. **d.** is the answer. (p. 365)

9. **b.** is the answer. (p. 368)

10. **b.** is the answer. (p. 367)

    a. This is the *accessing* of already learned information.

    c. Automatization is the process by which well-learned activities become routine and automatic.

    d. This is the ability to evaluate a task and to monitor and adjust one's performance on it.

11. **c.** is the answer. (p. 363)

12. **d.** is the answer. (p. 369)

    a. The sensory register stores incoming information for a split second.

    b. Working memory is the part of memory that handles current, conscious mental activity.

    c. Long-term memory stores information for days, months, or years.

13. **b.** is the answer. (p. 370)

14. **c.** is the answer. (pp. 381–382)

15. **a.** is the answer. (p. 387)

Matching Items

1. k (p. 368)	**5.** d (p. 366)	**9.** l (p. 370)
2. b (p. 359)	**6.** a (p. 369)	**10.** g (p. 387)
3. j (p. 363)	**7.** h (p. 367)	**11.** f (p. 363)
4. c (p. 359)	**8.** i (p. 367)	**12.** e (p. 363)

THINKING CRITICALLY ABOUT CHAPTER 12

1. **c.** is the answer. (p. 359)

    a., b., & d. Identity is the logical principle that certain characteristics of an object (such as the shape of a ball) remain the same even when other characteristics change.

2. **a.** is the answer. (p. 359)

    b., c., & d. Reversibility is the logical principle that something that has been changed (such as the height of lemonade poured from one glass into another) can be returned to its original shape by reversing the process of change (pouring the liquid back into the other glass).

3. **c.** is the answer. (p. 384)

4. **c.** is the answer. (pp. 367–369)

    a. This perspective emphasizes the logical, active nature of thinking during middle childhood.

    b. This perspective emphasizes the importance of social interaction in learning.

    d. This perspective does not address the development of cognitive skills.

5. **d.** is the answer. (p. 368)

6. **a.** is the answer. (p. 358)

7. **d.** is the answer. (p. 368)

    a. Selective attention is the ability to focus on important information and screen out distractions.

    b. Identity is the logical principle that certain characteristics of an object remain the same even when other characteristics change.

    c. Metacognition is the ability to evaluate a task and to monitor one's performance on it.

8. **c.** is the answer. (p. 369)

    a. Selective attention *is* a control process, but c. is more specific and thus more correct.

    b. Automatization refers to the tendency of well-rehearsed mental activities to become routine and automatic.

    d. Long-term memory is the part of memory that stores information for days, months, or years.

9. **a.** is the answer. (p. 363)

    b. & c. These exemplify conventional moral reasoning.

    d. This exemplifies stage two preconventional moral reasoning.

10. **b.** is the answer. Gilligan contends that females' morality of care makes them reluctant to judge right and wrong in absolute terms because they are socialized to be nurturant and caring. (p. 365)

11. **a.** is the answer. (p. 381)

    b. This approach encourages children to develop all their language skills at the same time.

    c. & d. These are approaches to bilingual instruction, not reading instruction, although reverse immersion was not discussed by name.

12. **d.** is the answer. (pp. 361–362)

13. **a.** is the answer. (p. 376)

14. **c.** is the answer. (p. 364)

15. **b.** is the answer. (p. 359)

KEY TERMS

Writing Definitions

1. The **No Child Left Behind Act** is a controversial law, enacted in 2001, that uses multiple assessments and achievement standards to try to improve public education in the United States. (p. 357)

2. During Piaget's stage of **concrete operational thought,** lasting from ages 7 to 11, children can think logically about direct experiences and perceptions but are not able to reason abstractly. (p. 357)

3. **Classification** is the process of organizing things into groups according to some common property. (p. 358)

4. In Piaget's theory, **identity** is the logical principle that certain characteristics of an object remain the same even when other characteristics change. (p. 359)

5. **Reversibility** is the logical principle that a transformation process can be reversed to restore the original conditions. (p. 359)

6. **Reciprocity** is the logical principle that two things can change in opposite ways in order to balance each other out. (p. 359)

7. Kohlberg's first level of moral reasoning, **preconventional moral reasoning**, emphasizes obedience to authority in order to avoid punishment (stage 1) and being nice to other people so they will be nice to you (stage 2). (p. 363)

8. Kohlberg's second level of moral reasoning, **conventional moral reasoning**, emphasizes winning the approval of others (stage 3) and obeying the laws set down by those in power (stage 4). (p. 363)

9. Kohlberg's third level, **postconventional moral reasoning**, emphasizes the social and contractual nature of moral principles (stage 5) and the existence of universal ethical principles (stage 6). (pp. 363–364)

10. According to Carol Gilligan, compared with boys and men, girls and women are more likely to develop a **morality of care** that is based on nurturance, compassion, and being nonjudgmental. (p. 365)

11. According to Carol Gilligan, compared with girls and women, boys and men are more likely to develop a **morality of justice** based on depersonalized and absolute standards of right and wrong. (p. 365)

12. **Information-processing theory** models human cognition after the computer, analyzing each component, step by step. (p. 366)

13. **Sensory memory** is the first component of the information-processing system that stores incoming stimuli for a split second, after which it is passed into working memory, or discarded as unimportant; sometimes called the *sensory register*. (p. 367)

14. **Working memory** is the component of the information-processing system that handles current, conscious mental activity; sometimes called short-term memory. (p. 367)

15. **Long-term memory** is the component of the information-processing system that stores unlimited amounts of information for days, months, or years. (p. 367)

16. The **knowledge base** is a broad body of knowledge in a particular subject area that has been learned and on which additional learning can be based. (p. 368)

17. **Control processes** (such as selective attention and metacognition) regulate the analysis and flow of information within the information-processing system. (p. 369)

18. **Metacognition** is the ability to evaluate a cognitive task to determine what to do and to monitor and adjust one's performance on that task. (p. 370)

19. **Code-switching** involves changing from one form of speech to another, as when children tailor their speech depending on whether they are speaking with adults or other children. (p. 371)

20. The **hidden curriculum** is the unofficial, unstated, or implicit rules and priorities that influence the academic curriculum and every other aspect of school learning. (p. 376)

21. The **TIMSS (Trends in Math and Science Study)** is an international assessment of math skills. (p. 377)

22. The **phonics approach** is a method of teaching reading by having children learn the sounds of letters before they begin to learn words. (p. 381)

23. The **whole-language approach** is a method of teaching reading by encouraging children to develop all their language skills simultaneously. (p. 381)

24. An **English-language learner (ELL)** is a person who is learning English. (p. 387)

25. **Total immersion** is an approach to bilingual education in which the child's instruction occurs entirely in the new language. (p. 387)

26. **ESL (English as a second language)** is an approach to bilingual education in which children are taught separately, and exclusively in English, to prepare them for attending regular classes. (p. 388)

Cross-Check

ACROSS	DOWN
3. control	**1.** knowledge base
7. justice	**2.** working
9. long-term	**3.** care
10. ESL	**4.** metacognition
11. stages	**5.** automatization
12. stages	**6.** myelination
14. logic	**8.** bilingual
16. conventional	**11.** prefrontal
17. Piaget	**13.** Gilligan
	15. concrete

Chapter Thirteen

The School Years: Psychosocial Development

Chapter Overview

This chapter brings to a close the unit on the school years. We have seen that from ages 7 to 11, the child becomes stronger and more competent, mastering the biosocial and cognitive abilities that are important in his or her culture. Psychosocial accomplishments are equally impressive.

Children's interaction with peers and others in their ever-widening social world is the subject of the first section. Although the peer group often is a supportive, positive influence on children, some children are rejected by their peers or become the victims of bullying.

The next section explores the ways in which families influence children, including the experience of living in single-parent, stepparent, and blended families. Although no particular family structure guarantees optimal child development, income and stability are important factors in the quality of family functioning.

The third section explores the growing social competence of children, as described by Freud and Erikson. The section continues with a discussion of the growth of social cognition and self-understanding. The chapter closes with a discussion of the ways in which children cope with stressful situations.

NOTE: Answer guidelines for all Chapter 13 questions begin on page 201.

Guided Study

The text chapter should be studied one section at a time. Before you read, preview each section by skimming it, noting headings and boldface items. Then read the appropriate section objectives from the following outline. Keep these objectives in mind and, as you read the chapter section, search for the information that will enable you to meet each objective. Once you have finished a section, write out answers for its objectives.

The Peer Group (pp. 395–405)

1. Discuss the importance of peer groups to the development of school-age children, focusing on how the culture of children separates itself from adult society.

2. Discuss the plight of two types of rejected children.

3. Discuss how friendship circles change during the school years.

4. (text and Issues and Applications) Discuss the special problems of bullies and their victims, and describe possible ways of helping such children.

9. (text and Issues and Applications) Explain how low income and high conflict can interfere with good family functioning, noting the effects on children of divorce and remarriage.

Families and Children (pp. 406–416)

5. Identify the essential ways in which functional families nurture school-age children.

The Nature of the Child (pp. 416–419)

10. Identify the themes or emphases of different theoretical views of the psychosocial development of school-age children.

6. Differentiate eleven family structures.

11. Describe the development of the self-concept during middle childhood and its implications for children's self-esteem.

7. Discuss family factors that affect the child's development.

Coping and Overcoming (pp. 419–425)

12. Discuss the concept of resilience, and identify the variables that influence the impact of stresses on schoolchildren.

8. Discuss the impact of blended families and other family structures on the psychosocial development of the school-age child.

13. Discuss several factors that seem especially important in helping children cope with stress.

Chapter Review

When you have finished reading the chapter, work through the material that follows to review it. Complete the sentences and answer the questions. As you proceed, evaluate your performance for each section by consulting the answers beginning on page 201. Do not continue with the next section until you understand each answer. If you need to, review or reread the appropriate section in the textbook before continuing.

The Peer Group (pp. 395–405)

1. Getting along with _____ is especially important during middle childhood. Compared to younger children, school-age children are _____ (more/less) deeply affected by others' acceptance or rejection. The inclination to compare themselves with others is called _____ _____ .

2. Peers create their own _____
_____ _____ , which includes the particular rules and rituals that are passed down from older to younger children and that _____ (mirror/do not necessarily mirror) the values of adults.

3. _____ (In some parts of the world/Throughout the world), the culture of children encourages _____ from adults. Generally, when it comes to codes of behavior, peer influence _____ (outweighs/is outweighed by) adult influence.

4. Research studies of social acceptance among schoolchildren reveal that approximately _____ (what proportion?) are popular, approximately _____ are aver-

age in popularity, and approximately _____ are unpopular.

5. Children who are not really rejected but not picked as friends are _____ . Children who are actively rejected tend to be either _____-_____ or _____-_____ .

Briefly explain why rejected children are disliked.

6. The ability to understand human interactions, called _____ _____ , begins in infancy with _____ _____ , continues in early childhood with _____ _____ _____ , and by middle childhood has developed into a set of _____ skills in children who are well-liked.

Gives some examples of the prosocial skills of well-liked children.

7. School children improve in _____ _____ , which is the power to modify their _____ and _____ .

8. Having a personal friend is _____ (more/less) important to children than acceptance by the peer group.

9. Friendships during middle childhood become more _____ and _____ . As a result, older children _____ (change/do not change) friends as often and find it _____ (easier/harder) to make new friends.

10. Middle schoolers tend to choose best friends whose _____ , _____ , and _____ are similar to their own.

11. Bullying is defined as _____ efforts to inflict harm through _____ , _____ , or _____ attacks. A key aspect in the definition of bullying is that harmful attacks are _____ .

12. Most bullies usually _____ (have/do not have) friends who admire them, and they are socially _____ but without _____ .

13. Victims of bullying are often _____ -rejected children. Less often, _____ -rejected children become _____-_____ . Bullies and their victims _____ (are/are not) usually of the same gender.

14. Boys who are bullies are often above average in _____ , whereas girls who are bullies are often above average in _____ . Boys who are bullies typically use _____ aggression, whereas girls use _____ aggression.

15. The origins of bullying may lie in _____ _____ or _____ impulses that are present at birth and then strengthened by _____ _____ , a stressful _____ life, hostile _____ , and other problems that intensify _____ impulses rather than teach _____ .

16. (Issues and Applications) One effective intervention in controlling bullying in Norway involved using an _____ approach to change the _____ within schools so that bully–victim cycles are not allowed to persist.

Families and Children (pp. 406–416)

17. It is generally accepted that about _____ (what proportion?) of a person's behavior can be traced to heredity.

18. Research demonstrates that _____ (shared/nonshared) influences on most traits are far greater than _____ (shared/nonshared) influences.

19. At every point in the life span, families _____ development. Children who have no families are likely to become _____ .

20. Family function refers to how well the family _____ _____ .

21. A functional family nurtures school-age children by meeting their basic _____ , encouraging _____ , fostering the development of _____ , nurturing peer _____ , and providing _____ and _____ .

22. (text and Table 13.2) Family structure is defined as the _____ _____ .

Identify each of the following family structures:

a. _____ A family that includes three or more biologically related generations, including parents and children.

b. _____ A family that consists of the father, the mother, and their biological children.

c. _____ A family that consists of one parent with his or her biological children.

d. _____ A family consisting of two parents, at least one with biological children from another union.

e. _____ In some nations, a family that consists of one man, several wives, and their children.

f. _____ A family that consists of one or more nonbiological children whom adults have legally taken to raise as their own.

g. _____ A family that consists of one or more orphaned, neglected, abused, or delinquent children who are temporarily cared for by an adult to whom they are not biologically related.

h. _____ A family that consists of a parent, his or her biological children, and his or her spouse, who is not biologically related to the children.

i. _____ A family that consists of one or two grandparents and their grandchildren.

j. _____ A family that consists of a homosexual couple and the biological or adopted children of one or both partners.

23. Although the _____ family is still the most common, about _____ (what percentage?) of all school-age children live in _____-_____ households.

Give several reasons for the benefits of the nuclear family structure.

24. Children in every type of family structure grow up very well and sometimes run into trouble. Thus, family _____ seems more critical than family _____ .

25. Family income _____ (correlates/does not correlate) with optimal child development. Economic distress _____ family functioning. According to the _____ _____ model, economic hardship in a family increases _____ , which often makes adults more _____ and _____ with their children.

26. A second factor that has a crucial impact on children is the _____ and _____ that characterizes family

interaction. Ideally, parents work cooperatively in a _____ _____ . This factor explains why _____ families are problematic for many children. Children are particularly affected when there are multiple _____ .

27. Single parents tend to be _____ (older/younger) than married parents.

28. Parents who use harsh discipline are usually categorized as _____ . In the United States, however, many _____ families use harsh discipline yet are also warm and accepting of their children. An important factor in the impact of this pattern on children is how _____ or _____ the family is.

29. (Issues and Applications) In addition to the problems caused by reduced income and parental conflict that occur with divorce, parents also intrude on the child's need for _____ and _____ . Parents may become controlling, not respecting the _____ between parent and child.

The Nature of the Child (pp. 416–419)

30. Freud describes middle childhood as the period of _____ , when emotional drives are _____ , psychosexual needs are _____ , and unconscious conflicts are _____ .

31. According to Erikson, the crisis of middle childhood is _____ _____ _____ .

32. As their self-understanding sharpens, children gradually become _____ (more/less) self-critical, and their self-esteem _____ (rises/dips). One reason is that they more often evaluate themselves through _____ _____ .

Coping and Overcoming (pp. 419–425)

33. Some children are better able to adapt within the context of adversity, that is, they seem to be more

_____ . This trait is a _____ process that represents a _____ adaptation to stress.

34. The impact of a given stress on a child (such as divorce) depends on three factors:

    a. _____

    b. _____

    c. _____

35. The importance of daily _____ explains why _____ is so difficult for children. One study found that children's coping depended more on their _____ of events than on the nature of the events themselves.

36. Another element that helps children deal with problems is the _____ _____ they receive.

37. During middle childhood, there are typically _____ (fewer/more) sources of social support. This can be obtained from grandparents or siblings, for example, or from _____ and _____ . In addition, _____ can also be psychologically protective for children in difficult circumstances.

Progress Test 1

Multiple-Choice Questions

Circle your answers to the following questions and check them with the answers on page 202. If your answer is incorrect, read the explanation for why it is incorrect and then consult the appropriate pages of the text (in parentheses following the correct answer).

1. Children who rarely play with other children:
   a. are at a disadvantage because they will not understand the culture of children.
   b. tend to become bullies.
   c. tend to become aggressive-rejected children.
   d. tend to become withdrawn-rejected children.

2. Which of the following is *not* among the highest values of middle-childhood?
   a. protect your friends
   b. don't tell adults what really goes on
   c. try not to be too different from other children
   d. don't depend on others

3. The best strategy for helping children who are at risk of developing serious psychological problems because of multiple stresses would be to:
   a. obtain assistance from a psychiatrist.
   b. increase the child's competencies or social supports.
   c. change the household situation.
   d. reduce the peer group's influence.

4. The culture of children refers to:
   a. the specific habits, styles, and values that reflect the rules and rituals of children.
   b. a child's tendency to assess her abilities by measuring them against those of her peers.
   c. children's ability to understand social interactions
   d. all of the above.

5. Girls who are bullies are often above average in _____ , whereas boys who are bullies are often above average in _____ .
   a. size; verbal assertiveness
   b. verbal assertiveness; size
   c. intelligence; aggressiveness
   d. aggressiveness; intelligence

6. As some rejected children get older:
   a. their problems often get worse.
   b. their problems usually decrease.
   c. they may become less rejected and more prosocial.
   d. their peer group becomes less important to their self-esteem.

7. Compared with average or popular children, rejected children tend to be:
   a. brighter and more competitive.
   b. affluent and "stuck-up."
   c. economically disadvantaged.
   d. socially immature.

8. School-age children advance in their awareness of classmates' opinions and accomplishments. These abilities are best described as advances in their:
   a. social comparison.
   b. social cognition.
   c. metacognition.
   d. pragmatic intelligence.

9. Resilience is characterized by all but which of the following characteristics?
   a. Resilience is a stable trait that a child carries throughout his or her life.
   b. Resilience represents a positive adaptation to stress.

c. Resilience is more than the absence of pathology.

d. Resilience is the capacity to develop optimally despite significant adversity.

10. Older schoolchildren tend to be _____ vulnerable to the stresses of life than children who are just beginning middle childhood because they _____ .

a. more; tend to overpersonalize their problems
b. less; have developed better coping skills
c. more; are more likely to compare their well-being with that of their peers
d. less; are less egocentric

11. Bully-victims are typically children who would be categorized as:
a. aggressive-rejected.
b. withdrawn-rejected.
c. isolated-rejected.
d. immature-rejected.

12. Bullying during middle childhood:
a. occurs only in certain cultures.
b. is more common in rural schools than in urban schools.
c. seems to be universal.
d. is rarely a major problem, since other children usually intervene to prevent it from getting out of hand.

13. During the school years, children become _____ selective about their friends, and their friendship groups become _____ .

a. less; larger   c. more; larger
b. less; smaller   d. more; smaller

14. Which of the following was *not* identified as a pivotal issue in determining whether divorce or some other problem will adversely affect a child during the school years?

a. how many other stresses the child is already experiencing
b. how the child interprets the stress
c. how much the stress affects the child's daily life
d. the specific structure of the child's family

15. Erikson's crisis of the school years is that of:
a. industry versus inferiority.
b. acceptance versus rejection.
c. initiative versus guilt.
d. male versus female.

True or False Items

Write T (*true*) or F (*false*) on the line in front of each statement.

_____ 1. As they evaluate themselves according to increasingly complex self-theories, school-age children typically experience a rise in self-esteem.

_____ 2. During middle childhood, acceptance by the peer group is valued more than having a close friend.

_____ 3. Children from low-income homes often experience more stress.

_____ 4. Bullies and their victims are usually of the same gender.

_____ 5. Children who are labeled "resilient" demonstrate an ability to adapt positively in all situations.

_____ 6. The quality of family interaction seems to be a more powerful predictor of children's development than the actual structure of the family.

_____ 7. Withdrawn-rejected and aggressive-rejected children both have problems regulating their emotions.

_____ 8. Most aggressive-rejected children clearly interpret other people's words and behavior.

_____ 9. School-age children are less able than younger children to cope with chronic stresses.

_____ 10. Children's ability to cope with stress may depend as much on their appraisal of events as on the objective nature of the events themselves.

_____ 11. Friendship circles become wider as children grow older.

Progress Test 2

Progress Test 2 should be completed during a final chapter review. Answer the following questions after you thoroughly understand the correct answers for the Chapter Review and Progress Test 1.

Multiple-Choice Questions

1. Children who are categorized as _____ are particularly vulnerable to bullying.

a. aggressive-rejected
b. passive-aggressive
c. withdrawn-rejected
d. passive-rejected

2. Environmental influences on children's traits that result from contact with different teachers and peer groups are classified as:
   a. shared influences.
   b. nonshared influences.
   c. epigenetic influences.
   d. nuclear influences.

3. Compared to parents in other family structures, married parents tend to be:
   a. wealthier.
   b. better educated.
   c. healthier.
   d. all of the above.

4. More than half of all school-age children live in:
   a. one-parent families.
   b. blended families.
   c. extended families.
   d. nuclear families.

5. Typically, children in middle childhood experience a decrease in self-esteem as a result of:
   a. a wavering self-theory.
   b. increased awareness of personal shortcomings and failures.
   c. rejection by peers.
   d. difficulties with members of the opposite sex.

6. A 10-year-old's sense of self-esteem is most strongly influenced by his or her:
   a. peers.   c. mother.
   b. siblings.   d. father.

7. Which of the following most accurately describes how friendships change during the school years?
   a. Friendships become more casual and less intense.
   b. Older children demand less of their friends.
   c. Older children change friends more often.
   d. Close friendships increasingly involve members of the same sex, ethnicity, and socioeconomic status.

8. Which of the following is an accurate statement about school-age bullies?
   a. They are socially perceptive but not empathic.
   b. They usually have a few admiring friends.
   c. They are adept at being aggressive.
   d. All of the above are accurate statements.

9. (Issues and Applications) One effective intervention to prevent bullying in the school is to:
   a. change the culture through community-wide and classroom education.
   b. target one victimized child at a time.
   c. target each bully as an individual.
   d. focus on improving the academic skills of all children in the school.

10. Which of the following most accurately describes the relationship between family income and child development?
   a. Adequate family income allows children to own whatever possessions help them to feel accepted.
   b. Because parents need not argue about money, household wealth provides harmony and stability.
   c. the basic family functions are enhanced by adequate family income.
   d. Family income is not correlated with child development.

11. Two factors that most often help the child cope well with multiple stresses are social support and:
   a. social comparison.
   b. religious faith.
   c. remedial education.
   d. referral to mental health professionals.

12. An 8-year-old child who measures her achievements by comparing them to those of her friends is engaging in social:
   a. cognition.   c. reinforcement.
   b. comparison.   d. modeling.

13. Family _____ is more crucial to children's well-being than family _____ is.
   a. structure; SES
   b. SES; stability
   c. stability; SES
   d. function; structure

14. According to Freud, the period between ages 7 and 11 when a child's sexual drives are relatively quiet is the:
   a. phallic stage.
   b. genital stage.
   c. period of latency.
   d. period of industry versus inferiority.

15. Children who are forced to cope with one serious ongoing stress (for example, poverty or large family size) are:
    a. more likely to develop serious psychiatric problems.
    b. no more likely to develop problems.
    c. more likely to develop intense, destructive friendships.
    d. less likely to be accepted by their peer group.

Matching Items

Match each term or concept with its corresponding description or definition.

Terms or Concepts

_____ 1. relational aggression
_____ 2. nuclear family
_____ 3. social comparison
_____ 4. provocative victim
_____ 5. foster family
_____ 6. aggressive-rejected
_____ 7. withdrawn-rejected
_____ 8. physical aggression
_____ 9. effortful control
_____ 10. blended family
_____ 11. extended family

Descriptions or Definitions

a. another term for a bully-victim
b. adults living with their children from previous marriages as well as their own biological children
c. a father, a mother, and the biological children they have together
d. used by boys who are bullies
e. children who are disliked because of their confrontational nature
f. evaluating one's abilities by measuring them against those of other children
g. three or more generations of biologically related individuals living together
h. children who are disliked because of timid, anxious behavior
i. used by girls who are bullies
j. a family in which one or more children are temporarily cared for by an adult individual or couple to whom they are not biologically related
k. the ability to regulate one's emotions

Thinking Critically About Chapter 13

Answer these questions the day before an exam as a final check on your understanding of the chapter's terms and concepts.

1. Concluding her presentation on bullying, Olivia notes that one factor in the possible development of bullying is:
   a. an inborn brain abnormality.
   b. insecure attachment.
   c. the presence of hostile siblings.
   d. any of the above.

2. Dr. Ferris believes that skill mastery is particularly important because children develop views of themselves as either competent or incompetent in skills valued by their culture. Dr. Ferris is evidently working from the perspective of:
   a. behaviorism.
   b. social learning theory.
   c. Erik Erikson's theory of development.
   d. Freud's theory of development.

3. The Australian saying that "tall poppies" are cut down underscores the fact that:
   a. older children often ignore their parents and teachers.
   b. culture influences standards of social comparison.
   c. middle childhood is a time of emotional latency.
   d. personal friendships become even more important in middle childhood.

4. Ten-year-old Ramón, who is disliked by many of his peers because of his antagonistic, confrontational nature, would probably be labeled as:
   a. a bully-victim.
   b. withdrawn-rejected.
   c. aggressive-rejected.
   d. resilient.

5. In explaining why some ethnic minority children in the United States become happy and successful despite the fact that their parent(s) use(s) harsh discipline, a developmentalist would point out that:
   a. such parents also tend to be warm and accepting of their children.
   b. immigrant and African American communities tend not to isolate single mothers.
   c. these children often are raised in communities in which many people help in child rearing.
   d. all of the above are true.

6. Sandra's family consists of her biological mother, her stepfather, and his two daughters from a previous marriage. Sandra's family would be classified as:
   a. nuclear.
   b. stepparent.
   c. blended.
   d. extended.

7. In discussing friendship, 9-year-old children, in contrast to younger children, will:
   a. deny that friends are important.
   b. state that they prefer same-sex playmates.
   c. stress the importance of loyalty and similar interests.
   d. be less choosy about who they call a friend.

8. Eight-year-old Henry is unpopular because he is a very timid and anxious child. Developmentalists would classify Henry as:
   a. aggressive-rejected.
   b. neglected-rejected.
   c. withdrawn-rejected.
   d. victim-rejected.

9. Concluding her presentation on resilient children, Brenda notes that:
   a. children who are truly resilient, are resilient in all situations.
   b. resilience is merely the absence of pathology.
   c. resilience is a stable trait that becomes apparent very early in life.
   d. resilience is a dynamic process that represents a positive adaptation to significant adversity or stress.

10. Of the following children, who is likely to have the lowest overall self-esteem?
    a. Karen, age 5   c. Carl, age 9
    b. David, age 7   d. Cindy, age 10

11. Ten-year-old Benjamin is less optimistic and self-confident than his 5-year-old sister. This may be explained in part by the tendency of older children to:
    a. evaluate their abilities by comparing them with their own competencies a year or two earlier.
    b. evaluate their competencies by comparing them with those of others.
    c. be less realistic about their own abilities.
    d. do both b. and c.

12. Kyle and Jessica are as different as two siblings can be, despite growing up in the same nuclear family structure. In explaining these differences, a developmentalist is likely to point to:
    a. shared environmental influences.
    b. nonshared environmental influences.
    c. genetic differences and shared environmental influences.
    d. genetic differences and nonshared environmental influences.

13. Of the following children, who is most likely to become a bully?
    a. Karen, who is taller than average
    b. David, who is above average in verbal assertiveness
    c. Carl, who is insecure and lonely
    d. Cindy, who was insecurely attached

14. I am an 8-year-old who frequently is bullied at school. If I am like most victims of bullies, I am probably:
    a. obese.
    b. unattractive.
    c. a child who speaks with an accent.
    d. anxious and insecure.

15. The impact of a stressor such as divorce on a child depends on:
- **a.** how many other stresses the child is experiencing
- **b.** how the stress affects the child's daily life.
- **c.** how the child interprets the stress.
- **d.** all of the above.

Key Terms

Using your own words, write a brief definition or explanation of each of the following terms on a separate piece of paper.

1. social comparison
2. culture of children
3. aggressive-rejected
4. withdrawn-rejected
5. social cognition
6. effortful control
7. bullying
8. bully-victim
9. family function
10. family structure
11. nuclear family
12. extended family
13. blended family
14. latency
15. industry versus inferiority
16. resilience

ANSWERS

CHAPTER REVIEW

1. peers; more; social comparison
2. culture of children; do not necessarily mirror
3. Throughout the world; independence; outweighs
4. one-third; one-half; one-sixth
5. neglected; aggressive-rejected; withdrawn-rejected

Aggressive-rejected children are disliked because of their confrontational behavior, while withdrawn-rejected children are timid, withdrawn, and anxious. Both types often misinterpret social situations, dysregulate their emotions, and are likely to be mistreated at home.

6. social referencing; theory of mind; prosocial

Well-liked children try to understand ambiguous situations. Given direct conflict with another, they seek compromise rather than revenge. Other prosocial skills include benign social perceptions, insight into relationships, and a tendency to help rather than to attack.

7. effortful control; impulses; emotions
8. more
9. intense; intimate; do not change; harder
10. interests; values; backgrounds
11. systematic; physical, verbal, social; repeated
12. have; perceptive; empathy
13. withdrawn; aggressive; bully-victims; are
14. size; verbal assertiveness; physical; relational
15. brain abnormalities; genetic; insecure attachment; home; siblings; aggressive; effortful control
16. ecological; culture
17. half
18. nonshared; shared
19. aid; self-destructive, lonely, and violent
20. works to meet the needs of its members
21. needs; learning; self-esteem; friendships; harmony; stability
22. genetic and legal relationships among related people living in the same household
- **a.** extended family
- **b.** nuclear family
- **c.** one-parent family
- **d.** blended family
- **e.** polygamous family
- **f.** adoptive family
- **g.** foster family
- **h.** stepparent family
- **i.** grandparents alone
- **j.** homosexual family
23. nuclear; one-fourth; single-parent

Parents in a nuclear family tend to be wealthier, better educated, psychologically and physically healthier, more willing to compromise, and less hostile than other parents.

24. function; structure
25. correlates; decreases; family stress; stress; hostile; harsh
26. harmony; stability; parental alliance; blended; transitions
27. younger
28. authoritarian; ethnic-minority; isolated; socially embedded
29. privacy; independence; boundaries

30. latency; quieter; repressed; submerged
31. industry versus inferiority
32. more; dips; social comparison
33. resilient; dynamic; positive
34. a. how many stresses the child is experiencing
     b. how the stress affects the child's daily life
     c. how the child interprets the stress
35. routines; homelessness; appraisal
36. social support
37. more; peers; pets; religion

PROGRESS TEST 1

Multiple-Choice Questions

1. a. is the answer. (p. 396)
2. d. is the answer. (p. 398)
3. b. is the answer. (pp. 421, 423)
4. a. is the answer. (p. 396)

    b. This is social comparison.

    c. This is social cognition.
5. b. is the answer. (p. 403)
6. a. is the answer. (p. 401)
7. d. is the answer. (p. 400)
8. b. is the answer. (p. 400)

    a. Social comparison is the tendency to assess one's abilities by measuring them against those of others, especially those of one's peers.

    c. Metacognition, which is not discussed in this chapter, is the ability to monitor and adjust one's cognitive processes.

    d. This term was not discussed in the chapter.
9. a. is the answer. Resilience is a dynamic, not a stable trait. (p. 420)
10. b. is the answer. (p. 424)
11. a. is the answer. (p. 403)

    b. Withdrawn-rejected children are frequently the victims of bullies, but rarely become bullies themselves.

    c. & d. There are no such categories.
12. c. is the answer. (p. 405)

    d. In fact, children rarely intervene, unless a best friend is involved.
13. d. is the answer. (p. 401)
14. d. is the answer. (p. 421)
15. a. is the answer. (p. 417)

True or False Items

1. F   In fact, just the opposite is true. (p. 418)
2. F   In fact, just the opposite is true. (p. 401)
3. T (p. 413)
4. T (p. 402)
5. F   A given child is not resilient in all situations. (p. 420)
6. T (p. 411)
7. T (p. 400)
8. F   Just the opposite is true: They tend to misinterpret other people's words and behavior. (p. 400)
9. F   Because of the coping strategies that many school-age children develop, they are better able than younger children to cope with stress. (p. 424)
10. T (p. 422)
11. F   Friendship circles become narrower because friendships become more selective and exclusive. (p. 401)

PROGRESS TEST 2

Multiple-Choice Questions

1. c. is the answer. (p. 403)

    a. These are usually bullies.

    b. & d. These are not subcategories of rejected children.
2. b. is the answer. (p. 406)

    a. Shared influences are those that occur because children are raised by the same parents in the same home.

    c. & d. There are no such influences.
3. d. is the answer. (p. 412)
4. d. is the answer. (p. 410)
5. b. is the answer. (p. 418)

    a. This tends to promote, rather than reduce, self-esteem.

    c. Only 10 percent of schoolchildren experience this.

    d. This issue becomes more important during adolescence.
6. a. is the answer. (p. 418)
7. d. is the answer. (p. 401)

    a., b., & c. In fact, just the opposite is true of friendship during the school years.
8. d. is the answer. (p. 403)
9. a. is the answer. (p. 404)
10. c. is the answer. (p. 413)

11. **b.** is the answer. (p. 423)

12. **b.** is the answer. (p. 396)

13. **d.** is the answer. (pp. 411–412)

14. **c.** is the answer. (p. 417)

15. **b.** is the answer. (pp. 421–422)

   c. & d. The text did not discuss how stress influences friendship or peer acceptance.

Matching Items

1. i (p. 403)	**5.** j (p. 410)	**9.** k (p. 400)
2. c (p. 411)	**6.** e (p. 400)	**10.** b (p. 412)
3. f (p. 403)	**7.** h (p. 400)	**11.** g (p. 411)
4. a (p. 314)	**8.** d (p. 403)	

THINKING CRITICALLY ABOUT CHAPTER 13

1. **d.** is the answer. (p. 403)

2. **c.** is the answer. The question describes what is, for Erikson, the crisis of middle childhood: industry versus inferiority. (p. 417)

3. **b.** is the answer. (p. 419)

4. **c.** is the answer. (p. 400)

5. **d.** is the answer. (pp. 414–415)

6. **c.** is the answer. (p. 410)

   a. A nuclear family consists of a husband and wife and their biological offspring.

   b. Although Sandra does live with a stepparent, because she also lives with the biological children from his previous marriage, her family would be classified as blended.

   d. An extended family includes children living with one or more of their biological parents, one or more grandparents, and often other relatives as well.

7. **c.** is the answer. (p. 401)

8. **c.** is the answer. (p. 400)

   a. Aggressive-rejected children are antagonistic and confrontational.

   b. & d. These are not classifications used by developmentalists.

9. **d.** is the answer. (p. 420)

10. **d.** is the answer. Self-esteem decreases throughout middle childhood. (p. 418)

11. **b.** is the answer. (p. 418)

   a. & c. These are more typical of preschoolers than school-age children.

12. **d.** is the answer. (p. 406)

13. **d.** is the answer. (p. 403)

   a. & b. It is taller-than-average *boys* and verbally assertive *girls* who are more likely to bully others.

   c. This is a common myth.

14. **d.** is the answer. (p. 403)

   a., b., & c. Contrary to popular belief, victims are no more likely to be fat or homely or to speak with an accent than nonvictims are.

15. **d.** is the answer. (p. 421)

KEY TERMS

1. **Social comparison** is the tendency to assess one's abilities, achievements, social status, and other attributes by measuring them against those of others, especially those of one's peers. (p. 396)

2. The **culture of children** refers to the specific habits, styles, and values that reflect the rules and rituals of children. (p. 396)

3. The peer group shuns **aggressive-rejected children** because they are overly confrontational. (p. 400)

4. **Withdrawn-rejected children** are shunned by the peer group because of their timid, withdrawn, and anxious behavior. (p. 400)

5. **Social cognition** is the ability to understand social interactions. (p. 400)

6. **Effortful control** is the ability to regulate one's impulses and emotions through effort, not simply through natural inclination. (p. 400)

7. **Bullying** is the repeated, systematic effort to inflict harm on a child through physical, verbal, or social attacks. (p. 402)

8. A **bully-victim** is a bully who has also been a victim of bullying, also called *provocative victim*. (p. 403)

9. **Family function** refers to the ways families work to foster the development of children by meeting their physical needs, encouraging them to learn, helping them to develop self-respect, nurturing friendships, and providing harmony and stability. (p. 409)

10. **Family structure** refers to the legal and genetic relationships among relatives in the same household. (p. 410)

11. A **nuclear family** consists of two parents and their mutual biological offspring under age 18. (p. 411)

12. An **extended family** consists of three or more generations of biologically related individuals living in one household. (p. 411)

13. A **blended family** consists of two parents, at least one with biological children from another union, and any children the adults have together. (p. 412)

14. In Freud's theory, middle childhood is a period of **latency,** during which emotional drives are quieter, psychosexual needs are repressed, and unconscious conflicts are submerged. (p. 417)

15. According to Erikson, the crisis of middle childhood is that of **industry versus inferiority**, in which children try to master many skills and develop views of themselves as either competent or incompetent and inferior. (p. 417)

16. **Resilience** is the capacity of some children to adapt positively despite adversity. (p. 420)

Chapter Fourteen

Adolescence:
Biosocial Development

Chapter Overview

Between the ages of 10 and 20, young people cross the great divide between childhood and adulthood. This crossing encompasses all three domains of development—biosocial, cognitive, and psychosocial. Chapter 14 focuses on the dramatic changes that occur in the biosocial domain, beginning with puberty and the growth spurt. The biosocial metamorphosis of the adolescent is discussed in detail, with emphasis on factors that affect the age of puberty and sexual maturation.

Although adolescence is, in many ways, a healthy time of life, the text addresses four health hazards that too often affect adolescence: accidental injury and death; sex too early; and the use of alcohol, tobacco, and other drugs; and poor nutrition.

NOTE: Answer guidelines for all Chapter 14 questions begin on page 217.

Guided Study

The text chapter should be studied one section at a time. Before you read, preview each section by skimming it, noting headings and boldface items. Then read the appropriate section objectives from the following outline. Keep these objectives in mind and, as you read the chapter section, search for the information that will enable you to meet each objective. Once you have finished a section, write out answers for its objectives.

Puberty Begins (pp. 432–439)

1. Outline the biological events of puberty.

2. Discuss the emotional and psychological impact of pubertal hormones.

3. Identify several factors that influence the onset of puberty.

The Transformations of Puberty (pp. 439–445)

4. Describe the growth spurt in both the male and the female adolescent, focusing on changes in body weight and height.

5. Describe the changes in the body's internal organs that accompany the growth spurt.

6. Discuss the effects of changing circadian and diurnal rhythms on the adolescent's physical and psychological well-being.

7. Discuss the development of the primary sex characteristics in males and females during puberty.

8. Discuss the development of the secondary sex characteristics in males and females during puberty.

Brain Development in Adolescence (pp. 445–449)

9. Describe the development of the brain during adolescence.

10. Explain why the brain's immaturity and asynchronous development partly account for adolescent risk taking.

Health Hazards (pp. 449–462)

11. Characterize the period of adolescence in terms of the adolescent's overall health.

12. Identify possible causes of the increase in injury and death in adolescence.

13. Discuss the potential problems associated with early sexual activity.

14. Discuss sexual abuse, noting its prevalence and consequences for development.

15. Discuss drug use and abuse among adolescents today, including their prevalence and significance for development.

16. Discuss the nutritional needs and problems of adolescents.

Chapter Review

When you have finished reading the chapter, work through the material that follows to review it. Complete the sentences and answer the questions. As you proceed, evaluate your performance for each section by consulting the answers beginning on page 217. Do not continue with the next section until you understand each answer. If you need to, review or reread the appropriate section in the textbook before continuing.

Puberty Begins (pp. 432–439)

1. The period of rapid physical growth and sexual maturation that ends childhood and brings the young person to adult size, shape, and sexual potential is called _____ . The physical changes of puberty typically are complete _____ (how long?) after puberty begins. Although puberty begins at various ages, the _____ is almost always the same.

    List, in order, the major physical changes of puberty in

    Girls: _____

    _____

    Boys: _____

    _____

2. The average girl experiences her first menstrual period, called _____ , between ages _____ and _____ , with age _____ being the average.

3. The average boy experiences his first ejaculation of seminal fluid, called _____ , between ages _____ and _____ , with age _____ being the average.

4. Menarche and spermarche signify the first release of _____ , including _____ and _____ .

5. Puberty begins when a hormonal signal from the _____ triggers hormone production in the _____ _____ , which in turn triggers increased hormone production by the _____ _____ and by the _____ , which include the _____ in males and the _____ in females. This route is called the _____ _____ .

6. The hormone _____ causes the gonads to dramatically increase their production of sex hormones, especially _____ in girls and _____ in boys.

7. The increase in the hormone _____ is dramatic in boys and slight in girls, whereas the increase in the hormone _____ is marked in girls and slight in boys. Conflict, moodiness, and sexual urges _____ (usually do/do not usually) increase during adolescence. This is due in part to the increasingly high levels of hormones such as _____ . The impact of hormones, however, depends profoundly on the adolescent's _____ _____ .

8. During puberty, hormones are quite _____ (consistent from child to child/erratic) in part due to the immaturity of the _____ .

9. Normal children begin to notice pubertal changes between the ages of _____ and _____ . Girls are about _____ (how many?) years ahead of boys in height.

10. Genes are an important factor in the timing of menarche, as demonstrated by the fact that _____ and _____ reach menarche at very similar ages.

11. Stocky individuals tend to experience puberty
_____ (earlier/later) than
those with taller, thinner builds.

12. Menarche seems to be related to the accumulation
of a certain amount of body _____ .

13. For both sexes, fat is limited by chronic
_____ , which therefore delays
puberty by several years.

14. Another influence on the age of puberty is
_____ .

15. Research from many nations suggests that family
stress may _____ (accelerate/
delay) the onset of puberty.

16. Stress may cause production of the hormones that
cause _____ . Support for this
hypothesis comes from a study showing that
early puberty was associated with
_____ and
_____ .

17. An evolutionary explanation of the stress-puberty
hypothesis is that ancestral females growing up
in stressful environments may have increased
their _____ _____ by
accelerating physical maturation.

18. For girls, _____
(early/late) maturation may be especially trou-
blesome.

Describe several common problems and developmental hazards experienced by early-maturing girls.

19. For boys, _____ (early/late/both
early and late) maturation may be difficult.
_____ (Early/Late) maturing boys
may have difficulty, in part because they are likely to join peer groups that rebel against
_____ and _____ .
_____ (Early/Late) maturing boys
may be teased.

The Transformation of Puberty (pp. 439–445)

20. A major _____ spurt occurs in late
childhood and early adolescence, during which
growth proceeds from the _____
(core/extremities) to the _____
(core/extremities). At the same time, children
begin to _____ (gain/lose) weight
at a relatively rapid rate.

21. The amount of weight gain an individual experiences depends on several factors, including
_____ , _____ ,
_____ , and _____ .

22. During the growth spurt, a greater percentage of
fat is retained by _____ (males/
females), who naturally have a higher proportion
of body fat in adulthood. The explanation for this
difference is _____ : Greater fat
made this gender appear more
_____ .

23. About a year after the height and weight changes
occur, a period of _____ increase
occurs, causing the pudginess and clumsiness of
an earlier age to disappear. In boys, this increase
is particularly notable in the _____ .

24. Internal organs also grow during puberty. The
_____ increase in size and capacity,
the _____ doubles in size, heart rate
_____ (increases/decreases), and
blood volume _____ (increases/
decreases). These changes increase the adolescent's physical _____ .

Explain why the physical demands placed on a
teenager, as in athletic training, should not be the
same as those for a young adult of similar height and
weight.

25. During puberty, one organ system, the
_____ system, decreases in size,
making teenagers _____
(more/less) susceptible to respiratory ailments.

26. One secondary sex characteristic that is mistaken-
ly considered a sign of womanhood and manli-
ness is _____ .

27. The hormones of puberty also affect the
_____ rhythm, causing, for instance,
changes in the level of the enzyme
_____ , which makes people more
_____ . One aspect of this rhythm is
the _____ cycle, which includes
changes in when the teenager needs the most
sleep. Adolescents typically get too
_____ (little/much) sleep.

28. Changes in _____
_____ _____
involve the sex organs that are directly involved
in reproduction. By the end of puberty, reproduction _____ (is/is still not) possible.

Describe the major changes in primary sex characteristics that occur in both sexes during puberty.

29. Sexual features other than those associated with
reproduction are referred to as _____
_____ _____ .

Describe the major pubertal changes in the secondary
sex characteristics of both sexes.

30. Although sex hormones trigger thoughts about
sexual intimacy, sexual behavior among teens
reflects _____ and
_____ more than biology.

Brain Development in Adolescence (pp. 445–449)

31. Many of the hallmarks of adolescent thinking and
behavior, including _____ ,
_____ , _____ skills,
and _____ solving, originate with
maturation of the _____ .

32. An adolescent's ability to plan, reflect, analyze,
and decide occurs because of maturation of the
_____ _____ .

33. Young people become faster and better at problem solving because of the development of more
_____ and better
_____ .

34. The limbic system, which includes the
_____ and the _____ ,
matures _____ (before/after) the
prefrontal cortex. The limbic system predominates in quick _____ reactions,
while the prefrontal cortex coordinates
_____ functions, including the
capacity for _____ control of
emotions.

35. One reason adolescents like intensity and excitement is that the maturing _____
system is attuned to these strong sensations, as
yet unchecked by the _____
_____ .

36. The executive functions of the brain
_____ (advance/recede) markedly
throughout adolescence and early adulthood.
This occurs along with new _____
of dendrites in the prefrontal cortex, making
some connections faster and increasing the
brain's _____ matter.

Health Hazards (pp. 449–462)

37. Girls usually reach their maximum height by age
_____ and boys by age
_____ . Death from disease is
_____ during adolescence. At the
same time, the proportion of deaths due to violence has _____ (increased/
decreased).

38. The leading cause of death from ages 1 to 45 is
_____ . The reasons include rapid
changes in _____
that correlate with increased _____
_____ . Another factor is that adolescents tend to _____ the joys of
the moment and to disregard _____ .
A third factor is the _____
_____ , which puts some adolescents—especially those who are
_____ from others—at greater risk
than others.

39. A major developmental risk for sexually active
adolescent girls is _____ . If this
happens within a year or two of menarche, girls
are at increased risk of many complications,
including _____
_____ . Another reason early
pregnancy is risky is that the younger a pregnant
girl is, the more likely her sexual experience is to
have been _____ and
_____ . A third reason is that the
younger she is, the more likely she is to have an
untreated _____
_____ _____ .

40. In every nation , adolescent pregnancy correlates
with _____ and _____
_____ .

41. Any activity in which an adult uses an unconsenting person for his or her own sexual stimulation or pleasure is considered
_____ _____ . When
such activity involves a young person, whether or
not genital contact is involved, it is called
_____ _____
_____ .

42. The damage done by sexual abuse depends on
many factors, including if it is _____
or _____ or if it impairs the child's
relationships with _____ .

43. More than _____ (how many?) of
child molesters are _____ .

44. The principal targets for victimization are young
adolescent _____ (girls/boys). If
_____ (girls/boys) are victims, they
feel shame at being weak.

45. Adolescent problems, such as pregnancy, drug
abuse, and suicide often are tied to past
_____ _____ .

46. Smoking in adolescence is linked to all kinds of
_____ , including
_____ , _____ ,
_____ , and _____ .

47. Drug _____ always harms physical
and psychological development. Drug
_____ is the need for more and
more of a drug.

48. Consuming _____ (how many?) or
more alcoholic drinks in a row sometime during
the past _____ (how many?) weeks
constitutes _____
_____ .

49. The younger people are when they first try a
drug, the more likely they are to become
_____ .

50. All psychoactive drugs interfere with development of the _____ , but
_____ may do the most damage.

51. By decreasing food consumption and the absorption of nutrients, tobacco can limit the adolescent
_____ _____ .

52. Alcohol impairs _____ and
_____ by damaging the brain's
_____ and
_____ _____ .

53. The idea that each new generations forgets what
the previous generation has learned about harmful drugs is referred to as _____
_____ .

54. Due to rapid physical growth, the typical adolescent needs about 50 percent more of the minerals _____ , _____ , and _____ during the growth spurt. Inadequate consumption of _____ is particularly troubling, because it is a good source of the _____ needed for bone growth.

55. Because of menstruation, adolescent females need additional _____ in their diets and are more likely to suffer _____ than any other subgroup of the population.

56. Adolescents' mental conception of, and attitude toward, their physical appearance is referred to as their _____ _____ . Most girls want to be _____ , and many boys want to look _____ and _____ .

57. Most teenagers eat _____ (few/most) meals at home. As a result, they are likely to consume too much _____ , _____ , and _____ .

58. Anorexia nervosa is a disease of the _____ context. Its diagnostic criteria include
    a. _____
    b. _____
    c. _____
    d. _____

59. Bulimia nervosa is _____ (more common/rarer) than anorexia nervosa. The symptoms of this disorder include a _____–_____ episode at least once a _____ for _____ (how many?) months. People who suffer from bulimia are usually close to _____ in weight.

Progress Test 1

Multiple-Choice Questions

Circle your answers to the following questions and check them with the answers on page 218. If your answer is incorrect, read the explanation for why it is incorrect and then consult the appropriate pages of the text (in parentheses following the correct answer).

1. Which of the following most accurately describes the sequence of pubertal development in girls?
   a. breasts and pubic hair; growth spurt in which fat is deposited on hips and buttocks; first menstrual period; ovulation
   b. growth spurt; breasts and pubic hair; first menstrual period; ovulation
   c. first menstrual period; breasts and pubic hair; growth spurt; ovulation
   d. breasts and pubic hair; growth spurt; ovulation; first menstrual period

2. Although both sexes grow rapidly during adolescence, boys typically gain more than girls in their:
   a. muscle strength.
   b. body fat.
   c. internal organ growth.
   d. lymphoid system.

3. For girls, the first readily observable sign of the onset of puberty is:
   a. the onset of breast growth.
   b. the appearance of facial, body, and pubic hair.
   c. a change in the shape of the eyes.
   d. a lengthening of the torso.

4. More than any other group in the population, adolescent girls are likely to have:
   a. asthma.
   b. acne.
   c. anemia.
   d. testosterone deficiency.

5. The HPA axis is the:
   a. route followed by many hormones to regulate stress, growth, sleep, and appetite.
   b. pair of sex glands in humans.
   c. cascade of sex hormones in females and males.
   d. area of the brain that regulates the pituitary gland.

6. For males, the secondary sex characteristic that usually occurs last is:
   a. breast enlargement.
   b. the appearance of facial hair.
   c. growth of the testes.
   d. the appearance of pubic hair.

7. For girls, the specific event that is taken to indicate fertility is _____ ; for boys, it is _____ .
   a. the growth of breast buds; voice deepening
   b. menarche; spermarche
   c. anovulation; the testosterone surge
   d. the growth spurt; pubic hair

8. The most significant hormonal changes of puberty include an increase of _____ in _____ and an increase of _____ in _____ .
   a. progesterone; boys; estradiol; girls
   b. estradiol; boys; testosterone; girls
   c. progesterone; girls; estradiol; boys
   d. estradiol; girls; testosterone; boys

9. In general, most adolescents are:
   a. overweight.
   b. satisfied with their appearance.
   c. dissatisfied with their appearance.
   d. unaffected by cultural attitudes about beauty.

10. Adolescents' improving ability to plan, reflect, and analyze is partly the result of maturation of the:
   a. hippocampus.
   b. amygdala.
   c. limbic system.
   d. prefrontal cortex.

11. The damage caused by sexual abuse depends on all of the following factors *except*:
   a. repeated incidence.
   b. the gender of the perpetrator.
   c. distorted adult–child relationships.
   d. impairment of the child's ability to relate to peers.

12. Early physical growth and sexual maturation:
   a. tend to be equally difficult for girls and boys.
   b. tend to be more difficult for boys than for girls.
   c. tend to be more difficult for girls than for boys.
   d. are easier for both girls and boys than late maturation.

13. Pubertal changes in growth and maturation typically are complete how long after puberty begins?
   a. one to two years
   b. two to three years
   c. three to five years
   d. The variation is too great to generalize.

14. The hypothalamus/pituitary/adrenal axis triggers:
   a. puberty.
   b. the growth spurt.
   c. the development of sexual characteristics.
   d. all of the above.

15. One reason adolescents like intensity, excitement, and risk taking is that:
   a. the limbic system matures faster than the prefrontal cortex.
   b. the prefrontal cortex matures faster than the limbic system.
   c. brain maturation is synchronous.
   d. puberty is occurring at a younger age today than in the past.

True or False Items

Write T (*true*) or F (*false*) on the line in front of each statement.

_____ 1. More calories are necessary during adolescence than at any other period during the life span.

_____ 2. During puberty, hormones have their greatest impact indirectly, rather than directly.

_____ 3. The first indicator of reproductive potential in males is menarche.

_____ 4. Lung capacity, heart size, and total volume of blood increase significantly during adolescence.

_____ 5. Puberty generally begins sometime between ages 8 and 15.

_____ 6. All the body systems function at an optimal level in adolescence.

_____ 7. Each culture and age cohort has its own patterns of drug use and abuse during adolescence.

_____ 8. Childhood habits of overeating and underexercising usually lessen during adolescence.

_____ 9. Early-maturing girls tend to have lower self-esteem.

_____ 10. Both the sequence and timing of pubertal events vary greatly from one young person to another.

Progress Test 2

Progress Test 2 should be completed during a final chapter review. Answer the following questions after you thoroughly understand the correct answers for the Chapter Review and Progress Test 1.

Multiple-Choice Questions

1. Which of the following is the correct sequence of pubertal events in boys?
   a. growth spurt, pubic hair, facial hair, first ejaculation, lowering of voice
   b. pubic hair, first ejaculation, growth spurt; lowering of voice, facial hair
   c. lowering of voice, pubic hair, growth spurt, facial hair, first ejaculation
   d. growth spurt, facial hair, lowering of voice, pubic hair, first ejaculation

2. Which of the following statements about adolescent physical development is *not* true?
   a. Hands and feet generally lengthen before arms and legs.
   b. Facial features usually grow before the head itself reaches adult size and shape.
   c. Oil, sweat, and odor glands become more active.
   d. The lymphoid system increases slightly in size, and the heart increases by nearly half.

3. In puberty, a hormone that increases markedly in girls (and only somewhat in boys) is:
   a. estradiol.   c. androgen.
   b. testosterone.   d. menarche.

4. Nutritional deficiencies in adolescence are frequently the result of:
   a. eating red meat.
   b. poor eating habits.
   c. anovulatory menstruation.
   d. excessive exercise.

5. In females, puberty is typically marked by a(n):
   a. significant widening of the shoulders.
   b. significant widening of the hips.
   c. enlargement of the torso and upper chest.
   d. decrease in the size of the eyes and nose.

6. Nonreproductive sexual characteristics, such as the deepening of the voice and the development of breasts, are called:
   a. gender-typed traits.
   b. primary sex characteristics.
   c. secondary sex characteristics.
   d. pubertal prototypes.

7. Puberty is initiated when hormones are released from the _____ , then from the _____ gland, and then from the adrenal glands and the _____ .
   a. hypothalamus; pituitary; gonads
   b. pituitary; gonads; hypothalamus
   c. gonads; pituitary; hypothalamus
   d. pituitary; hypothalamus; gonads

8. By age 17, what percent of adolescents have had intercourse?
   a. 25 percent
   b. 50 percent
   c. 90 percent
   d. The percentage is different in girls and boys.

9. Alcohol impairs memory and self-control by damaging the:
   a. hippocampus and prefrontal cortex.
   b. pituitary gland.
   c. hypothalamus.
   d. gonads.

10. The brain area that predominates in quick, emotional reactions is the:
    a. prefrontal cortex.
    b. limbic system.
    c. dendrite.
    d. axon.

11. Compounding the problem of sexual abuse of boys, abused boys:
    a. feel shame at the idea of being weak.
    b. have fewer sources of emotional support.
    c. are more likely to be abused by fathers.
    d. have all of the above problems.

12. The diagnostic criteria for anorexia nervosa include each of the following except:
    a. refusal to maintain body weight at least 85 percent of normal BMI.
    b. intense fear of gaining weight.
    c. disturbed body perception and denial of the problem.
    d. early menarche.

13. Puberty is *most accurately* defined as the period:
    a. of rapid physical growth that occurs during adolescence.
    b. during which sexual maturation is attained.
    c. of rapid physical growth and sexual maturation that ends childhood.
    d. during which adolescents establish identities separate from their parents.

14. Which of the following does *not* typically occur during puberty?
    a. The lungs increase in size and capacity.
    b. The heart's size and rate of beating increase.
    c. Blood volume increases.
    d. The lymphoid system decreases in size.

15. Teenagers' susceptibility to respiratory ailments typically _____ during adolescence, due to a(n) _____ in the size of the lymphoid system.
    a. increases; increase
    b. increases; decrease
    c. decreases; increase
    d. decreases; decrease

Matching Items

Match each term or concept with its corresponding description or definition.

Terms or Concepts

_____ 1. puberty
_____ 2. GnRH
_____ 3. testosterone
_____ 4. estradiol
_____ 5. growth spurt
_____ 6. primary sex characteristics
_____ 7. menarche
_____ 8. spermarche
_____ 9. secondary sex characteristics
_____ 10. body image

Descriptions or Definitions

a. onset of menstruation
b. period of rapid physical growth and sexual maturation that ends childhood
c. hormone that increases dramatically in boys during puberty
d. hormone that causes the gonads to increase their production of sex hormones
e. hormone that increases dramatically in girls during puberty
f. first sign is increased bone length
g. attitude toward one's physical appearance
h. physical characteristics not involved in reproduction
i. the sex organs involved in reproduction
j. first ejaculation containing sperm

Thinking Critically About Chapter 14

Answer these questions the day before an exam as a final check on your understanding of the chapter's terms and concepts.

1. Concluding her talk on adolescent alcohol use and brain damage, Maya notes that:
    a. studies have shown only that alcohol use is correlated with damage to the prefrontal cortex.
    b. thus far, studies have shown only that alcohol use is correlated with damage to the hippocampus.
    c. animal research studies demonstrate that alcohol does not merely correlate with brain abnormalities; it causes them.
    d. alcohol use causes brain abnormalities only in teens who are genetically vulnerable.

2. I am the hormone that causes the gonads to dramatically increase their production of sex hormones. Who am I?
    a. GnRH   c. estradiol
    b. cortisol   d. testosterone

3. Twelve-year-old Kwan is worried because his twin sister has suddenly grown taller and more physically mature than he. His parents should:
    a. reassure him that the average boy is about two years behind the average girl in the timing of puberty.
    b. tell him that within a year or less he will grow taller than his sister.
    c. tell him that one member of each fraternal twin pair is always shorter.
    d. encourage him to exercise more to accelerate the onset of his growth spurt.

4. Calvin, the class braggart, boasts that because his beard has begun to grow, he is more virile than his male classmates. Jacob informs him that:

   a. the tendency to grow facial and body hair has nothing to do with virility.

   b. beard growth is determined by heredity.

   c. girls also develop some facial hair and more noticeable hair on their arms and legs, so it is clearly not a sign of masculinity.

   d. all of the above are true.

5. Jennifer has a BMI of 18 and has lost more than 10 percent of her body weight during the past two months. Her physician suspects that Jennifer may be suffering from:

   a. bulimia nervosa.

   b. anorexia nervosa.

   c. the normal adolescent preoccupation with body image.

   d. an STI.

6. Which of the following students is likely to be the most popular in a sixth-grade class?

   a. Vicki, the most sexually mature girl in the class

   b. Sandra, the tallest girl in the class

   c. Brad, who is at the top of the class scholastically

   d. Dan, the tallest boy in the class

7. Regarding the effects of early and late maturation on boys and girls, which of the following is *not* true?

   a. Late-maturing boys are more likely to join peer groups that rebel against laws and traditions.

   b. Early puberty that leads to romantic relationships often leads to stress and depression among both girls and boys..

   c. Early-maturing girls may be drawn into involvement with older boys.

   d. Late puberty is often difficult for boys in schools where athletes are the local stars.

8. Teenagers whose parents are divorced and those who live in cities often experience puberty _____ than other teens, perhaps as a result of _____ .

   a. earlier; greater stress

   b. later; greater stress

   c. earlier; poor nutrition

   d. later; poor nutrition

9. Twenty-four-year-old Connie, who has a distorted view of sexuality, has gone from one abusive relationship with a man to another. It is likely that Connie:

   a. has been abusing drugs all her life.

   b. was sexually abused as a child.

   c. will eventually become a normal, nurturing mother.

   d. had attention-deficit disorder as a child.

10. When developmentalists say that hormones have an indirect effect on adolescent moods and emotions, they mean that:

    a. hormones directly affect appetite and nutrition, which dramatically influence emotionality.

    b. the variation in emotionality from teen to teen is too great to state that there is a direct impact.

    c. it is the social responses of others to hormonally triggered changes in appearance that trigger adolescent moods.

    d. all of the above occur.

11. Despite having normal body weight, 15-year-old Irena has a distorted body image and an uncontrollable urge to overeat. She also regularly engages in compulsive binge eating. Irena's symptoms are typical of people who suffer from:

    a. anorexia nervosa.

    b. bulimia nervosa.

    c. adrenal insufficiency.

    d. estradiol deficiency.

12. Of the following teenagers, those most likely to be distressed about their physical development are:

    a. late-maturing girls.

    b. early-maturing girls.

    c. early-maturing boys.

    d. girls or boys who masturbate.

13. Thirteen-year-old Kristin seems apathetic and lazy to her parents. You tell them:

    a. that Kristin is showing signs of chronic depression.

    b. that Kristin may be experiencing psychosocial difficulties.

    c. that Kristin has a poor attitude and needs more discipline.

    d. to have Kristin's iron level checked.

14. I am one of two glands, located above the kidneys, that produce "stress" hormones. What am I?

    a. pituitary gland   c. adrenal gland

    b. ovary   d. testes

15. Eleven-year-old Linda, who has just begun to experience the first signs of puberty, laments, "When will the agony of puberty be over?" You tell her that the major events of puberty typically end about _____ after the first visible signs appear.

    a. 6 years   **c.** 2 to 4 years

    b. 3 to 5 years   **d.** 1 year

Key Terms

Writing Definitions

Using your own words, write a brief definition or explanation of each of the following terms on a separate piece of paper.

1. puberty
2. menarche
3. spermarche
4. hormone
5. pituitary gland
6. adrenal glands
7. HPA axis
8. gonads
9. estradiol
10. testosterone
11. growth spurt
12. primary sex characteristics
13. secondary sex characteristics
14. sexually transmitted infections (STIs)
15. sexual abuse
16. child sexual abuse
17. drug abuse
18. drug addiction
19. binge drinking
20. generational forgetting
21. body image
22. anorexia nervosa
23. bulimia nervosa

Cross-Check

After you have written the definitions of the key terms in this chapter, you should complete the crossword puzzle to ensure that you can reverse the process—recognize the term, given the definition.

ACROSS

1. Glands near the kidneys that are stimulated by the pituitary at the beginning of puberty.
7. The first ejaculation of seminal fluid containing sperm.
12. The first menstrual period.
15. The ovaries in girls and the testes or testicles in boys.
17. Gland that stimulates the adrenal glands and the sex glands in response to a signal from the hypothalamus.
18. Event, which begins with an increase in bone length and includes rapid weight gain and organ growth, that is one of the many observable signs of puberty.
19. Ingestion of a drug, regardless of the amount or affect of ingestion.

DOWN

1. The period of biological, cognitive, and psychosocial transition from childhood to adulthood.
2. Organ system, which includes the tonsils and adenoids, that decreases in size at adolescence.
3. Area of the brain that sends the hormonal signal that triggers the biological events of puberty.
4. Widely abused gateway drug that loosens inhibitions and impairs judgment.
5. Dependence on a drug or a behavior in order to feel physically or psychologically at ease.
6. Drugs—usually tobacco, alcohol, and marijuana—whose use increases the risk that a person will later use harder drugs.
8. Ingestion of a drug to the extent that it impairs the user's well-being.
9. Body characteristics that are not directly involved in reproduction but that signify sexual development.
10. Main sex hormone in males.
11. Gateway drug that decreases food consumption, the absorption of nutrients, and fertility.
13. Main sex hormone in females.
14. Period of rapid physical growth and sexual maturation that ends childhood and brings the young person to adult size.
16. Sex organs that are directly involved in reproduction.

ANSWERS

CHAPTER REVIEW

1. puberty; three to five years; sequence

Girls: onset of breast growth, initial pubic hair, peak growth spurt, widening of the hips, first menstrual period, completion of pubic-hair growth, and final breast development

Boys: growth of the testes, initial pubic hair, growth of the penis, first ejaculation of seminal fluid, facial hair, peak growth spurt, voice deepening, and completion of pubic-hair growth

2. menarche; 10; 14; 12.8
3. spermarche; 10; 16; (just under) 13
4. gametes; sperm; ova
5. hypothalamus; pituitary gland; adrenal glands; gonads (sex glands); testes; ovaries; HPA axis
6. GnRH (gonadotropin-releasing hormone); estradiol; testosterone
7. testosterone; estradiol; usually do; testosterone; psychosocial context
8. erratic; brain
9. 8; 15; two
10. mothers; daughters
11. earlier

12. fat
13. malnutrition
14. stress
15. accelerate
16. puberty; conflicted relationships within the family; an unrelated man living in the home
17. reproductive success
18. early

Early-maturing girls may be teased about their big feet or developing breasts. Those who date early may begin "adult" activities at an earlier age, may be pressured by their dates to be sexually active, and may suffer a decrease in self-esteem.

19. both early and late; Early; laws; traditions; Late
20. growth; extremities; core; gain
21. gender; heredity; diet; exercise
22. females evolutionary; fertile
23. muscle; arms
24. lungs; heart; decreases; increases; endurance

The fact that the more visible spurts of weight and height precede the less visible ones of the muscles and organs means that athletic training and weight lifting should match the young person's size of a year or so earlier.

25. lymphoid; less
26. facial and body hair
27. circadian; MAO; careful; diurnal; little
28. primary sex characteristics; is

Girls: growth of ovaries and uterus and thickening of the vaginal lining

Boys: growth of testes and lengthening of penis; also scrotum enlarges and becomes pendulous

29. secondary sex characteristics

Males grow taller than females and become wider at the shoulders than at the hips. Females take on more fat all over and become wider at the hips, and their breasts begin to develop. About 65 percent of boys experience some temporary breast enlargement. As the lungs and larynx grow, the adolescent's voice (especially in boys) becomes lower. Head and body hair become coarser and darker in both sexes. Facial hair (especially in boys) begins to grow.

30. culture; cohort
31. impulsiveness; emotionality; analytical; problem; brain
32. prefrontal cortex
33. dendrites; myelination

34. hippocampus; amygdala; before; emotional; executive; effortful

35. limbic; prefrontal cortex

36. advance; pruning; white

37. 16; 18; rare; increased

38. accidents; size, shape, and hormone levels; risk taking; overrate; risks; social context; alienated

39. pregnancy; spontaneous abortion, high blood pressure, stillbirth, cesarean section, and a low-birthweight baby; unwanted; coercive; sexually transmitted infection (disease)

40. poverty; poor health

41. sexual abuse; child sexual abuse

42. repeated; coercive; peers

43. half; parents

44. girls; boys

45. sexual abuse

46. psychopathology; ADHD; conduct disorder; anxiety; depression

47. abuse; addiction

48. five; two; binge drinking

49. addicted

50. brain; alcohol

51. growth rate

52. memory; self-control; hippocampus; prefrontal cortex

53. generational forgetting

54. calcium; iron; zinc; milk; calcium

55. iron; anemia

56. body image; thinner; taller; stronger

57. few; salt; sugar; fat

58. social

    a. refusal to maintain body weight at least 85 percent of normal BMI

    b. intense fear of gaining weight

    c. disturbed body perception and denial of the problem

    d. lack of menstruation

59. more common; binge–purge; week; three; normal

PROGRESS TEST 1

Multiple-Choice Questions

1. a. is the answer. (p. 432)

2. a. is the answer. (p. 440)

    b. Girls gain more body fat than boys do.

c. & d. The text does not indicate that these are different for boys and girls.

3. a. is the answer. (p. 432)

4. c. is the answer. This is because each menstrual period depletes some iron from the body. (p. 458)

5. a. is the answer. (p. 433)

    b. This describes the gonads.

    c. These include estradiol and testosterone.

    d. This is the hypothalamus.

6. b. is the answer. (p. 443)

7. b. is the answer. (p. 432)

8. d. is the answer. (p. 434)

9. c. is the answer. (p. 459)

    a. Although some adolescents become overweight, many diet and lose weight in an effort to attain a desired body image.

    d. On the contrary, cultural attitudes about beauty are an extremely influential factor in the formation of a teenager's body image.

10. d. is the answer. (p. 447)

    a., b., & c. The hippocampus (a) and amygdala (b), which are both part of the limbic system (c), are important in quick emotional reactions.

11. b. is the answer. (p. 453)

12. c. is the answer. (p. 438)

13. c. is the answer. (p. 432)

14. d. is the answer. (p. 433)

15. a. is the answer. (p. 447)

    c. Brain maturation is asynchronous.

    d. This may be true, but it doesn't explain why adolescents have always liked intensity and excitement.

True or False Items

1. T (p. 458)

2. T (p. 435)

3. F The first indicator of reproductive potential in males is ejaculation of seminal fluid containing sperm (spermarche). Menarche (the first menstrual period) is the first indication of reproductive potential in females. (p. 432)

4. T (p. 440)

5. T (p. 435)

6. T (p. 449)

7. T (p. 454)

8. F These habits generally *worsen* during adolescence. (pp. 459–460)

9. T (p. 438)

10. F Although there is great variation in the timing of pubertal events, the sequence is very similar for all young people. (p. 432)

PROGRESS TEST 2

Multiple-Choice Questions

1. **b.** is the answer. (pp. 432)

2. **d.** is the answer. During adolescence, the lymphoid system *decreases* in size and the heart *doubles* in size. (p. 440)

3. **a.** is the answer. (p. 434)

   b. Testosterone increases markedly in boys.

   c. Androgen is another name for testosterone.

   d. Menarche is the first menstrual period.

4. **b.** is the answer. (p. 458)

5. **b.** is the answer. (pp. 432, 440)

   a. The shoulders of males tend to widen during puberty.

   c. The torso typically lengthens during puberty.

   d. The eyes and nose *increase* in size during puberty.

6. **c.** is the answer. (p. 443)

   a. Although not a term used in the textbook, a gender-typed trait is one that is typical of one sex but not of the other.

   b. Primary sex characteristics are those involving the reproductive organs.

   d. This is not a term used by developmental psychologists.

7. **a.** is the answer. (p. 433)

8. **b.** is the answer. (p. 444)

9. **a.** is the answer. (p. 457)

10. **b.** is the answer. (p. 447–448)

   a. The prefrontal cortex is responsible for planning, problem solving, and effortful control.

   c. & d. Dendrites and axons are parts of neurons.

11. **a.** is the answer. (p. 453)

   b. This was not discussed in the text.

   c. This is true of girls.

12. **d.** is the answer. (p. 460)

13. **c.** is the answer. (p. 432)

14. **b.** is the answer. Although the size of the heart increases during puberty, heart rate *decreases*. (p. 440)

15. **d.** is the answer. (p. 347)

Matching Items

1. b (p. 432) 5. f (p. 439) 9. h (p. 443)
2. d (p. 434) 6. i (p. 443) 10. g (p. 458)
3. c (p. 434) 7. a (p. 432)
4. e (p. 434) 8. j (p. 432)

THINKING CRITICALLY ABOUT CHAPTER 14

1. **c.** is the answer. (p. 457)

2. **a.** is the answer. (p. 434)

3. **a.** is the answer. (p. 436)

   b. It usually takes longer than one year for a prepubescent male to catch up with a female who has begun puberty.

   c. This is not true.

   d. The text does not suggest that exercise has an effect on the timing of the growth spurt.

4. **d.** is the answer. (p. 441)

5. **b.** is the answer. (p. 460)

   a. Persons with bulimia nervosa usually maintain normal, or near-normal body weight.

   c. Jennifer's BMI is too low, and her recent weight loss is too great and rapid to be considered normal.

6. **d.** is the answer. (p. 438)

   a. & b. Early-maturing girls are often teased and criticized by their friends.

   c. During adolescence, physical stature is typically a more prized attribute among peers than is scholastic achievement.

7. **a.** is the answer. This is true of early-maturing boys. (p. 438)

8. **a.** is the answer. (p. 437)

9. **b.** is the answer. (p. 453)

10. **c.** is the answer. (pp. 4334–435)

11. **b.** is the answer. (p. 461)

   a. People who suffer from anorexia are underweight.

   c. & d. Eating disorders are not caused by glandular or hormonal problems.

12. **b.** is the answer. (p. 438)

13. **d.** Kristin's symptoms are typical of anemia, which is more common in teenage girls than in any other age group. (p. 458)

14. **c.** is the answer. (p. 433)

   a. The pituitary, which is located in the brain, secretes hormones that regulate other glands, including the adrenals.

b. & d. The ovaries and testes secrete the sex hormones estradiol and testosterone.

15. **b.** is the answer. (p. 432)

KEY TERMS

1. **Puberty** is the period of rapid physical growth and sexual maturation that ends childhood and brings the young person to adult size, shape, and sexual potential. (p. 432)

2. **Menarche,** which refers to the first menstrual period, signals that the adolescent girl has begun ovulation. (p. 432)

3. **Spermarche,** which refers to the first ejaculation of sperm, signals sperm production in adolescent boys. (p. 432)

4. A **hormone** is an organic chemical messenger produced by one body tissue that travels via the bloodstream to another and influences thoughts, emotions, urges, and behaviors. (p. 433)

5. The **pituitary gland,** in response to a biochemical signal from the hypothalamus, produces hormones that regulate growth and control other glands. (p. 433)

6. The **adrenal glands** secrete epinephrine and norepinephrine, hormones that prepare the body to deal with emergencies or stress. (p. 433)

7. The **HPA axis** (hypothalamus/pituitary/adrenal axis) is the route followed by many hormones to trigger puberty and to regulate stress, growth, and other bodily changes. (p. 433)

8. The **gonads** are the paired sex glands in humans—the ovaries in females and the testes or testicles in males. (p. 433)

9. **Estradiol** is a sex hormone that is secreted in greater amounts by females than by males; considered the chief estrogen. (p. 434)

10. **Testosterone** is a sex hormone that is secreted more by males than by females; considered the best-known androgen. (p. 434)

11. The **growth spurt,** which is the relatively sudden and rapid physical growth of every part of the body, is one of the many observable signs of puberty. (p. 439)

12. During puberty, changes in the **primary sex characteristics** involve those sex organs that are directly involved in reproduction. (p. 443)

13. During puberty, changes in the **secondary sex characteristics** involve parts of the body that are not directly involved in reproduction but that signify sexual development. (p. 443)

14. **Sexually transmitted infections (STIs)** such as syphilis, gonorrhea, herpes, and AIDS, are those that are spread by sexual contact. (p. 451)

15. **Sexual abuse** is the use of an unconsenting person for one's own sexual pleasure. (p. 452)

16. **Child sexual abuse** is any erotic activity that arouses an adult and excites, shames, or confuses a child—even if the use does not involve physical contact. (p. 453)

17. **Drug abuse** is the ingestion of a drug to the extent that it impairs the user's biological or psychological well-being. (p. 456)

18. **Drug addiction** is a person's dependence on a drug or a behavior in order to feel physically or psychologically at ease. (p. 456)

19. **Binge drinking** entails consuming five or more drinks in a row. (p. 456)

20. **Generational forgetting** is the idea that each generation forgets what earlier generations had already learned about harmful drugs. (p. 457)

21. **Body image** is a person's concept of his or her body's appearance. (p.458)

22. **Anorexia nervosa** is an eating disorder characterized by self-starvation, a disturbed body image, and denial of the problem. (p. 460)

23. **Bulimia nervosa** is an eating disorder in which the person repeatedly binge eats and then purges through induced vomiting or laxative use. (p. 461)

Cross-Check

ACROSS

1. adrenal
7. spermarche
12. menarche
15. gonads
17. pituitary
18. growth spurt
19. drug use

DOWN

1. adolescence
2. lymphoid
3. hypothalamus
4. alcohol
5. drug addiction
6. gateway drugs
8. drug abuse
9. secondary
10. testosterone
11. tobacco
13. estradiol
14. puberty
16. primary

Chapter Fifteen

Adolescence: Cognitive Development

Chapter Overview

Chapter 15 describes the cognitive advances and limitations of adolescence. With the attainment of formal operational thought, the developing person becomes able to think in an adult way, that is, to be logical, to think in terms of possibilities, to reason scientifically and abstractly.

Even those who reach the stage of formal operational thought spend much of their time thinking at less advanced levels. The discussion of adolescent egocentrism supports this generalization in showing that adolescents have difficulty thinking rationally about themselves and their immediate experiences. Adolescent egocentrism makes them see themselves as psychologically unique and more socially significant than they really are.

The next section of the chapter explores teaching and learning in high school. As adolescents enter secondary school, their grades often suffer and their level of participation decreases. The rigid behavioral demands and intensified competition of most secondary schools do not, unfortunately, provide a supportive learning environment for adolescents. The chapter concludes with a discussion of the emerging intellectual flexibility that is the hallmark of cognition in late adolescence. College education advances this flexibility as students become more open-minded and less inclined to seek absolute truths.

NOTE: Answer guidelines for all Chapter 15 questions begin on page 229.

Guided Study

The text chapter should be studied one section at a time. Before you read, preview each section by skimming it, noting headings and boldface items. Then read the appropriate section objectives from the following outline. Keep these objectives in mind and, as you read the chapter section, search for the information that will enable you to meet each objective. Once you have finished a section, write out answers for its objectives.

Adolescent Egocentrism (pp. 465–472)

1. Discuss adolescent egocentrism, and give three examples of egocentric fantasies or fables.

2. Discuss possible reasons for the slump in academic performance and other problems that often appear during the transition from elementary school to middle school.

Thinking Processes During the Teen Years (pp. 472–480)

3. Describe evidence of formal operational thinking during adolescence, and provide examples of adolescents' emerging ability to reason deductively and inductively.

4. Explain adolescents' use of illogical, intuitive thought even when they are capable of logical thought.

Teaching and Learning in High School (pp. 481–487)

5. Evaluate the typical secondary school's ability to meet the cognitive needs of the typical adolescent.

6. Discuss three potential problems that stem from the mismatch between the typical high school environment and adolescents' needs.

Postformal Thought (pp. 487–491)

7. Identify the main characteristics of postformal thought, and describe how it differs from formal operational thought.

8. Discuss the relationship between cognitive growth and higher education.

Chapter Review

When you have finished reading the chapter, work through the material that follows to review it. Complete the sentences and answer the questions. As you proceed, evaluate your performance for each section by consulting the answers beginning on page 229. Do not continue with the next section until you understand each answer. If you need to, review or reread the appropriate section in the textbook before continuing.

1. Adolescents often combine _____ , _____ , and _____ in ways that contrast with the cognitive processes of older people.

Adolescent Egocentrism (pp. 465–472)

2. The adolescent's belief that he or she is uniquely significant and that the social world revolves around him or her is a psychological phenomenon called _____ _____ .

3. An adolescent's tendency to feel that he or she is somehow immune to the consequences of dangerous or illegal behavior is expressed in the _____ _____ .

4. An adolescent's tendency to imagine that her or his own life is unique, heroic, or even legendary and that she or he is destined for great accomplishments, is expressed in the _____ _____ .

5. Adolescents, who believe that they are under constant scrutiny from nearly everyone, create for themselves an _____ _____ .

6. Young people tend to become _____ , _____ , or _____ after leaving elementary school and entering _____ _____ . In addition, at about age 11, school grades tend to _____ (improve/worsen) and students' relationships with one another _____ (improve/ worsen).

7. Unlike in elementary school, aggressive children tend to be _____ in middle school.

These children tend to engage in
_____ aggression. Bullying becomes
_____ (more/less) frequent during
each year in elementary school but then
_____ (increases/decreases) during
he first year of middle school.

8. Because they were merely copies of high schools
and didn't meet the needs of middle school students, the first junior highs were developmentally
_____ . One problem with the typi-
cal middle school is that students' schedules are
too _____ .

Formal Operational Thought (pp. 472–480)

9. Piaget's term for the fourth stage of cognitive
development is _____
_____ thought.

10. Piaget devised a number of famous tasks to
demonstrate that formal operational adolescents
imagine all possible _____ of a
problem's solution in order to draw the appropriate _____ .

Briefly describe how children reason differently about
the "balance beam" problem at ages 7, 10, and 13.

11. The kind of thinking in which adolescents consider unproven possibilities that are logical but not
necessarily real is called _____
thought.

12. Adolescents become more capable of
_____ reasoning—that is, they can
begin with a general _____ or
_____ and draw logical
_____ from it. This type of reason-
ing is a hallmark of formal operational thought.

13. They also make great strides in _____
(inductive/deductive) reasoning.

14. Most developmentalists _____
(agree/disagree) with Piaget that adolescent
thought can be qualitatively different from children's thought. They disagree about whether the
change in thinking is _____ (grad-
ual/sudden) and whether it occurs in every
_____ , as Piaget thought.

15. According to information-processing theory, the
changes in adolescent thinking occur
_____ (suddenly/gradually).
Sociocultural theorists attribute these changes to
the adolescent's _____ , while epigenetic theorists see them as the result of
_____ changes.

16. In addition to advances in the formal, logical,
_____-_____ thinking
described by Piaget, adolescents advance in their
_____ cognition. Researchers
believe that the adult brain has two distinct pathways, called _____-_____
networks. If this is true, it might mean that
_____ and _____
build and develop independently.

17. In general, high levels of _____ produce a rush of _____ hormones that
slow down _____ thinking.

18. The first mode of thinking, which begins with a
prior _____ , is called
_____ . Theorists refer to hypothetical-deductive reasoning as _____
thought.

19. Although intuitive thinking generally is
_____ and _____ , it is
also often _____ .

20. Together, the _____ thinking that is
used in school and the _____ think-
ing used in one's personal life create a type of
_____ _____ .

Teaching and Learning in High School (pp. 481–487)

21. In most high schools, _____
_____ thinking is preferred over the
_____ thinking that students
themselves like. In addition, the link between

_____ and _____ is often ignored in the formal curriculum.

22. Another feature of the secondary school environment is _____-_____
_____ , so-called because the consequences of failing are so severe. This has raised special concerns about students who have
_____ _____ and those who come from families with low
_____ .

23. In the United States and other developed nations, boys get higher _____
_____ than _____
_____ . For girls, _____
(this pattern/the opposite pattern) holds.

24. A second problem with the high school environment involves student _____ ; many adolescents express _____ and
_____ with school.

25. Adolescents thrive on challenging intellectual activities that require _____
_____ within a _____
context.

26. A third problem that stems from the mismatch between the _____ curriculum of high schools and students' needs is the threat of
_____ .

Postformal Thought (pp. 487–491)

27. Some developmentalists believe that there is a fifth stage of thinking, called _____
_____ , that follows Piaget's final stage. This type of thinking focuses more on
_____ _____ than on
_____ _____ .

28. After high school, intellectual skills become harnessed to_____ and
_____ demands.

29. One hallmark of postformal thinking is that there are multiple _____ of the same phenomenon and that each problem has many potential _____ .

30. One by-product of this new intellectual flexibility is the fear-arousing awareness that one's
_____ or _____

might be misused to confirm another person's _____ about one's race, gender, or other group. This awareness is called
_____ _____ .

State some of the benefits that college-educated adults receive.

Progress Test 1

Multiple-Choice Questions

Circle your answers to the following questions and check them with the answers on page 230. If your answer is incorrect, read the explanation for why it is incorrect and then consult the appropriate pages of the text (in parentheses following the correct answer).

1. Many psychologists consider the distinguishing feature of adolescent thought to be the ability to think in terms of:
   a. moral issues.
   b. concrete operations.
   c. possibility, not just reality.
   d. logical principles.

2. Piaget's last stage of cognitive development is:
   a. formal operational thought.
   b. concrete operational thought.
   c. universal ethical principles.
   d. symbolic thought.

3. Many of the problems of adult life are characterized by ambiguity, partial truths, and extenuating circumstances, and therefore are often best solved using _____ thinking.
   a. formal   c. postformal
   b. reintegrative   d. executive

4. The adolescent who takes risks and feels immune to the laws of mortality is showing evidence of the:
   a. invincibility fable.   c. imaginary audience.
   b. personal fable.   d. death instinct.

5. Imaginary audiences, invincibility fables, and personal fables are expressions of adolescent:
   a. morality.
   b. thinking games.
   c. decision making.
   d. egocentrism.

6. The typical adolescent is:
   a. tough-minded.
   b. indifferent to public opinion.
   c. self-absorbed and hypersensitive to criticism.
   d. all of the above.

7. When adolescents enter middle school, many:
   a. experience a drop in their academic performance.
   b. are less motivated than they were in elementary school.
   c. are less conscientious than they were in elementary school.
   d. experience all of the above.

8. Research has shown that a typical outcome of college education is that students become:
   a. very liberal politically.
   b. less committed to any particular ideology.
   c. deeper, more flexible thinkers.
   d. less open-minded.

9. Thinking that begins with a general premise and then draws logical conclusions from it is called:
   a. inductive reasoning.
   b. deductive reasoning.
   c. intuitive thinking.
   d. hypothetical reasoning.

10. Serious reflection on important issues is a wrenching process for many adolescents because of their newfound ability to reason:
    a. inductively.
    b. deductively.
    c. hypothetically.
    d. symbolically.

11. Hypothetical-deductive thinking is to heuristic thinking as:
    a. rational analysis is to intuitive thought.
    b. intuitive thought is to rational analysis.
    c. experiential thinking is to intuitive reasoning.
    d. intuitive thinking is to analytical reasoning.

12. Many adolescents seem to believe that *their* lovemaking will not lead to pregnancy. This belief is an expression of the:
    a. personal fable.
    b. invincibility fable.
    c. imaginary audience.
    d. "game of thinking."

13. During middle school, aggressive children are often _____ and tend to engage in _____ aggression.
    a. unpopular; relational
    b. popular; relational
    c. unpopular; instrumental
    d. popular; instrumental

14. One problem with many high schools is that the formal curriculum ignores the fact that adolescents thrive on:
    a. formal operational thinking.
    b. intellectual challenges that require social interaction.
    c. inductive reasoning.
    d. deductive reasoning.

15. High levels of emotions produce a rush of stress hormones that:
    a. slow down rational thinking.
    b. accelerate analytic thinking.
    c. accelerate hypothetical-deductive thinking.
    d. slow down intuitive thinking.

True or False Items

Write T (*true*) or F (*false*) on the line in front of each statement.

_____ 1. The appropriateness of the typical high school's high-stakes testing environment has been questioned, especially for low-income students.

_____ 2. Older adolescents are generally better able than younger adolescents to recognize the validity of arguments that clash with their own beliefs.

_____ 3. Adolescents' egos sometimes seem to overwhelm logic.

_____ 4. Only about half of all students who enroll in college eventually graduate.

_____ 5. Adolescents often create an imaginary audience as they envision how others will react to their appearance and behavior.

_____ 6. Postformal thought is less absolute and less abstract than formal thought.

_____ 7. Adolescent egocentrism is always destructive.

_____ 8. Inductive reasoning is a hallmark of formal operational thought.

_____ 9. There is a sudden rise in psychopathology that occurs at about age 12.

_____ 10. The brain has two distinct processing networks.

Progress Test 2

Progress Test 2 should be completed during a final chapter review. Answer the following questions after you thoroughly understand the correct answers for the Chapter Review and Progress Test 1.

Multiple-Choice Questions

1. Adolescents who fall prey to the invincibility fable may be more likely to:
   a. engage in risky behaviors.
   b. suffer from depression.
   c. have low self-esteem.
   d. drop out of school.

2. Thinking that extrapolates from a specific experience to form a general premise is called:
   a. inductive reasoning.
   b. deductive reasoning.
   c. intuitive thinking.
   d. hypothetical reasoning.

3. Which approach to adult cognitive development "picks up where Piaget left off"?
   a. sociocultural
   b. epigenetic
   c. information-processing
   d. postformal

4. When young people overestimate their significance to others, they are displaying:
   a. concrete operational thought.
   b. adolescent egocentrism.
   c. a lack of cognitive growth.
   d. immoral development.

5. The personal fable refers to adolescents imagining that:
   a. they are immune to the dangers of risky behaviors.
   b. they are always being scrutinized by others.
   c. their own lives are unique, heroic, or even legendary.
   d. the world revolves around their actions.

6. The typical high school environment:
   a. has more rigid behavioral demands than the average elementary school.
   b. does not meet the cognitive needs of the typical adolescent.
   c. emphasizes competition.
   d. is described by all of the above.

7. As compared to elementary schools, most middle schools exhibit all of the following *except*:
   a. a more flexible approach to education.
   b. intensified competition.
   c. inappropriate academic standards.
   d. less individualized attention.

8. Compared to those with less education, college-educated adults:
   a. earn more.
   b. live longer
   c. have better emotional health.
   d. experience each of the above benefits.

9. In explaining adolescent advances in thinking, sociocultural theorists emphasize:
   a. the sudden change that occurs.
   b. underlying biological changes.
   c. the context in which these changes occur.
   d. the gradual emergence of changes.

10. Analytic thinking is to _____ thinking as emotional force is to _____ thinking.
    a. intuitive; egocentric
    b. egocentric; intuitive
    c. formal; intuitive
    d. intuitive; formal

11. One of the hallmarks of formal operational thought is:
    a. egocentrism.   c. symbolic thinking.
    b. deductive reasoning. d. all of the above.

12. Analytic thinking and experiential thinking:
    a. both use the same neural pathways in the brain.
    b. are really the same type of information processing.
    c. both improve during adolescence.
    d. are characterized by all of the above.

13. The pathways that form the brain's dual-processing networks involve the:
    a. hypothalamus and the amygdala.
    b. cerebellum and the corpus callosum.
    c. prefrontal cortex and the limbic system.
    d. left and right cerebral hemispheres.

14. Which of the following would be most helpful to know about a person in predicting that individual's level of cognitive development?
    a. age
    b. educational background
    c. household income
    d. Cognitive development is unpredictable from any of these factors.

15. To avoid a mismatch between its formal curriculum and the needs of adolescents, a middle school should:

- **a.** focus on cooperative rather than competitive learning.
- **b.** base grading on individual test performance.
- **c.** establish the same goals for every student.
- **d.** reduce the students' fragmented schedules.

Matching Items

Match each term or concept with its corresponding description or definition.

Terms or Concepts

_____ **1.** invincibility fable
_____ **2.** imaginary audience
_____ **3.** high-stakes testing
_____ **4.** hypothetical thought
_____ **5.** deductive reasoning
_____ **6.** inductive reasoning
_____ **7.** formal operational thought
_____ **8.** personal fable
_____ **9.** stereotype threat
_____ **10.** adolescent egocentrism

Descriptions or Definitions

- **a.** the tendency of adolescents to focus on themselves to the exclusion of others
- **b.** adolescents feel immune to the consequences of dangerous behavior
- **c.** adolescents feel destined for fame and fortune
- **d.** the idea held by many adolescents that others are intensely interested in them, especially in their appearance and behavior
- **e.** lower achievement resulting from concerns that another person has a prejudicial view of one's group
- **f.** reasoning about propositions that may or may not reflect reality
- **g.** the last stage of cognitive development, according to Piaget
- **h.** thinking that moves from premise to conclusion
- **i.** thinking that moves from a specific experience to a general premise
- **j.** an evaluation that is critical in determining success or failure

Thinking Critically About Chapter 15

Answer these questions the day before an exam as a final check on your understanding of the chapter's terms and concepts.

1. Summarizing her presentation on the mismatch between the needs of adolescents and the traditional structure of their schools, Megan notes that:

- **a.** most high schools feature intensified competition.
- **b.** the curriculum of most high schools emphasizes formal operational thinking.
- **c.** the academic standards of most schools do not reflect adolescents' needs.
- **d.** all of the above are true.

2. An experimenter hides a ball in her hand and says, "The ball in my hand is either red or it is not red." Most preadolescent children say:

- **a.** the statement is true.
- **b.** the statement is false.
- **c.** they cannot tell if the statement is true or false.
- **d.** they do not understand what the experimenter means.

3. Fourteen-year-old Monica is very idealistic and often develops crushes on people she doesn't even know. This reflects her newly developed cognitive ability to:

   a. deal simultaneously with two sides of an issue.
   b. take another person's viewpoint.
   c. imagine possible worlds and people.
   d. see herself as others see her.

4. Which of the following is the *best* example of a personal fable?

   a. Adriana imagines that she is destined for a life of fame and fortune.
   b. Ben makes up stories about his experiences to impress his friends.
   c. Kalil questions his religious beliefs when they seem to offer little help for a problem he faces.
   d. Julio believes that every girl he meets is attracted to him.

5. Which of the following is the *best* example of the adolescent's ability to think hypothetically?

   a. Twelve-year-old Stanley feels that people are always watching him.
   b. Fourteen-year-old Mindy engages in many risky behaviors, reasoning that "nothing bad will happen to me."
   c. Fifteen-year-old Philip feels that no one understands his problems.
   d. Thirteen-year-old Josh delights in finding logical flaws in virtually everything his teachers and parents say.

6. Frustrated because of the dating curfew her parents have set, Melinda exclaims, "You just don't know how it feels to be in love!" Melinda's thinking demonstrates:

   a. the invincibility fable.
   b. the personal fable.
   c. the imaginary audience.
   d. adolescent egocentrism.

7. Compared to her 13-year-old brother, 17-year-old Yolanda is likely to:

   a. be more critical about herself.
   b. be more egocentric.
   c. have less confidence in her abilities.
   d. be more capable of reasoning hypothetically.

8. Nathan's fear that his friends will ridicule him because of a pimple that has appeared on his nose reflects a preoccupation with:

   a. his personal fable.
   b. the invincibility fable.
   c. an imaginary audience.
   d. preconventional reasoning.

9. Thirteen-year-old Malcolm, who lately is very sensitive to the criticism of others, feels significantly less motivated and capable than when he was in elementary school. Malcolm is probably:

   a. experiencing a sense of vulnerability that is common in adolescents.
   b. a lower-track student.
   c. a student in a school that emphasizes rigid routines.
   d. all of the above.

10. The reasoning behind the conclusion, "if it waddles like a duck and quacks like a duck, then it must be a duck," is called:

    a. experiential thinking.
    b. heuristic thinking.
    c. inductive reasoning.
    d. deductive reasoning.

11. Which of the following is an example of responding to a stereotype threat?

    a. Because Jessie's older sister teases her for not being as good as she is at math, Jessie protects her self-concept by devaluing math.
    b. Feeling angered that others may think him less capable because of his ethnicity, Liam becomes flustered when trying to solve a problem in front of the class.
    c. Dave writes a scathing criticism of an obviously racist comment made by a local politician.
    d. As an elderly adult, Kathy takes pride in displaying her quick wit and intelligence to others.

12. Which of the following is an example of the principle of cognitive economy?

    a. Fifteen-year-old Alonza is too lazy to look up an unfamiliar word he encounters while reading.
    b. Sixteen-year-old Brittany loves to figure out "whodunit" crime mysteries.
    c. Fourteen-year-old Morgan, who has enjoyed unscrambling anagrams for years, prefers to follow his hunches rather than systematically evaluate letter combinations.

d. When taking multiple-choice tests, 13-year-old Trevor carefully considers every possible answer before choosing one.

13. After hearing that an unusually aggressive child has been in full-time day care since he was 1 year old, 16-year-old Keenan concludes that non-parental care leads to behavior problems. Keenan's conclusion is an example of:
    a. inductive reasoning.
    b. deductive reasoning.
    c. hypothetical thinking.
    d. adolescent egocentrism.

14. (Thinking Like a Scientist) Research demonstrates that which of the following are effective in reducing stereotype threat among college students?
    a. educational environments that include only students who have gender in common
    b. educational environments that include only students who have race in common
    c. interventions that help students internalize the concept that intelligence can change
    d. educational programs that sensitize men and ethnic-minority students to the effect of gender and ethnic stereotypes on other students

15. A neighbor wonders why depression, substance abuse, and eating disorders increase in middle school. You tell her that many social scientists believe that:
    a. the increase is caused by the physiological changes of puberty.
    b. genes for psychopathology become activated at about age 12.
    c. emotionally vulnerable children are pushed toward psychopathology by the social context and structure of middle schools.
    d. these internalizing and externalizing disorders only increase among adolescents in the United States.

Key Terms

Using your own words, write a brief definition or explanation of each of the following terms on a separate piece of paper.

1. adolescent egocentrism
2. invincibility fable
3. personal fable
4. imaginary audience
5. middle school
6. formal operational thought
7. hypothetical thought
8. deductive reasoning
9. inductive reasoning
10. intuitive thought
11. analytic thought
12. cognitive economy
13. high-stakes testing
14. postformal thought
15. stereotype threat

ANSWERS
CHAPTER REVIEW

1. ego; logic; emotion
2. adolescent egocentrism
3. invincibility fable
4. personal fable
5. imaginary audience
6. depressed, rebellious; apathetic; middle school; worsen; worsen
7. popular; relational; less; increases
8. regressive; fragmented
9. formal operational; is
10. determinants; conclusions

Preschoolers have no understanding of how to solve the problem. By age 7, children understand balancing the weights but don't know that distance from the center is also a factor. By age 10, they understand the concepts but are unable to coordinate them. By ages 13 or 14, they are able to solve the problem.

11. hypothetical
12. deductive; premise; theory; conclusions
13. inductive
14. agree; sudden; context
15. gradually; context; biological
16. hypothetical-deductive; intuitive; dual-processing; thoughts; emotions
17. emotions; stress; rational
18. belief or assumption; intuitive (or heuristic or experiential); analytic
19. quick; emotional; wrong

20. analytic; experiential; cognitive economy
21. formal operational; intuitive; logic; emotion
22. high-stakes testing; learning disabilities; incomes
23. test scores; school grades; the opposite pattern
24. motivation; boredom; unhappiness
25. social interaction; supportive
26. formal; violence
27. postformal thought; problem finding; problem solving
28. occupational; interpersonal
29. views; solutions
30. appearance; behavior; stereotype; stereotype threat

College-educated adults earn more, live longer, and have better emotional and physical health than do those with less education. They are also deeper, more flexible thinkers.

PROGRESS TEST 1

Multiple-Choice Questions

1. **c.** is the answer. (p. 473)

   a. Although moral reasoning becomes much deeper during adolescence, it is not limited to this stage of development.

   b. & d. Concrete operational thought, which *is* logical, is the distinguishing feature of childhood thinking.

2. **a.** is the answer. (p. 472)

   b. In Piaget's theory, this stage precedes formal operational thought.

   c. & d. These are not stages in Piaget's theory.

3. **c.** is the answer. (p. 487)

   a. Formal thinking is best suited to solving problems that require logic and analytical thinking.

   b. & d. These concepts are not discussed in the text.

4. **a.** is the answer. (p. 466)

   b. This refers to adolescents' tendency to imagine their own lives as unique, heroic, or even legendary.

   c. This refers to adolescents' tendency to fantasize about how others will react to their appearance and behavior.

   d. This is a concept in Freud's theory.

5. **d.** is the answer. These thought processes are manifestations of adolescents' tendency to see themselves as being much more central and important to the social scene than they really are. (pp. 466–467)

6. **c.** is the answer. (pp. 465–466)

7. **d.** is the answer. (p. 471)

8. **c.** is the answer. (p. 490)

9. **b.** is the answer. (p. 474)

   a. Inductive reasoning moves from specific facts to a general conclusion.

   c. By its very nature, intuitive thinking does not move logically either from a general conclusion to specific facts or from specific facts to a general conclusion.

   d. Hypothetical reasoning involves thinking about possibilities rather than facts.

10. **c.** is the answer. (p. 473)

11. **a.** is the answer. (p. 476)

    c. Heuristic thinking is both experiential *and* intuitive.

12. **b.** is the answer. (p. 466)

    a. This refers to adolescents' tendency to imagine their own lives as unique, heroic, or even mythical.

    c. This refers to adolescents' tendency to fantasize about how others will react to their appearance and behavior.

    d. This concept was not discussed in the text.

13. **b.** is the answer. (p. 469)

14. **b.** is the answer. (p. 494)

    a., c., & d. Adolescents are more likely to thrive on *intuitive* thinking.

15. **a.** is the answer. (p. 476)

True or False Items

1. T (pp. 481–482)
2. T (p. 478)
3. T (p. 465)
4. T (p. 490)
5. T (p. 487)
6. T (p. 469)
7. F The invincibility fable, for instance, can lead to brave deeds and heroic sacrifices. (p. 474)
8. F Deductive reasoning is a hallmark of formal operational thought. (p. 474)
9. T (p. 470)
10. T (p. 476)

PROGRESS TEST 2

Multiple-Choice Questions

1. **a.** is the answer. (p. 466)

   b., c., & d. The invincibility fable leads some teens to believe that they are immune to the dangers of risky behaviors; it is not necessarily linked to depression, low self-esteem, or the likelihood that an individual will drop out of school.

2. **a.** is the answer. (p. 474)

   b. Deductive reasoning begins with a general premise and then draws logical conclusions from it.

   c. By its very nature, intuitive thinking does not move logically either from a general conclusion to specific facts or from specific facts to a general conclusion.

   d. Hypothetical reasoning involves thinking about possibilities rather than facts.

3. **d.** is the answer. (p. 487)

4. **b.** is the answer. (p. 466)

5. **c.** is the answer. (p. 466)

   a. This describes the invincibility fable.

   b. This describes the imaginary audience.

   d. This describes adolescent egocentrism in general.

6. **d.** is the answer. (p. 481)

7. **a.** is the answer. (p. 481)

8. **d.** is the answer. (p. 489)

9. **c.** is the answer. (p. 475)

   a. This reflects Piaget's viewpoint.

   b. This reflects epigenetic theory.

   d. This reflects information-processing theory.

10. **c.** is the answer. (p. 476)

11. **b.** is the answer. (p. 474)

12. **c.** is the answer. (pp. 477–478)

13. **c.** is the answer. (p. 476)

14. **b.** is the answer. (p. 489)

15. **d.** is the answer. (p. 471)

Matching Items

1. b (p. 466)   5. h (p. 474)   9. e (p. 488)
2. d (p. 467)   6. i (p. 474)   10. a (pp. 465–466)
3. j (p. 481)   7. g (p. 472)
4. f (p. 473)   8. c (p. 466)

THINKING CRITICALLY ABOUT CHAPTER 15

1. **d.** is the answer. (p. 481)

2. **c.** is the answer. Although this statement is logically verifiable, preadolescents who lack formal operational thought cannot prove or disprove it. (p. 473)

3. **c.** is the answer. (p. 473)

4. **a.** is the answer. (p. 466)

   b. & d. These behaviors are more indicative of a preoccupation with the imaginary audience.

   c. Kalil's questioning attitude is a normal adolescent tendency that helps foster moral reasoning.

5. **d.** is the answer. (pp. 473–474)

   a. This is an example of the imaginary audience.

   b. This is an example of the invincibility fable.

   c. This is an example of adolescent egocentrism.

6. **d.** is the answer. (pp. 465–466)

7. **d.** is the answer. (p. 478)

8. **c.** is the answer. (p. 467)

   a. In this fable, adolescents see themselves destined for fame and fortune.

   b. In this fable, young people feel that they are somehow immune to the consequences of common dangers.

   d. This is a stage of moral reasoning in Kohlberg's theory, as discussed in Chapter 12.

9. **a.** is the answer. (p. 471)

10. **c.** is the answer. (p. 474)

    a. & b. Experiential (or heuristic) thinking, is more intuitive and less logical.

    d. Deductive thinking moves from from a general conclusion to specific principles; this example moves from particulars to a general conclusion.

11. **b.** is the answer. (p. 488)

12. **c.** is the answer. (p. 478)

    a. This is simply laziness.

    b. Solving mysteries is an example of deductive reasoning.

    d. This is an example of analytic thinking.

13. **a.** is the answer. (p. 474)

    b. Keenan is reasoning from the specific to the general, rather than vice versa.

    c. Keenan is thinking about an actual observation, rather than a hypothetical possibility.

    d. Keenan's reasoning is focused outside himself, rather than being self-centered.

14. **d.** is the answer. (p. 489)

15. **b.** is the answer. (p. 470)

KEY TERMS

1. **Adolescent egocentrism** refers to the tendency of adolescents to see themselves as much more socially significant than they actually are. (pp. 465–466)

2. Adolescents who experience the **invincibility fable** feel that they are immune to the dangers of risky behaviors. (p. 466)

3. Another example of adolescent egocentrism is the **personal fable**, through which adolescents imagine their own lives as unique, heroic, or even legendary. (p. 466)

4. Adolescents often create an **imaginary audience** for themselves, as they assume that others are as intensely interested in them as they themselves are. (p. 467)

5. **Middle school** refers to the years of school between elementary school and high school. (p. 469)

6. In Piaget's theory, the last stage of cognitive development, which arises from a combination of maturation and experience, is called **formal operational thought.** A hallmark of formal operational thinking is more systematic logic and the ability to think about abstract ideas. (p. 472)

7. **Hypothetical thought** involves reasoning about propositions and possibilities that may not reflect reality. (p. 473)

8. **Deductive reasoning** is thinking that moves from the general to the specific, or from a premise to a logical conclusion. (p. 474)

9. **Inductive reasoning** is thinking that moves from one or more specific experiences or facts to a general conclusion. (p. 474)

10. **Intuitive thought** is that which arises from a hunch or emotion, often triggered by past experiences, cultural assumptions, and sudden impulse. (p. 476)

11. **Analytic thought** is logical thinking that arises from rational analysis and the systematic evaluation of consequences and possibilities. (p. 476)

12. **Cognitive economy** is the idea that people generally use their minds as efficiently as possible, such as when adolescents prefer easier intuitive thought to the more difficult, analytic thought they are capable of. (p. 478)

13. **High-stakes testing** refers to exams and other forms of evaluation that are critical in determining a person's success or failure. (p. 481)

14. Proposed by some developmentalists as a fifth stage of cognitive development, **postformal thought** is suited to solving real-world problems and is more practical and flexible than formal operational thought. (p. 487)

15. **Stereotype threat** is the possibility that one's behavior may be misused to confirm another person's prejudiced attitude. (p. 488)

Chapter Sixteen

Adolescence: Psychosocial Development

Chapter Overview

Chapter 16 focuses on the adolescent's psychosocial development. The first section explores the paths that lead to the formation of identity, which is required for the attainment of adult status and maturity. The next section examines the influences of family and friends on adolescent psychosocial development, including the development of romantic relationships and sexual activity. Depression, self-destruction, and suicide—the most perplexing problems of adolescence—are then explored. The special problems posed by adolescent lawbreaking are discussed, and suggestions for alleviating or treating these problems are given. The chapter concludes with the message that although no other period of life is characterized by so many changes in the three domains of development, for most young people the teenage years are happy ones. Furthermore, serious problems in adolescence do not necessarily lead to lifelong problems.

NOTE: Answer guidelines for all Chapter 16 questions begin on page 244.

Guided Study

The text chapter should be studied one section at a time. Before you read, preview each section by skimming it, noting headings and boldface items. Then read the appropriate section objectives from the following outline. Keep these objectives in mind and, as you read the chapter section, search for the information that will enable you to meet each objective. Once you have finished a section, write out answers for its objectives.

Identity (pp. 495–505)

1. Describe the development of identity during adolescence.

2. Describe the four major identity statuses, and give an example of each.

3. Discuss the problems encountered in the formation of religious, gender, ethnic, and vocational identities, and describe cultural effects on identity formation.

Social Support (pp. 505–520)

4. Describe parental influence on identity formation, including the effect of parent–adolescent conflict and other aspects of parent–teen relationships.

5. Explain the constructive functions of peer relationships and close friendships during adolescence and the unique challenges faced by immigrants.

6. Discuss the development of male–female relationships during adolescence, including the challenges faced by gay and lesbian adolescents.

7. Discuss the various influences on teen sexual behavior, including schools, peers, and the media.

Sadness and Anger (pp. 520–527)

8. Discuss adolescent suicide, noting contributing factors and gender, ethnic, and national variations.

9. Discuss delinquency among adolescents today, noting its incidence and prevalence, significance for later development, and best approaches for prevention or treatment.

Conclusion (p. 527)

10. Describe the overarching theme of adolescent development.

Chapter Review

When you have finished reading the chapter, work through the material that follows to review it. Complete the sentences and answer the questions. As you proceed, evaluate your performance for each section by consulting the answers beginning on page 244. Do not continue with the next section until you understand each answer. If you need to, review or reread the appropriate section in the textbook before continuing.

Identity (pp. 495–505)

1. The momentous changes that occur during the teen years challenge adolescents to find their own

   _____ .

2. According to Erikson, the challenge of adolescence is _____-_____.
In this process, many adolescents experience _____ _____ , or various fantasies about what their futures might be if one or another course of action is followed.

3. Adolescents may take on a _____ _____ ; that is, they act in ways they know to be contrary to their true nature.

4. The ultimate goal of adolescence is to establish a new identity that involves both repudiation and assimilation of childhood values; this is called _____ _____ .

5. The young person who has few commitments to goals or values and is apathetic about defining his or her identity is experiencing _____ _____ .

6. The young person who prematurely accepts earlier roles and parental values without exploring alternatives or truly forging a unique identity is experiencing identity _____ .

7. An adolescent who adopts an identity that is the opposite of the one he or she is expected to adopt has taken on a _____ _____ .

8. A time-out period during which a young person experiments with different identities, postponing important choices, is called an identity _____ . An obvious institutional example of this in the United States is attending _____ .

9. Erikson described four arenas of identity: _____ , _____ , _____ , and _____ .

10. People _____ (can/generally cannot) achieve identity in one domain and still be searching for their identity in another.

11. The six signs that teenagers have successfully found their religious identity are that

   a. _____
   b. _____
   c. _____
   d. _____
   e. _____
   f. _____

12. A person's identification as either male or female is called _____ _____ .
Usually, a gender identity leads to a gender _____ and a sexual _____ .

13. A sex-typed occupation and pattern of behavior adopted by a person constitutes a _____ _____ . A person's sexual attraction to people of the same sex, other sex, or both sexes constitutes his or her _____ _____ .
Scholars _____ (agree/differ) about the extent to which male–female differences in behavior are _____ or _____ in origin.

14. There is some evidence that during the years of adolescence teenagers become _____ (more/less) flexible in their gender-role concepts and _____ (more/less) sex-typed. This pattern is called _____ .

15. Since Erikson's time, _____ identity has become more important than _____ identity, particularly for teenagers who are not _____-_____ or not of _____ descent. In addition, children of _____ experience the identity crisis with special intensity.

16. Ethnic identity has three characteristics: it depends on _____ and therefore may _____ ; it is _____ , meaning that it is both a _____ _____ and a _____ to others; and it is _____ .

17. Employment during adolescence is likely to impede _____ formation, _____ relationships, _____ achievement, and _____ success.

18. Adolescent employment _____ (varies/does not vary) cross-culturally.

19. In some nations, such as _____ , _____ , and _____ , almost no adolescent is employed or even does significant chores at home. In many _____ nations, adolescents choose between school and work. In _____ , adolescents choose a vocation and are then trained by an employer.

20. Whether or not an adolescent's job is meaningful or meaningless, research finds that adolescent employment of more than _____ hours a week is harmful.

Social Support (pp. 505–520)

21. People who focus on differences between the younger and older generations speak of a _____ _____ . This difference between generations is actually not very wide, especially for values regarding _____ , _____ , and _____ issues.

22. The idea that each generation views interactions from its own position and perspective is called the _____ _____ .

23. Parent–adolescent conflict is most common in the _____ and is particularly notable with _____ (mothers/fathers) and their _____ (sons/daughters). This conflict often involves _____ , which refers to repeated, petty arguments about daily habits.

24. In North America, ethnic variation is often found in the _____ of parent–child conflict. Internationally, some cultures value _____ _____ above all else and avoid conflict. Thus, the very idea of adolescent rebellion may be a _____ construction in Western culture.

25. Most research has found that some conflict between parents and teens is _____ ,

while too much conflict impairs _____ .

26. The dangers of _____ in parenting are increased in communities in which there is no _____ _____ to help teenagers.

27. Four other elements of parent–teen relationships that have been heavily researched include _____ , _____ , _____ , and _____ .

28. In terms of family control, a powerful deterrent to delinquency, risky sex, and drug abuse is _____ _____ . Too much interference, however, may contribute to adolescent _____ . Particularly harmful to teens are threats to withdraw love and support, or _____ _____ .

29. The largely constructive role of peers runs counter to the notion of _____ _____ . Social pressure to conform _____ (falls/rises) dramatically in early adolescence, until about age _____ , when it begins to _____ (fall/rise). Destructive peer pressure is strongest during times of _____ .

30. Two helpful concepts in understanding the influence of peers are _____ , meaning that peers _____ one another; and _____ , referring to the fact that peers encourage one another to do things that _____ .

31. Friends play a special role for adolescents whose parents are _____ .

Briefly outline the four-stage progression of heterosexual involvement.

32. Culture _____ (affect/do not affect) the _____ and _____ of these stages, but the basic _____ seems to be based on _____ factors. In modern developed nations, each stage typically lasts _____ (how long?).

33. Early pairing, especially when it decreases _____-_____ friendships, signifies _____ trouble.

34. For gay and lesbian adolescents, added complications usually _____ (slow down/speed up) romantic attachments.

35. Adolescents who discuss sex openly with their parents take fewer _____ , avoid _____ , and _____ .

36. Most American adults believe that high schools _____ (should/should not) teach sex education. In fact, most secondary schools _____ (provide/do not provide) sex education.

37. Worldwide, sex education evidence demonstrates that programs should be _____ and should precede sexual activity by _____ (how long?).

38. Most adolescents are not sexually active until _____ (how long?) after puberty. Most, however, _____ (are/are not) very well informed when it comes to sex. One reason is that teenagers do not readily use _____ _____ thinking for personal decisions. Another reason is that the _____ _____ may allow teens to deny responsibility for their behavior.

39. Sexual activity among adolescents _____ (is/is not) more diverse than it was 10 years ago.

40. The teen birth rate is _____ (increasing/decreasing). At the same time, contraceptive use has _____ (increased/decreased).

Sadness and Anger (pp. 520–527)

41. Adolescents who have one serious problem _____ (often have/do not usually have) others.

42. Cross-sequential research studies show that, from ages 6 to 18, people generally feel _____ (more/less) competent, on average, each year in most areas of their lives. The specifics depend on _____ , _____ , and _____ .

43. Clinical depression _____ (increases/decreases) at puberty, especially among _____ (males/females).

44. Thinking about committing suicide, called _____ _____ , is _____ (common/relatively rare) among high school students.

45. Adolescents under age 20 are _____ (more/less) likely to kill themselves than adults are.

46. Most suicide attempts in adolescence _____ (do/do not) result in death. A deliberate act of self-destruction that does not result in death is called a _____ .

47. List five factors that affect whether thinking about suicide leads to a self-destructive act or to death.

    a. _____

    b. _____

    c. _____

    d. _____

    e. _____

48. The rate of suicide is higher for adolescent _____ (males/females). The rate of parasuicide is higher for _____ (males/females).

49. Around the world, cultural differences in the rates of suicidal ideation and completion _____ (are/are not) apparent.

50. When a town or school sentimentalizes the "tragic end" of a teen suicide, the publicity can trigger _____ _____ .

(Table 16.2) Briefly describe ethnic differences in suicide rates in the United States.

51. Psychologists influenced by the _____ perspective believe that adolescent rebellion and defiance are normal.

52. Many children curse adults, engage in petty stealing, destroy property, and act in other destructive ways; they are diagnosed as having _____ _____ . In adolescence, these children usually become lawbreakers called _____ _____ .

53. Arrests are far more likely to occur during the _____ _____ of life than during any other time period. Although statistics indicate that the _____ (incidence/prevalence) of arrests is highest among this age group, they do not reveal how widespread, or _____ , lawbreaking is among this age group.

Briefly describe data on gender and ethnic differences in adolescent arrests.

54. The victims of crime tend to be _____ (teenagers/adults).

55. Experts find it useful to distinguish _____-_____ offenders, whose criminal activity stops by age 21, from _____-_____-_____ offenders, who become career criminals.

56. Developmentalists have found that it _____ (is/is not) currently possible to distinguish children who actually will become career criminals.

57. Adolescents who later become career criminals are among the first of their cohort to _____ . They also are among the least involved in _____ activities and tend to be _____ in preschool and elementary school. At an even earlier age, they show signs of _____ _____ , such as being slow in _____ development, being _____ , or having poor _____ control.

58. For most delinquents, residential incarceration in a prison or reform school usually _____ (is/is not) the best solution.

59. One innovative strategy for helping delinquents is _____ _____ _____ , in which violent youth are assigned to _____ families trained to teach anger management, school achievement, and responsible self-care.

Conclusion (p. 527)

60. For most young people, the teenage years overall are _____ (happy/unhappy) ones.

Progress Test 1

Multiple-Choice Questions

Circle your answers to the following questions and check them with the answers on page 245. If your answer is incorrect, read the explanation for why it is incorrect and then consult the appropriate pages of the text (in parentheses following the correct answer).

1. According to Erikson, the primary task of adolescence is that of establishing:
   a. basic trust.   c. intimacy.
   b. an identity.   d. integrity.

2. According to developmentalists who study identity formation, foreclosure involves:
   a. accepting an identity prematurely, without exploration.
   b. taking time off from school, work, and other commitments.
   c. opposing parental values.
   d. failing to commit oneself to a vocational goal.

3. When adolescents adopt an identity that is the opposite of the one they are expected to adopt, they are considered to be taking on a:
   a. foreclosed identity.
   b. diffused identity.
   c. negative identity.
   d. reverse identity.

4. The main sources of emotional support for most young people who are establishing independence from their parents are:
   a. older adolescents of the opposite sex.
   b. older siblings.
   c. teachers.
   d. peer groups.

5. For members of minority ethnic groups, identity achievement may be particularly complicated because:
   a. their cultural ideal clashes with the Western emphasis on adolescent self-determination.
   b. peers, themselves torn by similar conflicts, can be very critical.
   c. parents and other relatives tend to emphasize ethnicity and expect teens to honor their roots.
   d. of all of the above reasons.

6. In a crime-ridden neighborhood, parents can protect their adolescents by keeping close watch over activities, friends, and so on. This practice is called:
   a. generational stake.   c. peer screening.
   b. foreclosure.   d. parental monitoring.

7. Conflict between adolescent girls and their mothers is most likely to involve:
   a. bickering over hair, neatness, and other daily habits.
   b. political, religious, and moral issues.
   c. peer relationships and friendships.
   d. relationships with boys.

8. If there is a "generation gap," it is likely to occur in _____ adolescence and to center on issues of _____ .
   a. early; morality   c. early; self-control
   b. late; self-discipline d. late; politics

9. Adolescents who discuss sex openly with their parents:
   a. take fewer risks.
   b. avoid peer pressure to have unwanted sex.
   c. believe that their parents provide useful information.
   d. are characterized by all of the above.

10. Fifteen-year-old Cindy, who has strong self-esteem and is trying out a new, artistic identity "just to see how it feels," is apparently exploring:
    a. a false self.
    b. a possible self.
    c. an experimental self.
    d. a diffused self.

11. If the vast majority of cases of a certain crime are committed by a small number of repeat offenders, this would indicate that the crime's:
    a. incidence is less than its prevalence.
    b. incidence is greater than its prevalence.
    c. incidence and prevalence are about equal.
    d. incidence and prevalence are impossible to calculate.

12. Thirteen-year-old Adam, who never has doubted his faith, identifies himself as an orthodox member of a particular religious group. A developmentalist would probably say that Adam's religious identity is:
    a. achieved.
    b. foreclosed.
    c. in moratorium.
    d. oppositional in nature.

13. The early signs of life-course-persistent offenders include all of the following except:
    a. signs of brain damage early in life.
    b. antisocial school behavior.
    c. delayed sexual intimacy.
    d. use of alcohol and tobacco at an early age.

14. Regarding gender differences in self-destructive acts, the rate of parasuicide is _____ and the rate of suicide is _____ .
    a. higher in males; higher in females
    b. higher in females; higher in males
    c. the same in males and females; higher in males
    d. the same in males and females; higher in females

15. Conflict between parents and adolescent off-spring is:
    a. most likely to involve fathers and their early-maturing offspring.
    b. more frequent in single-parent homes.
    c. more likely between early-maturing daughters and their mothers.
    d. likely in all of the above situations.

True or False Items

Write T (*true*) or F (*false*) on the line in front of each statement.

_____ 1. A person can achieve identity in one domain but still be searching in another.

_____ 2. Most adolescents have political views and educational values that are markedly different from those of their parents.

_____ 3. Peer pressure is inherently destructive to the adolescent seeking an identity.

_____ 4. For most adolescents, group socializing and dating precede the establishment of true intimacy with one member of the opposite sex.

_____ 5. Worldwide, arrests are more likely to occur during the second decade of life than at any other time.

_____ 6. Most adolescent self-destructive acts are a response to an immediate and specific psychological blow.

_____ 7. Most adolescents break many minor laws.

_____ 8. In finding themselves, teens try to find an identity that is stable, consistent, and mature.

_____ 9. From ages 6 to 18, children feel more competent, on average, each year in most areas of their lives.

_____ 10. Increased accessibility of guns is a factor in the increased rate of youth suicide in the United States.

Progress Test 2

Progress Test 2 should be completed during a final chapter review. Answer the following questions after you thoroughly understand the correct answers for the Chapter Review and Progress Test 1.

Multiple-Choice Questions

1. Which of the following is *not* one of the arenas of identity formation in Erik Erikson's theory?
    a. religious   c. political
    b. sexual   d. social

2. Gender identity, gender role, and sexual orientation are:
    a. separate terms for the same developmental phenomenon.
    b. always aligned.
    c. correlated with biological sex but not entirely determined by either nature or nurture.
    d. social constructions.

3. Parent–teen conflict among Asian and Latino families often surfaces late in adolescence because these cultures:
    a. emphasize family closeness.
    b. value authoritarian parenting.
    c. encourage autonomy in children.
    d. do all of the above.

4. If the various cases of a certain crime are committed by many different offenders, this would indicate that the crime's:
    a. incidence is less than its prevalence.
    b. incidence is greater than its prevalence.
    c. incidence and prevalence are about equal.
    d. incidence and prevalence are impossible to calculate.

5. Thinking about committing suicide is called:
    a. cluster suicide.
    b. parasuicide.
    c. suicidal ideation.
    d. fratracide.

6. Which of the following was *not* noted in the text regarding peer relationships among gay and lesbian adolescents?
    a. Romantic attachments are usually slower to develop.
    b. In homophobic cultures, many gay teens try to conceal their homosexual feelings by becoming heterosexually involved.
    c. Many girls who will later identify themselves as lesbians are oblivious to these sexual urges as teens.
    d. Homosexual men report that they do not become aware of their interests until age 17.

7. The adolescent experiencing identity diffusion is typically:
    a. very apathetic.
    b. experimenting with alternative identities without trying to settle on any one.
    c. willing to accept parental values wholesale, without exploring alternatives.
    d. one who rebels against all forms of authority.

8. Cross-sequential studies of individuals from ages 6 to 18 show that:
   a. children feel less competent each year in most areas of their lives.
   b. the general emotional trend in adolescence is more downward than upward.
   c. self-esteem generally begins to decrease at about age 12.
   d. all of the above are true.

9. Crime statistics show that during adolescence:
   a. males and females are equally likely to be arrested.
   b. males are more likely to be arrested than females.
   c. females are more likely to be arrested than males.
   d. males commit more crimes than females but are less likely to be arrested.

10. Which of the following is the most common problem behavior among adolescents?
    a. pregnancy
    b. daily use of illegal drugs
    c. minor lawbreaking
    d. attempts at suicide

11. A time-out period during which a young person experiments with different identities, postponing important choices, is called a(n):
    a. identity foreclosure. c. identity diffusion.
    b. negative identity.   d. identity moratorium.

12. When adolescents' political, religious, educational, and vocational opinions are compared with their parents', the so-called generation gap is:
    a. much smaller than popularly believed.
    b. much wider than popularly believed.
    c. wider between parents and sons than between parents and daughters.
    d. wider between parents and daughters than between parents and sons.

13. Which of the following is *not* true regarding the rate of clinical depression among adolescents?
    a. At puberty the rate more than doubles.
    b. It affects a higher proportion of teenage boys than girls.
    c. Genetic vulnerability is a predictor of teenage depression.
    d. The adolescent's school setting is a factor.

14. Parent–teen conflict tends to center on issues related to:
    a. politics and religion.
    b. education.
    c. vacations.
    d. daily details, such as musical tastes.

15. According to a review of studies from various nations, suicidal ideation is:
    a. not as common among high school students as is popularly believed.
    b. more common among males than females.
    c. more common among females than among males.
    d. so common among high school students that it might be considered normal.

Matching Items

Match each term or concept with its corresponding description or definition.

Terms or Concepts

_____ 1. identity
_____ 2. identity achievement
_____ 3. foreclosure
_____ 4. negative identity
_____ 5. identity diffusion
_____ 6. identity moratorium
_____ 7. generation gap
_____ 8. generational stake
_____ 9. parental monitoring
_____ 10. parasuicide
_____ 11. cluster suicide

Descriptions or Definitions

a. premature identity formation
b. a group of suicides that occur in the same community, school, or time period
c. the adolescent has few commitments to goals or values
d. differences between the younger and older generations
e. self-destructive act that does not result in death
f. awareness of where children are and what they are doing
g. an individual's self-definition
h. a time-out period during which adolescents experiment with alternative identities
i. the adolescent establishes his or her own goals and values
j. family members in different developmental stages see the family in different ways
k. an identity opposite of the one an adolescent is expected to adopt

Thinking Critically About Chapter 16

Answer these questions the day before an exam as a final check on your understanding of the chapter's terms and concepts.

1. From childhood, Sharon thought she wanted to follow in her mother's footsteps and be a homemaker. Now, at age 40 with a home and family, she admits to herself that what she really wanted to be was a medical researcher. Erik Erikson would probably say that Sharon:
   a. adopted a negative identity when she was a child.
   b. experienced identity foreclosure at an early age.
   c. never progressed beyond the obvious identity diffusion she experienced as a child.
   d. took a moratorium from identity formation.

2. Fifteen-year-old David is rebelling against his devoutly religious parents by taking drugs, stealing, and engaging in other antisocial behaviors. Evidently, David has:
   a. foreclosed on his identity.
   b. declared an identity moratorium.
   c. adopted a negative identity.
   d. experienced identity diffusion.

3. Jennifer has a well-defined religious identity. This is true because she:
   a. self-identifies herself as a religious person.
   b. worships regularly.
   c. belongs to a fellowship of believers.
   d. does all of the above.

4. In 1957, 6-year-old Raisel and her parents emigrated from Mexico to the United States. Because her parents hold to the values and customs of their native land, Raisel is likely to have:
   a. an easier time achieving her own unique identity.
   b. a more difficult time forging her identity.
   c. a greater span of time in which to forge her own identity.
   d. a shorter span of time in which to forge her identity.

5. An adolescent exaggerates the importance of differences in her values and those of her parents. Her parents see these differences as smaller and less important. This phenomenon is called the:
   a. generation gap.   c. family enigma.
   b. generational stake.   d. parental imperative.

6. In our society, the most obvious examples of institutionalized moratoria on identity formation are:
   a. the Boy Scouts and the Girl Scouts.
   b. college and the military.
   c. marriage and divorce.
   d. bar mitzvahs and baptisms.

7. First-time parents Norma and Norman are worried that, during adolescence, their healthy parental influence will be undone as their children are encouraged by peers to become sexually promiscuous, drug-addicted, or delinquent. Their wise neighbor, who is a developmental psychologist, tells them that:
   a. peers are constructive as often as they are destructive.
   b. research suggests that peers provide a negative influence in every major task of adolescence.
   c. only through authoritarian parenting can parents give children the skills they need to resist peer pressure.
   d. unless their children show early signs of learning difficulties or antisocial behavior, parental monitoring is unnecessary.

8. Padma's parents are concerned because their 14-year-old daughter has formed an early romantic relationship with a boy. You tell them:
   a. not to worry, because boys are more likely to say they have a girlfriend than vice versa.
   b. early pairing can signify emotional trouble if it decreases same-sex friendships.
   c. by age 14, nearly all adolescents have had at least one romantic relationship.
   d. they should do everything they can to break up the relationship.

9. Commenting on a student's question regarding gender intensification, Professor Rivera notes that, during adolescence:
   a. teenagers become more flexible in their gender-role concepts.
   b. teenagers become less flexible in their gender-role concepts.
   c. girls become more flexible in their gender-role concepts than do boys.
   d. boys become more flexible in their gender-role concepts than do girls.

10. Rosaria is an adolescent in an immigrant family. In response to the conflict between the peer-group emphasis on adolescent freedom and the values of her family's culture, Rosaria is most likely to:
    a. rebel against her family, possibly leaving home.
    b. join a delinquent group.
    c. give in to parental control.
    d. ask to live with her grandparents.

11. Statistically, the person *least* likely to commit a crime is a(n):
    a. African American or Hispanic adolescent.
    b. middle-class white male.
    c. white adolescent of any socioeconomic background.
    d. Asian American.

12. Ray was among the first of his friends to have sex, drink alcohol, and smoke cigarettes. These attributes, together with his having been hyperactive and having poor emotional control, would suggest that Ray is at high risk of:
    a. becoming an adolescent-limited offender.
    b. becoming a life-course-persistent offender.
    c. developing an antisocial personality.
    d. foreclosing his identity prematurely.

13. Carl is a typical 16-year-old adolescent who has no special problems. It is likely that Carl has:
    a. contemplated suicide.
    b. engaged in some minor illegal act.
    c. struggled with "who he is."
    d. done all of the above.

14. Statistically, who of the following is *most* likely to commit suicide?
    a. Micah, an African-American female
    b. Yan, an Asian-American male
    c. James, a American Indian male
    d. Alison, a European-American female

15. Coming home from work, Malcolm hears a radio announcement warning parents to be alert for possible cluster suicide signs in their teenage children. What might have precipitated such an announcement?
    a. government statistics that suicide is on the rise
    b. the highly publicized suicide of a teen from a school in his town
    c. the recent crash of an airliner, killing all on board
    d. any of the above

Key Terms

Using your own words, write a brief definition or explanation of each of the following terms on a separate piece of paper.

1. identity
2. identity versus diffusion
3. possible selves
4. false self
5. identity achievement
6. identity diffusion
7. foreclosure
8. negative identity
9. identity moratorium
10. gender identity
11. gender role
12. sexual orientation
13. generation gap
14. generational stake
15. bickering
16. parental monitoring
17. peer pressure
18. clinical depression
19. suicidal ideation
20. parasuicide
21. cluster suicide
22. incidence
23. prevalence
24. adolescent-limited offender
25. life-course-persistent offender

ANSWERS
CHAPTER REVIEW

1. identity
2. identity versus diffusion; possible selves
3. false self
4. identity achievement
5. identity diffusion
6. foreclosure
7. negative identity
8. moratorium; college
9. religious; sexual; political; vocational
10. can
11. a. self-identify

b. specify a subcategory
c. belong to a fellowship of believers
d. pray daily
e. worship regularly
f. their faith affects their daily life

12. gender identity; role; orientation
13. gender role; sexual orientation; differ; biological; cultural
14. less; more; gender intensification
15. ethnic; political; native-born; European; immigrants
16. context; change; reciprocal; personal choice; response to others; multifaceted
17. identity; family; academic; career
18. varies
19. Japan; Africa; Germany
20. 20
21. generation gap; education; politics; social
22. generational stake
23. tweens; mothers; daughters; bickering
24. timing; family harmony; social
25. normal; development
26. permissiveness; collective efficacy
27. communication; support; connectedness; control
28. parental monitoring; depression; psychological control
29. peer pressure; rises; 14; fall; uncertainty
30. selection; choose; facilitation; none of them would do alone
31. immigrants

The progression begins with groups of same-sex friends. Next, a loose, public association of a girl's group and a boy's group forms. Then, a smaller, heterosexual group forms from the more advanced members of the larger association. Finally, more intimate heterosexual couples peel off.

32. affect; timing; manifestation; sequence; genetic; several years
33. same-sex; emotional
34. slow down
35. risks; peer pressure to have sex when they do not want to; believe their parents provide useful information
36. should; provide
37. multifaceted; one year or more
38. several years; are not; formal operational; personal fable

39. is

40. decreasing; increased

41. often have

42. less; cohort; culture; domain

43. increases; females

44. suicidal ideation; common

45. less

46. do not; parasuicide

47. **a.** the availability of lethal methods

    b. the extent of parental supervision

    c. the use of alcohol and other drugs

    d. gender

    e. cultural attitudes about suicide

48. males; females

49. are

50. cluster suicides

American Indian and Alaskan Native males have the highest rates, followed by European American males, Hispanic American and African American males, American Indian females, Asian American males, and so on.

51. psychoanalytic

52. conduct disorder; juvenile delinquents

53. second decade; incidence; prevalent

Adolescent males are three times as likely to be arrested as females, and African American youth are three times as likely to be arrested as European Americans, who are three times as likely to be arrested as Asian Americans. However, confidential self-reports find much smaller gender and ethnic differences.

54. teenagers

55. adolescent-limited; life-course-persistent

56. is

57. have sex and use drugs; school; antisocial; brain damage; language; hyperactive; emotional

58. is not

59. therapeutic foster care; foster

60. happy

PROGRESS TEST 1

Multiple-Choice Questions

1. **b.** is the answer. (p. 496)

   a. According to Erikson, this is the crisis of infancy.

   c. & d. In Erikson's theory, these crises occur later in life.

2. **a.** is the answer. (p. 497)

   b. This describes an identity moratorium.

   c. This describes a negative identity.

   d. This describes identity diffusion.

3. **c.** is the answer. (p. 498)

4. **d.** is the answer. (p. 509)

5. **d.** is the answer. (pp. 502–503)

6. **d.** is the answer. (p. 509)

   a. The generational stake refers to differences in how family members from different generations view the family.

   b. Foreclosure refers to the premature establishment of identity.

   c. Peer screening is an aspect of parental monitoring, but it was not specifically discussed in the text.

7. **a.** is the answer. (p. 507)

8. **c.** is the answer. (pp. 506–507)

9. **d.** is the answer. (p. 515)

10. **b.** is the answer. (p. 496)

    a. A false self involves acting in ways contrary to one's core being; there is no indication that Cindy is doing so.

    c. & d. These terms were not used to describe identity formation.

11. **b.** is the answer. Incidence is how often a particular circumstance (such as lawbreaking) occurs; prevalence is how widespread the circumstance is. A crime that is committed by only a few repeat offenders is not very prevalent in the population. (p. 525)

12. **b.** is the answer. Foreclosed members of a religious group have, like Adam, never really doubted. (p. 497)

    a. Because there is no evidence that Adam has asked the "hard questions" regarding his religious beliefs, a developmentalist would probably say that his religious identity is not achieved.

    c. Adam clearly does have a religious identity.

    d. There is no evidence that Adam's religious identity was formed in opposition to expectations.

13. **c.** is the answer. Most life-course-persistent offenders are among the earliest of their cohort to have sex. (p. 526)

14. **b.** is the answer. (p. 522)

15. **c.** is the answer. (p. 507)

a. In fact, parent–child conflict is more likely to involve mothers and their early-maturing offspring.

b. The text did not compare the rate of conflict in two-parent and single-parent homes.

True or False Items

1. T (p. 499)
2. F   Parent–teen conflicts center on day-to-day details, not on politics or moral issues. (p. 507)
3. F   Just the opposite is true. (p. 510)
4. T (p. 513)
5. T (p. 524)
6. F   Most self-destructive acts stem from many earlier developmental events. (p. 520)
7. T (p. 525)
8. T (pp. 496–498)
9. F   Just the opposite is true. (p. 520)
10. T (p. 522)

PROGRESS TEST 2

Multiple-Choice Questions

1. **d.** is the answer. (p. 499)
2. **c.** is the answer. (p. 501)
3. **a.** is the answer. For this reason, autonomy in their offspring tends to be delayed. (p. 507)
4. **c.** is the answer. (p. 525)

   a. This answer would have been correct if the question had stated, "If the majority of cases of a crime are committed by a small number of repeat offenders."

   b. Because it is simply the total number of cases of an event or circumstance (such as a crime), incidence cannot be less than prevalence.
5. **c.** is the answer. (p. 521)
6. **d.** is the answer. Homosexual men report that they become aware at age 11, but don't tell anyone until age 17. (p. 514)
7. **a.** is the answer. (p. 496)

   b. This describes an adolescent undergoing an identity moratorium.

   c. This describes identity foreclosure.

   d. This describes an adolescent who is adopting a negative identity.
8. **d.** is the answer. (p. 520)

9. **b.** is the answer. (p. 525)
10. **c.** is the answer. (p. 525)
11. **d.** is the answer. (p. 498)

    a. Identity foreclosure occurs when the adolescent prematurely adopts an identity, without fully exploring alternatives.

    b. Adolescents who adopt an identity that is opposite to the one they are expected to develop have taken on a negative identity.

    c. Identity diffusion occurs when the adolescent is apathetic and has few commitments to goals or values.
12. **a.** is the answer. (p. 505)

    c. & d. The text does not suggest that the size of the generation gap varies with the offspring's sex.
13. **b.** is the answer. (p. 521)
14. **d.** is the answer. (p. 507)

    a., b., & c. In fact, on these issues parents and teenagers tend to show substantial *agreement*.
15. **d.** is the answer. (p. 521)

Matching Items

1. g (p. 495)
2. i (p. 496)
3. a (p. 497)
4. k (p. 498)
5. c (p. 496)
6. h (p. 498)
7. d (p. 505)
8. j (p. 506)
9. f (p. 509)
10. e (p. 522)
11. b (p. 523)

THINKING CRITICALLY ABOUT CHAPTER 16

1. **b.** is the answer. Apparently, Sharon never explored alternatives or truly forged a unique personal identity. (p. 497)

   a. Individuals who rebel by adopting an identity that is the opposite of the one they are expected to adopt have taken on a negative identity.

   c. Individuals who experience identity diffusion have few commitments to goals or values. This was not Sharon's problem.

   d. Had she taken a moratorium on identity formation, Sharon would have experimented with alternative identities and perhaps would have chosen that of a medical researcher.
2. **c.** is the answer. (p. 498)
3. **d.** is the answer. (pp. 499–500)
4. **b.** is the answer. Ethnic adolescents struggle with finding the right balance between transcending their background and becoming immersed in it. (pp. 502–503)

   c. & d. The text does not suggest that the amount of time adolescents have to forge their identities varies from one ethnic group to another or has changed over historical time.

5. **b.** is the answer. (p. 506)

   a. The generation gap refers to actual differences in attitudes and values between the younger and older generations. This example is concerned with how large these differences are perceived to be.

   c. & d. These terms are not used in the text in discussing family conflict.

6. **b.** is the answer. (p. 499)

7. **a.** is the answer. (p. 510)

   b. In fact, just the opposite is true.

   c. Developmentalists recommend authoritative, rather than authoritarian, parenting.

   d. Parental monitoring is important for all adolescents.

8. **b.** is the answer. (p. 513)

   a. In fact, girls are more likely to say they have a boyfriend than vice versa.

   c. This is not true; one study found that less than half of eleventh-graders, most of whom would be older than 14, reported having had a romantic relationship.

   d. Doing so may backfire, increasing the risk of early pregnancy and elopement.

9. **b.** is the answer. (p. 502)

10. **c.** is the answer. Adolescent girls in immigrant families are most likely to live docilely at home until an early marriage. (p. 513)

    a. & b. Boys are most likely to do these things.

    d. This may be the parents' response to problems with their children.

11. **d.** is the answer. (p. 525)

12. **b.** is the answer. (p. 526)

13. **d.** is the answer. (pp. 496, 521, 525)

14. **c.** is the answer. (p. 523)

15. **b.** is the answer. (p. 523)

    a., c., & d. Cluster suicides occur when the suicide of a local teen leads others to attempt suicide.

KEY TERMS

1. **Identity,** as used by Erikson, refers to a person's consistent self-definition as a unique individual in terms of roles, attitudes, beliefs, and aspirations. (p. 495)

2. Erikson's term for the psychosocial crisis of adolescence, **identity versus diffusion,** refers to adolescents' need to combine their self-understanding and social roles into a coherent identity. (pp. 4495–496)

3. Many adolescents try out **possible selves,** or variations on who they are, who they might like to become, and who they fear becoming. (p. 496)

4. Some adolescents display a **false self,** acting in ways that are contrary to who they really are in order to be accepted, to please others, or to try out as a possible self. (p. 496)

5. In Erikson's theory, **identity achievement** occurs when adolescents attain their new identity by establishing their own goals and values and abandoning some of those set by their parents and culture and accepting others. (p. 496)

6. Adolescents who experience **identity diffusion,** according to Erikson, have few commitments to goals or values and are often apathetic about trying to find an identity. (p. 496)

7. In **foreclosure,** according to Erikson, the adolescent forms an identity prematurely, accepting parents' or society's roles and values wholesale, 497)

8. Adolescents who take on a **negative identity,** according to Erikson, adopt an identity that is the opposite of the one they are expected to adopt. (p. 498)

9. According to Erikson, in the process of finding a mature identity, many young people seem to declare an **identity moratorium,** a kind of time-out during which they experiment with alternative identities without trying to settle on any one. (p. 498)

10. **Gender identity** is a person's self-identification of being female or male. (p. 501)

11. A **gender role** is the sex-typed occupation and patterns of behavior that a person adopts. (p. 501)

12. **Sexual orientation** refers to a person's sexual attraction toward a person of the other sex, the same sex, or both sexes. (p. 501)

13. The **generation gap** refers to the alleged distance between generations in value and attitudes. (p. 505)

14. The **generational stake** refers to the need of each family member, because of that person's different developmental stage, to see family interactions in a certain way. (p. 506)

15. **Bickering** refers to the repeated, petty arguing that typically occurs in early adolescence about common, daily life activities. (p. 57)

16. **Parental monitoring** is parental awareness about where one's child is, what he or she is doing, and with whom. (p. 509)

17. **Peer pressure** refers to the social pressure to conform with one's friends in behavior, dress, and attitude. It may be positive or negative in its effects. (p. 510)

18. **Clinical depression** describes the syndrome in which feelings of hopelessness and lethargy last in a person for two weeks or longer. (p. 521)

19. **Suicidal ideation** refers to thinking about committing suicide, usually with some serious emotional and intellectual or cognitive overtones. (p. 521)

20. **Parasuicide** is a deliberate act of self-destruction that does not result in death. (p. 522)

21. A **cluster suicide** refers to a series of suicides or suicide attempts that are precipitated by one initial suicide and that occur in the same community, school, or time period. (p. 523)

22. **Incidence** is how often a particular circumstance (such as lawbreaking) occurs. (p. 525)

23. **Prevalence** is how widespread within a population a particular behavior or circumstance is. (p. 525)

24. **Adolescent-limited offenders** are juvenile delinquents whose criminal activity stops by age 21. (p. 525)

25. **Life-course-persistent offenders** are adolescent lawbreakers who later become career criminals. (p. 525)